Communicating Sustainability for the Green Economy

Communicating Sustainability for the Green Economy

Lynn R. Kahle and
Eda Gurel-Atay, Editors

SCP
SOCIETY FOR
CONSUMER
PSYCHOLOGY

M.E.Sharpe
Armonk, New York
London, England

Library of Congress Cataloging-in-Publication Data

Communicating sustainability for the green economy / edited by Lynn R. Kahle
and Eda Gurel-Atay.
pages cm
ISBN 978–0-7656–3680–5 (hardcover : alk. paper)—ISBN 978–0-7656–3681–2 (pbk. : alk. paper)
1. Sustainable development. 2. Consumption (Economics)—Environmental aspects.
3. Lifestyles—Environmental aspects. I. Kahle, Lynn R. II. Gurel-Atay, Eda, 1980–

HC79.E5.C61236 2013 338.9′27014—dc23
2013014856

Printed in the United States of America

The paper used in this publication meets the minimum requirements of
American National Standard for Information Sciences
Permanence of Paper for Printed Library Materials,
ANSI Z 39.48-1984.

∞

IBT (c) 10 9 8 7 6 5 4 3 2 1
SP (p) 10 9 8 7 6 5 4 3 2 1

Contents

Foreword

Diane M. Martin

Physical scientists have long understood the laws of thermodynamics and natural cycles. Our earth is an open system in terms of energy; the sun continues to warm the earth, adding solar energy to the system. Natural cycles of balanced consumption and reabsorption work well as long as humans do not systematically increase environmental concentrations of substances from the earth's crust, do not systematically increase environmental concentrations of synthetic substances, do not systematically increase ecosystem degradation, and create no systematic barriers to people meeting their own needs.[1] But the level of present-day consumption and disposal habits run counter to the natural cycles.

Environmental activists and social critics lay the problems of unsustainable consumption at the feet of marketing, arguing that excessive consumption is the result of product advertising. Marketing as we now know it may indeed be part of the problem. Moving toward balanced natural cycles requires a new thinking about consumers, consumption, and marketing communication.

The environmental movement of the 1960s and 1970s focused on the most obvious needs for a healthy and beautiful environment: air pollution, water pollution, solid waste disposal, and litter. Changing practices were primarily a function of state and federal legislation and gentle reminders to "Keep America Beautiful." More recently, globalization, increased population, and technology have led to concerns about food production, transportation issues, environmental toxins, and a plethora of unseen consequences of a hyperconsumption culture. Rather than making life on earth a little bit healthier and prettier, we are now concerned with sustaining current and future generations. Progress in public leadership has slowed as national governments look to protectionist policies. Multiple and changing definitions of "green" and "organic" suspiciously populate advertisements. Products are launched to take part in the landscape of fashionable sustainability, many in name only, without the benefit of actual product improvement. The burden of moving toward sustainable consumption has shifted from firms, mandated to follow environmental regulations or risk fines, to consumers who are asked to sift through spurious advertising claims and consider the total environmental and social implications of each purchase. Moving toward a consumer culture of sustainability takes more than a pretty highway marker or the fortification of current environmental protection laws. Marketing may be part of the problem, but it must also be part of the solution. This volume is a contribution to that cause.

In this book, the complexities of sustainability are investigated in the interdisciplinary crossroads of consumer psychology and advertising. Contributors offer empirical and theoretical arguments and, in doing so, invite the reader to find connections and overlaps, underscoring the mutual influences between humans and nonhumans, psychology and media, and social movement and physical science. Understanding the barriers to sustainable consumption through consumer psychology provides insights for marketing communication. Encouraging transparency and honesty in marketing communication engenders trust in consumers. Brand messages can educate as they differentiate. Consumer psychology and marketing communication research help to uncover what it means to be a responsible member of an increasingly environmentally aware culture.

"Culture eats strategy for breakfast," a remark attributed to management guru Peter Drucker, underscores the importance of culture in change efforts. Consumer culture, largely a creation of marketing, has the potential to make the road to sustainability either smoother or rockier. Currently, so-called green consumers largely constitute nonmainstream market segments and niches. However, by creatively managing marketing resources (e.g., merchandising and messaging), managers can begin to link sustainable products, services and practices to mainstream consumer activities (e.g., shopping and recycling), and concerns (e.g., quality, value, and family health and welfare).

Research that focuses on the gap between sustainable consumption intention and behavior; improving instruments, models, and measures; responses to sustainable messages; and other topics at the intersection of consumer psychology and marketing communication is an important step toward making marketing part of the solution. Each contribution brings researchers, consumers, and marketers a little bit closer to understanding the practices needed to bring society more in line with the balance of natural cycles.

Note

1. Based on the Natural Step, "The Four System Conditions," www.thenaturalstep.org/the-system-conditions/.

Preface

Communicating with consumers about sustainability in a psychologically sophisticated manner provides challenges that do not necessarily follow all the rules of other types of marketing communication. Marketing sustainability has unique combinations of tools that lead to unique patterns of psychological responses and therefore demand out-of-the-ordinary attention to a variety of marketing communication tactics. In some ways, the concept of sustainability challenges the core ideal of promoting consumption.

This book advances the understanding of the sustainability concept by bringing consumer psychology, advertising, and marketing communications together to bridge sustainable business practices and demand for those practices. Readers will learn some of the latest thinking in the areas of (a) understanding environmental sustainability (i.e., what it means to consumers), (b) determinants of sustainable consumption, (c) encouraging sustainable consumption, and (d) applications of environmental sustainability. This book refines and directs what we know about advertising and consumer psychology in relation to sustainability; it includes comprehensive reviews, innovative conceptual frameworks, and empirical studies based on rigorous data analyses; and it draws attention to diverse topics and perspectives such as greenwashing, persuasion and persuasion knowledge in sustainability marketing, social media and sustainability, lifestyles, voluntary simplicity, and green advertising and public policy.

This book is unique in that it provides both scholars and practitioners with the opportunity to (a) gain insights on the combination of consumer psychology, advertising, and marketing communications in relation to sustainable consumption; (b) accommodate a variety of quality work from respected researchers all over the world; and (c) revive academic interest in a popular practitioner topic. We hope that this information advances the conversation about how to communicate about sustainability.

The idea for this book emerged from the Society for Consumer Psychology Conference on Advertising and Consumer Psychology (ACP) held in Eugene, Oregon, May 2011. We (Lynn Kahle, chair; Eda Gurel-Atay, webmaster) were closely involved in the conference, which we organized as a forum for scholars to share emerging works on sustainable consumption. The range of contributors to the conference was impressive.

We thank the many people who helped us develop and improve this project, especially our colleagues and students at the University of Oregon, whose help during and after the ACP conference was tremendous. We appreciate the encouragement that we received from the Society for Consumer Psychology. Also, we thank our friends at M.E. Sharpe, especially Harry Briggs, for their invaluable support and assistance. Dr. Debra Eisert provided extensive substantive help. Finally, we thank our significant others for their continuous support, love, and patience.

Lynn R. Kahle
University of Oregon, Eugene, Oregon

Eda Gurel-Atay
University of Puget Sound, Tacoma, Washington

Communicating Sustainability for the Green Economy

1

Introduction to the Psychology of Communicating Sustainability

Lynn R. Kahle and Eda Gurel-Atay

Recent changes in the environment (e.g., climate change and decreases in nonrenewable resources) have persuaded many scholars that we cannot continue to use the world's resources without considering the consequences (Ottman, 1998; Wasik, 1996). As this environmental awareness increases, sustainable business practices gain in importance, leading to the emergence of a green economy as the world's new economic engine. In fact, many people believe that the next major world economic growth area is the green economy (e.g., Hawken, Lovins, & Lovins, 1999). However, although firms are adopting more sustainable business practices (as a result of both government sanctions and social marketing orientations), consumers seem to be lagging behind (Thøgersen & Crompton, 2009). In fact, it is suggested that "there is no 'sustainable consumer' who is taking social and ecological aspects into account in all fields of consumption" (Schäfer, Jaeger-Erben, & Santos, 2011, p. 179). Instead, consumers tend to engage in sustainable consumption in some aspects of their lives and ignore them in others (Brand, 2000). The reluctance of consumers across the board to engage in environmentally sustainable consumption (e.g., buying green products and recycling products at the end of their life cycle), in turn, raises several questions about the use of sustainable business practices by companies. Because those practices tend to be expensive, companies may begin to question their use if there is not enough demand for their green products. Accordingly, it is important for researchers and practitioners to identify the barriers that keep customers from engaging in environmentally sustainable consumption and find ways to bring down those barriers. The purpose of this book is to bring consumer psychology and marketing communications together to begin to bridge the gap between sustainable business practices and demand for those practices.

This introduction first provides an analysis of environmentally sustainable consumption by focusing on the factors that enhance and restrain environmentally sustainable consumption. The next section discusses some of the consumer psychology, advertising, and marketing communication theories that can be used to understand environmentally sustainable consumption. More specifically, based on means–end chain theory, it is suggested that social values, along with effective market segmentation, can be used to reach consumers and convince them to engage in a greater extent of green consumption. The last section overviews the chapters of this book.

An Analysis of Environmentally Sustainable Consumption

Environmentally sustainable consumption encompasses several consumer behaviors, including, but not limited to, buying green products, shopping at green retailers, supporting companies and charities that adopt or promote sustainable practices, adequately recycling products at the end of their life cycle, purchasing organic food, and wisely using energy resources that are based on renewable resources (e.g., installing solar energy panels on the roof of a house). Although some consumers want to minimize their impact on the earth by adopting at least one of these environmentally friendly consumer behaviors, the majority of the consumers are still reluctant to engage in those behaviors extensively. In this section, we discuss some of the major factors that influence environmentally sustainable, "green" consumption.

The most important factor in green consumption is probably *environmental awareness*. People who have the appropriate knowledge and information about sustainable consumption tend to understand the importance of green consumption and therefore change their practices in line with green consumption (Thøgersen, 2005; Valor, 2008). Accordingly, it is important to increase "environmental awareness" among regular/average customers through public policy and social marketing efforts. However, researchers have also found that some consumers, although they are knowledgeable about the importance of sustainable consumption, may not put it into practice, creating a "knowledge-to-action gap" (Markkula & Moisander, 2012). One reason for this gap is the burden placed on consumers from excessive amounts of information. Too much, sometimes contradictory, information about sustainable consumption can challenge consumers' capacity to process this information and come to an understanding about what they can personally do to advance environmental sustainability (Moisander, 2007). This problem suggests that closing the gap between knowledge and action will require consumers to receive more structured and better-planned education about sustainable consumption.

Consumers might also be more inclined to engage in green consumption if they know that they are making a difference. The theory of planned behavior (Ajzen, 1991) suggests that if people think that their own actions will not change the world (or reverse negative environmental changes), they will be less willing to engage in green consumption. Accordingly, public policy and social marketing efforts should communicate the message that even a single person or action can make a difference. Kaufman-Hayoz et al. (2012) call this method the planned behavior approach.

Another factor that discourages consumers from engaging in green consumption is the perception that green consumption practices are more time-consuming, costly, and stressful (Valor, 2008). Indeed, the majority of the green products are priced higher than non-green products, making them niche products targeted mainly to people with a higher disposable income (Markkula & Moisander, 2012). Making green consumption practices more affordable (e.g., financial incentives for using solar energy) may motivate more people to adopt those practices. However, these types of financial incentives are not without costs either. Because these incentives "can generate high, potentially inequitable and sometimes unpredictable costs," they may be perceived as "socially regressive instruments, unreliable sources of revenue for the public sector and unpopular measures both with the private sector and consumers alike" (Pape, Rau, Fahy, & Davies, 2011, p. 28). At the same time, the sole use of communication instruments, providing information to consumers to increase environmental awareness and sustainable behavior, can also backfire, especially if people have the knowledge but not the resources to engage in sustainable consumption (Stern, 1999). Accordingly, it is suggested that "instrument mixes that combine information, incentives, social influences and institutional supports" can be more effective in motivating people to consume more sustainably (Pape et al., 2011, p. 29).

It is also possible that people's everyday consumption routines interfere with the ability and willingness to engage in green consumption. Because everyday routines tend to be well-adapted to social demands, personal needs, financial and time resources, and accessible infrastructure, "they are effective strategies for minimizing the effort of organizing daily life, but are seldom consciously reflected upon, making it difficult to conceptualize policies or interventions aiming to motivate changes of habit behaviour towards sustainability" (Schäfer, Jaeger-Erben, & Bamberg, 2012, p. 2). Habit can prove a powerful inhibitor to positive change (Beatty & Kahle, 1988; Kahle & Beatty, 1987b; Kloekner & Matthies, 2004).

One approach to deal with the difficulty in changing everyday routines is to address people who are experiencing life-course transitions, such as graduating from college, getting married, moving to a new house, moving to another city, or giving birth (Schäfer et al., 2012, p. 2). Because these people are already in the process of changing their everyday routines, they may be more amenable to adopting more sustainable alternatives (e.g., installing solar panels at the new house, shopping at green retailers in the new city, or buying organic food for the new baby). A key concept is that any changes in routine must address lifestyle (Kahle & Valette-Florence, 2012; Reusswig, Lotze-Campen, & Gerlinger, 2005; Shove, 2005). Kaufman-Hayoz et al. (2012) call this sequential change the stage model approach.

In some cases green products may not exist. The range of green products is growing (Figueiredo, Gullen, & Zheng, 2012), but not all consumers have access to green products in all categories. What is a green product? Sometimes greenness is defined based on the manufacturing process. How is it built or rebuilt (e.g., Schuster, 2010)? Does it involve the use of green energy sources? Does it use recycled materials? Does it manufacture the final product in a way that minimizes the use of resources? At times, the greenness relates to the unique characteristics of the product: Is it organic? Is it fair trade (Toulouse, 2012)?

At the macro level, the real challenge may be to encourage consumers to consume less. In some respects, this idea seems contrary to the ideals of marketing, which generally follows an economic model regarding consumption that more is better. But positive psychology (e.g., Peterson, 2006) has shown that happiness does not always derive from obtaining more things. Perhaps consumers would experience more happiness if they enjoyed what they have rather than obtaining ever more products. One way of conceptualizing this idea is with "mindful consumption," in which consumers commit to more finite materialism (Sheth, Sethia, & Srinivas, 2011). Another perspective involves redefining the concept of marketing, which holds that companies should give consumers what they want, to one of viewing the goal as giving consumers what is good for them, perhaps educating them along the way to want what is good for them in a social sense (Crittenden, Crittenden, Ferrell, Ferrell, & Pinney, 2011; Hult, 2011).

Using Consumer Psychology Theories to Explain Environmentally Sustainable Consumption

Understanding the psychology of consumers is critical to expanding the green economy in democratic societies with an open economy. Theories of psychology, advertising, and marketing can be employed to persuade consumers to engage in green consumption (Jaeger-Erben, Schäfer, Dalichau, Dehmel, Goetz, Fischer, Homberg, Schulz, & Zundel, 2012). The literature on using theories of psychology to increase sustainable behavior is small but growing (e.g., Kahle & Valette-Florence, 2012; Kaufmann-Hayoz et al., 2012; Matthies, Kastner, Kleese, & Wagner, 2011; Steg & Norland, 2013; Stern, 2000).

Previous research has shown that values, personalities, and self-images of consumers dictate how they respond to brands and products (e.g., Batra, Homer, & Kahle, 2001; Kahle, Beatty, & Homer, 1986; Kahle & Valette-Florence, 2012). In fact, brands and products possess values and personalities that shape their perceived images (Aaker, 1997; De Chernatony, Drury, & Segal-Horn, 2004), and those perceived images influence how consumers respond to the brand or product (Da Silva & Syed Alwi, 2006). In general, consumers form stronger relationships with brands and products toward which they have more articulated attitudes (Fournier 1998; McAlexander, Schouten, & Koenig, 2002).

One idea on how to reach consumers, expressed in previous research, places social values at the center of consumer decision-making. In means–end chain theory, consumers want products that have certain attributes. When you ask a consumer why he or she bought a certain product, the answer usually involves a product attribute. For example, a consumer may buy a brand of bread because it has ample fiber. If you follow up with a question about why that attribute is important, the consumer will usually respond by citing a consequence of that attribute—for example, that high fiber in the bread aids digestion and promotes health. If you continue to ask the consumer questions about why the consequence is important, the response usually links to a core value held by the consumer. For example, efficient digestion is important because you need to have good health to accomplish what you want in life. If marketers can link a product to a core value held by a particular consumer, that product will be more attractive than one that merely has an attribute. Consumers respond more favorably if one of their core values is related to a product. This logic applies to green consumption as strongly as it does to other types of consumption.

Consider the case of marketing solar energy. Although using solar energy faces some important challenges (e.g., the high cost of solar panels, the difficulty of displacing petroleum products, a lack of familiarity with solar energy), doing so has benefits for consumers. Some of the reasons that someone might want to install a residential solar energy system include lower carbon emissions, greater safety, less dependence on foreign energy sources, widespread availability, individual control, participation in a movement, and incentives. Some of the core values to which these attributes might link include self-respect, a sense of accomplishment, security, being well respected, and warm relationships with others.

The problem with making linkages in any given instance is that not all people have the same core values. Thus one may need to use market segmentation to appeal to different target markets. For the person who values self-respect or a sense of accomplishment, the critical solar attributes might be lower carbon emissions, making a difference in the world, or even conspicuous consumption. For people who value security, the key attributes may be getting off the grid that requires dependence on others for supplies of energy or an increase in national independence from avoiding foreign sources of energy. For people who value being well respected, the opportunity to save money may be critical; thus, a feed-in tariff, which occurs when, for example, a utility company agrees to long-term compensation of a sustainable energy producer for energy supplied to the grid, or an incentive structure may prove critical in gaining acceptance to pro-sustainability policies. For people who value warm relationships with others, the opportunity to bond with other solar energy users may be critical.

Surveys make it possible to determine what combination of attributes, consequences, and values appeal to certain segments. For instance, Schäfer, Jaeger-Erben, and Santos (2011) conducted a survey in southern Brazil which identified five consumer segments and suggested ways in which to target these consumer segments with different sustainable products, services, and communication strategies. The authors, for example, suggested that while the "quality of life–oriented postmaterialists" would respond favorably to trendy bikes, community services for sharing products, and messages about the social and ecological implications of production, the "wannabe materialists" would respond more favorably to second-hand electronic devices and sustainable consumption patterns that reflect the lifestyles of the high-income class communicated through mass media. In fact, with advancing Internet technology, it is possible to direct people to ads or information sources that emphasize the values appropriate for a particular segment. Sustainable marketing will need to use these tools to reach the next wave of consumers interested in the new products of the green economy. Kaufman-Hayoz et al. (2012) call this method the norm-activation approach.

Other theoretical approaches abound. Minton, Lee, Orth, Kim, and Kahle (2012), for example, propose that the functional approach to attitudes is useful in the context of sustainable behavior. This approach holds that different attitudes and behaviors serve different psychological functions, and the change agent must first uncover the functions of sustainable attitudes and behaviors. Some people may want to impress or comply with friends, whereas others may have deeply felt, internalized commitments to preserving the environment. Kaufman-Hayoz et al. (2012) discuss rational choice and economic theory approaches.

Communicating Sustainable Consumption

Communication approaches differ widely (Banerjee, Gulas, & Iyer, 1995; Kaufman-Hayoz et al., 2012; Martin & Schouten, 2012; McDonagh, 1998; Minton et al., 2012). Some focus on advertising, while others emphasize social media (e.g., Minton et al., 2012). Some emphasize changing laws and jurisprudence, as well as providing incentives, as approaches to communicate the need to change to conform with broader societal goals. Others emphasize education. Some focus on individuals, whereas others emphasize consumption communities (Shoham & Kahle, 1996) and stakeholders (Cronin, Smith, Gleim, Ramirez, & Martinez, 2011). The strategy of communication encompasses public relations, publicity, sales promotion, personal selling, trade shows, customer relationship management, and direct marketing (Martin & Schouten, 2012).

Belz and Peattie (2009) maintain that communication is the most important element in the marketing mix because marketing sustainability requires developing long-term relationships with consumers. Consumers must accept not only a product's functional attributes but also ecological attributes. This task often involves opening the entire company's operation to consumer evaluation, rather than a simple focus on a product.

Martin and Schouten (2012) emphasize the importance of integrity in sustainability communication. Consumers need to trust the communication that they receive about sustainable products. Martin and Schouten identify several problems common in attempts to communicate sustainability. *Greenwashing* means exaggerating claims about sustainability. *Astroturfing* refers to creating a phony sense of public sentiment. *Greenmuting* involves underplaying contributions to sustainability when positive business activities might be controversial. For example, although consumers prefer organic wine in blind taste tests, vineyards that label their products as organic tend to have lower sales; therefore, organic wineries tend not to promote their sustainable production processes.

Before we go further, perhaps a brief note on the meaning communicated by concepts is in order. *Green marketing* refers to activities in selling that consider ecological or environmental consequences. It addresses the depletion of nonrenewable resources, but it also emphasizes other environmental issues, such as loss of species, destruction of habitat, and poverty (Martin & Schouten, 2012). *Sustainable marketing* expands the concept of green marketing to include the triple bottom line of economic, environmental, and social issues (Martin & Schouten, 2012). *Sustainability* implies the use of resources in a manner that can continue indefinitely. This ideal often remains elusive, but it is always the long-term goal, even if unstated.

Chapters in the Book

The chapters in this book make significant additional contributions to the understanding of sustainable consumption by bringing together consumer psychology, advertising, and marketing communications. The book is divided into four parts, with individual sections focusing on various aspects of sustainable consumption. Part I provides an overview of the meaning of sustainable consumption for consumers. In Part II, the authors introduce various determinants (e.g., religion and religiosity, social values and holistic thinking, ethnicity, and visual information) of sustainable consumption. Conceptual frameworks that may be used to increase sustainable consumption are discussed in Part III. Finally, Part IV introduces examples of environmental sustainability applications.

Part I. Understanding Environmental Sustainability: What It Means to Consumers

Chapter 2: Sustainability: Is Perception as Good as Reality?

Encouraging consumers to engage in sustainable consumption is closely related to what it means to a consumer to be sustainable. Using two studies, Parsons, Soo, and Berth attempt to provide a clear picture of what *sustainable* means for both consumers and businesses. Study 1, based on the Greenness Matrix developed by Simula, Lehtimaki, and Salo (2009), includes interviews with four chemical-based manufacturer businesses and corresponding business buyers to understand what high and low greenness (both actual and perceived) mean. As a result of the interviews, Parsons, Soo, and Berth constructed five greenness factors: sustainable credibility, environmental impact, consideration of stakeholders, resource and energy efficiency, and philosophy. These factors can help manufacturers and buyers place a business into one of the quadrants (i.e., green washer, sustainable superiority, honest–nongreen, and missed opportunity/strategic choice) of the Greenness Matrix. Study 2, based on the meaning transfer model (McCracken, 1986), focuses on the symbolic meanings of sustainable products to clarify why consumers choose them. Interviews conducted with seven consumers of a brand of sustainable household cleaning and body-care products uncovered symbolic meanings of virtue, personal and collective values, health, and trust. These meanings, in turn, are used by consumers to build and express a self-image based on being virtuous, responsible, contributing, and risk-averse members of society. These two studies can help researchers and marketers to understand the factors involved in determining the perceived and actual sustainability of businesses, how the self-image of a green consumer is created through the symbolic meanings of sustainability, and how the two can combine to determine segmentation in a market competing on sustainability issues.

Chapter 3: The Many Shades of Greenwashing: Using Consumer Input for Policy Decisions Regarding Green Advertisements

As the importance and popularity of sustainable consumption have increased, many companies started to promote their products as green although this green message may not be valid for some. To deal with these greenwashing practices, the Federal Trade Commission (FTC) updated its green guides through two sources of consumer input: open meetings and an online consumer survey. In Chapter 3, after reviewing these two consumer inputs and the resulting revised green guides of the FTC, Sheehan offers an alternative method, an online site called the Greenwashing Index, for consumers to give input. The Greenwashing Index allows visitors to assess advertisements posted on the Web site based on several criteria, including using misleading words and visuals, providing vague or un-provable claims, making exaggerations, and masking information. Sheehan analyzed the written comments on this Web site using a technique called Thematic Analysis. The results revealed two broad thematic categories: claims (based on language and images) and context. Visitors to the Web site believe that words like *green* and *clean*, visuals of trees and flowers, and the lack of contextual information make it difficult to assess authenticity of green claims made in advertisements. Based on these findings, Sheehan identifies gaps in FTC policy and offers suggestions to further strengthen the Green Guides to minimize the negative impacts of greenwashing. The findings can also help researchers to understand what *green* and *sustainable* mean for consumers.

Chapter 4: Product End-of-Life Decisions

Although the consumption cycle of products from a traditional perspective includes three stages (acquisition, use, and disposal), this cycle is more complex from a sustainability perspective as the cycle also involves reusing, recycling, donation, refurbishing, and so on. In this chapter, Kapitan, Bhargave, Trask, Sundie, and Silvera examine the link between disposal and second-hand acquisition through various subcultures (or consumer tribes) of consumption, such as thrift store shoppers, downshifters, and voluntary simplifiers. The authors suggest, based on a thorough literature review, that two pathways can be used to explore sustainable behaviors of these consumer tribes. First, these consumer tribes value consuming less and seek to maintain and consume used goods. Second, although the motivations for such practices are still unclear, it is possible that these practices are used to signal a certain lifestyle and image and are perceived as a source of pride for committed members of these consumer tribes. Accordingly, marketers can use these motivations as bases for their targeting strategies. Moreover, Kapitan, Bhargave, Trask, Sundie, and Silvera, after reviewing the literature on how endowment and attachment can make the process of parting with goods difficult, propose ways for consumers to navigate and ease the process of disposal. Finally, the authors examined why some consumers (such as those in the simplifier consumer subcultures) have less trouble participating in the used-goods market and suggest that an individual difference variable affects the responses to sensing the essence or personality of another consumer in a previously owned object.

Part II. Determinants of Sustainable Consumption

Chapter 5: Religion and Religiosity's Influence on Sustainable Consumption Behaviors

Although religion has not been one of the main variables used to understand consumer behavior, preliminary studies showed that religion does affect different aspects of consumer behavior (e.g., Bailey & Sood, 1993; Essoo & Dibb, 2004). In Chapter 5, Stickel provides support for the impact of religion on an important consumer behavior aspect: sustainable consumption. More specifically, this chapter treats religious affiliation and degree of religiosity as individual difference variables and investigates their impact on sustainable consumption practices (SCPs; both attitudes and behaviors). By using nationally representative secondary data from the General Social Survey 2010 dataset, Stickel examined the differences in sustainable consumption practices between Christian denominations (Baptists, Catholics, Lutherans, Methodists, Pentecostals, Presbyterians, and nondenominational Christians) as well as nonreligious respondents. She also included measures of religiosity (i.e., degree of belief) and some basic demographic and psychographic variables (e.g., age, gender, political orientation, and geographic location). Results revealed that nonreligious consumers are more likely than religious consumers to engage in sustainable consumption practices. Among religious consumers, those who belonged to denominations supporting an inerrant view of scripture are less likely to participate in SCPs than those who belonged to denominations that support human interpretation of scripture. Stickel's study also showed that higher religiosity is correlated with higher participation in sustainable consumption. Because the majority (if not all) of previous studies focused on main religious groupings (Christian, Muslim, Jew, Hindu, and so on), this study is different from those studies in terms of its focus. Accordingly, one of the key contributions of this study is its examination of differences in sustainable consumption practices at the level of religious denomination, not main religious grouping. The development of this comprehensive examination of religion, then, can help marketers to initiate segmentation practices for sustainable consumption on the basis of religious affiliation and prominent religious denominations.

Chapter 6: Sustainable Behavior and Holistic Thinking

Differences in cognitive processes of holistic and analytic thinkers tend to affect people's reactions to the social and ethical issues, including sustainability issues (e.g., Lee, Youn, & Nayakankuppam, 2011). In this chapter, a framework is proposed to stimulate sustainable behavior as a function of holistic thinking by Lee, Youn, and Nayakankuppam. Specifically, the authors suggest that holistic thinking, as opposed to analytic thinking, is associated with increased perceived importance of social values related to sustainability. This increased perceived importance, in turn, leads to greater willingness to enhance sustainability. Accordingly, based on three studies, the authors test the prediction that, when compared to analytic thinkers, holistic thinkers would hold more favorable attitudes toward sustainability and show greater willingness to help sustainable development. Study 1 treated thinking style as an individual difference and provided support for the positive impact of holistic thinking on attitudes toward a wildlife conservation program and donating to that program. In Study 2, holistic and analytic thinking were manipulated; still, the results replicated the first study. Study 3, however, examined how cognitive resources affect thinking styles on sustainability issues and showed that holistically primed participants tend to hold more favorable attitudes toward sustainability issues, and they are more likely to volunteer for programs related to sustainability when they are in the low cognitive-load condition. All these results suggest that sustainable behavior can be promoted as a function of holistic thinking. This knowledge can help marketers and public policy makers communicate about the importance of pro-social goals and override short-term self-interested benefits. However, as Lee, Youn, and Nayakankuppam showed in Study 3, holistic thinking requires cognitive resources. Accordingly, marketers and public policy makers should use strategies that can enhance cognitive resources for holistic thinkers.

Chapter 7: Green Advertising and Behavior: Non-Hispanics vs. Acculturating Hispanics

Because populations with different social and cultural characteristics may have different attitudes, knowledge, and behaviors regarding the environmental issues (e.g., Johnson, Bowker, & Cordell, 2004), and because the United States is becoming more ethnically diverse, it is important to understand how various ethnic groups in the United States approach environmental issues. In Chapter 7, Segev compares green behaviors and the drivers influencing them for non-Hispanic (i.e., native-born) and Hispanic immigrant consumers. Moreover, the Hispanic group is divided into four acculturation segments: assimilation, integration, separation, and marginalization. By focusing on four green behaviors (i.e., green purchase intention, actual green purchasing, conservation behavior, and environmentalism activism), Segev examines the mediating effect of perceived green advertising influence on the relationship between environmental awareness and these four environmentally friendly behaviors. Data collected from 587 Hispanic and 276 non-Hispanic participants in the Greater Miami metropolitan area were used to test this associative model. Results revealed differences among non-Hispanics and Hispanics as well as among four acculturation segments. For instance, the Hispanic integration group scored significantly higher on several green behaviors than did non-Hispanics and other Hispanics acculturation groups. The results also provided support for the hypothesized model across all groups: Awareness is positively associated with green behaviors tested (except environmental activism) through the perceived influence of green advertising. Overall, through these findings, Segev offers some preliminary insights for marketing professionals about the potential responsiveness of various consumer groups to green promotions and future communication practices directed at each group.

Chapter 8: The Influence of Visual Information on Environmentally Significant Behavior

In Chapter 8, Mosteller integrates research from two main aspects of environmentally significant behavior: the informational context of stimuli presented to inform behavior and factors that affect how consumers process and evaluate information presented. Contextual factors discussed in this chapter include product contexts in which attribute tradeoffs between social and environmental aspects of products can be critical; social dilemmas in which tradeoffs between attributes that benefit the self versus the environment are examined; values and ethics in which the perceptions of one's relationship with the environment serves as a guiding principle; and the choice context in which the context of information presented at the point of choice influences how consumers think about the decision. Mosteller also discusses three factors related to informational processes that may influence consumer decisions: negative versus positive valenced information, visual versus textual information, and concrete versus abstract information. Knowledge of these factors can be valuable to understanding consumers' attitudes and behaviors in relation to environmentally significant behavior.

Part III. Increasing Sustainable Consumption: Conceptual Frameworks

Chapter 9: Reluctant for a Reason? A Persuasion Knowledge Perspective on Green Advertising

In this chapter, Xie, Cavallero, and Cheng connect two streams of research—green advertising and persuasion knowledge—to explain the mechanisms responsible for consumer resistance to green advertising. By focusing on verbal claims in commercial advertisements (both broadcast and print) targeted at adult consumers, the authors first review the literature on green advertising, the Persuasion Knowledge Model (Friestad & Wright, 1994), and the green persuasion knowledge. Then, they provide recommendations for future research. Specifically, Xie, Cavallero, and Cheng discuss three issues (information processing, construal level, and perceived efficacy) related to the green persuasion knowledge that can have important theoretical, practical, and public policy implications. In terms of information processing, the authors suggest that the integration of the green persuasion knowledge with dual or tri-process models (e.g., central vs. peripheral or analytic vs. holistic) can enhance the effectiveness of the study of persuasion knowledge. The authors also suggest the integration of the green persuasion knowledge studies with the construal level studies as the types (e.g., substantive vs. associative) and frames (e.g., gain vs. loss) of green claims can interact with the construal level (abstract vs. concrete) when consumers assess those green claims. Finally, Xie, Cavallero, and Cheng propose that the perceptions of self-efficacy (how green tactics influence oneself) and other-efficacy (how green tactic influence other people) may be important factors in studying green persuasion knowledge. Based on these recommendations, researchers and marketers can conduct studies to understand consumers' resistance to both green advertising and sustainable consumption.

Chapter 10: Promoting Low-Carbon Policy to the Public: Message Framing Matters

As a result of recognizing climate change as an important environmental problem, many countries have introduced low-carbon policies (LCP) to encourage their citizens to use low-carbon energy systems. One factor that affects the success of these policies is the communication strategy used to promote LCP to the public (Scrase & Ockwell, 2010). In Chapter 10, Han, Yu, and Teng propose a model of message framing to address the communication problems related to promoting LCP to the public. Based on a hierarchical order of promotional goals from awareness to action (awareness → memory → attitude → intention → action), this model considers the impact of various moderators (i.e., target audience's self-regulation, subjective knowledge, culture, the level of involvement, and prior advertising messages) on the relationship between message framing and LCP promotional goals. In a way, the moderators included in this model construct the communication situation for the promotional campaign. Accordingly, marketers and public policy makers can use these moderators to perform situational analyses even before they start their campaigns to promote LCP to the public. The authors suggest, based on these situational analyses, that promotional messages can be planned and developed effectively by choosing appropriate message-framing strategies (e.g., gain vs. loss, promotion vs. prevention, positive vs. negative). The use of these message-framing strategies, in turn, can help marketers and public policy makers to convince the public of the necessity of LCP and lead citizens to take action to decrease their carbon footprint.

Chapter 11: Consumer Creativity and Its Implications for Sustainability Marketing

Although environmental sustainability issues have gained importance and popularity over the years, many consumers are still reluctant to engage in sustainable consumption (Thøgersen & Crompton, 2009). To deal with this problem, Yang, Bublitz, Wang, and Peracchio integrate the research on environmental sustainability and creativity and discuss how consumer creativity can encourage sustainable consumption. In other words, the authors suggest that creativity, conceptualized as a syndrome containing a number of elements, can be used to shift consumers toward innovations in sustainable consumption. Various factors that may promote creative solutions to environmental concerns are discussed in this chapter. Some of these factors include making consumers adopt a creative mindset, encouraging consumers to think at an abstract level, and inducing a visual processing style among consumers. Yang, Bublitz, Wang, and Peracchio also provide suggestions for identifying factors that lead consumers to convert their creative environmental ideas into actions as well as to use creative advertising (by marketers and public policy makers) to promote environmentally conscious behaviors. For instance, it is suggested that creative ads are more likely to activate a creative mindset among consumers, which will, in turn, help consumers find new and creative ways to engage in sustainable consumption. Overall, Yang, Bublitz, Wang, and Peracchio claim that encouraging consumer creativity may lead to more active involvement in environmentally conscious consumption.

Chapter 12: Consequences of Legislating Packaging Behavior: Germany's Green Dot Program and Its Communications

The Green Dot (GD) is a German program that requires manufacturers to take back post-consumer packaging waste from the products that they produce to recycle it. The program's goals are to encourage innovative packaging design and a higher recycling rate. In this chapter, Jones, Owen, and Kahle first examine the GD Program in Germany and the rest of Europe and evaluate its impact on progress toward sustainable development. More specifically, the authors discuss in detail the criticisms of the GD Program (e.g., not paying enough attention to avoiding waste in the first place, not promoting refillable bottles, misleading the public with the GD symbol, and being perceived as a barrier to trade). However, despite these criticisms, the GD Programs seems to be very successful in Germany and other European countries. Indeed, GD is considered a symbol of environmental responsibility throughout Europe. Can this program succeed in the United States, too? Jones, Owen, and Kahle conclude this chapter by identifying several factors that might affect the success of the program in the United States: resistance by municipal and state governments, industry cooperation in the venture, consumer attitudes toward recycling, and the recycling capacities and technologies currently available.

Part IV. Applications of Environmental Sustainability

Chapter 13: Preschool Children's Preference for Energy-Dense, Branded Foods: An Unsustainable Trajectory

Although food behavior is not one of the first issues that comes to mind when we think about sustainable consumption, certain food behaviors can have a direct impact on environmental degradation (Sager, 1995). In this chapter, Cornwell and McAlister focus on the development of food preferences and food choices in early childhood and provide insights for interventions that promote more sustainable food consumption habits. More specifically, because food preferences are established early in childhood, Cornwell and McAlister focus on preschool children and examine their responsiveness to marketing and advertising, how their thoughts and behaviors are shaped by their experiences with the market, and how sustainable behaviors (including sustainable food consumption) can be encouraged when they are still young. Based on a thorough literature review, the authors show that preschool children are affected by marketing and advertising practices when they are shaping their food consumption habits. For instance, it was found that preschool children develop particular food expectations (e.g., burger with fries) through advertising and marketing exposures and, as a result, actively seek to replicate these expectations when they dine at home and with other food and drinks. Cornwell and McAlister conclude the chapter by providing suggestions for parents, caregivers, and marketers: Parents and caregivers can remove all packaging to reduce food and brand associations, package healthy food choices in fun ways, reduce the commercial content available to children, and be aware of the commitment that they are making when they purchase meal deals with collectible toys. Marketers can also support the sustainable food consumption initiatives through methods such as offering only water as the default drink in kids' meals.

Chapter 14: Semantic Analysis of Energy-Related Conversations in Social Media: A Twitter Case Study

With the increasing adoption of social media, new opportunities are available for researching the impact on sustainable consumption of online conversation on environmental issues. In an attempt to show the feasibility of social media to detect awareness, describe attitudes, and infer influence about sustainability communication campaigns, in Chapter 14, Russell, Flora, Strohmaier, Pöschko, Perez, Yu, Smith, and Rubens examine the online conversation about energy efficiency behavior by using the data collected on Twitter through the analysis of the messages, users, and content hashtags in tweets over four months. More specifically, the authors analyze the eco-linguisticly filtered social media to understand the frequency, context, and potential persuasive influence of social media conversations about changing energy behaviors. Results indicate opportunities for text analysis on Twitter content to understand how to improve relevance of energy efficiency communications and demonstrate user-friendly tools to visualize the semantics of vast quantities of user-generated content about energy and sustainability. The authors conclude that studying Twitter communications can be an important tool for assessing engagement, identifying influencers, and identifying word-of-mouth communities that can accelerate change in energy efficiency behaviors.

Chapter 15: Oregon's Iconic Bottle Bill

The Oregon Bottle Bill (OBB) establishes a bottle return system that encourages participation by consumers and beverage companies, communicates that sustainability has a social value for everyone, and increases sustainable behaviors (cf. Kahle & Beatty, 1987). In 2011, the OBB was revised to include all glass, metal, and plastic containers; to open privately operated redemption centers; and to raise the current five-cent deposit to ten cents per container if participation rates fall below 80 percent. In this chapter, Moscowitz and Kahle examine the potential consequences and problems of the revised OBB from a comprehensive, marketing-based business perspective. The authors conducted telephone interviews with Oregon state politicians, beverage distributors, microbreweries, grocery retailers, and consumers to learn more about their responses to the OBB revisions. The results revealed that there are opposing thoughts on government intervention; consumer attitudes toward the bottle return program and recycling in general need to change; retailers support the availability of BottleDrop redemption centers as these centers give retailers the opportunity to increase their retail and inventory space; and problems associated with serving rural communities that use only specialized redemption centers. The authors also conducted secondary research through media accounts and compared bottle bills and container return programs in other states, such as California, Connecticut, Michigan, and Hawaii. Based on the phone interviews and state comparisons, Moscowitz and Kahle provide two specific recommendations, rebranding the Oregon's container-deposit return program and increasing the deposit fee, and discuss how the implementation of these recommendations can make the program more effective.

Chapter 16: Defining Livability: How Livable Communities Contribute to and Benefit from Social Cohesion

Livable communities, through enhancing residents' sense of community awareness and social bonding, contribute to sustainable communities and community identity. Other than the importance of livable communities in consumers' well-being, however, the concept of livable communities does not attract much attention. In this final chapter, Wiggin discusses how consumers select livable communities as well as the implications for consumers living in those communities. Using an Internet-based survey of 1,122 participants, the author finds that community members define values and attributes of a livable community differently, which creates different market segments, and that a livable community and the identification with that community improves community satisfaction and reduces mobility desires. Overall, Wiggin concludes that a livable community that provides a sense of social cohesion among community members drives sustainability in that community.

References

Aaker, J. (1997). Dimensions of brand personality. *Journal of Marketing Research, 34* (August), 347–357.

Ajzen, I. (1991). The theory of planned behavior. *Organizational Behavior and Human Decision Processes, 50*(2), 179–211.

Bailey, J., & Sood, J. (1993). The effects of religious affiliation on consumer behavior: A preliminary investigation. *Journal of Managerial Issues, 5*(3), 328–352.

Banerjee, S., Gulas, C. S., & Iyer, E. (1995). Shades of green: A multidimensional analysis of environmental advertising. *Journal of Advertising, 24*(2), 21–31.

Batra, R., Homer, P. M., & Kahle, L. R. (2001). Values, susceptibility to normative influence, and attribute importance weights: A nomological analysis. *Journal of Consumer Psychology, 11*(2), 115–128.

Beatty, S. E., & Kahle, L. R. (1988). Alternative hierarchies of the attitude-behavior relationship: The impact of brand commitment and habit. *Journal of the Academy of Marketing Science, 16*(Summer), 1–10.

Belz, F.-M., & Peattie, K. (2009). *Sustainability marketing: A global perspective*. Chichester, UK: John Wiley.

Brand, K. W. (2000). Environmental consciousness and behaviour: The greening of lifestyles. In M. Redclift & G. Woodgate (Eds.), *The international handbook on environmental sociology* (pp. 204–217). Cheltenham, UK: Edward Elgar.

Crittenden, V. L., Crittenden, W. F., Ferrell, L. K., Ferrell, O. C., & Pinney, C. C. (2011). Market oriented sustainability: A conceptual framework and propositions. *Journal of the Academy of Marketing Science, 39,* 71–85.

Cronin, J. J., Smith, J. S., Gleim, M. R., Ramirez, E., & Martinez, J. D. (2011). Green marketing strategies: An examination of stakeholders and the opportunities they present. *Journal of the Academy of Marketing Science, 39,* 158–174.

Da Silva, R. V., & Syed Alwi, S. F. (2006). Cognitive, affective attributes and conative, behavioral responses in retail corporate branding. *Journal of Product & Brand Management, 15*(5), 293–305.

De Chernatony, L., Drury, S., & Segal-Horn, S. (2004). Identifying and sustaining services brands' values. *Journal of Marketing Communications, 10*(2), 73–93.

Essoo, N., & Dibb, S. (2004). Religious influences on shopping behavior: An exploratory study. *Journal of Marketing Management, 20*(7), 683–712.

Figueiredo, J. N. de, Guillen, M., & Zheng, X. (2012). Mapping the universe of green products. In J. N. Figueiredo & M. Guillen (Eds.), *Green products: Perspectives on innovation and adoption* (pp. 1–16). Boca Raton, FL: CRC Press.

Fournier, S. (1998). Consumers and their brands: Developing relationship theory in consumer research. *Journal of Consumer Research, 24*(4), 343–373.

Friestad, M., & Wright, P. (1994). The persuasion knowledge model: How people cope with persuasion attempts. *Journal of Consumer Research, 21*(1), 1–31.

Hawken, P., Lovins, A., & Lovins, L. H. (1999). *Natural capitalism: Creating the next industrial revolution.* Boston: Little, Brown.

Hult, G. T. M. (2011). Market-focused sustainability: Market orientation plus! *Journal of the Academy of Marketing Science, 39,* 1–6.

Jaeger-Erben, M., Schäfer, M., Dalichau, D., Dehmel, C., Goetz, K., Fischer, D., Homberg, A., Schulz, M., & Zundel, S. (2012). Societal steering of consumption toward sustainability. In R. Defila, A. Di Giulio, & R. Kaufmann-Hayoz (Eds.), *The nature of sustainable consumption and how to achieve it* (pp. 113–142). Munich: Oekom.

Johnson, C. Y., Bowker, J. M., & and Cordell, K. H. (2004). Ethnic variation in environmental belief and behavior: An examination of the new ecological paradigm in social psychological context. *Environment and Behavior, 36*(2), 157–186.

Kahle, L. R., & Beatty, S. E. (1987a). Cognitive consequences of legislating postpurchase behavior: Growing up with the bottle bill. *Journal of Applied Social Psychology, 17,* 826–840.

Kahle, L. R., & Beatty, S. E. (1987b). The task situation and habit in the attitude-behavior relationship: A social adaptation view. *Journal of Social Behavior and Personality, 2*(2, pt. 1), 219–232.

Kahle, L. R., & Valette-Florence, P. (2012). *Marketplace lifestyles in an age of social media: Theory and method.* Armonk, NY: M.E. Sharpe.

Kahle, L R., Beatty, S. E., & Homer, P. M. (1986). Alternative measurement approaches to consumer values: The list of values (LOV) and the values and life style (VALS). *Journal of Consumer Research, 13*(4), 405–409.

Kaufmann-Hayoz, R., Brohmann, B., Defila, R., Di Giulio, A., Dunkleberg, E., Erdmann, L., Fuchs, D., Goelz, S., Homburg, A., Matthies, E., Nachreiner, M., Tews, K., & Weiss, J. (2012). Theoretical perspectives on consumer behavior—Attempt at establishing an order to the theories. In R. Defila, A. Di Giulio, & R. Kaufmann-Hayoz (Eds.), *The nature of sustainable consumption and how to achieve it* (pp. 81–112). Munich: Oekom.

Kloeckner, C. A., & Matthies, E. (2004). How habits interfere with norm directed behavior—A normative decision-making model for travel mode choice. *Journal of Environmental Psychology, 24,* 319–327.

Lee, Y., Youn, N., & Nayakankuppam, D. (2011). The content of a brand scandal moderating the effect of thinking styles on the scandal's spillover. In R. Ahluwalia, T. L. Chartrand, R. K. Ratner (Eds.), *Advances in Consumer Research* (Vol. 39, pp. 523–524). Duluth, MN: Association for Consumer Research.

Markkula, A., & Moisander, J. (2012). Discursive confusion over sustainable consumption: A discursive perspective on the perplexity of marketplace knowledge. *Journal of Consumer Policy, 35,* 105–125.

Martin, D., & Schouten, J. W. (2012). *Sustainable marketing.* Boston: Prentice Hall.

Matthies, E., Kastner, I., Kleese, A., & Wagner, H. J. (2011). High reduction potentials for energy user behavior in public buildings: How much can psychology-based interventions achieve? *Journal of Environmental Studies and Sciences, 1*(3), 241–255.
McAlexander, J., Schouten, J., & Koenig, H. (2002). Building brand community. *Journal of Marketing, 66*(1), 38–54.
McCracken, G. (1986). Culture and consumption: A theoretical account of the structure and movement of the cultural meaning of consumer goods. *Journal of Consumer Research, 13*(June), 71–84.
McDonagh, P. (1998). Toward a theory of sustainable communication in risk society: Relating issues of sustainability to marketing communications. *Journal of Marketing Management, 14,* 591–622.
Minton, E., Lee, C., Orth, U., Kim, C. H., & Kahle, L. R. (2012). Sustainable marketing and social media: A cross-country analysis of motives for sustainable behaviors. *Journal of Advertising, 41*(4), 71–87.
Moisander, J. (2007). Motivational complexity of green consumerism. *International Journal of Consumer Studies, 31*, 404–409.
Ottman, J. A. (1998). *Green marketing: Opportunity for innovation*. Lincolnwood, IL: NTC Business Books.
Pape, J., Rau, H., Fahy, F., & Davies, A. (2011). Developing policies and instruments for sustainable consumption: Irish experiences and futures. *Journal of Consumer Policy, 34*(1), 25–42.
Peterson, C. (2006). *A primer in positive psychology*. New York: Oxford University Press.
Reusswig, F., Lotze-Campen, H., & Gerlinger, K. (2005). Changing global lifestyle and consumption patterns: The case of energy and food. In G. Radhakrishna (Ed.), *Consumer behaviour: Effective measurement tools* (pp. 197–210). Hyderabad, India: ICFAI University Press.
Sager, G. (1995). "A burger and a coke" and other environmental problems: Reflections on diet and the environmental crisis. *Sustainable Development, 3,* 149–157.
Schäfer, M., Jaeger-Erben, M., & Bamberg, S. (2012). Life events as windows of opportunity for changing towards sustainable consumption patterns? Results from an intervention study. *Journal of Consumer Policy, 35,* 65–84.
Schäfer, M., Jaeger-Erben, M., & dos Santos, A. (2011). Leapfrogging to sustainable consumption? An explorative survey of consumption habits and orientations in southern Brazil. *Journal of Consumer Policy, 34*(1), 175–196.
Schuster, M. R. (2010). *Lofty pursuits: Repairing the world one building at a time*. Dallas: Brown Books.
Scrase, J., & Ockwell, D. (2010). The role of discourse and linguistic framing effects in sustaining high carbon energy policy—An accessible introduction. *Energy Policy, 38*(5), 2225.
Sheth, J. N., Sethia, N. K., & Srinivas, S. (2011). Mindful consumption: A customer-centric approach to sustainability. *Journal of the Academy of Marketing Science, 39,* 21–39.
Shoham, A., & Kahle, L. R. (1996). Spectators, viewers, readers: Communication and consumption communities in sport marketing. *Sport Marketing Quarterly, 5*(March), 11–19.
Shove, E. (2005). Changing human behavior and lifestyle: A challenge for sustainable consumption? In L. Repke & L. Reisch (Eds.), *The ecological economics of consumption* (pp. 111–132). Cheltenham, UK: Elgar.
Simula, H., Lehtimaki, T., & Salo, J. (2009). Managing greenness in technology marketing. *Journal of Systems and Information Technology, 11*(4), 331–346.
Steg, L., & Norland, A. (2013). Models to explain environmental behavior. In L. Steg, A. E. van den Berg, & J. I. M. de Groot (Eds.), *Environmental psychology: An introduction* (pp. 185–196). Chichester, UK: Wiley-Blackwell.

Stern, P. C. (1999). Information, incentives, and proenvironmental consumer behavior. *Journal of Consumer Policy, 22,* 461–478.

Stern, P. C. (2000). Toward a coherent theory of environmentally significant behavior. *Journal of Social Issues, 56,* 407–424.

Thøgersen, J. (2005). How may consumer policy empower consumers for sustainable lifestyles? *Journal of Consumer Policy, 28,* 143–178.

Thøgersen, J., & Crompton, T. (2009). Simple and painless? The limitations of spillover in environmental campaigning. *Journal of Consumer Policy, 32,* 141–163.

Toulouse, N. (2012). Institutionalization of the sustainable market: A case study of fair trade in France. In L. Penaloza, N. Toulouse, & L. M. Visconti (Eds.), *Marketing management: A cultural perspective* (pp. 475–488). New York: Routledge.

Valor, C. (2008). Can consumers buy responsibly? Analysis and solutions for market failures. *Journal of Consumer Policy, 31,* 315–326.

Wasik, J. F. (1996). *Green marketing and management: A global perspective.* Cambridge, MA: Blackwell.

Part I

Understanding Environmental Sustainability

What It Means to Consumers

Encouraging consumers to engage in sustainable consumption is closely related to what it means to a consumer to be sustainable. Accordingly, the chapters in this section attempt to clarify consumers' perceptions about sustainability and green practices.

Parsons, Soo, and Berth use two theoretical developments, the Greenness Matrix and the meaning transfer model, to explain what sustainability means to both consumers and businesses. Based on interviews, the authors identify five greenness factors that can help manufacturers and buyers place a business in one of the quadrants of the Greenness Matrix. Parsons, Soo, and Berth also examine the symbolic meanings of sustainable products to understand why consumers choose them and uncover symbolic meanings of virtue, personal and collective values, health, and trust. These two studies can help researchers and marketers to understand the factors involved in determining the perceived and actual sustainability of businesses and how the self-image of a green consumer is created through the symbolic meanings of sustainability.

Sheehan uses the data from an online site called the Greenwashing Index to understand consumers' perceptions of green advertisements. The analysis of the written comments provided by the visitors to the Web site revealed two broad thematic categories: claims (based on language and images) and context. Based on these findings, Sheehan identifies gaps in the revised Federal Trade Commission policy and provides suggestions to further strengthen the Green Guides to minimize the negative impacts of greenwashing.

Kapitan, Bhargave, Trask, Sundie, and Silvera focus on the extended consumption cycle and examine the link between disposal and secondhand acquisition through various consumer tribes. The authors suggest that two pathways can be used to explore sustainable behaviors among these consumer tribes. First, these consumer tribes value consuming less and seek to maintain and consume used goods. Second, these sustainable practices are used to signal a certain lifestyle and image, perceived as a source of pride for committed members of these consumer tribes. Moreover, Kapitan, Bhargave, Trask, Sundie, and Silvera propose ways for consumers to navigate and ease the process of disposal and parting with meaningful goods. Finally, the authors examine why some consumers have less trouble participating in the used-goods marketplace and suggest that an individual difference variable affects the responses to sensing the essence or personality of another consumer in a previously owned object.

2

Sustainability

Is Perception as Good as Reality?

Andrew G. Parsons, Samuel Soo, and Nicole Berth

During an episode of the popular television series *Mad Men* ("The Gold Violin," Episode 7, Season 2, AMC Network) set in the early 1960s, an advertising executive and his wife (the characters Don and Betty Draper) have a picnic on a pristine lawn in an idyllic park environment. At the conclusion of the picnic, the characters discard a drink container, shake off the trash from their picnic rug, and walk back to their car, letting the litter blow away in the breeze.

Regardless of whether this is an accurate portrayal of attitudes toward the environment at the time (and it has certainly given rise to debate on social media sites as to whether it was really conveying a deeper allegorical meaning), the perception "that is the attitude people had back in those days" struck a chord with many viewers. Words like "shocked," "horrified," and "disgusted" permeated the online discussions of the episode after it aired in 2008. Other perceptions of the time include the idea that environmentalists were all "hippies," advertising communications intended to increase consumption, and the catchphrase was "growth," not "sustainability."

This chapter is about today's perceptions—not about the green movement, environmentalism, recycling, or even littering; these are all areas discussed in other chapters, along with the debate over whether and how sustainable we need to be. Rather, the following discussion is about what it means to be sustainable and how the Drapers might act or perceive their actions today. We examine what businesses and consumers are seeking when they engage in sustainable practice. Over the past twenty or more years, we have seen a shift in consumer and business practices around the notion of sustainability, but what we have not seen is a clear understanding of where that shift has taken us in terms of what it means to a consumer and for a business to be sustainable.

Starting with a two-decade-old study looking at consumer attitudes toward socially responsible packaging (Parsons, 1988), we examine the literature to establish current thinking on sustainability and green marketing, symbolism and perceptions of sustainability, and strategies and behaviors that invoke sustainable practice. We then briefly present two studies of sustainability or green marketing. Study 1 is an empirical investigation of green marketing strategies in business organizations, designed to identify the "greenness factors" that put into practice Simula, Lehtimaki, and Salo's (2009) Greenness Matrix. We construct five themes that contribute to perceived greenness (as opposed to actual greenness). In study 2, we explore the symbolic meanings that consumers take from a brand of sustainable products, using McCracken's (1986) model of symbolic meaning transfer as the interpretation lens. We examine the use of these symbolic meanings in building a consumer's self-image related to sustainability and greenness. We conclude by combining the business and consumer perspectives to suggest what it means to be sustainable.

A Bygone Era . . .

A little over two decades ago, a study (Parsons, 1988) investigated the consumption behavior of people presented with two alternative forms of packaging for a fast-food burger—a polystyrene container, which was the prevalent form of packaging at the time, and a recycled-cardboard container, which became the norm in subsequent years. The polystyrene container was known to maintain the product's temperature longer but was recognized as an environmentally unfriendly item. Attitudes about social responsibility were measured, along with behavioral reactions to price manipulations. Two decades ago, consumers were unwilling to pay a premium for more sustainable packaging, believed that the immediate packaging benefit of polystyrene (warmth retention) outweighed the longer-term environmental hazard and did not perceive any social (peer-esteem) problem in being seen with the polystyrene container.

Parsons (1988) went further than simply examining packaging and price. In the studies conducted, 22 items were identified as meaningful or important to consumers at the time. Using the early works of Fishbein and Ajzen as a framework (for an excellent summary of this line of thinking, see Ajzen [2008]), the studies identified three general issues of social responsibility: (1) product-purchase specific, which have direct personal consequences; (2) organizational specific, which have indirect personal consequences; and (3) conservation specific, which also have indirect personal consequences. Applying attitude/behavior models with valence, Parsons found, unsurprisingly, that items with direct personal consequences were considered the most important to consumers. In other words, consumers considered themselves first, then the environment and wider society. In the burger case, consumers were conscious of things like taste and price well before consideration of whether packaging was recyclable.

Since that time, the "green" movement has become mainstream, the triple bottom line (Carter and Rogers, 2008; Elkington, 1997) gained credence in business circles, and the concept of sustainability has achieved traction with consumers and industry. Parsons's (1988) burgers now are not only unlikely to be presented in environmentally unfriendly packaging but are also subject to scrutiny over the sustainable farming practices for the beef, the nutritional value of the garnish, and the recyclability of the packaging. Businesses market themselves as operating sustainably, and consumers seek out products and businesses that are marketed as "green." Questions remain, though: What does it mean for a business to operate sustainably, and what does it mean for a consumer to behave (consume) sustainably? To help answer our questions, we present a brief overview of pertinent literature to set the scene for two studies from an ongoing program of research into sustainability, consumer behavior, and advertising.

Sustainability, Business to Consumer (B2C), and Business to Business (B2B)

Sustainability is one of the major concepts of modern business thinking (Peattie, 2001a, 2001b). It is widely promoted in the Brundtland Report, which defines sustainable development as a process that "meets the needs of the present without compromising the ability of future generations to meet their needs" (United Nations, 1987, p. 43). Sustainability deals with aspects such as increased consumption, population pressure, global warming, climate change, ozone depletion, and loss of habitats and species diversity (Charter et al., 2002).

B2C and Sustainable Consumption

Let us first consider the B2C perspective with regard to sustainability. The focus of this part of our discussion and our consumer study lies in sustainable consumption, which broadly refers to the purchase and use of more efficiently produced products (Seyfang, 2005) and environmentally friendly consumption practices (Halkier, 1999). We acknowledge the view that actions of consumption may not be necessarily sustainable in themselves, only that the nature of the consumption can be less unsustainable with respect to the resources used or environmental impacts generated. The term "sustainable consumption" first entered the international policy arena at the 1992 Earth Summit in Rio (Seyfang, 2005), in the action plan for sustainable development. Proposed solutions to sustainability issues included promoting eco-efficiency and using market instruments to shift consumption patterns (UNCED, 1992). Policy documents have frequently defined sustainable consumption as:

> the use of goods and services that respond to basic needs and bring a better quality of life, while minimizing the use of natural resources, toxic materials and emissions of waste and pollutants over the life cycle, so as not to jeopardize the needs of future generations. (European Environmental Agency, 2005, p. 13)

Many reviews have discussed what sustainable consumption means to different groups (see Cohen & Murphy, 2001; Jackson, 2006; Jackson & Michaelis, 2003; Seyfang, 2004). At present, there is no consensus on precisely what sustainable consumption entails, so it has been used as an umbrella term for a variety of social and environmental issues (Mont & Plepys, 2008). Despite this ambiguity it has become a core area of policy objectives in both national and international domains (Seyfang, 2005). Governments have increasingly incorporated sustainable consumption into policy, which demonstrates the growing importance of the issue and the necessity for solutions. To develop a solution, researchers need to understand the value individuals see in acts of consumption.

Dolan (2002) noted that previous conceptualizations of sustainable consumption did not incorporate the social and cultural meaning found in consumption practices. Soron (2010) adds that sustainable consumption has important communicative and identity-oriented functions that are missing from current conceptualizations. The ways in which individuals consume also house meanings and possess value that extends beyond the utilitarian. Thus, Dolan (2002) calls for sustainable consumption to fully encompass the sociological and anthropological meanings of consumption. Much of modern consumption is symbolic, so it is necessary to draw on theoretical frameworks that incorporate this meaning. Previous literature that has attempted to conceptualize sustainable consumption has not accounted for the symbolic meaning of products in the acts of consuming them.

Schaefer and Crane (2005) outline a number of views of consumption, each possessing a different relationship with the concept of sustainability. Here, the view of consumption that has been adopted for the research is "sociological and anthropological." Under this conceptualization, consumption is not examined from an information or psychological perspective but from a social and cultural one. This view emphasizes:

> less on how people perceive, evaluate and select different consumption options and more on the function that consumption has in their lives, both individually and as members of social groups. (Schaefer & Crane, 2005, p. 83)

The sociological and anthropological view of consumption emphasizes the importance of consumption in facilitating social and cultural expressions. Therefore, consumption can be conceptualized as an intrinsically positive force in allowing individuals to construct and express their self-image (Borgmann, 2001). The conceptualization is valuable as it recognizes that consumption has an important function in building one's self-image.

The literature on sustainable consumption has often focused on identifying who the green consumer is (e.g., Abeliotis, Koniari, & Sardianou, 2010; Diamantopoulos, Schlegelmilch, Sinkovics, & Bohlen, 2003). The green consumer was seen as a solution to consumption issues, so researchers were interested in identifying them. Some of the areas that they have sought to explore were the demographics of green consumers (Roberts, 1995; Schultz, Oskamp, & Mainieri, 1995; Straughan & Roberts, 1999), their personalities (Balderjahn, 1988; Kinnear, Taylor, & Ahmed, 1974), and their attitudes (Shrum, McCarty, & Lowrey, 1995). However, the problem with this focus on the consumer is that these studies have repeatedly contradicted one another (Kilbourne & Beckmann, 1998; Straughan & Roberts, 1999; Wagner,

1997). One explanation is that sustainable consumption behavior by itself is not consistent (Alwitt & Pitts, 1996; Moisander, 2007; Peattie, 1999; Thøgersen, 2004; Uusitalo, 1990). Green attitudes do not always correlate with green consumption behaviors. Researchers have called this the "attitude-behavior" gap.

The "attitude-behavior gap" has been extensively explored in a number of studies (Connolly & Prothero, 2003; Hughner, McDonagh, Prothero, Shultz, & Stanton, 2007; Kollmuss & Agyeman, 2002; Kraus, 1995; Padel & Foster, 2005; Vermeir & Verbeke, 2006; Young, Hwang, McDonald, & Oates, 2010). One example of this gap is that while just under half the population holds favorable attitudes toward organic produce, only about 10 percent of the population purchases organic produce (Hughner et al., 2007). Some explanations offered are that other factors, such as price, perception of performance, and convenience, take precedence in decision criteria (Carrigan & Attalla, 2001; Weatherell, Tregear, & Allinson, 2003). Others in the field state it is due to a lack of alternatives, a disbelief of claims, and a lack of information (de Pelsmacker, Driesen, & Rayp, 2005). This gap means that consumers do not always feel that they can trust the claims of manufacturers and brands. This situation compromises the consumers' commitment to social and ethical issues, one of which is sustainability. This attitude-behavior gap explains the disjuncture that Parsons (1988) found between the perception that recyclable packaging for his burgers was worthwhile and the behavior that rejected its use.

We assume that all consumers, rather than just green consumers, have some capacity and potential to make some or more sustainable consumption choices in their lives (Young et al., 2010). We do not attempt to provide an explanation for inconsistencies in the consumption of sustainable products. The focus of this part of our chapter moves away from who the consumer is and looks, instead, at the role for consumers in the process of consumption. Products and their consumption have important psychological roles that have been previously underestimated by sustainability researchers (van Dam & Apeldoorn, 1996). Study 2 identifies what symbolic value any consumer may obtain through the consumption of sustainable products.

Consumption activities have a distinct cultural significance that has been neglected in production-focused perspectives on sustainable consumption (Dolan, 2002). The practice of consumption is an individual's primary means of self-definition (Durning, 1994). This act of self-definition occurs because consumption is "inextricably linked with values and social meaning" and products act as "signifiers of cultural allegiance and social relationships" (Seyfang, 2004, p. 324). Sustainable consumption needs to start drawing from consumer research addressing consumption to understand the drivers and roles that it plays in self-image creation (Soron, 2010). Consumption is able to create self-image because products have symbolic meanings. We explore the symbolic meanings of sustainable products to develop an understanding of why consumers choose them. Developing this understanding of consumption is valuable as it supports a shift to a consumer culture that addresses sustainability concerns (Dolan, 2002).

Some authors have previously called for a major shift in the cultural values of consumption to address sustainability issues (Dolan, 2002; Michaelis, 2003). Consumer culture is seen as responsible for the growth of unsustainable consumption levels (Featherstone, 1990; Michaelis, 2003), however, shifting culture is not easy. Consumer culture is embedded in existing material and social infrastructure and therefore attempts to change it can face resistance (Heiskanen & Pantzar, 1997; Schein, 1997). Any attempt to initiate a shift in culture first needs to understand the nature and the role of consumption. Examining the consumption practices around sustainable products is a means of achieving this understanding through locating symbolic meanings.

The focus of our study into consumer sustainability perceptions lies in the symbolic value of sustainable products. The area of sustainability is a modern science, so consumer knowledge about it is not firmly rooted (Giddens, 1991). Consumers are not certain of the value of their actions on the environment. Consumers raise questions as to "whom to believe" and "how to decide whom to believe" (Macnaghten, 2003). Thus the choice to purchase sustainable products is difficult to make under the rational school of thought. Furthermore, other authors have noted that the rational and utilitarian consumer is unlikely to be the basis for addressing sustainability (van Dam & Apeldoorn, 1996). For these reasons, research on sustainable consumption needs to be developed from the symbolic and expressive perspective of consumer behavior.

Focusing on the symbolic value of products is useful because consumer behavior toward products is largely based on the ascribed symbolic meanings (Kleine & Kernan, 1991), so it is valuable to explore the symbolic meanings of sustainable products to understand why individuals select them over nonsustainable products. McCracken's (1986) focus on the transfer of symbolic meaning explains how products come to acquire symbolic meaning as well as how consumers use symbolic meaning, particularly through brands. Brands can be tools for shifting consumer attitudes to more sustainable consumption (Ottman, 1993; Pickett-Baker & Ozaki, 2008; Pooley & O'Connor, 2000). Affective processing has been shown to be a key means of converting passive green consumers into ones with sustainable consumption patterns (Ottman, 1998; Pooley & O'Connor, 2000). Exploring consumers' consumption of a particular brand of a sustainable product allows an opportunity for determining the motivation of such behavior.

Sustainable products have product attributes that imbue some symbolic meaning, but the branding of sustainable products grants far greater symbolic meaning. Consumers see value in the symbolic meaning of products as they can use them in their own way. These symbolic meanings can help consumers to manage their self-image.

Consumer products have long been considered extensions of the self (Belk, 1988; Dittmar, 1992; Sartre, 1943). Products can be used to construct a consumer's social world and then to define the consumer's place in it (Douglas, 1976). Consumers use these symbolic meanings to create, foster, and develop their identity

(Belk, 1988; Elliott & Wattanasuwan, 1998; Leigh & Gabel, 1992; McCracken, 1988; Solomon, 1983). These symbolic meanings allow individuals to express themselves and communicate with others (Dittmar, 1992; Douglas & Isherwood, 1978; Gabriel & Lang, 1995; McCracken, 1988; Wattanasuwan, 2005). Therefore, consumers choose products and brands with symbolic meanings that are perceived to be congruent with their personality (Aaker, 1999; Graeff, 1996; Kassarjian, 1971; Sirgy, 1982). Products can also serve as tangible linkages to family (Belk, 1988; Csikszentmihalyi & Rochberg-Halton, 1981; Muniz & O'Guinn, 2001) or past experiences (Prentice, 1987; Wallendorf & Arnould, 1988). Understanding the symbolic meanings of sustainable products is important, given that:

> The core of man's cultural activity lies in his capacity to generate meaning, to communicate, to transmit and to order those meanings; it lies in the creation of a specifically symbolic level of existence. (Silverstone, 1981, p. 2)

The centrality of symbolic meaning in a person's life indicates that it is important to consumers. Consumers value the self-image function of products. They deem products as significant based on what identities they enable and how important the product is in contributing to an overall sense of self (Kleine, Kleine, & Kernan, 1993). Exploring this sense of self allows researchers to understand the way in which consumers make choices in the context of symbolic meanings attached to brands (Onkvisit & Shaw, 1987). Connolly and Prothero (2003) suggest that if sustainable consumption is considered communication, it can be used in identity construction and could thus advance the prospect of a green commodity culture. A shift in consumption culture could be seen as what is necessary to address sustainability concerns.

A valuable starting point for understanding consumption culture is examining those who have already shifted. Consumers who are already using sustainable products have started using the products to build their self-image. Understanding the meaning of consumption and meaning obtained when individuals consume is vital for achieving sustainable consumption (Connolly & Prothero, 2003).

Sustainable products may have particular ideals, rituals, and traditions that feature in the act of consumption. This view merits attention, as it is these ideals, rituals, and traditions that may determine and highlight why they are consumed in preference to other products. Any differences between behaviors regarding sustainable as opposed to nonsustainable products may also give rise to differences in symbolic meaning.

B2B and Green Marketing

Let us turn briefly to the B2B perspective. For the business marketer, much of the emphasis has been on the concept of "green marketing." Basic frameworks on how to link sustainability and B2B marketing exist (e.g., Sharma et al., 2010), including a focus on sustainability related to supply chain activities, used to maintain and intensify collaborations between participants in the supply chain (Sharma et al., 2010; Sheu & Hu, 2008; Weber, 2001). Within the supply chain, remanufacturing activities and their implications for marketing are also of interest (Atasu, Sarvary, & Van Wassenhove, 2008). Remanufacturing captures the idea of examining and repairing a used product in order to extend its life (Sharma et al., 2010). Thus, it includes sustainable components that can be marketed within the supply chain. Furthermore, remanufacturing can moderately influence the manufacturer's ability to meet sustainable environment regulations. For the manufacturer, remanufacturing can open up a new group of key business customers. At the same time, the business customer benefits from lower prices for the remanufactured products, compared with products made with virgin materials (Ferrer & Whybark, 2000; Seitz & Peattie, 2004). Remanufacturing is practiced successfully throughout the automobile industry, in which parts such as motors are remanufactured and sold to business customers for a discounted price.

Another aspect discussed in the literature is integrating sustainability into the marketing processes for new product development (NPD) (Pujari, Peattie, & Wright, 2004). Additional activities have to be included into NPD when sustainability is the goal. These activities look at the environmental impact of the company's products and strive continuously to move NPD in the direction of sustainability (Pujari et al., 2004). Furthermore, organizational aspects influence NPD, such as support from top management, functional interfaces, and environmental policy. If organizational aspects and environmental impacts of products are incorporated into a company's NPD, sustainability can be generated.

Green marketing strategies can provide strong benefits. Business customers increasingly seek to buy environmentally friendly products and services (Drumwright, 1994; Min & Galle, 1997; Polonsky, Broks, & Henry, 1998; Pujari et al., 2004). They also emphasize environmentally responsible practices in their transactions with manufacturers (Sharma et al., 2010). Thus, environmental concern must be acknowledged as an important buying criterion for business customers. This needs to be considered in the development of successful marketing strategies for the B2B environment (Drumwright, 1994). Because they purchase large quantities, business customers are able to strongly influence manufacturers' operations. This influence allows business customers to question and discuss the manufacturer's performance in terms of sustainability (Peattie, 1992). Business customer expertise plays an important role, as it facilitates a profound examination and interpretation of the manufacturer's environmental claims (Iles, 2006; Prakash, 2002). The B2B environment represents the majority of all marketing activities, clearly outnumbering purchases by end-users (Pujari et al., 2004). Thus, the most significant impact of environmental concern is created in the B2B environment (Drumwright, 1994; Morton, 1996). Moreover, government regulations, environmental taxes, and legislation strongly influence companies in the B2B environment (Gurtoo & Antony, 2007; Hong, Kwon, & Roh, 2009; Prakash, 2002; Sharma et al., 2010; Vaccaro, 2009). Also, the public, shareholders, and investors expect companies to operate in a sustainable manner (Cetindamar, 2001; Hong et al., 2009). Companies with the most impact on the environment, such as manufacturers of chemicals, heavy metals, and oil, are the ones most affected by these pressures and regulations (Darnovsky, 1996; Ottman, 1998; Peattie, 1992).

Earl and Clift's (1999) case study outlines the importance of environmental features of electronic products, taking the manufacturer's perspective. Earl and Clift (1999) investigate the buying behavior of business customers regarding their willingness to pay a premium price for environmental product features. Furthermore, the authors examine whether environmental product features act as a selling attribute. Although the results are mixed, the authors find that business customers tend to pay more for a product with environmentally-friendly features. They found that mixed results stem from a business buyer's misperceptions of the green features of the product. This, in fact, weakens the effectiveness of the green marketing strategy. Business buyers do not understand the content and meaning of green product features so they do not react to the environmental features of the product. In addition, negative past experiences related to the performance of environmental friendly products influenced their buying behavior (Earl & Clift, 1999). This lack of understanding of how the degree of greenness is defined from the manufacturers' and business buyers' point of view is of major concern for marketing sustainability.

Crane (2000) integrates the entire supply chain. His study outlines the impacts of green alliances on relationships between supply chain members. These green alliances aim to achieve environmental objectives. However, the majority of the supply chain members react negatively to close green alliances because of companies' skepticism about sharing confidential information with other supply chain members. Nevertheless, after supply chain partners establish collaboration, environmental concerns, such as the use of products with green attributes, can be addressed more effectively. In a marketing environment dominated by government and stakeholder pressure, collaborations become attractive as a means of developing legitimacy and credibility for the entire industry. When such collaboration emerges on environmental issues, it can lead to mutual green marketing solutions to those issues (Crane, 2000).

Research in B2B marketing (as opposed to B2C marketing) that combines sustainability and green marketing is often related to manufacturers in specific industries, typically the technology sector (Simula et al., 2009) and the chemical industry (Iles, 2006; Peattie & Ratnayaka, 1992). These sectors face enormous pressure from government and stakeholders due to their strong potential impacts on the environment, society, and the economy.

In chemical manufacturing, competitive business advantages can be obtained by practicing green marketing while achieving sustainability (Iles, 2006). In his study of chemical manufacturers, Iles (2006) defines sustainability as "green chemistry," which studies the design of chemicals, processes, and impacts as well as energy conservation and resource efficiency. In order to link sustainability and green marketing, manufacturers must define and understand what business buyers see as the sustainable features of their products (Iles, 2006; Peattie & Ratnayaka, 1992). Thus, the business buyer's opinions and perceptions about the product must be considered in order for manufacturers to ensure that the product image matches the true content of the product (Peattie, 1992; Simula et al., 2009) and to enhance the important sustainable features and benefits of the product to match the expectations of the business buyer (Simula et al., 2009).

Simula et al. (2009) describe four approaches for a B2B organization trying to associate green marketing and sustainability with their products. The authors look at organizations in the B2B technology sector that consider sustainability and green marketing in the development of new products. Simula et al. (2009) focus on the development of green marketing strategies to benefit all dimensions of sustainability and recognize that when firms are developing a green marketing strategy, business buyer's preference for green products must be well understood. Thus, Simula et al. (2009) assume that before a new product can be developed, all efforts should be focused on the business buyer's needs and responses. These efforts ensure that manufacturers and their products are perceived as green (Peattie & Crane, 2005). Simula et al. (2009) developed a four-quadrant Greenness Matrix (see below and Figure 2.1) that illustrates how business buyers and manufacturers perceive the greenness of new products. The manufacturer's perceived greenness, called "actual greenness," relates to the objective greenness of the manufacturer and its products. The business buyer's perceived greenness, called "perceived greenness," describes how the business buyer evaluates the manufacturer's greenness and products. Simula et al. (2009) compare the level of actual greenness of the manufacturer with the business buyer's perceived greenness and suggest that a B2B organization consider its own level of greenness in comparison to the level of greenness perceived by the business buyer.

We now briefly turn our attention to two studies that attempt to clarify business's, buyers', and consumers' perceptions and reality with respect to sustainability.

Study 1: Factors of Greenness for Business Organizations

A review of the sustainability and green marketing literature aimed at finding a framework for sustainability from a marketing perspective leads us to the Greenness Matrix of Simula et al. (2009). This framework suggests that when establishing strategies engaging in sustainable practices, businesses consider their actual greenness in comparison to their perceived (by buyers) greenness. The authors, however, fail to define what it means to have "high" greenness or "low" greenness, which makes it impossible for organizations to put this concept into operation.

To rectify this, we conducted a thematic analysis of interviews with four chemical-based manufacturing businesses and corresponding business buyers. We used constructivism as our epistemological philosophy. The businesses are in the hygiene, pharmaceuticals, environmental protection systems, and plastics industries. Participants were marketing managers and business buyers for manufacturers. Participants were selected on the basis of purposive sampling.

The manufacturers were selected if they satisfied the following criteria:

- They are manufacturers.
- They use chemicals in the production process.
- They are based in New Zealand (for practicality as the researchers are New Zealand-based).
- They operate in a B2B environment.

A search of the homepage of www.madefromnewzealand.co.nz was conducted to search for companies that met the selection criteria, yielding four manufacturers. Subsequently, manufacturers were contacted via telephone or e-mail to obtain contact details of the person who could most knowledgably contribute to the research, in this case the marketing manager, who was then contacted via e-mail to inform them about the research project and the ethics and expectations of the participants.

The business customers were selected if they satisfied the following criteria:

- They were business buyers for a manufacturer (above) based in New Zealand that uses chemicals in the production process.
- They operate in a B2B environment.

Business customers were contacted to obtain contact details for the most knowledgeable person. They were also contacted with details about the research, ethics, and expectations of participants.

We constructed five greenness factors, based upon overarching themes identified, which were considered for each of the quadrants in the Greenness Matrix. Each factor outlines the characteristics that manufacturers and buyers would assign to a company with low or high greenness.

The first factor is *sustainable credibility*, related to environmental certifications, compliance with government regulations, a sustainable procurement policy, and environmental management systems. *Greenwashing* activities are not acceptable.

The second factor is the *environmental impact* of the company and the product(s). Emissions, air quality, noise pollution, and the carbon footprint are the most discussed by participants, with concerns over recyclability, biodegradability, and reuse options also raised. The entire product life cycle should also be considered in this context.

The third factor is *consideration of stakeholders*. Stakeholders must include the local and wider community, with particular attention to supply chain partners.

The fourth factor constructed is *resource and energy efficiency*, looking at environmental preservation while achieving cost benefits. Material consumption and material source are also part of this factor.

The final factor is *philosophy*. The philosophy not only describes the business's

Figure 2.1 **The Greenness Factors Defining the Greenness Matrix**

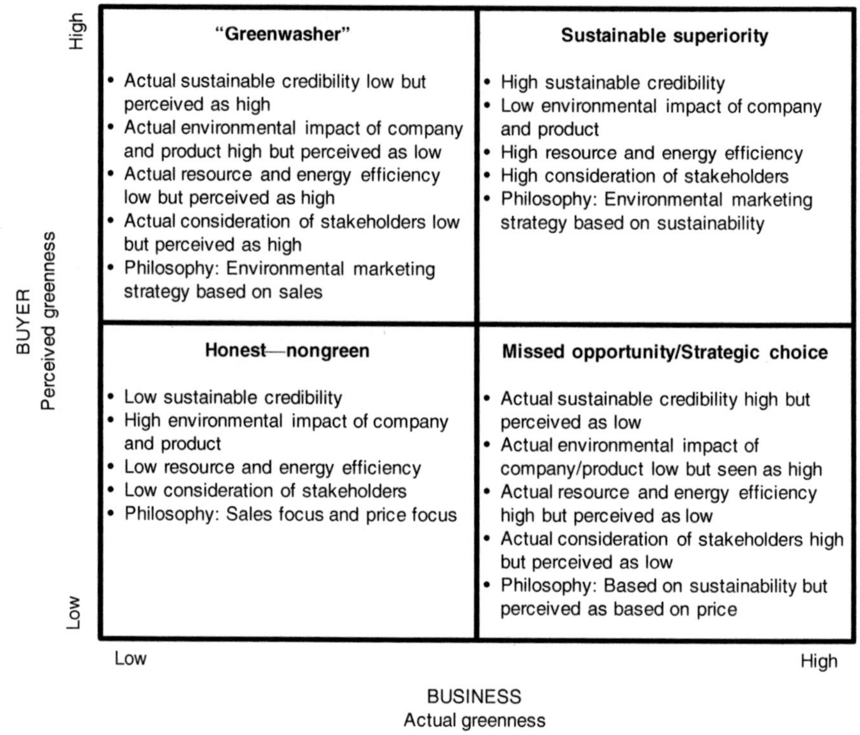

attitude toward sustainability and greenness but helps to determine which quadrant of the matrix the business is assigned to, and, most importantly, it influences the other greenness factors in either having high or low greenness. Four different philosophies are identified: (1) sales focus—not concerned with sustainability; (2) sustainability—a triple bottom line holistic approach; (3) price focus—a buyers' perspective similar to the sales focus; and (4) environmental marketing strategy—aims to communicate greenness to position the company as sustainable and environmentally conscious in the market.

These factors allow us to define Simula et al.'s (2009) matrix as shown in Figure 2.1.

Study 2: The Consumer View

While we may have some insight into business's actual and perceived sustainability, how does the consumer view a sustainable business? Study 2 considers the interaction between consumer and product as modeled by McCracken's (1986) symbolic meaning transfer. Interviews of seven consumers of Ecostore products were thematically analyzed. Participants were recruited at the site of the Ecostore retail operation. Ecostore is a brand of sustainable household cleaning and body-care products; it fits the "sustainable superiority" quadrant of the Greenness Matrix in Study 1. The questions were informed by the model of symbolic meaning transfer and sought to allow participants to tell their consumption stories and rituals of the product.

The findings uncovered symbolic meanings of *virtue, personal and collective values, health,* and *trust* (in Ecostore products). Consumers use these symbolic meanings to create their self-image through the ritual of consumption, including the actions of buying, using, gift-giving, and disposing. The self-image built expressed that they are virtuous, responsible, contributing, and risk-adverse members of society. Furthermore, the personal and collective values of consumers could be expressed through the consumption of the product. The ability to build this self-image from Ecostore products is important to consumers and contributed to their decision to select this brand over others.

If we consider the Greenness Matrix as defined from Study 1, Ecostore benefits from its position in the sustainable superiority quadrant if the green consumer is looking for acknowledgment of the symbolism sought. If the consumer does not require acknowledgement then the strategic choice offer is potentially better as it offers the building of the same self-image at a lower price. If consumers are not only seeking the self-image to be built from the symbolic transfer but also/instead want their projected (public) image to be acknowledged, then the business in the strategic choice quadrant may miss that market because they are "below the radar." Conversely, the consumer seeking a green public image who is happy to have an alter-self-image is unlikely to question a green washer too closely. Finally, despite the shift in consumption and business practices since the days of the polystyrene burger container, there are those who still value the price and other attributes of a product over the sustainability or greenness; these consumers will happily buy from the honest-nongreen business. There are also those who do so as counterculture proponents, wearing the public consumption of nongreen products as a badge of honor.

So. . . . What Can We Say?

Our two studies help explain the factors involved in determining the perceived and actual sustainability of businesses, how the self-image of a green consumer is created through the symbolic meanings of sustainability, and how the two might combine to determine the segmentation in a market competing on sustainability issues. In this respect, perception and reality become united for the consumer and the business.

Furthermore, it appears that there has been a shift in those perceptions about what reality actually is. Two decades ago, Parsons (1988) suggested in his conclusions that marketers interested in social responsibility, the forerunner of sustainability, may need to look at moving the perceptions of what is important to consumers to those items he had identified as having indirect personal consequences. The fictionalized account of 1960s attitudes toward, and the 1980s studies of, perceptions about sustainability issues suggest that a disjuncture between perceptions and reality existed. Parsons (1988) showed that while consumers recognized that issues of social responsibility were important, the prevailing attitude was that more immediate, direct consequences were more important. The studies conducted today, however, suggest that the old perceptions that conservation and organizational issues had only indirect consequences have changed and that in reality sustainability issues do have a direct and immediate effect on the individual.

To businesses, green marketing is important and valid. For the business buyer, credible evidence of sustainable practices is now required. And, for the consumer, the ability to identify with and actualize a self-image through sustainability actions is a legitimate and coherent process of consumption.

References

Aaker, J. L. (1999). The malleable self: The role of self-expression in persuasion. *Journal of Marketing Research, 36*(1), 45–57.

Abeliotis, K., Koniari, C., & Sardianou, E. (2010). The profile of the green consumer in Greece. *International Journal of Consumer Studies, 34,* 153–160.

Ajzen, I. (2008). Consumer attitudes and behavior. In C.P. Haugtvedt, P.M. Herr, and F.R. Kardes (Eds.), *Handbook of consumer psychology* (pp. 525–548). New York: Psychology Press, Taylor and Francis Group.

Alwitt, L. F., & Pitts, R. E. (1996). Predicting purchase intentions for an environmentally sensitive product. *Journal of Consumer Psychology, 5*(1), 49–64.

Appadurai, A. (1986). *The social life of things: Commodities in cultural perspective.* Cambridge: Cambridge University Press.

Atasu, A., Sarvary, M., & Van Wassenhove, L. N. (2008). Remanufacturing as a marketing strategy. *Management Science, 54*(10), 1731–1746.

Balderjahn, I. (1988). Personality variables and environmental attitudes as predictors of ecologically-responsible consumption patterns. *Journal of Business Research, 17,* 51–56.

Belk, R. W. (1988). Possessions and the extended self. *Journal of Consumer Marketing, 15*(September), 139–168.

Borgmann, A. (2001). The moral complexion of consumption. *Journal of Consumer Research, 26,* 418–422.

Carrigan, M., & Attalla, A. (2001). The myth of the ethical consumers: Do ethics matter in purchase behavior? *Journal of Consumer Marketing, 18*(7), 560–577.

Carter, C., & Rogers, D. (2008). A framework of sustainable supply chain management: Moving towards a new theory. *International Journal of Physical Distribution and Logistics Management, 38*(5), 360–387.

Cetindamar, D. (2001). The role of regulations in the diffusion of environment technologies: micro and macro issues. *European Journal of Innovation Management, 4*(4), 186–193.

Charter, M., Peattie, K., Ottman, J. A., & Polonsky, M. (2002). Marketing and sustainability. Association with the Centre of for Sustainability Design, Centre for Business Relationships, Accountability, Sustainability and Society (BRASS), Cardiff.

Cohen, M. J., & Murphy, J. (2001). *Exploring sustainable consumption: Environmental policy and the social sciences.* New York: Pergamon.

Connolly, J., & Prothero, A. (2003). Sustainable consumption: consumption, consumers and the commodity discourse. *Consumption Markets & Culture, 6*(4), 275–291.
Crane, A. (2000). Facing the backlash: Green marketing and strategic reorientation in the 1990's. *Journal of Strategic Marketing, 8*(3), 277–296.
Csikszentmihalyi, M., & Rochberg-Halton, E. (1981). *The meaning of things: Domestic symbols and the self.* Cambridge: Cambridge University Press.
Darnovsky, M. (1996). The green challenge to consumer culture: The movement, the marketers, and the environmental imagination. PhD diss., University of California, Santa Cruz.
de Pelsmacker, P., Driesen, L., & Rayp, G. (2005). Do consumers care about ethics? Willingness to pay for fair-trade coffee. *Journal of Consumer Affairs, 39*(2), 363–385.
Diamantopoulos, A., Schlegelmilch, B. B., Sinkovics, R. R., & Bohlen, G. M. (2003). Can socio-demographics still play a role in profiling green consumers? A review of the evidence and an empirical investigation. *Journal of Business Research, 56*(6), 465–480.
Dittmar, H. (1992). *The social psychology of material possessions: To have is to be.* New York: St. Martin's Press.
Dolan, P. (2002). The sustainability of "sustainable consumption." *Journal of Macromarketing, 22*(2), 170–181.
Douglas, M. (1976). Relative poverty, relative communication. In A. Halsey (Ed.), *Essays in honour of Violet Butler.* Malden, MA: Blackwell.
Douglas, M., & Isherwood, B. (1978). *The world of goods: Towards an anthropology of consumption.* London: Allen Lane.
Drumwright, M. (1994). Socially responsible organizational buying: Environmental concern as a non-economic buying criterion. *Journal of Marketing, 58*(3), 1–19.
Durning, A. T. (1994). *How much is enough?* London: Earthscan.
Earl, G., & Clift, R. (1999). Environmental performance: What is it worth? A case study of "business-to-business" consumers. In M. Charter & M. J. Polonsky (Eds.), *Greener marketing: A global perspective on greening marketing practice* (pp. 255–274). Sheffield, UK: Greenleaf.
Elkington, J. (1997). *Cannibals with forks: The triple bottom line of the 21st century.* Oxford: Capstone.
Elliott, R., & Wattanasuwan, K. (1998). Brands as symbolic resources for the construction of identity. *International Journal of Advertising, 17*(2), 131–145.
European Environmental Agency. (2005). *Household consumption and the environment.* EEA Report No. 11/2005. Copenhagen: EEA. www.eea.europa.eu/publications/eea_report_2005_11/.
Featherstone, M. (1990). Perspectives on consumer culture. *Sociology, 24*(1), 5–22.
Ferrer, G., & Whybark, D. C. (2000). From garbage to goods: Successful remanufacturing systems and skills. *Business Horizons, 43*(2), 55–64.
Gabriel, Y., & Lang, T. (1995). *The unmanageable consumer: Contemporary consumption and its fragmentation.* London: Sage.
Giddens, A. (1991). *Modernity and self-identity.* Cambridge, UK: Polity.
Graeff, T. R. (1996). Using promotional messages to manage the effects of brand and self-image on brand evaluations. *Journal of Consumer Marketing, 13*(3), 4–18.
Gurtoo, A., & Antony, S. J. (2007). Environmental regulations: Indirect and unintended consequences on economy and business. *Management of Environmental Quality: An International Journal, 18*(6), 626–642.
Halkier, B. (1999). Consequences of the politicization of consumption: The example of environmentally friendly consumption practices. *Journal of Environmental Policy & Planning, 1,* 25–41.
Heiskanen, E., & Pantzar, M. (1997). Toward sustainable consumption: Two new perspectives. *Journal of Consumer Policy, 20,* 409–442.

Hong, P., Kwon, H.-B., & Roh, J. J. (2009). Implementation of strategic green orientation in supply chain: An empirical study of manufacturing firms. *European Journal of Innovation Management, 12*(4), 512–532.

Hughner, R. S., McDonagh, P., Prothero, A., Shultz, C. J., & Stanton, J. (2007). Who are organic food consumers? A compilation and review of why people purchase organic food. *Journal of Consumer Behaviour, 6,* 94–110.

Iles, A. (2006). Shifting to green chemistry: The need for innovations in sustainability marketing. *Business Strategy and the Environment, 17*(8), 524–530.

Jackson, T. (2006). *The earthscan reader in sustainable consumption.* Sterling, VA: Earthscan.

Jackson, T., & Michaelis, L. (2003). *Policies for sustainable consumption.* Oxford: Sustainable Development Commission.

Kassarjian, H. H. (1971). Personality and consumer behavior: A review. *Journal of Marketing Research, 8*(November), 409–418.

Kilbourne, W. E., & Beckmann, S. C. (1998). Review and critical assessment of research on marketing and the environment. *Journal of Marketing Management, 14,* 513–532.

Kinnear, T. C., Taylor, C. R., & Ahmed, S. A. (1974). Ecologically concerned consumers: Who are they? *Journal of Marketing, 38*(April), 20–24.

Kleine, R. E., & Kernan, J. B. (1991). Contextual influences on the meanings ascribed to ordinary consumption objects. *Journal of Consumer Research, 18*(3), 311–324.

Kleine, R. E., Kleine, S. S., & Kernan, J. B. (1993). Mundane consumption and the self: A social-identity perspective. *Journal of Consumer Psychology, 2*(3), 209–235.

Kollmuss, A., & Agyeman, J. (2002). Mind the gap: Why do people act environmentally and what are the barriers to pro-environmental behavior? *Environmental Educational Research, 8*(3), 239–260.

Kraus, S. J. (1995). Attitudes and the prediction of behavior—A meta-analysis of the empirical literature. *Personality and Social Psychology Bulletin, 21*(1), 58–75.

Leigh, J. H., & Gabel, T. G. (1992). Symbolic interactionism: Its effects on consumer behavior and implications for marketing strategy. *Journal of Consumer Marketing, 9*(Winter), 27–38.

McCracken, G. (1986). Culture and consumption: A theoretical account of the structure and movement of the cultural meaning of consumer goods. *Journal of Consumer Research, 13*(June), 71–84.

McCracken, G. (1988). *Culture and consumption: New approaches to the symbolic character of consumers goods and activities.* Bloomington: Indiana University Press.

Macnaghten, P. (2003). Embodying the environment in everyday life practices. *Sociological Review, 51*(5), 63–84.

Michaelis, L. (2003). The role of business in sustainable consumption. *Journal of Cleaner Production, 11,* 915–921.

Min, H., & Galle, W. P. (1997). Green purchasing strategies: Trends and implications. *International Journal of Purchasing and Material Management, 21*(9), 1222–1238.

Moisander, J. (2007). Motivational complexity of green consumerism. *International Journal of Consumer Studies, 31*(4), 404–409.

Mont, O., & Plepys, A. (2008). sustainable consumption progress: Should we be proud or alarmed? *Journal of Cleaner Production, 16,* 531–537.

Morton, B. (1996). The role of purchasing and supply management in environmental improvement. In *Proceedings of the 1996 Business Strategy and the Environment Conference* (pp. 136–141). Leeds: ERP Environment.

Muniz, A. M., & O'Guinn, T. C. (2001). Brand community. *Journal of Consumer Research, 27*(March), 898–913.

Onkvisit, S., & Shaw, J. (1987). Self-concept and image congruence: Some research and managerial implications. *Journal of Consumer Marketing, 4,* 13–23.

Ottman, J. A. (1993). *Green marketing.* Lincolnwood, IL: NTC Business Books.

Ottman, J. A. (1998). *Green marketing: Opportunity for innovation*. Chicago: NTC Business Books.
Padel, S., & Foster, C. (2005). Exploring the gap between attitudes and behaviour: Understanding why consumers buy or do not buy organic food. *British Food Journal, 107*(8), 606–625.
Parsons, A. (1988). Societal responsibility and consumer behaviour: An application of attitude/behaviour theory. Master's thesis, University of Auckland.
Peattie, K. (1992). *Green marketing*. London: Pitman.
Peattie, K. (1999). Trappings versus substance in the greening of marketing planning. *Journal of Strategic Marketing, 7,* 131–148.
Peattie, K. (2001a). Golden goose or wild goose? The hunt for the green consumer. *Business Strategy and the Environment, 10*(4), 187–199.
Peattie, K. (2001b). Towards sustainability; The third age of green marketing. *Marketing Review, 2*(2), 129–146.
Peattie, K., & Crane, A. (2005). Green marketing: Legend, myth, farce or prophesy? *Qualitative Market Research, 8*(4), 357–370.
Peattie, K., & Ratnayaka, M. (1992). Responding to the green movement. *Industrial Marketing Management, 21*(2), 103–110.
Pickett-Baker, J., & Ozaki, R. (2008). Pro-environment products: Marketing influence on consumer purchase decision. *Journal of Consumer Marketing, 25*(5), 281–293.
Polonsky, M. J., Broks, H., & Henry, P. (1998). An explanatory examination of environmentally responsible straight rebuy purchases in large Australian organizations. *Journal of Business & Industrial Marketing, 13*(1), 54–69.
Pooley, J. A., & O'Connor, M. (2000). Environmental education and attitudes: Emotions and beliefs are what is needed. *Environmental and Behavior, 32*(5), 711–723.
Prakash, A. (2002). Green marketing, public policy and managerial strategies. *Business Strategy and the Environment, 11*(5), 285–297.
Prentice, D. A. (1987). Psychological correspondence of possessions, attitudes and values. *Journal of Personality and Social Psychology, 53*(6), 993–1003.
Pujari, D., Peattie, K., & Wright, G. (2004). Organizational antecedents of environmental responsiveness in industrial new product development. *Industrial Marketing Management, 33*(5), 381–391.
Roberts, J. A. (1995). Profiling levels of socially responsible consumer behavior: A cluster analytic approach and its implications for marketing. *Journal of Marketing and Practice, 3*(4), 97–118.
Sahlins, M. (1972). The spirit of the gift. In M. Sahlins (Ed.), *Store-age economics* (pp. 149–183). Chicago: Aldine.
Sartre, J. (1943). *Being and nothingness: An essay on phenomenological ontology*. New York: Philosophical Library.
Schaefer, A., & Crane, A. (2005). Addressing sustainability and consumption. *Journal of Macromarketing, 25*(1), 76–92.
Schein, E. (1997). *Organizational culture and leadership* (2nd ed.). San Francisco: Jossey-Bass.
Schultz, W. P., Oskamp, S., & Mainieri, T. (1995). Who recycles and when? A review of personal and situational factors. *Journal of Environmental Psychology, 15,* 105–121.
Seitz, M., & Peattie, K. (2004). Meeting the closed-loop challenge: The case of remanufacturing. *California Management Review, 46*(2), 74–89.
Seyfang, G. (2004). Consuming values and contested cultures: A critical analysis of the UK strategy for sustainable consumption and production. *Review of Social Economy, 62*(3), 323–338.
Seyfang, G. (2005). Shopping for sustainability: Can sustainable consumption promote ecological citizenship? *Environmental Politics, 14*(2), 290–306.

Sharma, A., Gopalkrishnan, Iyer, G. R., Mehrotra, A., & Krishnan, R. (2010). Sustainability and business-to-business marketing: A framework and implications. *Industrial Marketing Management, 39*(2), 330–341.

Sheu, J.-B., & Hu, T.-L. (2008). Channel power, commitment and performance toward sustainable channel relationship. *Journal of Industrial Marketing Management, 38*(1), 17–31.

Shrum, L. J., McCarty, J. A., & Lowrey, T. M. (1995). Buyer characteristics of the green consumer and their implications for advertising strategy. *Journal of Advertising, 24*(2), 71–82.

Silverstone, R. (1981). *The message of television: Myth and narrative in contemporary culture*. London: Heinemann.

Simula, H., Lehtimaki, T., and Salo, J. (2009). Managing greenness in technology marketing. *Journal of Systems and Information Technology, 11*(4), 331–346.

Sirgy, M. J. (1982). Self-concept in consumer behavior: A critical review. *Journal of Consumer Research, 9*(December), 287–300.

Solomon, M. R. (1983). The role of products as social stimuli: A symbolic interactionism perspective. *Journal of Consumer Research, 10*(3), 319–329.

Soron, D. (2010). Sustainability, self-identity and the sociology of consumption. *Sustainable Development, 18*(18), 172–181.

Straughan, R. D., & Roberts, J. A. (1999). Environmental segmentation alternatives: A look at green consumer behavior in the new millennium. *Journal of Consumer Marketing, 16*(6), 558–575.

Thøgersen, J. (2004). A cognitive dissonance interpretation of consistencies and inconsistencies in environmentally responsible behavior. *Journal of Environmental Psychology, 24,* 93–103.

United Nations. (1987). *Report of the World Commission on Environment and Development—Our Common Future.* Brundtland Report, United Nations General Assembly. www.worldinbalance.net/agreements/1987-brustland.php.

United Nations Conference on Environment and Development (UNCED). (1992). *Agenda 21: The United Nations Program of Action from Rio.* New York: UN Publications.

Uusitalo, L. (1990). Consumer preferences for environmental quality and other social goals. *Journal of Consumer Policy, 13,* 231–251.

Vaccaro, V. L. (2009). B2B green marketing and innovation theory for competitive advantage. *Journal of Systems and Information Technology, 11*(2), 315–330.

van Dam, Y. K., & Apeldoorn, P. A. C. (1996). Sustainable marketing. *Journal of Macromarketing* (Fall), 45–64.

Vermeir, I., & Verbeke, W. (2006). Sustainable food consumption: Exploring the Consumer "attitude—behavioral intention" gap. *Journal of Agricultural and Environmental Ethics, 19,* 164–194.

Wagner, S. A. (1997). *Understanding green consumer behaviour.* London: Routledge.

Wallendorf, M., & Arnould, E. J. (1988). My favorite things: A cross-cultural inquiry into object attachment, possessiveness, and social linkage. *Journal of Consumer Research, 14*(March), 531–547.

Wattanasuwan, K. (2005). The self and symbolic consumption. *Journal of American Academy of Business, Cambridge, 6*(1), 179–184.

Weatherell, C., Tregear, A., & Allinson, J. (2003). In search of the concerned consumer: UK public perceptions of food, farming and buying local. *Journal of Rural Studies, 19*(2), 233–244.

Weber, J. A. (2001). Partnering with resellers in business markets. *Journal of Industrial Marketing Management, 30*(2), 87–99.

Young, W., Hwang, K., McDonald, S., & Oates, C.J. (2010). Sustainable consumption: Green consumer behaviour when purchasing products. *Sustainable Development, 18,* 20–31.

3

The Many Shades of Greenwashing

Using Consumer Input for Policy Decisions Regarding Green Advertisements

Kim Bartel Sheehan

Soda bottles made out of plant-based material. Cars that run on water. Recycled leather handbags. Compostable snack food bags. It is hard to read a magazine, surf the Web, or watch your favorite TV show without seeing an advertisement promoting the environmental benefits of a product or service. This growth of green products and green product messages is attributed to Americans' increasing desire to take action to help the planet. According to the most recent tracking poll by Integrated Marketing Services, half of consumers surveyed say they switch brands of the products that they purchase based on environmental criteria in order to select one that they see as environmentally friendly. Furthermore, more than 40 percent of all consumers are willing to pay extra for products with green characteristics (Green Home, 2011).

One unintended effect of this attention to green purchasing, though, is that many companies adjust their marketing to position their products as green in order to get their share of the green pie even if a "green" message is arguably inappropriate. For some of these products, for example, the green positioning may be touting an unoriginal positioning (such as when a suntan lotion positions itself as "friendly to the earth" because it is oil free, but the majority of suntan lotions are oil free). For other green products, the environmental commitment of a company may be exaggerated (e.g., when a company says it is green because it has one plant that uses solar energy even if six of its plants do not).

The Federal Trade Commission (FTC) recently issued revisions to its policies on environmental communications known as the Green Guides. These revisions reflected recommendations based on a consumer survey regarding green messaging. This chapter reviews the FTC survey and the resultant guidelines and suggests that a secondary method of consumer analysis, a thematic analysis of commentary in a Web site devoted to green advertising, may provide a level of data that can help refine and clarify the Green Guides.

A Brief History of Greenwashing

The term *greenwashing* was first used in 1986 in an essay by environmentalist Jay Westerveld (Hayward, 2009). In the essay, Westerveld questioned the hotel industry's practice of promoting the reuse of towels as part of the industry's commitment to saving the environment, because this practice resulted primarily in cost reductions (from decreased labor, water, and electricity) that led to increased profits for hotels. Such practices led to the definition of *greenwashing* as environmentally conscientious acts with a greater, underlying purpose of increasing profits. Today, the term tends to refer to exaggerated benefits or unsupported claims in support of the environment in advertising and other persuasive communications.

In 1993, David F. Welsh expressed a high level of concern over the green marketing practices. The percentage of products using green advertising increased from less than 1 percent of all products in 1985 to 9 percent in 1990. Welsh connected the growth in new green products to the public's increasing awareness of and concern over the environmental problems facing the world (Welsh, 1993). He also believed that many companies were greenwashing in these messages, given the ambiguity of existing laws on deceptive advertising at the state level, coupled with minimal resources provided to prosecute marketing violations. In addition, Welsh was concerned about the lack of consistency in state regulations. As an example, he showed how the definition of the term *biodegradable* in Pennsylvania (i.e., that a product must eventually break down naturally into nonharmful materials) differed from that in California (that a product will decompose naturally within one year into nontoxic soil, water, or carbon dioxide). As an added complexity, Rhode Island banned use of the term *biodegradable*. Similar concerns over the inconsistency in definition existed with the terms *recyclable* and *compostable*.

Welsh also questioned the value of FTC policy making on a case-by-case basis and argued that this method was time-consuming given the agency's caseloads. Moreover, he argued that FTC policy did little to separate grossly exaggerated claims from ones that only bordered on deceptive and blamed this on the absence of definitions that would allow consistent and understandable policy. He further argued that unclear national standards confused consumers, making it difficult for them to assess strengths and weaknesses of different products. He concluded with the assertion that the lack of standards made it hard for authentically green companies to craft green messages. As a result, these companies were hesitant to talk about their green products and practices, which, Welsh argued, added to problems with consumer confusion, as consumers would be less knowledgeable about their product choices. Clearly, more government involvement in green messaging was needed.

The FTC Green Guides

The FTC issued the first Green Guides in 1992, although it had had jurisdiction over environmental claims since 1922 with the passage of the Wheeler–Lea Act, which authorized the agency to investigate and bring law enforcement actions against deceptive, false, and misleading marketing claims (FTC, 2008). Although the Green Guides are intended as guidelines for voluntary compliance and do not constitute laws, the FTC can bring action against a company that is believed to violate prohibitions against unfair or deceptive practices.

The Green Guides, and other guidance on deceptive advertising, use three criteria for determining what distinguishes a legitimate advertising claim from one that is unfair or deceptive. First is substantiation: Advertisers must provide reliable evidence to support assertions about a product. Second is specificity and clarity: Advertisers should avoid broad claims and terms unless the specific meaning is made clear. For example, if a product calls itself "eco-friendly," the reason that claim can be made should be provided. Third, claims should not be overstated. An example of an overstatement is a product that calls itself eco-friendly because some of the people who manufacture the product carpool to work.

In 2007, the FTC announced plans to review the 1995 update to the Green Guides after noticing the increase in messages using green claims. This update process included two forms of information gathering regarding the current use of green messages. The FTC held a series of public meetings and workshops on several different topics, including the marketing of carbon offsets and renewable energy certificates, green packaging claims, and building and textile claims. These meetings included informational sessions, sessions on consumer perceptions of claims, and discussions on the need for revised guidance.

In addition, the FTC used a consumer survey to gather broader consumer input, a technique outlined by Hastak, Mazis, and Morris (2001) in their article describing the role of consumer research in the evaluation of public policy issues. Hastak, Mazis, and Morris found that consumer research for policy decision making is used to help evaluate specific topics in multiple phases of policy making. Surveys can be used to identify specific problems and assess their effects on society. Moreover, consumer surveys can be used to build a policy mandate: that is, to indicate the importance of a problem to a range of constituents. Surveys can also be used to explore and evaluate policy options and to help identify optimal execution strategies for policy decisions. Finally, consumer surveys can be used to assess the outcome of a policy by answering the question "does the policy do what it was intended to do?"

Hastak, Mazis, and Morris (2001) identified several challenges to using consumer research in policy development. First, they found that surveys are used inconsistently across the policy development process: Surveys are relied on most often in identifying a problem and building a policy mandate and used less often in exploring options. Second, survey use varied depending on perceived stakeholder support for policy initiatives: the more support for policy development, the less reliance on consumer surveys. Third, the more complex the problem, the more often surveys were used. Finally, the lack of consumer surveys at the execution and enforcement stages was seen as problematic, and the authors argue that consumer research can have a much greater potential to make a contribution in these areas: identifying optimal execution methods and tracking whether the policy is doing what it was intended to do.

The FTC announced a survey in the Federal Register to "examine consumer perceptions of environmental marketing claims" in May 2009 (FTC, 2009). According to the Federal Register Notice, the survey had several goals:

- to evaluate consumer perceptions of various environmental marketing claims, including general environmental benefits claims (such as the term *eco-friendly*) and claims including a specific representation (such as "this product is green, made with renewable materials";
- to evaluate how consumers translate claims into benefits;
- to identify whether claims suggest benefits over and above provided benefits;
- to identify how claims connect with consumer awareness of product life cycles; and
- to evaluate how consumers perceive claims about the purchase of renewable energy, carbon neutrality, and carbon offsets.

The suggested sample size was 3,700 Americans.

Harris Interactive conducted the survey during August and September 2009 using its existing online consumer panel (FTC, 2010a). An initial pretest showed that most respondents were not very familiar with the topics addressed in the survey (e.g., carbon offsets) but that the survey questions were clear enough for the majority of respondents to understand. A total of 3,777 adults completed the online survey, suggesting a response rate of 9 percent based on information provided by the research firm.

The consumer survey revealed how these consumers viewed unqualified green claims like being "eco-friendly." The study found that unqualified claims (e.g., "this wrapping paper is eco-friendly") provoked a range of different interpretations such as "the wrapping paper is made from recycled materials" or "the wrapping paper is nontoxic." In contrast, when a green claim was qualified (e.g., "the wrapping paper is eco-friendly because it is made with recycled materials"), not surprisingly the number of implied or nonqualified claims decreased substantially.

The survey also identified some key terms that were confusing to respondents. For example, when asked what the word *sustainable* meant, 13 percent said it meant nothing, 8 percent said they did not know what it meant, 19 percent said it means a product is durable or long-lasting, and relatively few indicated that it was related to any environmental benefit.

Summary of Proposed Revised Green Guides

The hearings and the consumer survey resulted in the proposed revision to the existing Green Guides that was announced to the public in October 2010. Large portions of the proposed Green Guides revise existing guidance. A smaller portion addresses new types of green claims. A comment period was open until December 2010, with final guidance released in 2012.

In terms of revising existing guides, the following revisions were made (FTC 2012):

- Regarding general environmental benefits such as using the terms *green* and *eco-friendly*, the guides indicate that marketers should not make unqualified general environmental benefit claims because they are difficult to substantiate. This changes previous guidance that marketers can make claims as long as they can substantiate them. In addition, the new proposals say that any qualifications should be clear and prominent and should limit the claim to a specific benefit. Marketers should ensure that the advertisement's context does not imply deceptive environmental claims.
- Regarding certifications and seals of approval, the guides provide more detail on the appropriate use of certificates and seals outlined in existing guides. Marketers are cautioned not to use unqualified certifications or seals if they do not state the basis for certification. The Guides also indicate that certifications and seals do not eliminate a marketer's obligation to substantiate claims.
- The guides provide an enhanced definition of the term *degradable* (now defined as meaning that waste must break down within a year) and of the term *compostable* (now defined as meaning that materials must break down in approximately the same time as the materials with which it is composted).
- The guidelines provide information about defining how recyclable a product or its packaging is based on availability of local recycling facilities in the market where the product is sold.
- The guides suggest that the claim "free of" (as in the phrase "free of PVC") is deceptive if the product or its packaging use a substitute material that is equally dangerous or if the product never contained the material in the first place.
- The guidelines extend the definition of *nontoxic* to relate to both human beings and the environment in general.

The revision provides several areas of new guidance, including:

- guidance identifying the types of appropriate qualifying claims in messages about products made with renewable energy or materials (percentage of product, what types of materials, how it is sourced, and why it is renewable).
- guidance about renewable energy claims when the company sells renewable energy credits.
- guidance defining appropriate evidence in carbon-offset claims, including appropriate accounting methods, when emission reductions occur, and in situations where offsets are required by law.

Alternative Consumer Input: The Greenwashing Index

While the FTC's consumer survey apparently informed some of the policies proposed in the new guidance, the information collection techniques (consumer survey and meetings) used for this specific policy issue seem somewhat limited. First, this type of survey will gather data only on the topics deemed important by the data collectors. Although the topics presented by the FTC seem an appropriate list of areas about which to gather data, any additional consumer concerns not covered in the survey may not be identified and addressed in the policies. The composition of the survey panel may also limit the quality of the information received: It was an online panel made up of people who self-selected to participate in surveys. No attempts were made to determine how important sustainability messages were to the people answering the survey. It would be helpful to see whether people who are trying to live a greener lifestyle had different responses to the questions in order to make the Green Guides more meaningful for companies who direct messages to different consumers. Moreover, the relatively low response rate (9 percent) may create concern over validity. While the public meetings offered an opportunity to air actual consumer concerns, these workshops tend to be attended more by industry representatives and not-for-profit groups.

As a result, the revisions do not address some of the areas contained in the survey, specifically Life Cycle Assessment (LCA). The survey contained several questions about LCA, which is a technique to assess environmental impacts associated with all the stages of a product's life (i.e., from raw material extraction through materials processing, manufacture, distribution, use, repair and maintenance, and disposal or recycling). However, the revised Green Guides contain no guidance or recommendation about LCA messages. This is surprising, because a majority of respondents to the online survey reported that they considered multiple stages of the product life cycle when assessing messages (62 percent of respondents answering questions about products including laundry baskets, kitchen flooring, and wrapping paper) (FTC, 2010b).

Another source of consumer opinions on green messages and greenwashing is the Greenwashing Index (www.greenwashingindex.com). This site, established in 2008, allows individuals to rate advertisements that they and others upload. The rating scale was developed by a group of professors from the University of Oregon and professionals working at the marketing firm EnviroMedia. The Greenwashing Index Scoring Criteria ask visitors to assess advertisements on criteria including whether the advertisement misleads with words, misleads with visuals, provides vague or improvable claims, makes exaggerations, or masks information. The criteria were based on information from several other rating procedures used by academia and industry, including Terra Choice, Greenpeace, and the British Code of Advertising, Sales Promotion, and Direct Marketing. After individuals rate an advertisement, a form allows them to express their opinions about the advertisement or to indicate why they scored the advertisement the way they did.

These comments, along with the ratings and other information on the site, have the potential to educate consumers about how to read and interpret advertisements with green messages. The site encourages consumers to decide for themselves whether what they are seeing is greenwashing: The site highlights advertisements that are not seen as greenwashed, and the comment box allows people to indicate why they think the advertisement is authentic. Thus, the Greenwashing Index can influence industry by encouraging the development and accountability of green messages.

The Greenwashing Index hosts more than 300 advertisements with over 700 ratings, rated by more than 500 different individuals. The consumers who visit the site may be very different from the Harris panel that responded to the FTC survey. Like the Harris survey, the Greenwashing Index visitors self-select to participate on the site, but many Greenwashing Index visitors bring a green orientation to the site. Many are highly aware of issues with greenwashing and are eager to share and educate others. In addition, many visitors are students participating in sustainability classes who were required to post and rate advertisements on the site, bringing additional types of insight and information to the site. As a result, it can be argued that this group is not a generalizable group to the U.S. population. However, this group does provide an additional voice in policy development that can be useful. These comments provide a wealth of data that is available to analyze and compare to the data in the FTC survey as well as to the proposed Green Guides.

This rich array of data has several benefits. Open-ended questions are responses that individuals give spontaneously (Reja, Manfreda, Hlebec, & Vehovar, 2003), and responses are provided in "real world" terminology rather than laboratory or marketing jargon. Respondents are answering from their own frame of reference. Similarly, open-ended questions may suggest alternatives not listed in a closed-ended data acquisition questionnaire. Reja et al. (2003) found that open-ended questions produced a much more diverse set of answers. In addition, open-ended questions produce more missing data than closed-ended ones.

Analysis of Greenwashing Index Data

In order to identify key concerns with greenwashing among people visiting the Greenwashing Index site, the written comments reported in there were analyzed using a technique called Thematic Analysis (Aronson, 1994). Specific patterns in the comments were identified in a preliminary subset of data, and then the full set of comments was evaluated to see how it fit into these patterns. Themes were identified by "bringing together components or fragments of ideas or experiences, which often are meaningless when viewed alone" (Leininger, 1985, p. 60). Themes that emerge from comments are pieced together to form a comprehensive picture of visitors' collective experience with green messages. The "coherence of ideas rests with the analyst who has rigorously studied how different ideas or components fit together in a meaningful way when linked together" (Leininger, 1985, p. 60). Finally, validation of the themes based on existing information about the Green Guides and FTC process was performed. Three individuals familiar with the Green Guides participated in this thematic analysis process.

Two different broad thematic categories were found: claims and context.

Claims

The first category, claims, can be broken down into two subcategories: claims based on language and claims based on images. Both language and images were generally discussed in the Greenwashing Index rating scale directions, however, the open-ended comments provided a level of specificity that can help inform policy.

In terms of language, open-ended comments identified key words that seemed to signal the presence of greenwashing in an advertisement. In particular, two words appeared repeatedly, indicating that they were highly problematic in terms of how they communicated a "green" benefit: *clean* and (not surprisingly) *green*.

For example, one informant took issue with a claim that Fiji Water was green. This person wrote:

> While Fiji is doing a good job at reducing their carbon emissions (going carbon neutral), this is not an excuse for making people think that drinking bottled water is a "green" thing to do. Trumpet your accomplishments, but don't pretend that bottled water itself can be completely green, because it has fundamentally unsustainable characteristics.

Similarly, concerns regarding the word *clean* were raised, for example, in the phrase *clean coal*. Wrote one individual:

> They are not even saying something more subtle like "cleaner." I don't consider mercury leeching into the water supply clean, but I guess it's just a matter of semantics.

Another individual, reviewing a shampoo advertisement with the theme "Pure Clean," indicated that there was no support for the "clean" claim, indicating that the word *clean* is very difficult to define.

An advertisement for an online marketing firm positioning itself as a green company inspired this comment:

> This company is just saying that since their business is all Internet related they don't cut down trees, which is green marketing. Doesn't really make much sense now, does it? It's just kind of pointless; they are just using the term *green* because it's the thing to do now.

The complexity of using the word *green* becomes apparent when three companies (HP, Dell, and Vulcan) appeared on the index for advertisements using the phrase *go green* when the marketing message had nothing to do with the environment. HP's "go green" advertisement touted a computer peripheral product that showed a green light when a high level of data protection was achieved (green was supposed to mean safety). The Dell "go green" advertisement featured a computer with a green case. The advertisement for the Vulcan motorcycle encouraged people to "go green" and showed a motorcycle painted green to promote a sale (green signifying money). Although close attention to these advertisements would correct any initial misperceptions that the products were environmentally friendly, the comments suggested that the advertisements were problematic because that initial consumer interpretation would be that the product was environmentally friendly.

Written (or spoken) claims tend to be accompanied by some type of visual image that supports or enhances the message. The "colors and images" subtheme found evidence that images (such as the color green and natural images such as those of trees, flowers, and animals) strongly suggest that a product may have an ecological advantage over other products, even if such a claim is not expressly stated in written or spoken words. An individual wrote this comment about an advertisement for Malaysian Palm Oil:

> Flowery imagery of nature makes you want to think it's just as natural as can be and doesn't harm the environment, but it is completely vague about the product itself, as well as its true effects on the environment.

A Shell Oil print advertisement portraying flowers being emitted from factory smokestacks in place of pollutants garnered a comment suggesting a strong link between imagery and claims:

> It seems like they are saying the pollutants we emit are flowers-nature friendly. Their message definitely misleads the public into thinking their pollutants and smog in some way are healthy for the environment.

An advertisement for one Clorox Greenworks cleaning product featured the bottle in the middle of a natural scene. Wrote one individual (who used capital letters to indicate emphasis):

> The PLASTIC bottle is placed in the middle of trees and flowers giving it an environmentally friendly concept. . . . I find it hard to believe they place a non-degradable plastic bottle in the middle of trees while claiming to be "natural." Now they are not misleading because they explain that the content of the bottle is what is "natural," yet they are giving their product credit that may only be supported if the entire thing was GREEN.

A comment on a brand of bottled water that featured a visual of a tree was:

> The tree is literally a cliché that should be legally banned from advertising that isn't about trees.

Simply using the color green was a signal to some people that the company was making a green claim that they may or may not be able to support. A print advertisement for Toyota's Rav-4 Diesel used a green background, which generated this comment:

> Toyota is pushing a nature theme onto this advertisement. While it doesn't specifically say that the car is green, the coloring (a green background) is enough for people to perceive it that way.

The implied claim using the color green was also noted in a comment for an advertisement for bottled water:

> The largest claim that I find issue with on the Web site, however, is in bold print outlined by a green border with leaves. For the next 16.9 ounces, you can be an environmentalist without even thinking about it.

Context

All advertising claims must be supported: The FTC has had that requirement as part of its deceptive advertising regulations for years. However, even a supported claim can be misleading if there is a lack of context to assess that claim. Visitors to the Greenwashing Index site found that it was often difficult to find contextual information to assess green claims made in advertisements. An example of this is raised by a comment for an advertisement for Sara Lee's Eco-Grain bread. This advertisement suggested that Eco-Grain is greener than regular organic grain because farmers of eco-grains reduced their use of chemical fertilizer by 15 percent. One individual wrote that the claim itself was an exaggeration of how green the product really is because the government mandated 100 percent reduction of such fertilizers in all organic products. This individual then provided the source of this data and commented that Sara Lee did not provide the context for helping the consumer evaluate the claim for him- or herself.

Similarly, some automotive advertisements rated poorly when advertisements provided miles-per-gallon (MPG) information in support of green claims yet failed to provide contextual information (such as comparisons to other brands) so that a consumer could evaluate the information. This problem occurred not only for cars such as Hummers but also for diesel and hybrid cars.

Context became a major problem in terms of the context of a product over its life cycle. Many messages that do not take the broader life cycle into account were seen as highly problematic. For example, a comment on an advertisement for BMW's hydrogen-powered car (which has no harmful emissions) read: "where will it [the car itself] come from and how will it be made?" The lack of information about the emissions for the manufacturing process, as well as an indication of emissions from transporting the car from factory to dealer, made this claim problematic.

A similar problem with LCA and context arose regarding an advertisement for the retail store Banana Republic and its "green" bag promotion. Consumers who purchase a green bag from Banana Republic and then use it to carry home products that they purchased at Banana Republics would get a 10 percent discount. One individual, though, questioned the value of the creation and green value of the bag:

> All it is promoting is a reusable bag, but how green is that? Is it made of recycled material? Doubtful. To me, it looks like all they did was greenwash by creating another product out of new materials, which, while it may be reusable, just is still overall contributing to the problem by using more resources and energy. Why not make it out of recycled clothing or cloth materials? It's totally bogus that this is green in reality; it's only bogus seen through green sunglasses.

A lack of context for advertising claims in bottled water advertisements also raised concern:

> The energy that it requires to manufacture the single-use bottles (the product) claim its bottles require 50% less non-renewable energy than PET bottles, but that is still 100% more than for tap water with a reusable container.

Another visitor wrote about bottled water in a container made of plant-based materials:

> There are different phases in the life cycle of bottled water that contribute to its overall impact. First there is extraction of resources, then production of the bottle and manufacturing, shipping and transportation, consumption and disposal. . . . While the plant-based bottle can be argued as a better alternative to petroleum, this Florida-based company still uses plenty of petroleum to ship its product to market.

Discussion

Based on an analysis of comments from the Greenwashing Index site, it is clear that although the proposed Green Guides can address some of these concerns, the actual guides do not take some proposed guidelines as far as they could to ensure that green messages are authentic. In addition, the Green Guides avoid talking about LCA issues, which are clearly a concern for consumers. Finally, the Guides spend time on some areas, like renewable energy credits, that do not seem to be a concern at all because this type of information seems to appear rarely in advertisements.

The Green Guides encourage marketers to qualify all green claims. What they do not require, though, is that marketers provide the proper context for claims to be evaluated. Without this context, it is difficult for a consumer to determine the validity of a green claim. For example, supporting a green claim for an automobile with MPG information may meet the "letter" of the guides but does not help a consumer assess that claim and use it in a purchasing decision without some comparable data.

Similarly, when a company reduces energy use or packaging, without some idea of appropriate industry standards, it is difficult to evaluate that information.

The proposed Green Guides do not address certain cues, such as imagery or well-known phrases. It is apparent that imagery can carry green connotations as well, if not better, than words (the persuasive aspect of imagery is addressed in, e.g., Goodyear-Smith et al., 2008; Hoffman, 2009; Sojka & Giese, 2006). Colors and imagery, as well as phrases such as *go green*, are highly compelling but extremely difficult to regulate. However, given the strong connection of green imagery and phrases with the environmental movement, the potential exists for these to deceive consumers. In addition, phrases such as *go green* generally appear in headlines of ads, which are read as many as ten times more often than the body copy (Witt, 1999). Understanding that consumers immediately interpret such cues as environmental claims means that the Green Guides must address them, regardless of whether they lead to a green claim.

The lack of guidance on LCA is highly problematic, particularly because this came up as a consumer concern in the original survey and in the Greenwashing Index commentary. Of course, a one-page magazine advertisement or a 30-second television commercial may not provide sufficient space to address all the issues associated with LCA. However, marketers could be required to have links to information about the environmental impacts of a product over its life cycle. This level of transparency has a precedent in marketing for prescription drugs, where full product information must be available to all consumers who wish to access this information.

Finally, the proposed Green Guides spend significant space and effort talking about messaging concerns that do not seem to appear in green consumer advertising or to be of concern to consumers. Topics such as renewal energy credits, carbon offsets, and post–consumer waste information simply do not appear in consumer advertising and do not seem to be of interest to consumers.

Conclusion

The proposed Green Guides provide a higher level of specificity on green messages than ever before. Unfortunately, some of this specificity is focused in the wrong direction: away from what many green consumers are thinking about and reacting to when seeing green messages. The FTC must be congratulated for encouraging consumer input in policy development. Now, it needs to address limitations with current practices and ensure that a range of voices and concerns are heard about green messaging.

Clearly, this will not be easy. The FTC must find ways to provide guidance on areas that have not been addressed in any previous FTC guidance, e.g., imagery and larger contextual issues. Some type of consumer education campaign should also be considered as part of this effort to provide more authenticity in messages and more accountability among marketers. The revised Green Guides are a first step, but it is the first step down a long road.

References

Aronson, J. (1994). A pragmatic view of thematic analysis. *Qualitative Report, 2*(1), Spring. www.nova.edu/ssss/QR/BackIssues/QR2–1/aronson.html (accessed July 20, 2011).

Federal Trade Commission (FTC). (2008). Complying with the Environmental Marketing Guides. www.ftc.gov/bcp/grnrule/guides92.htm (accessed June 24, 2011).

Federal Trade Commission. (2009). *Federal Register 74*(90) (Tuesday, May 12), Notices.

Federal Trade Commission. (2010a). Environmental Marketing Consumer Perception Study Background Information. www.ftc.gov/bcp/edu/microsites/energy/green-consumer-perception-study.shtml (accessed April 15, 2011).

Federal Trade Commission (2010b). Proposed Revisions to the Green Guides. www.ftc.gov/or/fedreg/2012/ocrober/1001006greenguidesfrn.pdf (accessed April 15, 2011).

Federal Trade Commission. (2012). Green Guides. www.ftc.gov/or/2012/10/greenguides.pdf (accessed November 15, 2012).

Goodyear-Smith, F., Arroll, B., Chan, L., & Jackson, R. (2008). Patients prefer pictures to numbers to express cardiovascular benefit from treatment. *Annals of Family Medicine, 6*(3), 213–217.

Green Home. (2011). Green Commerce. www.greenhome.com/info/articles/is_ecommerce_green/68/ (accessed April 15, 2011).

Hastak, M., Mazis, M. B., & Morris, L. A. (2001). The role of consumer surveys in public policy decision making. *Journal of Public Policy & Marketing, 20*(2), 170–185.

Hayward, P. (2009). The real deal? Hotels grapple with green washing. *Lodging Magazine* (February). www.ahla.com/uploadedFiles/AHLA/Programs_and_Initiatives/Green/The%20Real%20Deal.pdf (accessed August 10, 2011).

Hoffman, K. S. (2009). A picture speaks a thousand words: Presidential rhetoric and visual communication. Paper presented at the annual meeting of the Midwest Political Science Association 67th Annual National Conference, Palmer House Hilton, Chicago.

Leininger, M. M. (1985). Ethnography and ethnonursing: Models and modes of qualitative data analysis. In M. M. Leininger (Ed.), *Qualitative research methods in nursing* (pp. 33–72). Orlando, FL: Grune & Stratton.

Reja, U., Manfreda, L., Hlebec, V., & Vehovar, V. (2003). Open ended vs. close ended questions in web questionnaires. *Advances in Methodology and Statistics, 19,* 159–177.

Sojka, J. Z., & Giese, J. (2006). Communicating through pictures and words: Understanding the role of affect and cognition in processing visual and verbal information. *Psychology and Marketing, 23,* 995–1014.

Welsh, D. F. (1993). Environmental marketing and federal preemption of state law: Eliminating the "gray" behind the "green." *California Law Review, 81,* 991.

Witt, G. (1999). What to say after you've got their attention: Creating effective messages. Marketing Psychology Web site. www.marketingpsychology.com/article9.htm/ (accessed April 21, 2011).

4

Product End-of-Life Decisions

Sommer Kapitan, Rajesh Bhargave, Kristin Trask, Jill M. Sundie, and David H. Silvera

Three stages define the consumption cycle, forming the drumbeat of consumer behavior research studies: Acquisition, use, and disposal (MacInnis & Folkes, 2010). Yet from the perspective of sustainability, the cycle is far richer and more complex, involving reuse, sharing, refurbishing, donation, recycling, leasing, and postponement of purchases. In this chapter, we focus on underlying mechanisms in the link that turns disposal into secondhand acquisition or prolonged product life. Such activity contributes to sustainable endeavors by ensuring that consumer goods are given a new life with a second (or third or fourth) owner, while delaying acquisition of new items to slow the consumption cycle.

We explore reuse and the used-goods market through two themes: first, how sellers of meaningful possessions disassociate themselves from their goods in the secondhand market; and, second, how consumer essences "in" a consumer good can affect buyers' responses to used goods. We begin this discussion via an examination of the world of thrift-store shoppers, downshifters, and voluntary simplifiers—subcultures of consumption for whom ownership of outdated, vintage, or secondhand goods, such as older model cars (Craig-Lees & Hill, 2002), becomes an important identity marker. Consistent with the focus of this book, we also specifically explore advertising tactics that might prove fruitful in reaching members of sustainable subcultures. In each of the three arenas above, we review key areas of literature and propose research opportunities.

Subcultures of Consumption

On a recent day of local postings back and forth at freecycle.org, one metropolitan community of downshifters offered and accepted gifts of used printers, children's clothing, coffeemakers, treadmills ("in working condition!"), barstools, sunglasses, mattresses, keyboards, window air-conditioner units, and a set of the board game Battleship. The simple living movement, also described in the literature as "downshifting" and "voluntary simplicity," involves minimizing consumption, making do with fewer acquisitions, eliminating new acquisitions, and gifting or donating seldom-used but viable goods to other consumers within a social network, such as the freecycle.org network (Nelson, Rademacher, & Paek, 2007). The freecycle network, comprising 8.5 million members, circulates e-mails to members when someone requests or offers a "gift" of a secondhand good. Still other related subcultures revel in used goods and antique consumption, forming a community around their local thrift store or vintage shop. Such groups call themselves vintage aficionados or thrift-store romantics and network via Facebook groups or blogs, sharing details of their latest purchases and snapshots of experiments with such vintage styles as the 1940s hairstyle known as "victory rolls." Facebook groups such as the Australian Vintage Marketplace, the Houstonian Retro Revival, the London-based Vintage Mafia, and hundreds of fan pages for local shops created by thrift-store romantics attest to the vibrancy of these consumer tribes.

Nelson et al. (2007) argue that the self-concept consumers struggle to separate from their possessions when selling, gifting, or donating in traditional senses fades from the equation for downshifters. Downshifters and voluntary simplifiers focus on consuming less or consuming already-extant goods and resources in ways such as maintaining and repairing aging appliances, car sharing, and growing food in gardens (McDonald, Oates, Young, & Hwang, 2006). Downshifters in Nelson et al.'s study (2007) reportedly disengaged notions of identity from their possessions and more easily parted with goods that they were not consistently using. However, it remains likely that the self and the self-image are just as tangled up in these product decisions for downshifters, retro-, and vintage tribes. Community was the moderator for a conceptual separation of self from object in Albinsson and Perera's (2009) study of clothing-exchange networks: Through organized connection, exchanges were held at a member's home, and each person brought secondhand items from which others could choose. One of Albinsson and Perera's informants, who attended her first clothing exchange with initial resistance because of the "energy" in other people's possessions, left satisfied after making friends of the members of the exchange and deeming it "acceptable" to claim their used possessions from the pile and recommend her castaway items to others. The informant became comfortable with the exchange only after she had become acquainted with members of the group and had gained some visibility and status with fellow exchangers.

What is clear in these subcultures of consumption or consumer tribes—formed around any brand or consumption activity (Schouten & McAlexander, 1995)—is that some groups pride themselves on relying on older models, retaining presently owned goods longer, or sharing no-longer-needed goods within a network to simplify the consumption cycle. The literature points to two possible mechanisms for these consumption preferences within such subcultures. First, vintage tribes and voluntary simplifiers by definition seek to maintain and consume used goods, focusing on the stated functionality of products (Etzioni, 1998). Such activity serves as an automatic barrier to resist psychological product wear-out and boredom, a principal driver behind perceptions of relative obsolescence that often lead to consumer upgrades of products that have not yet outlived their usefulness and capacity (Cooper, 2005). Second, ownership of older models and vintage styles, such as older cars, accessories, and appliances, helps some enhance their voluntary simplifier, thrift-store, or vintage lifestyle and image (Craig-Lees & Hill, 2002). Thus, for such subcultures, ownership of aging but well-maintained, cared-for products is a status-bearing act of conspicuous consumption, a source of pride for committed members of these consumer tribes.

This is an intriguing point for marketers of sustainability, a potential key for targeting specific consumer tribes and popularizing the notion of retaining older goods until they can no longer be used. In implicit association tests, "old" is more readily associated with "bad" (while "new" is implicitly viewed as "good"), and that is a strong, ingrained psychological force to overcome (Greenwald, McGhee, & Schwartz, 1998). However, if older products are associated with a retro, thrifty, or vintage image that is popularized, sustainable behavior marketers might have an opportunity in targeting the status-conferring value of retro products, repair, care, and maintenance in the mass market. Or more compellingly, linking such activities to environmentalist or green behaviors could improve the status of vintage. Griskevicius, Tybur, and Van den Bergh (2010) find that activating status concerns leads to increased purchases of green or environmental products. Although respect for vintage and simplified-consumption values might not yet be mainstream, reuse and refashioning comprise a sustainable method that might benefit from the same aura of status if clearly classified as environmentally correct behavior.

Another area of research into consumer tribes presents an opportunity for those targeting sustainability, though such marketing tactics might affect any tribe. The examination above of the online activity surrounding thrift-store, vintage, and simplifier tribes attests to the ways in which society today facilitates social connections via consumption. Western society no longer revolves around townhall meetings and church socials (Belk, 1985). In the modern consumer society, instead, those in need of social interaction self-select into identity subgroups that become part social, part image projection, and, at their base, material driven. In a subculture of consumption formed around any brand or consumption activity, from riding Harley-Davidson motorcycles and skateboarding to quilting bees, rock climbing, kayaking, and listening to heavy metal, the "hard-core" members at the center of the subculture are the opinion leaders (Schouten & McAlexander, 1995). They are the cultural disseminators who strictly set, maintain, and adhere to a code of conduct for their group and enforce its rules among junior members (Fox, 1987). As keepers of the faith, the hard-core members are role models for the aspirant peripheral culture and probationary soft-core members who revolve around their leadership (Schouten & McAlexander, 1995).

Aspiring, fringe members and those among the mainstream who are lured to the periphery of any consumption subculture are hopeful about their possible entry into the hard core. Their reverence and adulation of the hard core supports the concentric structure of the subculture (Fox, 1987). In this way, hard-core members can be viewed as operating with a prevention focus in their subculture (Higgins,

1998), being sensitive to the duties and obligations of maintaining values and on guard for negative outcomes for themselves. The preventive focus can also lead to ejection of nonfollowers formally or via social ostracism. Their role is of vigilant avoidance, which Semin, Higgins, Gil de Montes, Estourget, and Valencia (2005) associate with regulatory focus. Fringe members and peripheral aspirants flirting with the subculture of consumption are hopeful and aspiring, toward the hard-core and attuned to what Semin et al. (2005) note is the positive outcome orientation and eager approach of the promotion-focused strategy.

This points to an unexplored yet intriguing link between level of naïveté or expertise in a consumer specialty and response to message framing via goal approach. Semin et al. chart responses to the different goals-based language strategies of prevention- and promotion-focused individuals that offer insight into research on consumption subcultures and brand communities. Prevention-focused consumers are more responsive to concrete, avoidance language, whereas promotion-focused consumers are more responsive to abstract, approach-oriented language.

Because individuals speak in different ways depending on their goals, consumers are more influenced by wording that matches their goal focus. This is especially the case in a subculture formed around a particular brand or an activity dominated by a few specialty brands. Those in the outer rings of membership are hopeful and need encouragement from brands to pursue those hopes and rise to the ideals of the subcultures. Those in the hard-core inner circle no longer need such encouragement to stay with the brand or consumption activity but, instead, are focused on the penalties of losing touch with the group or their responsibilities now that they are at the top of their game. The most hard core among the downshifters are prone to grow food in their own gardens, use tool and toy libraries, and car share or drive an older model car (Etzoni, 1998; McDonald et al., 2006). Those hard-core downshifters are continually seeking new ways to consume less and to remain as committed as possible, while "apprentice simplifiers" might start with fair-trade coffee and buying organics in the hope of one day growing their own backyard garden (McDonald et al., 2006).

Distinct goals drive the apprentice and the expert in a particular consumer tribe, and the goal orientation, matching language, and image appeals might be particularly compelling to members of a tribe depending on their level of entrée into the activity or brand lifestyle. Key to future research, then, is uncovering if these hypothesized goal orientations translate to differences in attraction to brands, causes, activities, and services from within the hierarchy of a consumer tribe.

It is possible that marketing that simply mentions or honors a consumption subculture, from thrift-store romantics and distance runners to rug-hooking "hookers" in craft circles and Harley-Davidson riders, makes enough impact that goal focus is irrelevant to judgment, preference, and ultimate choice. But we still find compelling cause for a careful consideration of the role of the hard-core members in any consumer tribe: Those who turn to a more experienced member of a tribe for advice are handed down tested and hallowed word-of-mouth advice about solutions, brands, styles, and preferences that apprentices are inclined to heed in their quest to become more complete members of their self-selected subcultures.

As we have indicated, two pathways to exploring consumer tribes are poised to provide valuable insight into sustainable behaviors. Sustainable consumer tribes value consuming less, consuming older and secondhand items, and reuse and refashioning practices, yet the motives for such consumption practices remain unclear. Consumer tribes also form in concentric circles (Fox, 1987; Schouten & McAlexander, 1995) in which the hard-core committed members tend to disseminate information about preferences, styles, and practices. Future researchers should seek to understand more about the motives behind tribes focused on reuse of older products, whether such motives revolve around status as a reuser or key in on the main function of consumer tribes devoted to vintage, thrift, or simplification. Interested researchers might also examine whether and how the concentric hierarchy of a tribe results in influence and how targeted messaging might affect consumer tribe members at differing levels within the hierarchy.

Attachment and Selling

Lessons from the sustainable consumer tribe movement are informative even for those consumers not interested in owning only "100 things" (Bruno, 2010) or in restricting their shopping to secondhand markets. Consumers today own more than they ever have: The average U.S. consumers are spending more and more of their disposable income on *stuff*, thus encountering ownership of twice as many possessions as they did in the 1970s as a normal state of life (Mooallem, 2009). Parting with owned goods is a stressful issue (Kahneman, Knetsch, & Thaler, 1991), but one that seems to speak to the same sustainable effort to achieve a healthy balance and learn to let go of some ownership issues. In this section, we review how endowment and attachment can make the process of parting with meaningful goods difficult and propose ways in which consumers might navigate the process of disposal. We also explore the rituals that consumers attend to that allow their singularized owned goods to be converted into secondhand goods with market value as commodities. Within those rituals, issues arise that can pose a strong counterpoint to hoarding behaviors with the anti-attachment impulse of those who continually buy and sell used goods.

The endowment effect encapsulates the somewhat perverse human need to hold on to what is owned, never to part with possessions. Kahneman, Knetsch, and Thaler (1991) chart this trend as the result of an inherent and nonrational loss aversion, or the weighing of losses more heavily than gains, that stems from the pain of parting ways with anything that we own. The literature shows that sellers typically set their selling price at twice what average buyers are willing to pay, except when they treat items they own as exchange goods, like currency (Novemsky & Kahneman, 2005), or happen to be feeling exceedingly sad or disgusted at the time of sale (Lerner, Small, & Loewenstein, 2004).

From an adaptation perspective, loss aversion might first have emerged as a matter of survival: The less humans living in subsistence environments had to last them through the winter, the lower their chance of survival due to starvation or illness (Lumsdem & Wilson, 1981). But nomadic and traditional societies with no refrigeration, closets, attics, or rental storage units also encountered far fewer advantages from a surplus that they would have had to carry, store, and protect (Betzig & Turke, 1986; Kaplan & Hill, 1985). Thus, while a gain was less important to humanity's early adaptation, a loss triggers distress, which is an appropriate response in matters of survival. Ariely, Huber, and Wertenbroch (2005) ascribe some of the effects of loss aversion to the power of learned possession attachment: Modern humans learn early in their consumer lives to protect, care for, and cherish our possessions. They conclude that this results in an overwhelming force in consumer life: Even when contemplating ownership in a context such as bidding in an auction, consumers can adopt to-be-owned items as part of their "psychic endowment" and fear losing the bid.

Nayakankuppam and Mishra (2005) show that sellers of non–exchange-endowed goods, who face losing the benefits of ownership and gaining only cash, focus on the positive features of their products, to the detriment of any negative features. This positive-feature bias for sellers is so pronounced that they do not even recall any nonpositive features. The buyers in Nayakankuppam and Mishra's studies, though demonstrating greater recall for negative features, show evidence of weighing both the positives and negatives of a product that they are asked to contemplate purchasing.

Yet sellers who are cleaning out the closet after an identity change—after college, divorce, death of a parent, children growing up and moving out—must focus on some negatives of their possessions in order to part with them. Lastovicka and Fernandez (2005) examine divestment of meaningful goods in a detailed study of garage sales and online auctions to chart three pathways to disposal. Goods that are "never-me" are negative reminders of an undesirable past self and thus are the easiest identity markers to part with. Possessions that are "not-me-now," however, are positively charged items that consumers have simply outgrown or no longer have room for. It is time to remove these items from the endowment, yet owners typically must find a way of preserving private meaning while selling off the vessel of that meaning itself—a divestment ritual of sorts that helps sellers past the emotional difficulty of giving up an item they were once attached to (Lastovicka & Fernandez, 2005). Thus, a wedding band or shared furnishings after a divorce are the "never-me" items consumers can reject, because they are negatively charged and easier to part with, despite the central role that such possessions once played in consumers' lives. But the "not-me-now" children's toys with which a parent must part after the children leave for college, the starter furnishings that a young couple agrees to sell after they have money for finer things, and the deceased parent's car that runs-like-new but has no place in the child's garage all incur a set of mixed emotions that complicate the selling process.

These mixed emotions could motivate consumers to convince themselves of the reduced benefits of continued ownership, thus focusing—unlike Nayakankuppam and Mishra's (2005) sellers—on both the positive and negative aspects of the item, no matter how deeply they were once attached to such possessions. In Mandel's (2002) terms, such sellers of attached goods exhibit "transaction demand" and are willing to settle on a lower selling price, once they deem themselves ready to be divested of these goods.

Consumer ambivalence seems to concern secondhand sellers. Mixed emotions about selling a meaningful possession that consumers are ready to part with might force sellers of such goods to weigh the merits and faults of the item. This consideration of the negative aspects of continued ownership could be anticipated to lower the selling price in accordance with Mandel's (2002) prediction that sellers exhibiting transaction demand are more willing to divest themselves of their endowments. Likewise, consumers who are saddened or disgusted by their situation might require a change in state that drives contemplation of selling meaningful goods for lower prices. This aligns with Lerner, Small, and Loewenstein's (2004) participants, who, primed with sadness or disgust, asked for lower prices for their goods.

Yet not all sellers of meaningful goods might be willing to weigh the negative aspects of their possessions. When sellers of attached goods have not yet, as Lastovicka and Fernandez (2005) point out, engaged in an "iconic transfer ritual" to transfer the personal meaning of a possession away from the carrier of the meaning (the possession itself), then they might simply show an endowment effect with heightened loss aversion and be even more reticent to sell their goods. This can occur when an owner is forced to consider selling meaningful goods for economic reasons or life changes, such as pawning jewelry after a job loss, selling furnishings to move into a small apartment following a divorce, or clearing out items after a death in the family. It could be the case that this kind of seller's demand would be for a similar or perhaps even higher selling price than that which a regularly endowed seller will demand.

Consumers are molded into possession attachment from the moment our collective cultural mothers caution us to take pride and care with our belongings, to treat possessions as special (Ariely et al., 2005; Kleine & Baker, 2004). When consumers begin to outgrow possessions or no longer need to be defined by a certain set of consumption goods, however, they must negotiate the binding forces of such attachment and the looming loss of the benefits of ownership or face a costly hoarding habit. The consumer propensity toward accumulation of possessions is quantifiable: As real disposable income has doubled over the past 40 years in the United States, American consumers have been spending all but 3 percent of that rising income (Mooallem, 2009). The key to survival in this consumer jungle is a psychological mechanism that allows consumers to break down the barriers of endowment, loss aversion, and possession attachment in order to divest themselves of no-longer-wanted goods at a time when the costs (both financial and psychological) of maintaining ownership outweigh the benefits of ownership.

The literature of sustainable practices in consumer selling of possessions also concerns the conversion of possessions into commodities. Young and Wallendorf (1989) describe disposition as the process of "detachment" from self. Lastovicka and Fernandez (2005) also note that a meaningful possession can be a vessel, a bearer for private meanings. It is incumbent upon the seller to fully restore "public meanings" and discharge the singularized possession meanings from a used good, however, in order to convert his or her singularized object into a market commodity. Many owners in Lastovicka and Fernandez's (2005) study first boxed up or stored such possessions in basements, attics, or closets, successfully removing these goods from the living areas of the home to a transitory location. Items to sell were eventually selected from those locations. As part of being prepared for sale, goods were washed, cleaned, folded, pressed, tied with string, and affixed with a price tag, which returned the once-personalized, decommodified object to a commodity.

Denegri-Kott and Molesworth (2009) found that the same cleansing ritual was key to online auction site e-Bay users' processes for turning singularized possessions into commercial, market valuables. Cleansing, repackaging, even professional-style photography of the object to present it online created for their e-bay viewers the sense of possessions as stock from which commodity value can be extracted. Activating commodity values restores public meanings and transports the good from singularized, private domain to the domain of commodity exchange. This disposition choice, however, involves copious work and effort that not all consumers are willing to expend to restore such public meaning, from cleansing to postage to maintenance and advertising for a public online profile (Denegri-Kott & Molesworth, 2009). The consumers who successfully turn their possessions into market commodities are able to sell their goods in a sustainable way, extending the life of the product to a new owner. But inherent in this practice is also its potential for abuse: Denegri-Kott and Molesworth (2009) also raise the specter of the potential "promiscuity" of possessions, in which personalized goods are objectified for their resale value, and several owners might attach little meaning to their possessions. Collectibles, autographed sports and movie memorabilia, and items specifically sold and labeled as being "authentic" antiques or historical artifacts seem particularly susceptible to such promiscuity. In effect, these objects subvert attachment and by their very value as a to-be-sold item hold no meaning or redeeming value to sellers who buy such goods only for the pleasure of selling them.

In this section, we reissue a call raised by Novemsky and Kahneman (2005): Loss aversion is present but obviously does not halt all transactions in the market between endowed sellers and buyers (or else no exchanges would ever take place in a secondhand market). What mechanisms allow average consumers to overcome loss aversion and sell their goods? We are particularly interested in how members of a consumer society choose to sell things that matter to them. This represents a sustainable urge to own less, and within this process of "letting go" of meaningful possessions might lie a key to encouraging a healthier balance in the amount of consumer goods purchased and amount of disposable income spent on possessions.

Future researchers should seek to uncover the distinction and the mechanism involved here. That includes outlining both the difference in demanded price between a seller of a meaningful good and the seller of a less-meaningful good, and determining the driver of the mechanism, whether affective state (disgust, sadness) or cognitive calculation (weighing of both positive and negative features). A salient area of unexplored research emerges as the literature also considers which consumers are more willing to invest the time to restore public, market values to privatized objects. We recommend that future researchers examine and explain the underlying psychological process that helps consumers part with their dearly beloved goods, whether those processes are emotional or cognitive. And akin to hoarders who are unable to let go of their possessions and are too attached to their purchases, there might exist a class of promiscuous sellers who are obsessed with reselling and acquiring only to resell, who remain far too aloof from their possessions and suffer negative consequences as a result.

Contamination Essences in a Used Good

Sustainable consumer tribes exhibit an extraordinary willingness to share tools, cars, bicycles, and toys; to buy or accept gifts of secondhand goods; and to sell their own items in the used-goods market. Yet to some consumers, used goods are undesirable and not only for their depreciation or potential damage but for perceptively gross or disgusting qualities (Rozin, Millman, & Nemeroff, 1986). The key question becomes why some consumers, such as those in the vintage or simplifier consumer subcultures, have less trouble participating in the used-goods market. An answer might have something to do with what essences adhere in a used good.

The presence of a real or imagined social actor can affect how a consumer feels about a good in a retail setting, especially in a secondhand market. Argo, Dahl, and Morales (2006, 2008) expand on a theory of consumer contamination stemming from consumer touch in the retail environment. If a product has been touched or perceived to be touched (a blouse hanging in a dressing room, the display or tester version of a household appliance), consumers are more likely to feel that the product is now unclean, dirty, or gross and report lower purchase intentions (Argo, Dahl, & Morales, 2006). Although, by contrast, if the source of such contamination is positive, such as an attractive member of the opposite sex or a celebrity, purchase intentions rise (Argo, Dahl, & Morales, 2008; Rozin, Millman, & Nemeroff, 1986).

Observed touch can also significantly alter behavior and encourage negative-contamination responses. Morales and Fitzsimons (2007) document contagion of unwanted qualities from one object to another. In their studies, offensive properties are transferred from items in a shopping cart that either touch or are in proximity to more pleasing objects. A package of cooking lard next to a package of ricecakes not only makes the ricecakes less desirable to consumers but also changes the way consumers view the product, rating it as less healthy than a control group that observes the ricecakes in a shopping cart with no lard in sight. Similarly, a package of tampons makes a nearby bundle of cookies less appealing.

But importantly, contamination from moral or social undesirables, including hidden prejudices, is also shown to transfer to product evaluation and purchase intent. In field studies of an online auction in which a light- or dark-skinned hand held an iPod for sale in a featured product photograph, Doleac and Stein (2010) uncover a result that is suggestive of social contamination. Dark-skinned hands garnered lower inquiries and 17 percent fewer offers, roughly the same decrease as a hand with a visible wrist tattoo, a societal taboo that has been documented as incurring moral disgust (Nemeroff & Rozin, 1994; Rozin & Singh, 1999).

What emerges from these studies is a sense that people and other objects contain properties that can be invisibly transferred to goods and possessions. This essence can be good or bad, and can stem from observed touch (Doleac & Stein, 2010; Morales & Fitzsimons, 2007) or imagined touch (Argo, Dahl, & Morales, 2006, 2008). The underlying mechanism for each of these interactions seems to stem from our evolutionary response to sources of disgust (Rozin, 1999). Since some objects carry pestilence and disease, such as feces and insects, it was important for survival to feel revulsion and reject contact with such sources of disgust (Rozin & Fallon, 1987; Rozin, Millman, & Nemeroff, 1986). In modern times, such disgust has evolved as a survival response against sexual, physical, death-related, and even social and moral sources from AIDS to cigarette smoke to symbols of fear and prejudice (Nemeroff & Rozin, 1994; Olatunji & Sawchuk, 2005; Rozin & Singh, 1999). Responses to disgusting items align with the evolutionary adaptation of disgust: namely, avoidance or rejection of the disgusting stimuli. Although the average consumer is not necessarily a threat to one's health, the thought of an unknown or undesirable source coming into contact with a good can lower evaluations of that good.

Although such studies chart a response to contamination by other consumers, the degree of sensitivity to the tangible essence or presence of others' properties in a consumer good that others have touched, used, or owned might be expected to vary. As Haidt, McCauley, and Rozin (1994) showed in the disgust sensitivity scale, responses to sources of disgust vary as an individual difference. It is highly likely that consumers might have more or less sensitivity to residual contamination in consumer objects in much the same way, either viewing possessions as carriers of their owners' or users' personality traits or "essence" or viewing possessions as inanimate objects with manufactured qualities that are unaltered by a previous user. The literature so far lacks insight into how consumers respond to such residual content in possessions, especially considering how these responses might drive thought processes, responses, and decision making in settings involving objects that have been previously handled, used, or owned by others. We suggest that there is an individual difference at work driving the response to sensing the "essence" or personality of another consumer in an object once touched, used, or owned by another. A consumer either recognizes such essence as an alteration of the object by another consumer or fails to perceive how a previous user could alter the good.

If brands with appealing personalities can "rub off" on people who seek to signal that they possess the same appealing traits (Park & John, 2010), can people "rub off" on their objects in the same way? Park and John find that carrying a Victoria's Secret bag, even when empty, helped female shoppers at the mall feel more glamorous and attractive. Using a pen emblazoned with the MIT logo made MBA students feel more hard-working and intelligent. Would the same results occur if female shoppers carried a handbag once owned by their favorite actress, or if students used the dean's pen for a week? More intriguing, can the reverse effects occur? Does the dean feel that decisions signed off on with his pen are less effective if a student has used it for a week, or does an actress feel that her purse is less glamorous if her personal assistant carries it for a few days? Understanding how sensitive consumers are to the residual taint or "rub off" of another consumer into an object could pilot a basic understanding of how consumers think about objects previously used by another.

The perception of another's essence or taint is apparent in consumer studies. Respondents had a natural aversion to wearing a sweater owned by an unfamiliar stranger as opposed to purchasing the same sweater new (Rozin, Markwith, & McCauley, 1994). Researchers found that the acceptability of the used sweater decreased significantly if the same sweater was once worn by a man who had tuberculosis, had been maimed, was a murderer, or had AIDS. Contamination is also evident in the positive-contagion direction: Although respondents were unwilling to wear a laundered blouse once worn by a disliked person, they rated the laundered blouse once worn by a liked person as more valuable (Rozin, Milliman, & Nemeroff, 1986).

From the work of these disgust theorists, we know that people imbue objects with the personality or traits of their owners. To clarify, we suggest that an important goal for consumer behavior is understanding relationships to possessions, particularly how and why secondhand use via the understudied arenas of sharing or disposal occurs (MacInnis & Folkes, 2010). A component of that puzzle is understanding both how objects might or might not retain their users' characteristics or essences and why and when others perceive and react to that residual taint. It is suggested that some consumers see their identity as being reflected in meaningful possessions (Belk, 1988). If they indeed see themselves in some objects, to what degree might they see other consumers reflected in possessions to which they are or were once attached? This individual difference might be cultural or could be cross-cultural universal. How does this alter judgments and valuations about used goods, as well as determine consumers' level of participation in the secondhand market? And what is the mediating effect that transfers essences from a previous user to a consumer good: Is it a physical model of disgust transfer, a mere association based on symbolic interactions, or something else? The answers could provide salient clues to active, sustainable consumer behaviors and individual dispositions toward flea-market shopping, antiquing, Saturday morning yard-sale hopping, online classifieds purchasing, sharing, leasing, borrowing, and donation.

Conclusion

In this chapter, we draw together threads in related areas of research that each informs a mindful consumption practice around reuse, resale, and refashioning. Sustainable consumer tribes, such as vintage aficionados, thrift-store romantics, and voluntary simplifiers, seek out such practices as a way of affecting the environment, gaining control over a fast-paced consumer culture, and showing their own status as simplified consumers. What is most intriguing to learn from these consumer tribes is how they part with their goods and mitigate the stress of detaching from meaningful possessions and how they navigate the possible essences (both positive and negative) of other consumers in the used goods that they value and purchase. Further research into these arenas might help uncover clues to increasing the sustainable practices of reuse, refashioning, and delayed purchasing of new goods.

References

Albinsson, P.A., & Perera, B.Y. (2009). From trash to treasure and beyond: The meaning of voluntary disposition. *Journal of Consumer Behavior, 8,* 340–353.

Argo, J.J., Dahl, D.W., & Morales, A.C. (2006). Consumer contamination: How consumers react to products touched by others. *Journal of Marketing, 70,* 81–94.

Argo, J.J., Dahl, D.W., & Morales, A.C. (2008). Positive consumer contagion: Responses to attractive others in a retail context. *Journal of Marketing Research, 45,* 690–701.

Ariely, D., Huber, J., & Wertenbroch, K. (2005). When do losses loom larger than gains? *Journal of Marketing Research, 42,* 134–138.

Belk, R.W. (1985). Trait aspects of living in the material world. *Journal of Consumer Research, 12*(3), 265–280.

Belk, R.W. (1988). Possessions and the extended self. *Journal of Consumer Research, 15*(2), 139–168.

Betzig, L. L., & Turke, P. W. (1986). Food sharing on Ifaluk. *Current Anthropology, 27,* 397–400.

Bruno, D.M. (2010). *The 100 thing challenge: How I got rid of almost everything, remade my life, and regained my soul.* New York: Harper.

Cooper, T. (2005). Slower consumption: Reflections on product life spans and the "throw-away society." *Journal of Industrial Ecology, 9*(1–2), 51–67.

Craig-Lees, M., & Hill, C. (2002). Understanding voluntary simplifiers. *Psychology & Marketing, 19*(2), 187–210.

Denegri-Kott, J., & M. Molesworth (2009). I'll sell this and I'll buy them that: eBay and the management of possessions as stock. *Journal of Consumer Behavior, 8,* 305–315.

Doleac, J.L., & Stein, L.C.D (2010). The visible hand: Race and online market outcomes. JEL working paper series. Last revised March 25, 2011. http://ssrn.com/abstract=1615149/.

Etzioni, A. (1998). Voluntary simplicity: Characterization, select psychological implication, and societal consequences. *Journal of Economic Psychology, 19,* 619–643.

Fox, K.J. (1987). Real punks and pretenders: The social organization of a counterculture. *Journal of Contemporary Ethnography, 16*(October), 344–370.

Greenwald, A. G., McGhee, D. E., & Schwartz, J. K. L. (1998). Measuring individual differences in implicit cognition: The Implicit Association Test. *Journal of Personality and Social Psychology, 74,* 1464–1480.

Griskevicius, V., Tybur, J.M., & Van den Bergh, B. (2010). Going green to be seen: Status, reputation and conspicuous consumption. *Journal of Personality and Social Psychology, 98*(3), 392–404.

Haidt, J., McCauley, C., & Rozin, P. (1994). Individual differences in sensitivity to disgust: A scale sampling seven domains of disgust elicitors. *Personality and Individual Differences, 16*(5), 701–713.

Higgins, E.T. (1998). Promotion and prevention: Regulatory focus as a motivational principle. *Advances in Experimental Social Psychology, 30,* 1–46.

Kahneman, D., Knetsch, J.L., & Thaler, R. (1991). The endowment effect, loss aversion, and the status quo bias. *Journal of Economic Perspectives, 5*(1), 193–206.

Kaplan, H., & Hill, K. (1985). Food sharing among Ache foragers: Tests of explanatory hypotheses. *Current Anthropology, 26,* 223–246.

Kleine, S.S., & Baker, S.M. (2004). An integrative review of material possession attachment. *Academy of Marketing Science Review, 2004*(1). www.amsreview.org/articles/kleine01-2004.pdf.

Lastovicka, J.L., & Fernandez, K.V. (2005). Three paths to disposition: The movement of meaningful possessions to strangers. *Journal of Consumer Research, 31,* 813–823.

Lerner, J.S., Small, D.A., & Loewenstein, G. (2004). Heart string and purse strings: Carryover effects of emotions on economic decisions. *Psychological Science, 15*(5), 337–341.

Lumsden, C. J., & Wilson, E. O. (1981). *Genes, mind, and culture: The coevolutionary process.* Cambridge: Harvard University Press.

MacInnis, D.J., & Folkes, V.S. (2010). The disciplinary status of consumer behavior: A sociology of science perspective on key controversies. *Journal of Consumer Research, 36,* 899–914.

Mandel, D.R. (2002). Beyond mere ownership: Transaction demand as a moderator of the endowment effect. *Organizational Behavior and Human Decision Processes, 88,* 737–747.

McDonald, S., Oates, C.J., Young, C.W., & Hwang, K. (2006). Toward sustainable consumption: Researching voluntary simplifiers. *Psychology & Marketing, 23*(4), 515–534.

Mooallem, J. (2009, September 9). The self-storage self. *New York Times Magazine*, p. MM24. www.nytimes.com/2009/09/06/magazine/06self-storage-t.html?pagewanted=all/.

Morales, A.C., & Fitzsimons, G.J. (2007). Product contagion: Changing consumer evaluations through physical contact with "disgusting" products. *Journal of Marketing Research, 44*(2), 272–283.

Nayakankuppam, D., & Mishra, H. (2005). The endowment effect: Rose-tinted and dark-tinted glasses. *Journal of Consumer Research, 32,* 390–395.

Nelson, M.R., Rademacher, M.A., & Paek, H. (2007). Downshifting consumer = upshifting citizen? An examination of a local freecycle community. *ANNALS of the American Academy of Political and Social Science, 611,* 141–156.

Nemeroff, C., & Rozin, P. (1994). The contagion concept in adult thinking in the United States: Transmission of germs and of interpersonal influence. *Ethos, 22*(2), 158–186.

Novemsky, N., & Kahneman, D. (2005). The boundaries of loss aversion. *Journal of Marketing Research, 42,* 119–128.

Olatunji, B.O., & Sawchuk, C.N. (2005). Disgust: Characteristic features, social manifestation, and clinical implications. *Journal of Social and Clinical Psychology, 24*(7), 932–962.

Park, J.K., & John, D.R. (2010). Got to get you into my life: Do brand personalities rub off on consumers? *Journal of Consumer Research, 37,* 655–669.

Rozin, P. (1999). The process of moralization. *Psychological Science, 10,* 218–221.

Rozin, P., & Fallon, A.E. (1987). A perspective on disgust. *Psychological Review, 94,* 23–41.

Rozin, P., & Singh, L. (1999). The moralization of cigarette smoking in the United States. *Journal of Consumer Psychology, 8*(3), 321–337.

Rozin, P., Markwith, W., & McCauley, C. (1994). Sensitivity to indirect contacts with other persons: AIDS aversion as a composite of aversion to strangers, infection, moral taint and misfortune. *Journal of Abnormal Psychology, 103*(3), 495–504.

Rozin, P., Millman, L., & Nemeroff, C. (1986). Operation of the laws of sympathetic magic in disgust and other domains. *Journal of Personality and Social Psychology, 50*(4), 703–712.

Schouten, J.W., & McAlexander, J.H. (1995). Subcultures of consumption: An ethnography of the new bikers. *Journal of Consumer Research, 22,* 43–61.

Semin, G.R., Higgins, T., Gil de Montes, L., Estourget, Y., & Valencia, J.F. (2005). Linguistic signatures of regulatory focus: How abstraction fits promotion more than prevention. *Journal of Personality and Social Psychology, 89*(1), 36–45.

Young, M. M. & Wallendorf, M. (1989). Ashes to ashes, dust to dust: Conceptualizing consumer disposition of possessions. In T. Childers, R. Bagozzi, P. Peter, A. Firat, C. Kumcu, A. Sawyer, J. Frazier, M. Rothschild, & M. Strong (Eds.), *Marketing Theory and Practice*, AMA Winter Educators Conference (pp. 33–38). Chicago: American Marketing Association.

Part II

Determinants of Sustainable Consumption

When the purpose is to increase sustainable consumption among consumers, it is important to understand which factors affect, either negatively or positively, engaging in green practices. The chapters in this section introduce various determinants of sustainable consumption.

Stickel treats religious affiliation and degree of religiosity as individual difference variables and investigates their impact on sustainable consumption practices (both attitudes and behaviors). By focusing on Christian denominations and nonreligious respondents, Stickel shows that nonreligious consumers are more likely than religious consumers to engage in sustainable consumption practices. Among religious consumers, those who belonged to denominations supporting an inerrant view of scripture are less likely to participate in SCPs than those who belonged to denominations supporting human interpretation of scripture. Stickel's study also showed that higher religiosity is correlated with higher participation in sustainable consumption.

Lee, Youn, & Nayakankuppam focus on the differences in cognitive processes of holistic and analytic thinkers and propose a framework to stimulate sustainable behavior as a function of holistic thinking. Based on three studies, the authors suggest that holistic thinking, as opposed to analytic thinking, is associated with increased perceived importance of social values related to sustainability. This increased perceived importance, in turn, leads to a greater willingness to enhance sustainability.

Segev deals with the impact of ethnicity on sustainable practices by comparing green behaviors and the drivers influencing them for non-Hispanic (i.e., native-born) consumers and Hispanic immigrant consumers (examined through four acculturation segments: assimilation, integration, separation, and marginalization). In addition to revealing differences among non-Hispanics and Hispanics as well as among four acculturation segments in terms of engaging in green behaviors (e.g., green purchase intention, actual green purchasing, and conservation behavior),

Segev also shows that environmental awareness is positively associated with green behaviors through the perceived influence of green advertising.

Mosteller integrates research from two main aspects of environmentally significant behavior: the informational context of stimuli presented to inform behavior and factors that affect how consumers process and evaluate information presented. Contextual factors discussed in this chapter include product contexts, social dilemmas, values and ethics, and the choice context. Three informational factors that may influence sustainable consumption are also discussed: negative versus positive valenced information; visual versus text information; and concrete versus abstract information. The knowledge of these factors can be valuable for understanding consumers' attitudes and behaviors in relation to environmentally significant behavior.

5

Religion and Religiosity's Influence on Sustainable Consumption Behaviors

Elizabeth Minton

For many people, religion is the backbone of everyday behavior. World population, which currently totals almost 6.9 billion (U.S. Census Bureau, 2011), includes approximately 2.2 billion Christians, 1.2 billion Muslims, 350 million Buddhists, 1 billion Hindus, 16 million Jews, and 6 million Confucians/Daoists, along with many followers of other small religions (Hunt & Penwell, 2008). Approximately 70 percent of the world's population follows one of these seven prominent world religions (Hunt & Penwell, 2008). In the United States, 62 percent of citizens self-classify as "highly religious" and are confident that God exists, and 82 percent self-classify as at least somewhat confident that God exists (New Strategist, 2010).

Moreover, research shows that 70.7 percent of Americans carry their religious beliefs into other aspects of life (New Strategist, 2010), such as into the consumption of sustainable goods and services. For these Americans and many others throughout the world, religion represents far more than just attendance at religious services once a week. Religion influences, for instance, what consumers value, with whom they spend time, from where they get information, and in which activities are deemed acceptable to participate.

Specifically in the realm of sustainability, consumption of sustainable products and services in the United States produced $28 billion in revenue in 2010, which is expected to increase to $60 billion by 2014 (Chestney, 2010). Because such extensive growth is expected, the market for sustainable products and services is a pertinent subject to study. Also, differences in references to sustainability in religious doctrine provide theoretical support for differing views of sustainable consumption.

As the field of consumer behavior acknowledges the importance of religion, the field should follow the pragmatic belief that what is important is not whether religious beliefs are true but, rather, the effect these beliefs have on human behavior (James, 1902/2004). Following this pragmatic belief, religion can be considered an individual difference variable, a predictor of sustainable consumption practices, or a basis for market segmentation. Therefore, the purpose of this chapter is to investigate a new stream of research focusing on how religion influences consumer behavior as an individual difference variable, specifically with sustainable consumption practices. This chapter reviews prominent findings from consumer behavior studies addressing religion, related sustainability findings in other fields, and provides support for sustainable consumption differences among religious affiliations through a nationally representative study.

Religion and General Consumer Behavior

Despite religion's prominence in the world, relatively little research has been conducted that assesses how religion influences consumer behavior. Nearly every study relating religion to consumer behavior highlights the study's exploratory nature and makes no attempt to replicate previous research. Also, previous studies lack a theoretical foundation.

A possible explanation for this lack of research is the sensitivity of the topic, which is widely considered somewhat taboo (Bailey & Sood, 1993; Kahle, Kau, Tambyah, Tan, & Jung, 2005; Mokhlis, 2006; Rindfleisch, Wong, & Burroughs, 2010). Lack of realization that religion can affect consumer behavior is another possible explanation; researchers believe that religion primarily affects the prominently studied areas of sociology, anthropology, and political science (Hirschman, 1983). Regardless of the reasoning for this lack of studies relating religion to consumer behavior, the field of marketing is missing a significant component of consumer behavior: religion.

Religion is a key element of culture that contributes to a person's values and thereby influences his or her behavior (Bailey & Sood, 1993; Fam, Waller, & Erdogan, 2004; Harrell, 1986; Schiffman & Kanuk, 2007). Religion and associated value systems permeate society and influence both believers and nonbelievers (Khraim, 2010).

Discussion of religion is found infrequently in the consumer behavior literature, due in part to the fact that religion is seen as an adjoining discipline but not part of the consumption process (MacInnis & Folkes, 2010). However, when religion is viewed as an individual difference variable rather than just a correlational element for the marketization of religious goods, religion can be incorporated directly into a consumer's acquisition, consumption, and disposal of goods and services in the market, which MacInnis and Folkes (2010) identify as within the bounds of consumer behavior.

According to Sheth's (1983) shopping preference theory, shopping motives are influenced directly by personal values, social values, and epistemic values. Because religion serves broadly as the foundation for personal values (Bailey & Sood, 1993; Fam et al., 2004), religion should directly influence shopping motives, according to Sheth's (1983) theory. Several studies in the consumer behavior literature have supported Sheth's (1983) shopping preference theory identifying religion as a component of personal values that influences shopping and consumption behavior (McDaniel & Burnett, 1990; Mokhlis, 2006; Swimberghe, Sharma, & Flurry, 2009).

Religion can be divided into two main components: (1) religious affiliation (e.g., Buddhist, Hindu, Christian, Muslim) and (2) religiosity (i.e., degree of belief). There is no all-encompassing definition of religion (Hood, Hill, & Spilka, 2009); instead, the definition is adjusted based on the needs of the study (Wilkes, Burnett, & Howell, 1986). For the purpose of this study, religion is defined based on previous research (Delener, 1990; Fam et al., 2004; Hill et al., 2000; Himmelfarb, 1975; Kale, 2004) as "a commonly held set of beliefs and values that guide external behavior and an internal search for meaning and may include institutional practices such as religious services or religious social networks." Religiosity is then defined, for the purpose of this study, as "the degree to which one holds religious beliefs and values through both an internal spiritual connection and external religious practices and behaviors."

Research addressing religion's influence on consumer behavior is important to marketers and vital for a comprehensive understanding of what causes consumers to behave as they do (Essoo & Dibb, 2004; Hirschman, 1981). Also, religion is an easily observable construct and therefore can be used by marketing academics and practitioners alike (McDaniel & Burnett, 1990). An extensive review of the literature both in and outside the field of marketing since a seminal article by Engle (1976) revealed only 70 publications that have addressed the topic of religion's (religious affiliation or religiosity) influence on consumer behavior. Based on numerous empirical studies, religion and religiosity clearly influence consumer behavior.

Religion has the ability to influence consumer behavior in two main ways: directly through explicit prohibitions in religious books and by religious leaders (e.g., rules for producing and consuming Muslim *halal* or Jewish *kosher* foods) or indirectly through the values that are impressed on by religious scripture and religious leaders (Harrell, 1986). Several studies have looked at the former explicit prohibitions on general consumer behavior (Alserhan, 2010; Muhamad & Mizerski, 2007), but few studies assess the psychological relationship between these prohibitions and religious values and market sustainability behaviors.

Religion and Sustainability

As previously stated, the purchase of sustainable products and services is expected to increase to $60 billion in revenue by 2014 (Chestney, 2010), which is part of sustainable consumption behaviors, which encompass the purchase, use, and disposal of sustainable products and services as well as the purchase, use, and disposal of products and services in a sustainable manner (e.g., recycling). Because attitudes often do not directly correspond with behaviors, distinguishing between sustainable consumption behaviors (SCBs), such as purchasing alternative energy vehicles, and sustainable consumption attitudes (SCAs), such as believing that there is a need for alternative energy, is important. Together, SCBs and SCAs constitute sustainable consumption practices (SCPs), which theory would lead one to expect to be influenced by religious affiliation.

One of the earliest religious scholars identified several distinct differences between Western religious doctrine (e.g., Christianity and the Bible, Judaism and the Torah, Islam and the Qur'an) and Eastern religious doctrine (e.g., Hinduism and the Vedas, Buddhism and the Tripitaka and Jatakas) including varying views toward sustainability (James, 1902/2004). Western religions believe that God created nature and that the physical world will come to a distinct end, compared to Eastern religions, which hold a pantheistic view that God is one with nature (James, 1902/2004; Sarre, 1995). Therefore, these distinctions provide theoretical support that Eastern religious adherents should be more apt to participate in SCPs because caring for nature is equivalent to caring for God, compared to Western religious adherents, who believe the world is merely a temporary holding place on the way to heavenly life.

Differences in SCPs within Western and Eastern religions are also expected based on varying views on the inerrancy and infallibility of the scripture. This study focuses specifically on Christian denominations due to the availability of data with sufficient sample sizes. Religious scholars have shown that the literalist ideology of denominations that believe that the Bible is inerrant and infallible drives behaviors, attitudes, and religious convictions based on doctrine (Hoffmann & Bartkowski, 2008; Sherkat & Ellison, 1997). To better understand the field of consumer behavior and defend religion as an individual difference variable, it would be useful to apply this relationship between literal biblical ideology and behavior to the context of consumer behavior.

Baptists, Catholics, Pentecostals, and Presbyterians comprise Christian denominations that believe that the Bible is inerrant, infallible, and the authoritative word for faith and conduct (Bowman, 2003; Rhodes, 2005). In particular, Baptists are described by a prominent, well-respected Christian theologian as believing that the Bible "contains truth without any mixture of error" (Rhodes, 2005, p. 69). In contrast, Lutherans and Methodists believe that the Bible must be interpreted by the reader in light of tradition and human reason (Bowman, 2003; Rhodes, 2005). Finally, nondenominational churches (i.e., churches that adhere only to basic Christian doctrine) vary significantly on their views toward scripture inerrancy. By contrast, the nonreligious are expected to believe in basing life's actions on human reason rather than scriptural dictates (Peterson & Liu, 2008). This separation between denominations based on belief regarding the inerrancy of scripture also correlates with views toward social and political issues, such as abortion and homosexuality, with inerrancy-supporting denominations much less likely to support abortion or homosexuality (Pew Forum on Religion and Public Life, 2008).

Therefore, significant differences in attitudes and behaviors are expected between denominations based on differences in views toward inerrancy of the scripture and associated sociopolitical attitudes. Denominations that view the Bible as inerrant are expected to strictly follow the Western religious belief that sustainability is less important because God created the physical world as only a passing condition on the way to heavenly life (Eckberg & Blocker, 1989; White, 1967). Participation in SCPs is expected to increase for denominations that support an interpretation of scripture based on tradition and human reason, with SCPs highest for nonreligious consumers who believe that the world is not a transitional phase and, as a result, needs to be cared for through SCPs.

Hypothesis 1: Consumers who adhere to Christian denominations that believe that the Bible is inerrant and infallible (Baptists, Catholics, Pentecostals, and Presbyterians) participate in fewer SCPs than consumers who adhere to Christian denominations that believe that the Bible should be interpreted in light of tradition and human reason (Lutherans and Methodists), nondenominational Christians, or nonreligious consumers. Nonreligious consumers participate in more SCPs than consumers who adhere to a Christian denomination.

Previous studies from other disciplines show significant differences in environmental concern among religiosity levels (Woodrum & Wolkomir, 1997). Higher religiosity levels indicate higher levels of adherence to denomination beliefs and often higher levels of scriptural knowledge (Dejong, Faulkner, & Warland, 1976). Therefore, highly religious consumers should be more likely to follow the expected relationship between Christian denomination and SCPs than less religious consumers.

Hypothesis 2: Religiosity moderates the relationship between Christian denomination and participation in SCPs.

Previous studies in other disciplines are missing a key component of the interaction between religion and environmental behaviors that is particularly pertinent to the field of marketing: purchasing and consumption-related environmental attitudes and behaviors. In all identified religion and sustainability studies, religious affiliation is not categorized beyond main religious groupings (e.g., Hindu, Buddhist, Muslim, Christian, Jew; Protestant, Catholic, Jew; liberal, moderate, fundamentalist), if any measure of religious affiliation is included at all. For sustainability preferences based on religious groupings to be useful to marketers, clear and targetable segments (e.g., highly devout Baptists) need to be identified. Therefore, this research fills a gap in the literature by analyzing the relationship between religion (both religious affiliation and religiosity) and sustainable consumption at the religious denomination level using a theoretical foundation.

Method

This study uses data from the General Social Survey (GSS) 2010 dataset to analyze differences in sustainable consumption attitudes (SCAs) and behaviors (SCBs) among Christian denominations to determine whether differences in views toward scriptural inerrancy predict SCAs and SCBs. The GSS 2010 dataset has 2,044 respondents who were randomly sampled and collected via face-to-face interviews, phone interviews, and, more recently, computer-assisted personal interviewing (National Opinion Research Center, 2009).

Principle components analysis with varimax rotation was run using 13 sustainable consumption variables. Two factors were identified that explained 38.22 percent of the variability in sustainable consumption. Factor 1 includes variables addressing the behavioral component of sustainable consumption: (1) eats chemical-free fruits and vegetables, (2) drives less for environmental reasons, (3) reduces water use for environmental reasons, (4) avoids buying products for environmental reasons, (5) recycles, (6) pays higher prices to help the environment, (7) pays higher taxes to help the environment, (8) accepts cut in living standards to help the environment, and (9) reduces fuel for environmental reasons. Factor 2 includes variables addressing the attitudinal component of sustainable consumption: (1) believes car pollution is dangerous for the environment, (2) believes pesticides are dangerous for the environment, (3) believes industrial air pollution is dangerous for the environment, and (4) believes water pollution is dangerous for the environment. Scales were created to represent both factors. The behavior scale consisting of nine items has an alpha of .805. The attitudinal scale consisting of four items has an alpha of .801.

Responses were included in the analysis only if all sustainability attitude and behavior questions, as well as all religiosity questions were answered, leaving 985 respondents. Also, Judeo-Christian denominations with fewer than 30 respondents were eliminated from the analysis, thereby excluding 15 Jews and 20 Episcopalians. Finally, respondents with missing responses to individual difference variables were eliminated, leaving 855 respondents for regression analysis. Christian denominations with sufficient sample sizes included in this analysis were Baptists, Catholics, Lutherans, Methodists, Pentecostals, Presbyterians, and nondenominational Christians. Nonreligious respondents were also included as a comparison group.

A measure of religiosity was included to determine how the strength of religious belief influences the degree to which a respondent adheres to his or her denomination's beliefs, specifically as these beliefs relate to SCAs and SCBs. The six-item composite religiosity variable has a Cronbach's alpha of .820 and is composed of a measure of (1) confidence in the existence of God, (2) frequency of prayer, (3) self-perceived strength of religious affiliation, (4) attendance at religious services, (5) self-perceived carrying of beliefs into other dealings, and (6) self-perceived appraisal as a religious person.

Literature-supported individual difference variables were also included to determine how religious affiliation and religiosity serve as predictors of sustainable consumption attitudes and behaviors above and beyond basic demographic and psychographic characteristics. Individual difference variables included in this analysis consist of age (Babakus, Cornwell, Mitchell, & Schlegelmilch, 2004;

Table 5.1

Bivariate Correlation Matrix, Means, and Standard Deviations for Sustainable Consumption Behaviors and Attitudes, Religious Measures, and Individual Difference Variables

	SCA	SCB	REL	AGE	FEM	INC	MAR	EDU	CON	STH	Mean	SD
SCA	1	13.06	2.69									
SCB	.428***	1	22.07	5.78								
REL	–.024	–.066	1	21.03	6.78							
AGE	–.032	.034	.182***	1	46.42	16.44						
FEM	.152***	.102**	.166***	–.008	1	0.55	0.50					
INC	–.159***	–.009	–.002	.148***	–.093**	1	17.14	5.62				
MAR	–.035	–.038	.184***	.510***	.042	.258***	1	0.71	0.45			
EDU	–.074*	.105**	–.030	.014	.054	.348***	–.007	1	13.89	2.99		
CON	–.253***	–.261***	.322***	.098**	–.121***	.055	.125***	–.053	1	4.03	1.44	
STH	–.018	–.037	.176***	–.012	.030	.003	–.008	.020	.048	1	0.26	0.44
DEN												
NON	.105**	.134***	–.706***	–.163***	–.045	–.039	–.152***	.104**	–.251***	–.091**	0.23	0.42
CAT	–.030	.038	.112**	–.044	–.019	.074*	–.026	–.096**	.048	–.194***	0.28	0.45
BAP	.006	–.129***	.320***	.042	.049	–.084*	.014	–.127***	.041	.278***	0.20	0.40
MET	–.002	.004	.088*	.159***	.036	.050	.100**	.039	–.006	.035	0.06	0.24
LUT	–.049	–.043	.031	.100**	–.062	.071*	.112**	.028	.054	–.015	0.05	0.22
PRE	–.123***	–.053	.119***	.159***	.008	.072*	.067	.107**	.065	–.002	0.04	0.20
PEN	.075*	–.020	.110**	–.012	.053	–.115**	.046	–.079*	.060	.044	0.03	0.17
NDN	–.033	.002	.156***	–.058	.008	–.018	.002	.084*	.109**	.004	0.11	0.31

Note: $N = 855$. ***significance at .001 level or lower; **significance at .01; *indicates .05. Bivariate correlations between religious denomination dummy variables have no meaning and are omitted. SCA = sustainable consumption attitudes; SCB = sustainable consumption behaviors; REL = religiosity; AGE = age; FEM = femaleness; INC = income; MAR = married; EDU = years of education; CON = conservativeness; STH = located in the Bible belt in Southeastern United States; DEN = denomination that includes dummy variables of NON = not religious, CAT = Catholic, JEW = Jewish, BAP = Baptist, MET = Methodist, LUT = Lutheran, PRE = Presbyterian, EPI = Episcopal, PEN = Pentecostal, and NDN = nondenominational.

Muhamad & Mizerski, 2007; Ong & Moschis, 2006), income (Bailey & Sood, 1993), gender (Babakus et al., 2004; Bailey & Sood, 1993; Wilkes et al., 1986), years of education (Bailey & Sood, 1993; Muhamad & Mizerski, 2007), marital status (Muhamad & Mizerski, 2007), political orientation (Wolkomir, Futreal, Woodrum, & Hoban, 1997), and geographic location (Siguaw & Simpson, 1997; Taylor, Halstead, & Haynes, 2010).

Linear regression was run using a four-block design with denominational affiliation in block 1 (Presbyterians, a highly inerrancy-supporting denomination, as reference group); religiosity in block 2, basic demographic individual difference variables in block 3 (age, income, gender, years of education, and marital status); and individual difference variables expected to be highly correlated with religiosity in block 4 (political orientation and geographic location); see Table 5.1 for descriptive statistics. Two separate linear regression models were run: one for SCBs and another for SCAs to determine whether attitudes lead to behaviors.

Results

Denominational affiliation is a significant predictor of both sustainable consumption attitudes (SCAs) ($F(7,847) = 4.070, p < .001, R^2 = .033$) and behaviors (SCBs) ($F(7,847) = 4.152, p < .001, R^2 = .033$) in model 1; see Table 5.2. Both religious affiliation and religiosity together significantly predict SCAs ($F(8,846) = 4.089, p < .001, R^2 = .037$) and SCBs ($F(8,846) = 4.135, p < .001, R^2 = .038$) in model 2. Religiosity significantly adds to the predictive power of the attitudinal model ($F(1,846) = 4.114, p = .043, R^2 = .005$) and behavioral model ($F(1,846) = 3.910, p = .048, R^2 = .004$) in model 2, though only slightly.

Model 3, including basic demographic individual difference variables in addition to religious affiliation and religiosity, significantly predicts both SCAs ($F(13,841) = 5.147, p < .001, R^2 = .074$) and SCBs ($F(13,841) = 4.403, p < .001, R^2 = .064$). Basic demographic individual difference variables significantly add to the predictive power of both the attitudinal model ($F(5,841) = 6.623, p < .001, R^2 = .036$) and the behavioral model ($F(5,841) = 4.687, p < .001, R^2 = .026$) in model 3.

The full model, model 4, which includes the addition of individual difference variables known to significantly correlate with religiosity (political orientation and geographic location) also significantly predicts both SCAs ($F(15,839) = 8.104, p < .001, R^2 = .127$) and SCBs ($F(15,839) = 7.568, p < .001, R^2 = .119$). Political orientation and geographic location significantly add to both the attitudinal ($F(2,839) = 25.386, p < .001, R^2 = .053$) and behavioral model ($F(2,839) = 26.410, p < .001, R^2 = .055$) in model 4.

Discussion

Results from this analysis reveal significant differences among Christian denominations in views and behaviors related to sustainable consumption. The correlations

Table 5.2

OLS Regression Coefficients and Standard Errors for Models Predicting Sustainable Consumption Behaviors and Attitudes Using Denominational Religious Grouping

	Attitudes				Behaviors			
Variables	Model 1	Model 2	Model 3	Model 4	Model 1	Model 2	Model 3	Model 4
NON	2.12***	2.62***	2.37***	2.30***	2.89**	3.94**	4.11***	3.94**
	(0.49)	(0.55)	(0.54)	(0.53)	(1.05)	(1.17)	(1.18)	(1.14)
CAT	1.48**	1.58**	1.47**	1.38**	1.83	2.05*	2.71*	2.54*
	(0.48)	(0.48)	(0.48)	(0.47)	(1.03)	(1.04)	(1.05)	(1.02)
BAP	1.64**	1.62**	1.40**	1.26**	–0.02	–0.05	0.57	0.19
(0.49)	(0.49)	(0.49)	(0.48)	(1.06)	(1.06)	(1.07)	(1.04)	
MET	1.58**	1.64**	1.51**	1.35*	1.57	1.70	1.88	1.49
	(0.58)	(0.58)	(0.47)	(0.56)	(1.25)	(1.24)	(1.23)	(1.20)
LUT	1.03	1.15	1.19*	1.18 *	0.38	0.63	1.17	1.16
	(0.61)	(0.61)	(0.60)	(0.58)	(1.30)	(1.30)	(1.30)	(1.26)
PEN	2.79***	2.77***	2.31**	2.36**	0.78	0.74	1.43	1.51
	(0.71)	(0.70)	(0.71)	(0.69)	(1.51)	(1.51)	(1.53)	(1.48)
NDN	1.35*	1.39**	1.27*	1.32*	1.50	1.57	2.09	2.18*
	(0.53)	(0.53)	(0.53)	(0.51)	(1.13)	(1.13)	(1.14)	(1.10)
REL		0.04*	0.03	0.06**		0.08*	0.05	0.12**
		(0.02)	(0.02)	(0.02)		(0.04)	(0.04)	(0.04)
AGE			0.01	0.01			0.04**	0.04**
			(0.01)	(0.01)			(0.01)	(0.01)
FEM			0.74***	0.51**			1.16**	0.66
			(0.19)	(0.18)			(0.40)	(0.40)
INC			–0.06**	–0.05**			–0.03	–0.02
			(0.02)	(0.02)			(0.04)	(0.04)

(continued)

Table 5.2 *(continued)*

	Attitudes				Behaviors			
Variables	Model 1	Model 2	Model 3	Model 4	Model 1	Model 2	Model 3	Model 4
			(0.24)	(0.23)			(0.52)	(0.50)
EDU			–0.03	–0.05			0.18*	0.15*
			(0.03)	(0.03)			(0.07)	(0.07)
CON				–0.46***				–1.02***
				(0.07)				(0.14)
STH				–0.12				0.05
				(0.21)				(0.45)
Intercept	11.46	10.47	11.81	13.20	20.60	18.53	15.00	18.08
R-square	.033	.037	.074	.127	.033	.038	.064	.119
F	4.070***	4.089**	5.147***	8.104***	4.152***	4.135***	4.403***	7.568***
F Change	—	4.114*	6.623***	25.386***	—	3.910*	4.687***	26.410***

Note: $N = 855$. Values in parentheses are standard errors. Variables representing religious groups are dummy variables with Presbyterian as baseline group; each slope represents the difference in group means for the dependent variable between a given group and Presbyterian. REL = religiosity; AGE = age; FEM = femaleness; INC = income; MAR = married; EDU = years of education; CON = conservativeness; STH = located in the Bible belt of south central of southeast U.S.; DEN = denomination which includes dummy variables of NON = not religious, CAT= Catholic, JEW = Jewish, BAP = Baptist, MET = Methodist, LUT = Lutheran, PRE = Presbyterian, EPI = Episcopal, PEN = Pentecostal, and NDN = non-denominational.*significance at .05 level; **significance at .01 level; *** significance at < .001 level.

in Table 5.1 initially suggest that nonreligious respondents are positively correlated with holding SCAs and with participating in SCBs, while denominations that support an inerrant view of the scripture, such as Baptists and Presbyterians, are negatively correlated with SCAs and SCBs, thereby supporting H1.

As expected, conservative respondents are positively correlated with SCAs and SCBs. Despite a positive correlation between SCAs and SCBs, several variables in the model show a disconnect between SCAs and SCBs. For example, the more education a respondent has completed, the less likely he or she is to hold SCAs but the more likely he/she is to participate in SCBs. However, no disconnect is found in regression results for either Christian denominations or degree of religiosity.

Regression results show that respondents who are nonreligious, Catholic, and nondenominational Christian are significantly more likely than the baseline Presbyterian respondents to hold SCAs and participate in SCBs, providing partial support for H1. Interestingly, Baptists are also significantly more likely to hold SCAs than Presbyterians, who were hypothesized to have the same views toward scripture inerrancy. Possibly, differences in church views toward inerrancy (such as differences between the Presbyterian Church in America and the Presbyterian Church USA) could explain these findings. Future research should assess national church/convention adherence under each denomination to minimize variability within denominations, which is a limitation of this research as seen through high standard errors for all religious denominations.

As full models, both religious affiliation and religiosity significantly predict participation in SCAs and SCBs, providing partial support for H1 and full support for H2. Contrary to expectations, higher religiosity is correlated with higher participation in SCAs and SCBs. Possibly, consumers of higher religiosity feel a commitment to care for God's creation, as has been supported in previous studies (Granzin & Olsen, 1991; Noomene, 2011). However, in comparison to religiosity, denominational affiliation adds almost 3 percent more to the explanatory power of both the SCA and SCB model. The final model including all individual difference variables show that, in addition to the significant predictors of religion and religiosity, respondents who are female, have less income, and hold more liberal (as opposed to conservative) political views are more likely to hold SCAs. Similar results hold true for SCBs except that income is not a significant predictor, and higher education leads to more SCBs.

Although all denominations are more likely to participate in SCAs and SCBs than Presbyterians, this does not mean that all denominations participate in SCAs and SCBs. The correlation matrix in Table 5.1 and beta weights in Table 5.2 suggest that Pentecostals and nonreligious respondents are more likely to participate in SCAs than other denominations. Pentecostals were hypothesized to be less participatory in SCAs and SCBs than other denominations that believe the Bible is not inerrant or infallible. These differing results could be due to personal views of flexibility toward church practices leading to more flexibility to adapt to modern culture advocating for SCAs and SCBs (Sheppard, 2007).

One of the limitations of this study is inadequate sample sizes of non-Christian denominations. Future research should assess SCAs and SCBs across a wider variety of Judeo-Christian denominations in addition to denominations from other Western and Eastern religions. Also, future studies should include primary, experimental research assessing specific sustainable consumption behaviors (e.g., differences in purchasing green cleaning products, products using environmentally friendly packaging) as well as consumption differences based on the conspicuousness of the product (e.g., religious differences in the purchase of a jacket made from recycled material in comparison to bed linens made from recyclable material).

An interesting future study would address the distinction between SCAs and SCBs focusing on differences between the Western creational and Eastern pantheistic religious doctrine (James, 1902/2004). As shown in this study, both religious affiliation and religiosity significantly influence consumer behavior and, more specifically, the theory that views toward scriptural inerrancy predict participation in SCAs and SCBs.

Conclusion

Religion is an important predictor of SCAs and SCBs and needs to be given more attention in the marketing literature. This study represents only the beginning of a stream of research addressing how one's religious affiliation and degree of religiosity influence consumer behaviors, specifically in relation to environmental sustainability. According to MacInnis and Folkes's (2010) definition of consumer behavior, religion needs to be included in consumer behavior research as an individual difference variable. Currently, studies linking religion to consumer behavior are extremely limited. Due to the nature of the sample (with inadequate sample sizes of Jews, Muslims, Hindus, and Buddhists), the findings from this study are generalizable only to Christian denominations. Future studies should continue this stream of research, conducting studies across a broader range of religious affiliations.

Development of a comprehensive understanding of religion's influence on consumer behavior, specifically in the realm of sustainability, will allow marketers to initiate segmentation practices on the basis of religious affiliation. For example, findings from this study show that Catholics are most likely to participate in SCBs. The monthly magazine *Catholic Digest* is just one way that Catholics could be specifically targeted with environmentally friendly products and services. Also, denominations associated with minimal SCAs and SCBs (e.g., Baptists and Presbyterians) could be targeted with social marketing campaigns encouraging sustainability, though such campaigns should be cautious so as not to offend or directly ridicule religious doctrine.

Knowledge of the prominent religious denominations that purchase a company's products and services is also beneficial for better matching offerings and communications with customer values and minimizing the risk of offending valuable customers. Religious magazines, denominational conferences, and religious social media groups are among the many ways that segmentation by religious affiliation can be easily implemented by marketers in an area where targeted marketing for environmentally friendly products and services is limited.

Acknowledgments

I thank Dr. Lynn Kahle for his frequent, constructive feedback on this paper as well as motivation to pursue research in the area of religion and consumer behavior. I also thank Dr. Bettina Cornwell and Dr. Matt O'Hern for their constructive feedback.

References

Alserhan, B. A. (2010). Islamic branding: A conceptualization of related terms. *Journal of Brand Management, 18*(1), 34–49.

Babakus, E., Cornwell, T., Mitchell, V., & Schlegelmilch, B.B. (2004). Reactions to unethical consumer behavior across six countries. *Journal of Consumer Marketing, 21*(4), 254–263.

Bailey, J., & Sood, J. (1993). The effects of religious affiliation on consumer behavior: A preliminary investigation. *Journal of Managerial Issues, 5*(3), 328–352.

Bowman, R. M. (2003). *Denomination comparison.* Torrance, CA: Rose.

Chestney, N. (2010, October 6). U.S. sustainability spending seen doubled by 2014. Reuters. www.reuters.com/article/2010/10/06/us-climate-business-united-states-idUS-TRE6951ZE20101006/.

Dejong, G. F., Faulkner, J. E., & Warland, R. H. (1976). Dimensions of religiosity reconsidered: Evidence from a cross-cultural study. *Social Forces, 54*(4), 866–889.

Delener, N. (1990). The effects of religious factors on perceived risk in durable goods purchase decisions. *Journal of Consumer Marketing, 7*(3), 27–38.

Eckberg, D. L., & Blocker, T. J. (1989). Varieties of religious involvement and environmental concerns: Testing the Lynn White thesis. *Journal for the Scientific Study of Religion, 28*(4), 509–517.

Engel, J. (1976). Psychographic research in a cross-cultural nonproduct setting. *Advances in Consumer Research, 3*, 98–101.

Essoo, N., & Dibb, S. (2004). Religious influences on shopping behavior: An exploratory study. *Journal of Marketing Management, 20*(7), 683–712.

Fam, K. S., Waller, D. S., & Erdogan, B. Z. (2004). The influence of religion on attitudes towards the advertising of controversial products. *European Journal of Marketing, 38*(5/6), 537–555.

Granzin, K. L., & Olsen, J. E. (1991). Characterizing participants in activities protecting the environment: A focus on donating, recycling, and conservation behaviors. *Journal of Public Policy & Marketing, 10*(2), 1–27.

Harrell, G. (1986). *Consumer behavior.* San Diego: Harcourt Brace Jovanovich.

Hill, P. C., Pargament, K. I., Hood, R. W., McCullough, M. E., Swyers, J. P., Larson, D. B., & Zinnbauer, B. J. (2000). Conceptualizing religion and spirituality: Points of commonality, points of departure. *Journal for the Theory of Social Behavior, 30*(1), 51–77.

Himmelfarb, H. S. (1975). Measuring religious involvement. *Social Forces, 53*(4), 606–618.

Hirschman, E. C. (1981). American Jewish ethnicity: Its relationship to some selected aspects of consumer behavior. *Journal of Marketing, 45*(3), 102–110.

Hirschman, E. C. (1983). Religious affiliation and consumption processes: An initial paradigm. *Research in Marketing, 6,* 131–170.
Hoffmann, J. E., & Bartkowski, J. E. (2008). Gender, religious tradition and biblical literalism. *Social Forces, 86*(3), 1245–1272.
Hood, R., Hill, P., & Spilka, B. (2009). *The psychology of religion: An empirical approach.* New York: Guilford Press.
Hunt, J., & Penwell, D. (2008). *AMG's handi-reference world religions and cults.* Chattanooga, TN: AMG.
James, W. (1902/2004). *The varieties of religious experience.* New York: Touchstone.
Kahle, L. R., Kau, A.-K., Tambyah, S.-K., Tan, S.-J., & Jung, K. (2005). Religion, religiosity, and values: Implications for consumer behavior. Paper presented at the Australian and New Zealand Marketing Academy Conference.
Kale, S. H. (2004). Spirituality, religion, and globalization. *Journal of Macromarketing, 24*(2), 92–107.
Khraim, H. (2010). Measuring religiosity in consumer research from Islamic perspective. *International Journal of Marketing Studies, 2*(2), 166–179.
MacInnis, D. J., & Folkes, V. S. (2010). The disciplinary status of consumer behavior: A sociology of science perspective on key controversies. *Journal of Consumer Research, 36*(6), 899–914. doi: 10.1086/644610.
McDaniel, S., & Burnett, J. (1990). Consumer religiosity and retail store evaluative criteria. *Journal of the Academy of Marketing Science, 18*(2), 101–112.
Mokhlis, S. (2006). The effect of religiosity on shopping orientation: An exploratory study in Malaysia. *Journal of American Academy of Business, 9,* 64–74.
Muhamad, N., & Mizerski, D. (2007). Muslim religious commitment related to intention to purchase taboo products. *Journal of Business and Policy Research, 3,* 74–85.
National Opinion Research Center. (2009, December 2). General social survey. www.norc.org/GSS+Website/.
New Strategist. (2010). *American attitudes: Who thinks what about the issues that shape our lives* (6th ed.). Ithaca, NY: New Strategist.
Noomene, R. (2011). Consumers' recycling attitudes: Towards socially responsible consumption. Paper presented at the 85th Annual Conference of the Agricultural Economics Society, Warwick University, United Kingdom.
Ong, F. S., & Moschis, G. P. (2006). Religiosity and consumer behavior: A cross-cultural study. Paper presented at the International Conference on Business and Information, Singapore.
Peterson, M. N., & Liu, J. G. (2008). Impacts of religion on environmental worldviews: The Teton Valley case. *Society & Natural Resources, 21*(8), 704–718.
Pew Forum on Religion and Public Life. (2008). *U.S. religious landscape survey.* Washington DC: Pew Research Center.
Rhodes, R. (2005). *The complete guide to Christian denominations.* Eugene, OR: Harvest House.
Rindfleisch, A., Wong, N., & Burroughs, J. E. (2010). God & mammon: The influence of religiosity on brand connections. In S. H. K. Wuyts, M. G. Dekimpe, E. Gijsbrecths & R. Pieters (Eds.), *The connected customer: The changing nature of consumer and business markets,* (pp. 163–201). Mahwah, NJ: Lawrence Erlbaum.
Sarre, P. (1995). Towards global environmental values: Lessons from Western and Eastern experience. *Environmental Values, 4*(2), 115–127.
Schiffman, L. G., & Kanuk, L. L. (2007). *Consumer behavior* (9th ed.). Upper Saddle River, NJ: Pearson Prentice-Hall.
Sheppard, K. (2007). Pentecostalism and sustainability: Conflict or convergence? PhD diss., Murdoch University, Perth, Australia.

Sherkat, D. E., & Ellison, C. G. (1997). The cognitive structure of a moral crusade: Conservative Protestantism and opposition to pornography. *Social Forces, 75*(3), 957–980.

Sheth, J. N. (1983). An integrative theory of patronage preference and behavior. In W. R. Darden & R. F. Lusch (Eds.), *Patronage behavior and retail management* (pp. 9–28). New York: North-Holland.

Siguaw, J., & Simpson, P. (1997). Effects of religiousness on Sunday shopping and outshopping behaviours: A study of shopper attitudes and behaviours in the American South. *International Review of Retail, Distribution and Consumer Research, 7*(1), 23–40.

Swimberghe, K., Sharma, D., & Flurry, L. (2009). An exploratory investigation of the consumer religious commitment and its influence on store loyalty and consumer complaint intentions. *Journal of Consumer Marketing, 26*(5), 340–347.

Taylor, V., Halstead, D., & Haynes, P. (2010). Consumer responses to Christian religious symbols in advertising. *Journal of Advertising, 39*(2), 79–92.

U.S. Census Bureau. (2011). World POPClock Projection. www.census.gov/ipc/www/popclockworld.html (accessed February 9, 2011).

White, L. (1967). The historical roots of our environmental crisis. *Science, 155*(3767), 1203–1207.

Wilkes, R., Burnett, J., & Howell, R. (1986). On the meaning and measurement of religiosity in consumer research. *Journal of the Academy of Marketing Science, 14*(1), 47–56.

Wolkomir, M., Futreal, M., Woodrum, E., & Hoban, T. (1997). Denominational subcultures of environmentalism. *Review of Religious Research, 38*(4), 325–343.

Woodrum, E., & Wolkomir, M. J. (1997). Religious effects on environmentalism. *Sociological Spectrum, 17*(2), 223–234.

6

Sustainable Behavior and Holistic Thinking

Yun Lee, Nara Youn, and Dhananjay Nayakankuppam

In recent years, the significance of sustainable development has unprecedentedly increased in our society. Sustainability is defined as development of a capable system by which environmental, social, and economic well-being can be maintained long term without compromising the ability of future generations to meet their own needs (Chabowski, Mena, & Gonzalez-Padron, 2011; Huang & Rust, 2011; Jackson, 2006; Seyfang, 2009; World Commission on Environment and Development, 1987). In the past decade, people have increasingly acknowledged that it is vitally important to actively respond to the challenge of sustainable development in order to reconcile the limited environmental resources available. More than ever, business companies, investors, customers, and policy makers not only regard sustainability as a profoundly important goal for our current and future lives (Chabowski et al., 2011; Crittenden et al., 2011; Engardio Capell, Carey, & Hall, 2007; Peloza & Shang, 2011; Pfeffer, 2010; Sheth, Sethia, & Srinivas, 2011; Werbach, 2009), but they also seek to develop a system to enhance sustainability (Bansal, 2005; Elkington, 1998). Within this emerging megatrend of sustainability (Lubin & Esty, 2010), corporate social responsibility (CSR) (Brown & Dacin, 1997; Luo & Bhattacharya, 2006; Matten & Moon, 2008; Russell & Russell, 2010; Sen & Bhattacharya, 2001; Torelli, Monga, & Kaikati, 2011; Varadarajan, 2010), corporate citizenship (Maignan, Ferrell, & Hult, 1999; Matten & Crane, 2005), environmentalism (Banerjee, Iyer, & Kashyap, 2003; Cronin et al., 2011), enviropreneurial marketing (Menon & Menon, 1997), and sustainable consumption (Jackson, 2006; Tukker, Cohen, Hubacek, & Mont, 2010; Young, Hwang, McDonald, & Oates, 2010) have emerged as important topics responding to these vibrant movements aimed at sustainability (Chabowski et al., 2011). Corporate social and environmental responsibility has also been one of the important criteria used to evaluate business firms' performance (Chabowski et al., 2011). With these advances, marketing researchers have suggested various conceptual frameworks for facilitating sustainability. For example, Hult (2011) proposes a framework of market-based sustainability that strategically aligns sustainability issues with consumer needs and wants and interests of multiple stakeholders. In a different approach, Sheth, Sethia, and Srinivas (2011) introduce the concept of mindful consumption, which links a consumer mindset concerning the self, the community, and nature with sustainable consumption and behavior.

Consumer responses toward corporate sustainability efforts, however, have been inconsistent. Some have shown that consumers evaluate sustainable products positively and are willing to pay more for ethically produced products (e.g., Brown & Dacin, 1997; Trudel & Cotte, 2008), whereas others have documented that a positive corporate social responsibility (CSR) record has negative effects (e.g., Luo & Bhattacharya, 2006; Sen & Bhattacharya, 2001). Extending these studies that show the different consumer responses toward corporate sustainability efforts, recent research has identified important factors that determine consumer preferences toward sustainable products. For example, Luchs et al. (2010) point out that consumer reactions toward sustainable products with a positive social or environmental impact vary depending on the type of benefits that consumers tend to associate with ethical and sustainable products. According to them, consumers are inclined to connect gentleness-related attributes with ethical products, but they have a tendency to link strength-related attributes with nonethical products. As a result, when strength-related attributes are valued, consumer preferences toward sustainable products are reduced, whereas when gentleness-related attributes are valued, consumer preferences toward sustainable products are enhanced. In a recycling-related communication context, White, MacDonnell, and Dahl (2011) investigate how consumer mindset influences recycling behavior. For example, the authors prime abstract versus concrete mindsets by using temporally distant (i.e., inducing an abstract mindset) versus proximal taglines (i.e., inducing a concrete mindset) in a recycling advertisement and examine how these different types of mindsets affect consumers' recycling intentions in response to the advertisement appeals framed either by gains or losses. Their results indicate that consumers' recycling intentions and behavior are enhanced when consumers with concrete mindsets process loss-framed messages and when those with abstract mindsets process gain-framed messages. In a CSR-related communication context, Torelli, Monga, and Kaikati (2011) examine the role of consumer mindset on consumer responses toward CSR activities of a luxury brand. The authors demonstrate that an abstract (versus concrete) mindset decreases consumers' luxury brand evaluations when the brand information is presented with CSR activities. They explain that this is because a luxury brand's self-enhancement concept is in conflict with the CSR information's self-transcendence concept, and an abstract (versus concrete) mindset accentuates this conceptual conflict (Liberman, Sagristano, & Trope, 2002).

Torelli, Monga, and Kaikati (2011)'s results suggest that there are conflicting motives in communicating corporate social responsibility, such as self-enhancement motives focusing on self-interested benefits versus self-transcendent motives focusing on public and societal welfare. The CSR messages linked with luxury brands entail these conflicting motives and, in turn, lead to consumers' negative responses toward the CSR efforts. Overcoming these conflicting motives between selfish inclinations and pro-social goals would encourage individuals to engage in sustainable behavior.

Literature on pro-social behavior suggests that failure to engage in socially desirable behavior is the default response, and thus people do not always engage in pro-social and ethical behavior (DeWall, Baumeister, Gailliot, & Maner, 2008; Gilovich, Medvec, & Savitsky, 2000; Weigel, Hessing, & Elffers, 1999). The prevailing explanation for this is that behaving in socially desirable ways often entails motivational conflicts between pro-social motives and selfish impulses, which induce a social dilemma in which individuals are tempted to take a free ride by leaving the social responsibilities to others (Biel & Dahlstrand, 2005; Chatzidakis, Hibbert, & Smith, 2007; Dovidio et al., 1991; Moisander, 2000, 2007; Uusitalo, 1990; Wiener & Doesher, 1991; Young et al., 2010). To enable socially desirable goals, people need to override selfish inclinations (DeWall et al., 2008) by deliberating relevant issues' social and ethical values and public consequences of their behavior (Des Jardins, 1997; Harre, Brockmeier, & Mülhaüser, 1999; Moisander, 2000, 2007; Webster, 1975) based on deontological considerations of individuals' social roles and obligations (Moisander, 2007). Enabling socially desirable goals by overriding selfish motives may require adopting a psychological process, such as holistic thinking.

Nisbett and his colleagues have proposed that people generally adopt analytic or holistic styles of thinking in their cognitive processes (Nisbett, Peng, Choi, & Norenzayan, 2001). According to Nisbett et al. (2001), holistic thinkers tend to focus on the relationships between a focal object and its field and prefer to explain and predict events on the basis of such relationships. In contrast, analytic thinkers tend to detach a focal object from its context and prefer to use rules about categories to explain and predict the object's behavior. Recent research suggests that these distinct cognitive tendencies between holistic and analytic thinkers may lead to different reactions to the issues related with social and ethical values; holistic thinkers, for example, tend to be more sensitive than analytic thinkers to a person's social roles and obligations (Choi, Dalal, Kim-Prieto, & Park, 2003; Miller, 1984; Shweder & Bourne, 1982). In tandem with this perspective, recent research has demonstrated that holistic thinkers are more susceptible to brand scandals related with corporate ethics and social responsibility, whereas analytic thinkers are more susceptible to brand scandals related with brand quality and performance (Lee, Youn, & Nayakankuppam, 2011a). Further, Lee, Youn, & Nayakankuppam (2011b) have found that thinking holistically enhances the perceived importance of social values relevant to sustainability issues and thus leads to greater willingness to help sustainable development than does thinking analytically.

Given these findings, in this chapter, we propose a framework in which sustainable behavior can be stimulated as a function of holistic thinking. The rest of this chapter is organized as follows. First, we provide a more detailed discussion of the relevant literature, from which we derive the conceptual framework. Next, we summarize the findings that provide evidence supporting the relationships between holistic thinking and sustainable behavior. We then conclude with a discussion of the implications and opportunities for future research.

Holistic and Analytic Styles of Thinking

Holistic thinking is defined as "involving an orientation to the context or field as a whole, including attention to relationships between a focal object and the field, and a preference for explaining and predicting events on the basis of such relationships" (Nisbett et al., 2001, p. 293). In contrast, analytic thinking "involves a detachment of the object from its context, a tendency to focus on attributes of the object to assign it to categories, and a preference for using rules about the categories to explain and predict the object's behavior" (Nisbett et al., 2001, p. 293). These two different types of cognitive processing styles differ in their field dependence, which indicates the degree of attention paid to contextual information. The field-dependent style of thinking points to the cognitive tendency, focusing on the relationships between objects and the field and thus relying more on external referents (i.e., contextual information). In contrast, the field-independent style of thinking refers to the cognitive tendency that ignores contextual information and pays more attention to the focal objects out of the field. Holistic thinkers are more likely to be field dependent in processing information and use external context–based theories, whereas analytic thinkers are more likely to be field independent in cognitive processing and use internal object–based theory exclusively (Norenzayan, Choi, & Nisbett, 2002). Thus, analytic thinkers are more known to engage in rule-based categorization than do holistic thinkers (Norenzayan, Choi, & Nisbett, 2002). Analytic thinkers group objects based on category membership or shared attributes (e.g., an off-road vehicle and boat are grouped together), whereas holistic thinkers group objects based on thematic interdependence (e.g., a table and chair are grouped together) (Chiu, 1972).

This distinction between analytic and holistic thinking styles is supported by a substantial amount of previous research. For example, in a study on student achievement, holistic thinkers regarded effort (a contextual factor) as most important, whereas analytic thinkers considered the internal, natural abilities of the student more important (Stevenson & Stigler, 1992). In another example, when analytic thinkers were presented with a picture of fish moving in relation to one another, they thought that the fish's behavior was caused by internal factors, unlike holistic thinkers, who thought it was caused by movements of other fish (a contextual factor) (Morris & Peng, 1994). In visual-scene-processing tasks, when individuals were asked to compare two consecutively presented images, individuals who observed the images analytically detected more changes in focal objects of the scenes, whereas those who observed the images holistically detected more changes in the background of the scenes (Masuda & Nisbett, 2001). These systematic variations between context-inclusive attention and object-oriented attention were also found in artistic styles and aesthetic preferences of visual images (Masuda, Gonzalez, Kwan, & Nisbett, 2008), such that holistic thinkers see visual images contextually, attending more to background and to relations between images, while analytic thinkers focus more on the salient objects and their properties. In line with these findings, Masuda and Nisbett (2001) showed that when holistic thinkers were exposed to the scenes of animals and other animated objects, they recalled more statements about the background environment and relationships between the animal and the environment than did analytic thinkers.

Social psychologists have suggested that a person's social surroundings induce a particular style of cognitive process (Nisbett et al., 2001). Holistic processing is observed more among people embedded in many relationships, which leads to the belief that everything in the universe is interrelated. In contrast, people from an environment with fewer relationships exhibit analytic processing, which leads to the belief that objects and events are independent of each other. Most of the research to date on thinking styles, therefore, has focused on cross-cultural differences, comparing individuals in East Asian countries (e.g., Chinese, Japanese, Koreans), who tend to be holistic thinkers, with individuals in Western countries (e.g., Americans), who tend to be analytic thinkers. Recent research, however, has demonstrated that there are differences within cultures in analytic and holistic thinking, which emerge as a result of individual differences or contextual factors (Choi, Koo, & Choi, 2007; Lee, Youn, & Nayakankuppam, 2011a, 2011b; Monga & John, 2008, 2010).

Motivational Conflicts, an Individual-Collective Paradox, and Sustainable Behavior

Our society has esteemed and admired individuals for their acts of helping sustainable development, because it has been regarded as vitally important for current and future lives. People have values that support helping and enhancing sustainability.

It is generally recognized, however, that there is a fundamental barrier to engaging in socially desirable behavior—motivational conflicts, which arise from the incompatibility between pro-social goals and selfish inclinations (Biel & Dahlstrand, 2005; Chatzidakis et al., 2007; DeWall et al., 2008; Dovidio et al., 1991; Graziano, Habashi, Sheese, & Tobin, 2007; Moisander, 2007; Penner, Fritzsche, Craiger, & Freifeld, 1995; Uusitalo, 1990; Weigel et al., 1999; Wiener & Doesher, 1991; Young et al., 2010). A large body of literature supports the notion that individuals are more concerned with the benefits that directly affect their daily lives. Individuals' impulsive selfishness has been deemed the most relevant construct that strongly influences individuals' decision making related to engaging in pro-social behavior (Russell & Russell, 2010; Weigel et al., 1999). Selfish impulses often override pro-social and ethical motives and make people allocate more resources to themselves or their in-group (versus out-group) members (Diekmann, 1997). People usually fail to overcome these selfish motives (DeWall at al., 2008; Gilovich et al., 2000) because they tend to behave to maximize their own gains, and thus their every action is motivated by self-interested benefits (Russell & Russell, 2010; Weigel et al., 1999). Such natural inclinations that select and favor behavior that brings themselves direct benefits (Cialdini, 1991; DeWall et al., 2008) have been "the starting point of all conflicts" in individuals' decision making (Mannion, 2003, p. 193). People engage less in pro-social and ethical behavior, as the cost of being pro-social and ethical increases (DeWall et al., 2008; Graziano et al., 2007; Penner et al., 1995). Thus many researchers have tried to understand individuals' decision making based on selfishness (Niebuhr, 1932; Russell & Russell, 2010). Marketing managers have also increasingly tried to link personal relevance and self-interested benefits with social marketing programs (Morales, 2005; Reed, Aquino, & Levy, 2007). As a result, society has shown a tendency toward personal greed (Dickinson & Hollander, 1991; Russell & Russell, 2010).

Consistent with the theory suggesting that selfish impulses tend to override pro-social and ethical motives and thus prevent people from being pro-social and ethical, environmentally responsible behavior entails a social dilemma in which individuals are tempted to become free riders by leaving the social and environmental responsibilities to others (Uusitalo, 1990, p. 170). Dawes explains that this is because "the social payoff to each individual for defecting behavior is higher than the payoff for cooperative behavior" (1980). This means that people believe that behaving in environmentally and socially responsible ways is for a collective public good, such as clean air, fresh water, or wilderness, which is for everyone but can be produced by others who are willing to cooperate to achieve it (Moisander, 2007). This individual–collective paradox usually lures people to become free riders because they often feel that their contributions to a public collective good have a marginal impact, and helping sustainable development costs more in money, time, and effort (Moisander, 2007; Uusitalo, 1990). People often fail to behave in socially desirable ways when helping involves some cost to the self, such as an expenditure of energy, time, money, or other precious resources (DeWall et al., 2008). Pro-social and sustainable goals will be achieved only if people can overcome these short-term self-interested motives.

Sustainable Behavior as a Function of Holistic Thinking

Considerable literature on pro-social and ethical judgment and decision making has suggested that people can overcome the conflicting motives between selfish inclinations and pro-social goals, first, by taking into account the public consequences of their behavior (Des Jardins, 1997; Dickinson & Hollander, 1991; Harre et al., 1999; Moisander, 2000, 2007; Webster, 1975) and, second, by carefully considering the values of the pro-social and ethical issues (Des Jardins, 1997; Moisander, 2000, 2007; Uusitalo, 1990; Young et al., 2010). Producing the greatest good for all people involved is derived from deliberations of individuals' social roles and responsibilities (Des Jardins, 1997; Moisander, 2000, 2007). Helping sustainable development also requires ascribing objective values to adopt moral and ethical obligations to protect all living things on earth based on deontological and eco-centric ethical considerations (Moisander, 2007). A sufficient understanding of the ethical and social values relevant to sustainability issues encourages individuals to override selfishness and tempting self-interested benefits and, in turn, increases willingness to use some personal resources (e.g., time, money, effort) to care for the environment (Des Jardins, 1997; Moisander, 2000, 2007; Uusitalo, 1990; Young et al., 2010).

Adopting a cognitive process, such as holistic thinking, may be required for this change to occur. Holistic thinkers tend to focus on the relationships between a focal object and its contextual information and prefer to explain and predict events on the basis of such relationships, thus they are involved in relatively systematic cognitive processing (Gilbert, Pelham, & Krull, 1988; Lieberman et al., 2005; Monga & John, 2008; Nisbett et al., 2001). In contrast, analytic thinkers tend to focus more on attributes of an object by detaching the focal object from its context and prefer to use rules about categories to explain and predict the object's behavior, thus they are involved in relatively automatic cognitive processing (Lieberman, Gaunt, Gilbert, & Trope, 2002; Monga & John, 2008; Nisbett et al., 2001). Much of existing research on thinking styles has demonstrated that these distinct differences between holistic and analytic thinking styles entail different reactions toward pro-social and ethical issues, such that holistic thinkers tend to consider more information to explain and predict a person's pro-social behavior in terms of the person's social roles and obligations than do analytic thinkers (Choi et al., 2003; Miller, 1984; Shweder & Bourne, 1982). Recent research has also found results that are consistent with this perspective, such that holistic thinkers are more susceptible to brand scandals related with corporate ethics and social responsibility than are analytic thinkers (Lee, Youn, & Nayakankuppam, 2011a).

In support of these findings, Lee, Youn, & Nayakankuppam (2011b) recently demonstrated that holistic thinking enhances the perceived importance of social values relevant to sustainable issues and, in turn, leads to greater willingness to help enhance sustainability. Across three studies, the authors tested the prediction that holistic thinkers would show more favorable attitudes toward sustainability and greater willingness to help sustainable development than would analytic thinkers.

To test this prediction, study 1 was conducted as part of a series of marketing surveys containing a number of unrelated filler studies. The main stimulus for the study was a fundraising advertisement for a wildlife organization. After reviewing the fundraising advertisement, participants rated their attitudes toward the wildlife conservation program. Participants were then asked to select the financial amount that they would be willing to donate to it. Next, as part of a seemingly unrelated study, participants responded to ten statements of the holistic thinking measure. A holism scale measures individually different thinking tendencies (Choi et al., 2003).

The scale asks participants to indicate the extent to which they agree or disagree with 10 statements, such as "Everything in the universe is somehow related" and "Nothing is unrelated." Participants' responses to the ten statements of the holism scale were averaged, and a median split was performed to identify analytic and holistic thinkers. The results indicated that holistic thinkers had more favorable attitudes toward the wildlife conservation program than did analytic thinkers and were willing to donate more to it than were analytic thinkers. The results of a series of regression analyses confirmed that thinking style is a significant predictor of participants' attitudes toward the wildlife conservation program and their willingness to donate to it.

In study 2, styles of thinking were manipulated. Participants were presented with a picture of a farm where children and their parents are feeding llamas. The picture had smaller objects (e.g., toothbrush, bow tie, screwdriver, ice skate) embedded in the scene. Analytic thinking was manipulated by asking participants to find the objects hidden in the picture, and holistic thinking was manipulated by asking participants to describe the scene of the picture and its background. Participants were then presented with a fundraising advertisement for a healthy planet program and asked to evaluate it. To examine the mechanism underlying the impact of thinking styles on attitudes and willingness to help sustainable development, it was investigated whether holistic thinking enhances perceived importance of social values relevant to sustainability issues and, in turn, leads to greater willingness to support sustainability. To test this prediction, participants were asked to indicate the degree to which they think the issues related with sustainability are important. The results replicated the results of study 1. Holistic thinkers had more favorable attitudes toward the healthy planet program than did analytic thinkers and were willing to donate more to it than were analytic thinkers. More important, the results of mediation analyses confirmed that the effect of thinking styles on attitudes toward the healthy planet program and willingness to donate to it was mediated by the perceived importance of social values.

Study 3 investigated how cognitive resources affect the effect of thinking styles on attitudes toward sustainability and willingness to support sustainable development. Prior research suggests that analytic thinking, which involves context-irrelevant cognitive processes focusing on detachment of an object from its field, is relatively automatic and requires few cognitive resources (Lieberman et al., 2002). Conversely, holistic thinkers' context-relevant cognitive processes, focusing on the relationships between a focal issue and its background information and predicting the causes and consequences of an event based on such relationships (Nisbett et al., 2001), require cognitive efforts (Gilbert et al., 1988; Lieberman, Jarcho, & Obayashi, 2005). Further, Monga and John (2008) demonstrated that holistic thinkers cannot use contextual information under a high cognitive load. These findings suggest that the effect of holistic versus analytic thinking on helping to enhance sustainability should be diminished under a high cognitive load because the cognitive resources necessary for holistic thinking are not available. An adequate amount of cognitive resources should be available for holistic thinkers, so they can spend their cognitive efforts on deliberations of sustainability issues and their societal values with ethical considerations of individuals' social roles and obligations to protect environmental resources on earth. However, analytic thinkers should not vary in their evaluations of a sustainability program regardless of cognitive load, because they are not usually involved in context-relevant, effortful cognitive processing.

To examine this perspective, study 3 manipulated thinking styles using the identical method as that in study 2. Cognitive load was manipulated by asking participants to memorize 2-digit (low load) versus 10-digit (high load) numbers and recall the memorized numbers at the end of the study. They were then asked to evaluate the advertisement of the Nature Conservancy's volunteer program. After reviewing the ad, participants rated their attitudes toward the program and indicated the perceived importance of social values, as in study 2. Participants were then asked to indicate how much they would be willing to volunteer to support sustainable development. The results indicated that cognitive resources influenced holistic thinkers, but not analytic thinkers. Holistically primed participants in the low-cognitive-load condition were more favorable toward the Nature Conservancy's volunteer program and were more willing to volunteer to help sustainable development than were holistically primed participants in the high-cognitive-load condition. However, analytic thinkers' attitudes and willingness to volunteer to support sustainability were not significantly different across the high- versus low-cognitive-load conditions. The results of mediation analyses confirmed that the effect of thinking styles on attitudes toward the Nature Conservancy's volunteer program and willingness to volunteer was mediated by the perceived importance of social values.

These results suggest that sustainable behavior can be promoted as a function of holistic thinking. Compared to analytic thinkers, holistic thinkers are more favorable toward sustainability and are more willing to help sustainable development. This effect emerged when analytic and holistic thinking was examined as an individual difference and as a manipulated cognitive style. These differences occurred because holistic thinkers perceived greater importance of social values relevant to sustainability issues than did analytic thinkers. Further, this process required cognitive resources. Decreasing cognitive resources that are necessary for holistic thinkers to consider the importance of social values negatively affected individuals' attitudes toward sustainability and willingness to help enhance sustainability.

General Discussion

In this chapter, we propose a framework in which sustainable behavior can be enhanced by thinking holistically. For this purpose, we reviewed the relevant literature and studies that suggest the predicted relationships between different styles of thinking and sustainable behavior. The proposed framework of sustainable behavior as a function of holistic thinking contributes to the knowledge of how and why different styles of thinking influence individuals' attitudes and willingness to support sustainable development and have implications for related research areas and future research.

First, it adds to a better understanding of the mechanism underlying the framework by which sustainable behavior can be enhanced as a function of holistic thinking. Thinking holistically encourages individuals to perceive a greater importance of social values relevant to sustainability issues and, in turn, leads to more favorable attitudes and greater willingness to help sustainable development than does thinking analytically. It has been generally recognized that engaging in sustainable behavior is often restrained by motivational conflicts between selfish inclinations and pro-social motives. These conflicting motives usually entail an individual–collective paradox, which lures individuals to become free riders by leaving social and ethical obligations and responsibilities to others (Biel & Dahlstrand, 2005; Chatzidakis et al., 2007; DeWall et al., 2008; Dovidio et al., 1991; Graziano et al., 2007; Moisander, 2007; Penner et al., 1995; Uusitalo, 1990; Wiener & Doesher, 1991; Young et al., 2010). Thus engaging in socially responsible behavior requires people to overcome the temptation to pursue short-term self-interested benefits (DeWall et al., 2008; Moisander, 2007) based on sufficient understanding of ethical and social values and deliberations of individuals' social roles and duties (Des Jardins, 1997; Moisander, 2000, 2007; Uusitalo, 1990; Young et al., 2010). The framework of sustainable behavior as a function of holistic thinking that we propose in this chapter sheds light on this line of research by highlighting the role of holistic thinking, which encourages individuals to consider social values and thus have more positive attitudes toward sustainability. It appears that holistic thinkers are more likely to perceive the importance of social values relevant to sustainability issues, which may help them to focus on pro-social goals and override short-term self-interested benefits. Thus holistic thinkers are more likely to show favorable attitudes toward sustainability and greater willingness to help sustainable development than are analytic thinkers. Marketing managers can effectively communicate with individuals in order to promote sustainable behavior by using strategies to influence their style of thinking. If marketing managers encourage consumers to have context-relevant holistic thinking, those consumers would perceive a greater importance of social values and thus become more willing to help sustainable development.

Further, our framework of sustainable behavior, which depends on different styles of thinking, suggests that holistic thinkers are involved in effortful cognitive processing, which helps them to assign a greater importance to social values and thus have more favorable attitudes toward sustainability. This perspective is consistent with the previous research that demonstrated that an adequate amount of cognitive resources is required to overcome selfish inclinations that conflict with pro-social motivations (Baumeister & Vohs, 2007; DeWall et al., 2008) and to adopt context-relevant holistic thinking (Gilbert et al., 1988; Lieberman et al., 2005; Monga & John, 2008). Prior research on thinking styles has suggested that analytic thinking involves relatively automatic cognitive processing, which requires few cognitive resources (Lieberman et al., 2002; Monga & John, 2008), whereas holistic thinking involves relatively systematic cognitive processing, which requires greater cognitive efforts (Gilbert et al., 1988; Lieberman et al., 2005; Monga & John, 2008). Recent research on pro-social behavior has demonstrated that overcoming motivational conflicts requires cognitive resources. With an adequate amount of cognitive resources, people can be involved in "the inner process that enables them to override short-term and selfish inclinations to bring behavior in line with more desirable long-term goals and ideals, such as behaving prosocially toward others" (DeWall et al., 2008, p. 1660). Consistent with these motivational conflict and limited resource explanations of pro-social behavior and the findings showing the differential effects of cognitive resources on analytic-versus-holistic thinking styles, we suggest that the effectiveness of the framework of sustainable behavior as a function of holistic thinking can depend on whether cognitive resources are available for holistic thinkers. Limited cognitive resources can negatively affect holistic thinkers' cognitive efforts to view and evaluate social values relevant to sustainable issues and thus influence their attitudes toward sustainability. It is important that marketing managers use strategies that enhance cognitive resources for holistic thinkers, but not limit them, so that holistic thinking can use their cognitive efforts to consider and evaluate the importance of social issues.

The literature and studies reviewed in this chapter support a conceptual framework in which sustainable behavior can be stimulated as a function of holistic thinking. The studies explored here, however, have several limitations that will provide useful avenues for further investigation. For example, none of the studies reviewed in this chapter systematically varied the costs of engaging in sustainable behavior. Previous evidence suggests that pro-social behavior dramatically decreases as the cost of engaging in socially responsible behavior increases (e.g., Dovidio et al., 1991; Graziano et al., 2007; Penner et al., 1995). It is possible that the cost of helping sustainable development may interact with cognitive resources and holistic thinking.

Another potential limitation is that none of the studies reported in this chapter observed actual sustainable behavior enhanced by holistic versus analytic thinking. Because people tend to make an effort to present themselves in socially desirable ways (Vohs, Baumeister, & Ciarocco, 2005), the effect of thinking styles on helping enhance sustainability might be partly due to this motivational effort. Although some previous studies demonstrate that there is convergent validity between self-reported responses and actual behavior (DeWall et al., 2008; Robinson & Clore, 2001), future research would benefit from observing actual sustainable behavior facilitated by holistic thinking.

Last, social psychologists have identified many different motives for pro-social behavior from empathy to self-esteem, social acceptance, or mood. Some motives for pro-social behavior may be linked more closely with holistic thinking and may require more cognitive resources than others. For example, a self-presentational function (e.g., the desire to gain social approval), one of the most important motives for pro-social behavior (Benabou & Tirole, 2006; Brown & Smart, 1991; Grant & Gino, 2010; Rege & Telle, 2004) entails using strategies to express oneself to others in a socially desirable way, and this may involve adopting a holistic thinking style over an analytic thinking style and requires greater cognitive efforts to achieve it. None of the studies discussed in this chapter identified which motives might lead individuals to help enhance sustainability and how they are related to holistic versus analytic thinking under the condition of depleted versus nondepleted cognitive resources. Consequently, future research might profitably explore this issue more closely.

Sustainability is important for efficiently managing the limited natural resources and maintaining the ecosystem. Our society needs to ensure that the environmental, social, and economic systems provide a healthy and sustainable future for the planet. The framework of sustainable behavior as a function of holistic thinking suggests that holistic thinking increases the chances that individuals perceive greater importance of social values, which may help them to overcome conflicting motivations between short-term self-interested benefits and pro-social goals and thus encourages them to be more willing to help sustainable development. Future research on the limitations mentioned above would provide a much fuller understanding of the proposed framework in which individuals are encouraged to behave in socially and ethically responsible ways by thinking holistically and how its effectiveness is related to the costs of engaging in actual sustainable behavior and different types of pro-social motivations, depending on depleted versus nondepleted cognitive resources.

References

Banerjee, S. B., Iyer, E. S., & Kashyap, R. K. (2003). Corporate environmentalism: Antecedents and influence of industry type. *Journal of Marketing, 67*(2), 106–122.

Bansal, P. (2005). Evolving sustainably: A longitudinal study of corporate sustainable development. *Strategic Management Journal, 26*(3), 197–218.

Baumeister, R. F., & Vohs, K.D. (2007). Self-regulation, ego depletion, and motivation. *Social and Personality Psychology Compass, 1,* 115–128.

Benabou, R., & Tirole, J. (2006). Incentives and prosocial behavior. *American Economic Review, 96,* 1652–1678.

Biel, A., & Dahlstrand, U. (2005). Values and habits: A dual-process model. In S. Krarup & C. S. Russell (Eds.), *Environment, information and consumer behaviour* (pp. 33–50). Cheltenham, UK: Edward Elgar.

Brown, T. J., & Dacin, P. A. (1997). The company and the product: Corporate associations and consumer product responses. *Journal of Marketing, 61*(1), 68–84.

Brown, J. D., & Smart, S. A. (1991). The self and social conduct: Linking self-representations to prosocial behavior. *Journal of Personality and Social Psychology, 60*(3), 368–375.

Chabowski, B. R., Mena, J. A., & Gonzalez-Padron, T. L. (2011). The structure of sustainability research in marketing, 1958–2008: A basis for future research opportunities. *Journal of Academy of Marketing Science, 39,* 55–70.

Chatzidakis, A., Hibbert, S., & Smith, A.P. (2007). Why people don't take their concerns about fair trade to the supermarket: The role of neutralization. *Journal of Business Ethics, 74,* 89–100.

Chiu, L.-H. (1972). A cross-cultural comparison of cognitive styles in Chinese and American children. *International Journal of Psychology, 7*(4), 235–242.
Choi, I., Koo, M., & Choi, J. A. (2007). Individual differences in analytic versus holistic thinking. *Personality and Social Psychology Bulletin, 33,* 691–705.
Choi, I., Dalal, R., Kim-Prieto, C., & Park, H. (2003). Culture and judgment of causal relevance. *Journal of Personality and Social Psychology, 84,* 46–59.
Cialdini, R. B. (1991). Altruism or egoism? That is (still) the question. *Psychological Inquiry, 2,* 124–126.
Crittenden, V. L., Crittenden, W. F., Ferrell, L. K., Ferrell, O. C., & Pinney, C. C. (2011). Market-oriented sustainability: A conceptual framework and propositions. *Journal of Academy of Marketing Science, 39,* 71–85.
Cronin, J. J., Smith, J. S., Gleim, M. R., Ramirez, E., & Martinez, J. D. (2011). Green marketing strategies: An examination of stakeholders and the opportunities they present. *Journal of Academy of Marketing Science, 39,* 158–174.
Dawes, R. (1980). Social dilemmas. *Annual Review of Psychology, 31,* 69–93.
Des Jardins, J.R. (1997). *Environmental ethics.* Belmont, CA: Wadsworth.
DeWall, C. N., Baumeister, R. F., Gailliot, M. T., & Maner, J. K. (2008). Depletion makes the heart grow less helpful: Helping as a function of self-regulatory energy and genetic relatedness. *Personality and Social Psychology Bulletin, 34,* 1653–1662.
Dickinson, R., & Hollander, S. C. (1991). Consumer votes. *Journal of Business Research, 23*(1), 9–20.
Diekmann, K. A. (1997). Implicit justifications and self-serving group allocations. *Journal of Organizational Behavior, 18*(1), 3–16.
Dovidio, J. F., Piliavin, J. A., Gaertner, S. L., Schroeder, D. A., & Clark, R. D., III. (1991). The arousal cost-reward model and the process intervention: A review of the evidence. In M. S. Clark (Ed.), *Review of Personality and Social Psychology* (Vol. 12, pp. 86–118). Newbury Park, CA: Sage.
Elkington, J. (1998). *Cannibals with forks: The triple bottom line of 21st century business.* Stony Creek, CT: New Society.
Engardio, P., Capell, K., Carey, J., & Hall, K. (2007). Beyond the green corporation: Imagine a world in which eco-friendly and socially responsible practices actually help a company's bottom line. It's closer than you think. *Business Week, 29,* 50.
Gilbert, D. T., Pelham, B. W., & Krull, D. S. (1988). On cognitive busyness: When person perceivers meet persons perceived. *Journal of Personality and Social Psychology, 54,* 733–740.
Gilovich, T., Medvec, V. H., & Savitsky, K. (2000). The spotlight effect in social judgment: An egocentric bias in estimates of the salience of one's own actions and appearance. *Journal of Personality and Social Psychology, 78*(2), 211–222.
Grant, A. M., & Gino, F. (2010). A little thanks goes a long way: Explaining why gratitude expressions motivate prosocial behavior. *Journal of Personality and Social Psychology, 98*(6), 946–955.
Graziano, W. G., Habashi, M. M., Sheese, B. E., & Tobin, R. M. (2007). Agreeableness, empathy, and helping: A person × situation perspective. *Journal of Personality and Social Psychology, 93,* 583–599.
Harre, R., Brockmeier, J., & Mülhaüser, P. (1999). *Greenspeak: A study of environmental discourse.* Thousand Oaks, CA: Sage.
Huang, M., & Rust, R. T. (2011). Sustainability and consumption. *Journal of the Academy of Marketing Science, 39,* 40–54.
Hult, G. T. (2011). Market-focused sustainability: Market orientation plus! *Journal of the Academy of Marketing Science, 39,* 1–6.
Jackson, T. (2006). Readings in sustainable consumption: Introduction. In T. Jackson (Ed.), *The Earthscan reader in sustainable consumption* (pp. 1–23). London: Earthscan.

Lee, Y., Youn, N., & Nayakankuppam, D. (2011a). The content of a brand scandal moderating the effect of thinking styles on the scandal's spillover. In R. Ahluwalia, T. L. Chartrand, & R. K. Ratner (Eds.), *Advances in consumer research*, Vol. 39. Duluth, MN: Association for Consumer Research.

Lee, Y., Youn, N., & Nayakankuppam, D. (2011b). What makes people care about sustainability? The influence of styles of thinking and cognitive resources on attitudes and willingness to support sustainable development. Working paper.

Liberman, N., Sagristano, M. D., & Trope, Y. (2002).The effect of temporal distance on level of mental construal. *Journal of Experimental Social Psychology, 38*(6), 523–534.

Lieberman, M. D., Gaunt, R., Gilbert, D. T., & Trope, Y. (2002). Reflection and reflexion: A social cognitive neuroscience approach to attributional inference. *Advances in Experimental Social Psychology, 34,* 199–249.

Lieberman, M. D., Jarcho, J. M., & Obayashi, J. (2005). Attributional inference across cultures. *Personality and Social Psychology Bulletin, 31,* 889–901.

Lubin, D. A., & Esty, D. C. (2010). The sustainability imperative. *Harvard Business Review, 88*(5), 42–50.

Luchs, M. G., Naylor, R. W., Irwin, J. R. & Raghunathan, R. (2010). The sustainability liability: Potential negative effects of ethicality on product preference. *Journal of Marketing, 74,* 18–31.

Luo, X., & Bhattacharya, C. B. (2006). Corporate social responsibility, customer satisfaction, and market value. *Journal of Marketing, 70,* 1–18.

Maignan, I., Ferrell, O. C., & Hult, G. T. M. (1999). Corporate citizenship: Cultural antecedents and business benefits. *Journal of the Academy of Marketing Science, 27*(4), 455–469.

Mannion, G. (2003). *Schopenhauer, religion and mortality: The humble path to ethics.* Burlington, VT: Ashgate.

Masuda, T., & Nisbett, R. E. (2001). Attending holistically versus analytically: Comparing context sensitivity of Japanese and Americans. *Journal of Personality and Social Psychology, 81,* 922–934.

Masuda, T., Gonzalez, R., Kwan, L., & Nisbett, R. E. (2008). Culture and esthetic preference: Comparing the attention to context of East Asians and Americans. *Personality and Social Psychology Bulletin, 38,* 1260–1275.

Matten, D., & Crane, A. (2005). Corporate citizenship: Toward an extended theoretical conceptualization. *Academy of Management Review, 30*(1), 166–179.

Matten, D., & Moon, J. (2008). "Implicit" and "explicit" CSR: A conceptual framework for a comparative understanding of corporate social responsibility. *Academy of Management Review, 33*(2), 404–424.

Menon, A., & Menon, A. (1997). Enviropreneurial marketing strategy: The emergence of corporate environmentalism as market strategy. *Journal of Marketing, 61*(1), 51–67.

Miller, J. (1984). Culture and the development of everyday social explanation. *Journal of Personality and Social Psychology, 46,* 961–978.

Moisander, J. (2000). Group identity, personal ethics, and sustainable development: Suggesting new directions for social marketing research. In E. Jochem, J. Sathaye, & D. Bouille (Eds.), *Society, behaviour, and climate change mitigation* (pp. 127–156). Dordrecht: Kluwer Academic.

Moisander, J. (2007). Motivational complexity of green consumerism. *International Journal of Consumer Studies, 31*(4), 404–409.

Monga, A. B., & John, D. R. (2008). When does negative brand publicity hurt? The moderating influence of analytic versus holistic thinking. *Journal of Consumer Psychology, 18,* 320–332.

Monga, A. B., & John, D. R. (2010). What makes brands elastic? The influence of brand concept and styles of thinking on brand extension evaluation. *Journal of Marketing, 74,* 80–92.

Morales, A. C. (2005). Giving firms an "E" for effort: Consumer responses to high-effort firms. *Journal of Consumer Research, 31*(4), 806–812.

Morris, M. W., & Peng, K. (1994). Culture and cause: American and Chinese attributions for social and physical events. *Journal of Personality and Social Psychology, 67,* 949–971.

Niebuhr, R. (1932). *Moral man and immoral society*. New York: Charles Scribner's Sons.

Nisbett, R. E., Peng, K.P., Choi, I., & Norenzayan, A. (2001). Culture and systems of thought: Holistic versus analytic cognition. *Psychological Review, 108*(4), 291–310.

Norenzayan, A., Choi, I., & Nisbett, R. E. (2002). Cultural similarities and differences in social inference: Evidence from behavioral predictions and lay theories of behavior. *Personality and Social Psychology, 28,* 109–120.

Peloza, J., & Shang, J. (2011). How can corporate social responsibility activities create value for stakeholders? A systematic review. *Journal of the Academy of Marketing Science, 39,* 117–135.

Penner, L. A., Fritzsche, B. A., Craiger, J. P., & Freifeld, T. S. (1995). Measuring the prosocial personality. In J. N. Butcher & C. D. Spielberger (Eds.), *Advances in personality assessment* (Vol. 10, pp. 147–163). Hillsdale, NJ: Erlbaum.

Pfeffer, J. (2010). Building sustainable organizations: The human factor. *Academy of Management Perspectives, 24*(1), 34–45.

Reed, A., Aquino, K., & Levy, E. (2007). Moral identity and judgments of charitable behaviors. *Journal of Marketing, 71*(1), 178–193.

Rege, M., & Telle, K. (2004). The impact of social approval and framing on cooperation in public good situations. *Journal of Public Economics, 88*, 1625–1644.

Robinson, M. D., & Clore, G. L. (2001). Simulation, scenarios, and emotional appraisal: Testing the convergence of real and imagined reactions to emotional stimuli. *Personality and Social Psychology Bulletin, 27,* 1520–1532.

Russell, D.W., & Russell, C. A. (2010). Here or there? Consumer reactions to corporate social responsibility initiatives: Egocentric tendencies and their moderators. *Marketing Letters, 21,* 65–81.

Sen, S., & Bhattacharya, C.B. (2001). Does doing good always lead to doing better? Consumer reactions to corporate social responsibility. *Journal of Marketing Research, 38*(5), 225–243.

Seyfang, G. (2009). *The new economics of sustainable consumption.* New York: Palgrave Macmillan.

Sheth, J. N., Sethia, N. K., & Srinivas, S. (2011). Mindful consumption: A customer-centric approach to sustainability. *Journal of Academy of Marketing Science, 39,* 21–39.

Shweder, R. A., & Bourne, E. J. (1982). Does the concept of the person vary cross-culturally? In R. A. Shweder (Ed.), *Thinking through cultures: Expeditions in cross-cultural psychology* (pp. 113–155). Cambridge: Harvard University Press.

Stevenson, H. W., & Stigler, J. W. (1992). *The learning gap: Why our schools are failing and what can we learn from Japanese and Chinese education.* New York: Summit Books.

Torelli, C. J., Monga, A. B., & Kaikati, A. M. (2011). Doing poorly by doing good: Corporate social responsibility and brand concepts. *Journal of Consumer Research, 38*(5), 948–963.

Trudel, R., & Cotte, J. (2008, May 12). Does being ethical pay? Companies spend huge amounts of money to be socially responsible. Do consumers reward them for it? And how much? *Wall Street Journal.* http://online.wsj.com/article_email/SB121018735490274425-lMyQjAxMDI4MTEwMjExODI3Wj.html.

Tukker, A., Cohen, M. J., Hubacek, K., & Mont, O. (2010). Sustainable consumption and production. *Journal of Industrial Ecology, 14,* 1–3.

Uusitalo, L. (1990). Consumer preferences for environmental quality and other social goals. *Journal of Consumer Policy, 13,* 231–251.

Varadarajan, P.R., (2010). Strategic marketing and marketing strategy: Domain, definition, fundamental issues and foundational premises. *Journal of the Academy of Marketing Sciences, 38*, 119–140.

Vohs, K. D., Baumeister, R. F., & Ciarocco, N. J. (2005). Self-regulation and self-presentation: Regulatory resource depletion impairs impression management and effortful self-presentation depletes regulatory resources. *Journal of Personality and Social Psychology, 88*, 632–657.

Webster, F. E. (1975). Determining the characteristics of the socially conscious consumer. *Journal of Consumer Research, 2*, 188–196.

Weigel, R. H., Hessing, D. J., & Elffers, H. (1999). Egoism: Concept, measurement and implications for deviance. *Psychology, Crime & Law, 5*(4), 349–378.

Werbach, A. (2009). *Strategy for sustainability: A business manifesto.* Boston: Harvard Business School Press.

White, K., MacDonnell, R., & Dahl, D. W. (2011). It's the mind-set that matters: The role of construal level and message framing in influencing consumer efficacy and conservation behaviors. *Journal of Marketing Research, 48*(3), 472–485.

Wiener, J. L., & Doesher, T. A. (1991). A framework for promoting cooperation. *Journal of Marketing, 5*, 38–47.

World Commission on Environment and Development. (1987). *Our common future*. Oxford: Oxford University Press.

Young, W., Hwang, K., McDonald, S., & Oates, C. J. (2010). Sustainable consumption: Green consumer behavior when purchasing products. *Sustainable Development, 18*(1), 20–31.

7

Green Advertising and Behavior

Non-Hispanics vs. Acculturating Hispanics

Sigal Segev

Environmentalism has become an increasingly visible public concern during the past four decades, and an ever-increasing public concern for the environment leads individuals to pursue or consider more environmentally friendly lifestyles and products (Grillo, Tokarczyk, & Hansen, 2008). The green movement is now moving from niche consumer markets into the mainstream (Brown & Wahlers, 1998) due to the extensive attention mass media and advertising have been placing on environmental issues (Grillo et al., 2008; Iyer & Banerjee, 1993). Further, environmentalism may be increasingly linked to people's civic life (Deng, Walker, & Swinnerton, 2006). Of course, there may be significant nuances among populations. It has been argued that populations with distinct social practices and cultural characteristics, such as immigrants, may have different values, attitudes, or levels of knowledge about environmental issues that may lead to differences in environmental behavior (e.g., Johnson, Bowker, & Cordell, 2004).

One approach to comparing such attitudes, knowledge, or behaviors lies in research dealing with acculturation, the sociocultural change that immigrants go through when in contact with the host culture (Pfeffer & Stycos, 2002). As the United States is becoming extremely ethnically diversified, comparing various ethnic groups with regard to their stand on environmentalism is of growing importance (Leung & Rice, 2002; Schultz, Unipan, & Gamba, 2000). In the United States today, Hispanics are the largest and fastest-growing ethnic group, comprising 50.5 million people, or 16.3 percent of the total population. This group is projected to account for most of the country's population growth, so by 2050, Hispanics will make up 29 percent of the overall population (Pew Research Center, 2008). Because of their ever-increasing demographic and economic power, Hispanics are affecting every aspect of U.S. society, including its culture, politics, economy, and consumer market (McCabe & Corona, 2011). Therefore, understanding their environmental behaviors and drivers relative to those of the mainstream, host population is of considerable importance, as it can have implications for future environmental consumer behavior in the United States.

This chapter proposes an associative model for understanding non-Hispanic, native-born, and Hispanic immigrant consumers' green behaviors and the drivers influencing them, across various levels of acculturation, with three primary objectives. First, the chapter identifies the cognitive factors that can be associated with pro-environmental behaviors. Second, it explores whether differences exist among mainstream consumers as opposed to Hispanic consumers with respect to these factors and the resulting environmental behaviors, while acknowledging the role of acculturation in determining their extent. Third, by examining the role of environmental awareness and the perceived influence of green advertising on a series of pro-environmental behaviors, this study may shed light on the effectiveness of communicating information about environmental issues in changing actual behaviors. These findings may provide some preliminary insights for advertising and marketing professionals about the potential responsiveness of various consumer groups to green promotions and help facilitate future communication practices directed at each group.

Modeling Environmentalism

Debate has long raged around the degree to which foreign-born U.S. residents differ from those born and raised in the United States in terms of their environmental attitudes and behaviors. Perspectives range from stereotyping immigrants as lacking concern about the environment to highlighting their greater environmental awareness when compared to those born in the United States. At one end of this continuum, the postmaterialist approach views immigrants' concern for the environment as a secondary concern, which becomes important only after material issues such as physical and economic security have been resolved (e.g., Inglehart, 1990). According to this view, immigrants, who are, for the most part, citizens of poorer countries, are preoccupied with materialist values, while those from developed countries have postmaterialist values, such as environmentalism (Pfeffer & Stycos, 2002; Whittaker et al., 2005). This view has led to some highly criticized calls for regulating immigration as a means of protecting the environment (Zuckerman, 1999). At the other end of the continuum, others argue that immigrants show high levels of environmental concerns because those who immigrate inherently hold postmaterialist values (e.g., Kidd & Lee, 1997). This chapter poses an additional question in terms of the extent to which environmental attitudes change when people emigrate from the country of their birth (Schultz et al., 2000). Moreover, it attempts to address the challenge of exploring the differences in immigrants' environmental behaviors (rather than just concerns) through the lens of cultural adjustment (Pfeffer & Stycos, 2002) by comparing immigrant groups to mainstream (native-born) residents.

One of the key factors that determines environmental behavior is the extent of an individual's awareness of and knowledge about environmental issues (Schuhwerk & Lefkoff-Hagius, 1995). In this context, the mass media and advertising are considered major influences in heightening public awareness of environmental issues. However, to date, little is known about the relative persuasiveness of green advertising for different audiences (Schuhwerk & Lefkoff-Hagius, 1995) and how environmental awareness interacts with perceptions about green advertising in affecting green behavior. Researchers argue that while consumers rely heavily on the mass media for environmental information, they often do not find this information believable or reliable (Iyer & Banerjee, 1993). At the same time, for immigrant consumers, mass media and advertising help them learn how to function in the new marketplace and often influence their resulting consumer behavior (Lee, 1993). Thus, the two cognitive variables—environmental awareness and the perceived influence of green advertising—are integrated into the model, and the extent of their contribution to and relationship with green behaviors are investigated with respect to the populations under study.

Against the previous background, this chapter attempts to provide a better understanding of the ways in which various factors affect the green behaviors of non-Hispanics compared to acculturating Hispanics. Specifically, this model depicts positive relationships between environmental awareness and the perceived influence of green advertising, resulting in various green behaviors, including conservation, environmental activism, intention to buy green products, and actual green purchasing (see Figure 7.1). The perceived influence of green advertising is viewed as a mediator between environmental awareness and the various green behaviors. In addition, direct associations between environmental awareness and the various green behaviors are also tested. Given that immigrants go through a process of cultural change and adjustment through contact with the host culture (Berry, 1997), the possible influence of acculturation on the relationships in this model is analyzed here. In this way, the Hispanic group is "unbundled," and the model is examined across four acculturation segments: assimilation, integration, separation, and marginalization.

Theoretical Framework

Acculturation and Environmental Attitudes

Acculturation has been recognized as a core construct in social and behavioral research dealing with ethnic groups and various behaviors (Ogden, Ogden, & Schau, 2004). Therefore, it provides a viable theoretical framework for the study of the environmental views of immigrants from both perspectives, intracultural (within the immigrant group) and intercultural (immigrant vs. host population). Acculturation refers to the process of cultural and psychological change that occurs as a result of continuous, direct contact between cultures (Berry, 1997). The process revolves around the core question of the extent of immigrants' adaptation to the host culture attitudinally (ethnic identity) or behaviorally (choices about language, media, and ethnic food consumption), but many definitions focus on changes at the

Figure 7.1 **A Theoretical Model for the Determinants of Consumers' Green Behavior**

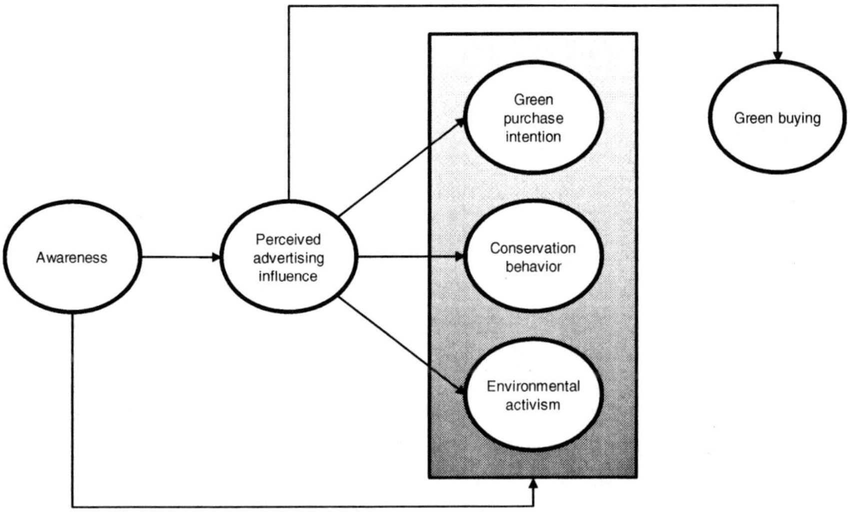

individual level with respect to attitudes, values, behaviors, and sense of cultural identity (Cuéllar, Arnold, & Maldonado, 1995). Similarly, while individuals go through cultural change over time, the resulting culture is not necessarily identical to the new culture (Berry, 1997).

Advanced stages of the acculturation process are referred to as assimilation, in which individuals adopt behavioral patterns reflecting the dominant values, norms, and attitudes of the host culture (Berry, 1997; Ogden et al., 2004). Although related concepts, acculturation and assimilation are not synonymous. Acculturation is a process of change, while assimilation is the end result of that process, characterized by a total adoption of the host culture and the loss of the original culture. Thus assimilation is viewed as a unidirectional movement from the individual's original culture to the new, host culture (Ogden et al., 2004). Acculturation, by contrast, does not necessarily presume the loss of one's original culture and does not necessarily lead to a complete adoption of the host culture, but refers to the process of integration. So, acculturation occurs when some elements of the host culture are added to the original culture, while maintaining the original culture (Berry, 1997). Recognizing that individuals may alternate between two cultures, the bidirectional model presents a more realistic approach to acculturation, allowing for individuals to identify with more than one culture (Cleveland, Laroche, Pons, & Kastoun, 2009).

Berry (1997) proposed a widely accepted model that captures the bidimensional nature of acculturation. This model features two independent continua. One is related to the degree to which individuals maintain their original culture. The other describes the degree to which individuals conform to the attitudes, values, and behaviors associated with the host culture. Changes occur on the two independent axes to varying degrees, so each individual moves independently along each axis. When these axes intersect, four different acculturation modes emerge (Berry, 1997):

1. *Assimilation* occurs when individuals abandon their original cultural identity and acquire the new, host cultural identity;
2. *Integration* occurs when individuals develop a bicultural orientation of maintaining their original culture while successfully integrating into the host culture;
3. *Separation* occurs when individuals value maintaining their original culture and avoid interacting with the new culture; and
4. *Marginalization* occurs when there is little interest in or sense of belonging to either the original culture or the host culture.

Research on Hispanics' environmentalism and acculturation is relatively scarce and focuses mainly on attitudes rather than concrete, pro-environmental behaviors. These studies indicate that acculturation plays an important role in shaping immigrants' environmental attitudes. For example, studies have demonstrated that there is a relationship between Hispanics' levels of acculturation and their attitudes about "showing respect for the forest" (Carr & Williams, 1993), general environmental attitudes (Caro & Ewert, 1995), and the interrelatedness of humans and the natural environment (Schultz et al., 2000). In addition, a study about the relationships among acculturation, environmental attitudes, and recycling behavior revealed that the most acculturated group scored lower on environmental attitudes and recycling behavior than the less acculturated group (Mukherji, 2005). Thus these studies have demonstrated that less acculturated Hispanics scored higher than more acculturated Hispanics with regard to environmental attitudes.

Cognitive Determinants of Pro-Environmental Behavior

Perceived Environmental Awareness

Environmental researchers have long argued that environmental awareness is a key prerequisite for pro-environmental acts (e.g., Grunert & Kristensen, 1994). Thus the more conscious people are of the state of their environment, the more pro-environmentally they will act (Grob, 1995). Environmental awareness includes two domains: abstract and concrete (Hines, Hungerford, & Tomera, 1987). The abstract domain is related to knowledge about causes, problems, and solutions, while the concrete domain refers to behavioral knowledge that can be used and acted upon. According to Schlegelmilch, Bohlen, and Diamantopoulos (1996), capturing individuals' level of factual information about specific or general aspects of the environment is important, as it is more closely related to green behavior than either sociodemographic or personality characteristics.

The literature reports conflicting results about the nature of the relationship between environmental knowledge and concrete behavior. For example, Schlegelmilch and colleagues (1996) showed that environmental awareness was closely linked to environmentally friendly purchasing behavior. Similarly, a meta-analysis of 128 studies revealed an average correlation of 0.30 between abstract ecological knowledge and behavior (Hines et al., 1987). This moderately positive association was also evident in Grunert's (1993) study regarding the purchase of green products. Finally, Simmons and Widmar (1990) concluded that among people who had positive attitudes toward conservation, lack of knowledge was a substantial barrier to recycling, underscoring the key role of environmental awareness in driving recycling behavior. In contrast, a number of studies have shown no significant link between environmental awareness and actual behaviors (e.g., Grob, 1995; Schahn & Holzer, 1990). For example, a study of water conservation (Watson, Kilfoyle, Murphy & Moore, 1999) showed no correlation between knowledge and attitude or knowledge and intention. Similarly, Grob (1995) found that factual knowledge had no effect on environmental behavior.

The contradictory evidence with respect to the relationship between environmental awareness and behavior implies that a more complex relationship might exist (Bohlen, Schlegelmilch, & Diamantopoulos, 1993; Chan, 2001), perhaps in part because consumers know little about particular environmental problems and solutions (Cope & Winward, 1991). In addition, some of the studies were conducted in different countries where there might be certain country-specific factors, such as levels and types of pollution, environmental legislation, and the availability of green products that might have affected the operationalization of the environmental-consciousness construct (Schlegelmilch et al., 1996). In order to address these challenges, the environmental awareness component in this model is represented in self-reports about general knowledge about environmental issues. Rather than testing individuals' knowledge of very specific issues, it captures individuals' perceived awareness of environmental problems and their recognition of pro-environmental laws (solutions).

Perceived Influence of Green Advertising

Increasing environmental awareness is often attributed to mass media coverage and educational initiatives (e.g., Dunlap & Van Liere, 2008; Jain & Kaur, 2004; Thøgersen, 2006). In this context, advertising is seen as playing an instrumental role in promoting environmentalism and generating eco-friendly sentiments among consumers and organizations (Grillo et al., 2008; Iyer & Banerjee, 1993). Nevertheless, only a few studies have explored the effect of advertising on green consumer behavior, which in these studies generally refers to purchase intentions. Furthermore, inconsistent results emerge from the literature. For example, studies that examined consumers' responses toward green ads based on the concept of involvement (e.g., Chan, Leung, & Wong, 2006; D'Souza & Taghian, 2005; Schuhwerk & Lefkoff-Hagius, 1995) show mixed results. Chan et al. (2006) found that environmental claims were effective for both low- and high-involvement services, but substantive environmental claims for high-involvement services were more effective than associative environmental claims. D'Souza and Taghian (2005) showed that consumers differed in their responses to green advertising. While very involved consumers did not find green ads convincing enough, those who were less involved were quite likely to disregard the ads. In contrast, Schuhwerk and Lefkoff-Hagius (1995) found that only consumers who were less involved were positively affected by green appeals in the ads. Finally, Newell, Goldsmith, and Banzhaf (1998) established an association between higher levels of perceived deception in green ads and lower levels of corporate credibility, less favorable attitudes toward the advertised brand, and a drop in intentions to purchase the advertised product.

In a study that examined environmental awareness, attitudes, and behaviors among Indian consumers, researchers found that consumers were strongly influenced by advertising that promotes green behavior (Jain & Kaur, 2004). While this study did not test the relationship between the perceived influence of green advertising and green behaviors, individuals' self-evaluation of the extent of the influence of green advertising provides a viable way to explore advertising as a driver of consumers' green behavior. While the perceived influence of green advertising has not been fully explored in empirical studies, it represents a cognitive reaction to the substance of green communications.

Thus the literature on the effect of green advertising on consumer behavior is both scarce and disparate. In addition, most of these studies equate consumer behavior with purchase intentions, even though green behavior covers a wide variety of acts whose goals are to protect the environment. This study uses the perceived influence of green advertising as a possible mediator in the relationship between environmental awareness and environmentally friendly behaviors.

The Proposed Model

Figure 7.1 proposes a model to explain environmentally friendly behaviors among non-Hispanics and acculturating Hispanics. This partial mediation model posits that environmental awareness (*awareness*) affects various green behaviors directly as well as through the mediating role of the perceived influence of green advertising (*AdInfluence*). Green behaviors include conservation behavior (*conservation*), environmental activism (*activism*), and green purchase intentions (*green PI*), with the last item mediating *AdInfluence* and actual green purchasing (*green buying*). As it has been well established in consumer behavior theory that purchase intentions predict subsequent purchases (Ajzen & Fishbein, 1980), this model hypothesizes that *AdInfluence* is linked to green buying through the mediating variable of *green PI*. Furthermore, the model posits that differences in levels of acculturation among immigrants and native-born individuals will lead to differences among them with respect to all of the model's variables, as well as differences in the nature of the associations among these variables. The model will be tested using a sample of non-Hispanics and Hispanics from the four acculturation groups described previously.

Methodology

Sample and Data Collection

Data were collected from 587 Hispanic participants (68 percent of the sample) and 276 non-Hispanics participants (32 percent) through self-administered questionnaires distributed with no compensation to a convenience sample of individuals from the Greater Miami metropolitan area. Given the challenges involved in reaching Hispanic participants from all acculturation levels due to issues related to language barriers, cultural differences, and immigration status (Marin & Vanoss, 1991), a snowball sampling method was used.

In the Hispanic sample, 55 percent were female and 45 percent were male, with ages ranging from 18 to 85, averaging 34 (SD = 14) years old. The vast majority of the Hispanics in the sample were white (94 percent), and 56 percent were first generation (born outside the United States), 37 percent were second generation (born in the United States), and 5 percent were third generation (born in the United States with either grandparent born outside the United States). Participants also declared themselves to be fairly well educated and affluent. The non-Hispanic sample was 48 percent male and 52 percent female, with ages ranging from 19 to 79, averaging 33 (SD = 12.40) years old. Participants reported themselves to be both educated and affluent.

Materials

Hispanic participants could choose between English and Spanish versions of the same survey based on their language competency. The original English version of the questionnaire was translated into Spanish and then back into English to ensure equivalence. The questionnaire was pretested with a group of bilingual students with various Latin American nationalities to ensure clarity, proper word usage, and maximum comprehension by all Spanish speakers. All variables in the questionnaire were measured by using previously validated scales with items rated on a five-point Likert-type scale (1 = strongly disagree to 5 = strongly agree) for acculturation, environmental awareness, perceived advertising influence, and the green behaviors.

Measurement

Acculturation was measured using the Acculturation Scale for Mexican Americans II (Cuéllar et al., 1995), which was modified slightly to address all Hispanic participants, regardless of their national origin. Given that acculturation entails change in three areas—affective, behavioral, and cognitive (Ward, 2001)—this scale effectively captures individuals' acculturation in all three areas. The scale includes 30 items that were rated on a five-point scale ranging from 1 (not at all) to 5 (almost always).

Environmental awareness was measured using two items from Jain and Kaur's (2004) Perceived Personal Environmental Awareness and Concern scale. Because environmental issues are complex, and it is difficult to produce a series of questions that are balanced in terms of their difficulty level across the range of questions (Bohlen et al., 1993), it was decided to use a self-reported general perception of environmental awareness as represented by responses to the following two items:

1. I am fully aware of environmental issues/problems, and
2. I am aware of laws in the United States that protect the environment.

The perceived influence of green advertising was measured using a four-item subscale from Jain and Kaur's (2004) nine-item Perceived Personal Environmental Awareness and Concern scale. This four-item scale was slightly modified to measure the extent to which participants were influenced by advertising that promoted various environmentally friendly behaviors.

Green consumer behaviors were measured by integrating items from the Environmentally Conscious Consumer Behavior (ECCB) scale (Roberts, 1996) with items developed by Jain and Kaur (2004). Items were organized into three distinct green behaviors following the structure provided by Jain and Kaur (2004), which was modified slightly for this study. The green behavior subscales included conservation behavior, green purchase behavior, environmental activism, and intention to buy green. Conservation behavior was measured using eight items from Roberts's (1996) ECCB scale. Green purchase behavior was operationalized using nine items from Roberts's (1996) ECCB scale that captured concrete purchase decision-making situations with environmental implications. Environmental activism was assessed using four items from Jain and Kaur's (2004) subscale that measured the extent of individuals' personal involvement and participation in activities aimed at protecting the environment. Items were rated on a five-point Likert-type scale ranging from 1 (never) to 5 (frequently). Intention to buy green products was measured by two items from Schlegelmilch et al.'s (1996) general purchasing behavior scale. Participants rated their responses on a five-point Likert-type scale ranging from 1 (strongly disagree) to 5 (strongly agree). All measurements used previously validated scales, and reliabilities were equal to or more than 0.70.

Results

The measures of the cognitive variables (i.e., *awareness* and *AdInfluence*) as well as the four green behaviors (i.e., *conservation, activism, green PI*, and *green buying*) were compared across the five groups (i.e., non-Hispanics and Hispanics with four acculturating modes). Scores on these scales are shown in Table 7.1. A

Table 7.1

Means Standard Deviations and MANOVA Results for Acculturation Types and Green Behaviors

	Non-Hispanics	Hispanics assimilation	Hispanics integration	Hispanics separation	Hispanics marginalization	*F*
Measure	(*N* = 280)	(*N* = 167)	(*N* = 122)	(*N* = 144)	(*N* = 149)	
Awareness	3.48	3.60	3.68	3.38	3.39	2.36
	(0.93)	(0.90)	(0.98)	(1.04)	(0.89)	
AdInfluence	3.44	3.60	4.03	3.91	3.50	14.35**
	(0.90)	(0.86)	(0.76)	(0.96)	(0.82)	
Green PI	3.37	3.49	3.85	3.52	3.37	6.34**
	(0.90)	(0.95)	(0.92)	(1.02)	(0.96)	
Conservation	3.24	3.27	3.53	3.53	3.30	5.62**
	(0.86)	(0.71)	(0.76)	(0.72)	(0.72)	
Activism	2.00	1.81	2.05	1.36	1.78	16.35**
	(0.90)	(0.85)	(1.02)	(0.48)	(0.83)	
Green Buying	2.79	2.88	3.19	2.77	2.78	4.75**
	(0.98)	(0.95)	(0.99)	(0.95)	(0.93)	

*$p \leq .05$; **$p \leq .001$

one-way multivariate analysis of variance (MANOVA) comparing the five groups on the dependent variables revealed a significant overall effect (F (24, 3420) = 7.11; *Pillai's* = 1.9, $p < 0.00$). Follow-up univariate tests revealed significant differences among all groups on all variables under study ($p < 0.05$). Results showed differences among non-Hispanics and Hispanics across acculturation levels with respect to their green behaviors, level of environmental awareness, and perceived influence of green advertising.

Tested at the 0.01 level, post-hoc comparisons of the five groups indicate that the Hispanic integration group scored significantly higher on green purchase intentions (mean = 3.85) than non-Hispanics (mean = 3.37) and the marginalization group (mean = 3.37). The Hispanic integration group also scored higher on green buying (mean = 3.19) than the non-Hispanics (mean = 2.79), the separation (mean = 2.77), and the marginalization (mean = 2.78) groups, as well as higher on *AdInfluence* (mean = 4.03) than the assimilation (mean = 3.60) and marginalization (mean = 3.50) groups. The separation group scored significantly higher (mean = 3.91) than most groups under study with respect to *AdInfluence*, while exhibiting significantly lower scores than all other groups on activism (mean = 1.36). In addition, non-Hispanics showed significantly lower scores on conservation behavior (mean = 3.24) than the separation (mean = 3.53) and integration (mean = 3.53) groups. No significant differences were found on environmental awareness across all groups.

Using Structural Equation Modeling (SEM), a partial mediation model in which *awareness* and *AdInfluence* were associated with *conservation, activism, green PI,* and *green buying* was tested separately for each group. The hypothesized model fit the data well (χ^2 = 1,302.80, degrees of freedom [df] = 630, $p < 0.05$; root mean square error of approximation [RMSEA] = 0.03; Normed fit index (NFI) = 0.93; Comparative Fit Index (CFI) = 0.94). Table 7.2 presents the regression weights and the explained variances for the non-Hispanics and the four Hispanic acculturation groups as well as the fit measures of the hypothesized model.

Using the partial mediation model across all groups demonstrated that in general, the level of environmental awareness was positively associated with *AdInfluence* for the non-Hispanics ($\gamma = .48$), and the four acculturation groups, assimilation ($\gamma = 0.50$), integration ($\gamma = 0.46$), separation ($\gamma = 0.28$), and marginalization ($\gamma = 0.62$). In addition, among non-Hispanics, *AdInfluence* had a significant association ($p < 0.05$) with green PI ($\beta = 0.54$), conservation ($\beta = 0.53$), and activism ($\beta = 0.31$).

As Table 7.2 shows, for the assimilation group, *AdInfluence* was positively associated with *activism* ($\beta = 0.27$) and *green PI* ($\beta = 0.48$), which, in turn, was positively associated with green buying ($\beta = 0.39$). However, there was no significant relationship between *AdInfluence* and conservation. For the integration group, *AdInfluence* was positively associated with *activism* ($\beta = 0.28$), *conservation* ($\beta = 0.52$), and *green PI* ($\beta = 0.54$), which was positively associated with *green buying* ($\beta = .039$). For the separation group, *AdInfluence* was positively associated with *conservation* ($\beta = 0.44$) and *green PI* ($\beta = 0.57$), which was positively associated with *green buying* ($\beta = 0.52$). However, there was no significant relationship between

Table 7.2

Standardized Regression Weights, Explained Variance (%) and Fit Measures of the Structural Model

From	To	Non-Hispanics	Assimilation	Integration	Separation	Marginalization
Awareness	*AdInfluence*	0.48**	0.50**	0.46**	0.28*	0.62**
		R^2 = 23	R^2 = 25	R^2 = 22	R^2 = 8	R^2 = 39
AdInfluence	*Green PI*	0.54**	0.48**	0.54**	0.57**	0.42**
		R^2 = 51	R^2 = 45	R^2 = 41	R^2 = 37	R^2 = 46
AdInfluence	*Conservation*	0.53**	0.27	0.52**	0.44**	0.27
		R^2 = 47	—	R^2 = 44	R^2 = 22	—
AdInfluence	*Activism*	0.31**	0.27*	0.28*	0.21	0.31*
		R^2 = 28	R^2 = 22	R^2 = 15	—	R^2 = 12
Green PI	*Green Buying*	0.23**	0.39**	0.39**	0.52**	0.19
		R^2 = 57	R^2 = 50	R^2 = 42	R^2 = 39	—
AdInfluence	*Green Buying*	0.37**	0.26*	0.13	0.09	0.22
						—
Awareness	*Green PI*	0.28**	0.29*	0.19	0.11	0.33**
				—	—	R^2 = 46
Awareness	*Green Buying*	0.30**	0.17	0.26*	0.11	0.32*
			—		—	R^2 = 40
Awareness	*Activism*	0.30**	0.27*	0.16	0.06	0.06
				—	—	—
Awareness	*Conservation*	0.26**	0.66**	0.24	0.07	0.31
			R^2 = 69	—	—	—

Fit measures: $\chi^2(df)$; p = 1032.80 (630); 0.00 NFI; CFI; TLI; RMSEA: .93; .94; .91; .03.
*$p < 0.05$ **$p < 0.01$.
R^2 values were rounded to the nearest integer.

AdInfluence and *activism*. In the marginalization group, *AdInfluence* was positively associated with *activism* ($\beta = 0.31$) and *green PI* ($\beta = 0.42$). In this group, there was no significant relationship between *green PI* and *green buying* or *AdInfluence* and *conservation*.

Given the mixed results reported in the literature about the relationship between environmental awareness and behavior, the analysis also tested the direct relationship between environmental awareness and the green behaviors constructs. As Table 7.2 indicates, some associations were positive and significant, while others were nonsignificant. For example, among non-Hispanics, the relationships between *awareness, conservation, activism, green PI,* and *green buying* were moderate but significant ($\beta = 0.26$; $\beta = 0.30$; $\beta = 0.28$; $\beta = 0.30$). In the assimilation group, awareness was directly associated with *conservation* ($\beta = 0.66$), *activism* ($\beta = 0.27$), and *green PI* ($\beta = 0.29$) but not with green buying. In the marginalization group, there were significant relationships only between *awareness* and *green PI* ($\beta = 0.33$) and between *awareness* and *green buying* ($\beta = 0.32$). However, there was no direct relationship between *awareness* and the other behavior variables. Among the integration group, there was a significant relationship only between *awareness* and *green buying* ($\beta = 0.26$). However, the most comprehensive results emerged from the separation group. In this group alone, all the direct associations between *awareness* and the four green behaviors were insignificant ($p > 0.05$), implying that for this group, *AdInfluence* fully mediated the relationship between *awareness* and green behavior.

The analysis also showed that *green PI* mediated the relationship between *AdInfluence* and *green buying* among all groups except the marginalization group. However, *AdInfluence* was also directly associated with *green buying* in the non-Hispanic ($\beta = 0.37$) and assimilation ($\beta = 0.26$) groups. In the separation and integration groups, *green buying* was exhibited only through the mediating role of *green PI*, while the direct relationship between *AdInfluence* and *green buying* was insignificant in these groups. As for the marginalization group, there were no significant relationships between *green PI* and *green buying*, or *AdInfluence* and *green buying*, implying that in this group, *AdInfluence* was not associated with *green buying* either directly or through a mediator variable.

Discussion

Results from testing the model with Hispanics and non-Hispanics demonstrate that both score above average on most constructs under study. In fact, Hispanics do not behave according to the postmaterialist assumption, with certain acculturation groups scoring significantly higher than non-Hispanics on green PI, green buying, and conservation. This is in line with previous studies on acculturation and environmental attitudes (Noe & Snow, 1990; Schultz et al., 2000). Although these arguments were not tested directly, the results imply that concern for the environment is a global phenomenon shared by both immigrants and native-born populations. Furthermore, the environmental attitudes documented in previous studies are closely reflected in the green behavior found in this study.

As for the associative model, the analysis shows that, in general, awareness is positively associated with the various green behaviors through the perceived influence of green advertising. Through its persuasive style, advertising translates awareness into concrete actions. However, the non-Hispanic and assimilation groups also demonstrated a direct relationship between awareness and the various behaviors, though to lesser degrees. For these groups, environmental awareness is key to performing green behaviors even without the presence of *AdInfluence*. However, the latter has the potential to further enhance such behaviors.

In this respect, the separation and integration groups warrant special attention. In the former group, the various green behaviors are manifested *only* through the mediating role of *AdInfluence*. For those who are less acculturated, awareness seems to be a necessary condition for performing green behavior but is not sufficient for driving it, so awareness alone cannot predict pro-environmental behaviors. This seems to be the case, too, for the integration group in which the direct relationship between awareness and green behaviors was insignificant, except for green buying. These findings are in line with previous studies showing that environmental knowledge alone cannot predict environmental attitudes and norms (Bamberg & Möser, 2007) or environmental behavior (Grob, 1995). In addition, this study confirms previous speculations about acculturation as a source for similarities and differences in environmental attitudes and perceptions about nature among Hispanics and non-Hispanics (Lynch, 1993; Noe & Snow, 1990).

A possible explanation for the role of *AdInfluence* in predicting behaviors lies in the literature on acculturation and perceptions about advertising. Previous research has already shown that strong Hispanic identifiers (low acculturation) have favorable attitudes toward advertising in general (Donthu & Cherian, 1992), see advertising as a valuable source of information (Korgaonkar, Karson, & Lund, 2000), and respond more favorably to specific ads (Torres & Briggs, 2005) than weak Hispanic identifiers (high acculturation). These differences are also evident in the relatively higher scores of the separation and integration groups with respect to *AdInfluence* compared to the other groups. Part of the reason lies in the role advertising plays in the social learning of acculturating individuals (Lee, 1993; O'Guinn, Lee, & Faber, 1986). Given that this group lacks experience with the host culture, and the availability of other rival sources of information is limited, low-acculturation individuals are more likely to be receptive to messages from the mass media, especially from advertising (Lee, 1993), which ultimately affect specific behaviors.

Another set of relationships that demand attention is that between *AdInfluence*, green PI, and green buying. For most of the groups under study, *AdInfluence* is associated with green purchase behavior directly as well as through the mediation of purchase intentions. For non-Hispanics, and the assimilation and marginalization groups, perceived *AdInfluence* is a stronger predictor of green buying than green

PI, emphasizing the role of advertising in driving purchase behavior, even with a lack of intention. However, for the integration and separation groups, *AdInfluence* alone cannot predict green buying. The presence of intention is necessary. A possible explanation for this difference could be that more risk is involved in unplanned purchases that are based solely on advertising prompts. Especially for the separation group, a lack of experience and familiarity with the host market, insufficient knowledge about the available green products as well as the premium prices attached to them, all make such decisions nontrivial ones. Thus, as Ajzen and Fishbein's (1980) theory of reasoned action argued, a set of hierarchical steps must precede actual green purchases. Therefore, advertisers need to pay more attention to the separation group in order to better inform and educate its members about the available green products, their features, functions, and benefits for both the consumer and the environment.

Finally, across all groups, the relationship between awareness and *AdInfluence* and environmental activism was relatively weak or nonsignificant in some instances. However, for the separation group, there was no relationship between these variables and activism. While this finding is consistent with previous studies that show little involvement in environmentally related political behaviors among minority groups (e.g., Greenberg & Schneider, 1996; McCabe & Corona, 2011; Pfeffer & Stycos, 2002), the current findings underscore the challenges that green movements face today and will face in the future in mobilizing immigrants into community-oriented activities that go beyond personal, daily green practices. One media-centered solution may be to enhance the informative, persuasive communication directed at immigrants in ways that resonate with them culturally, given the importance of media industries in raising awareness of such issues and the links between awareness, perceptions, and behaviors.

Conclusions, Limitations, and Future Research

Although the empirical results provide support for the model, two observations call for further investigation. First, this study relies on a convenience sample taken from a specific geographic region, so generalizations must be limited. Second, this model focuses on two cognitive antecedents, awareness and *AdvInfluence*, that were directly linked to green behaviors. As noted above, the theory of reasoned action views a hierarchical flow from cognition to affect to behavior in determining corresponding behavior. To expand this model and gain a deeper understanding about the process that leads to green behavior, follow-up studies should include variables that measure environmental effect as well as different measures of attitudes toward green advertising.

Although unrelated phenomena, environmentalism and immigration are becoming increasingly apparent in the United States and the Western world. As a result, governments, environmental movements, and marketers face challenges in terms of educating and promoting pro-environmental lifestyles among native and immigrant populations. Because both groups see advertising as a powerful factor in their green behavior decision making, it has the potential to spearhead social change and mobilize groups into becoming more pro-environmental.

References

Ajzen, I., & Fishbein, M. (1980). *Understanding attitudes and predicting behavior.* Englewood Cliffs, NJ: Prentice-Hall.

Bamberg, S. & Möser, G. (2007). Twenty years after Hines, Hungerford and Tomera: A new meta-analysis of psychosocial determinants of pro-environmental behavior. *Journal of Environmental Psychology, 27,* 14–25.

Berry, J. W. (1997). Immigration, acculturation, and adaptation. *Applied Psychology, 46*(1), 5–34.

Bohlen, G., Schlegelmilch, B. B., & Diamantopoulos, A. (1993). Measuring ecological concern: A multi-construct perspective. *Journal of Marketing Management, 9,* 415–430.

Brown, J. D., & Wahlers, R. G. (1998). The environmentally concerned consumer: An exploratory study. *Journal of Marketing Theory and Practice, 6*(2), 39–47.

Caro, V., & Ewert, A. W. (1995). The influence of acculturation on environmental concerns: An exploratory study. *Journal of Environmental Education, 26,* 13–21.

Carr, D. S., & Williams, D. R. (1993). Understanding the role of ethnicity in outdoor recreation experiences. *Journal of Leisure Research, 25*(1), 22–38.

Chan, R. Y. K. (2001). Determinants of Chinese consumers' green purchase behavior. *Psychology and Marketing, 18*(4), 389–413.

Chan, R. Y. K., Leung, T. K. P., & Wong, Y. H. (2006). The effectiveness of environmental claims for services advertising. *Journal of Services Marketing, 20*(4), 233–250.

Cleveland, M., Laroche, M., Pons, F., & Kastoun, R. (2009). Acculturation and consumption: Textures of cultural adaptation. *International Journal of Intercultural Relations, 33*(3), 196–212.

Cope, D., & Winward, J. (1991). Information failures in green consumerism. *Consumer Policy Review, 1*(2), 83–86.

Cúellar, I. Arnold, B., & Maldonado, R. (1995). Acculturation rating scale for Mexican Americans-II: A revision of the original ARSMA scale. *Hispanic Journal of Behavioral Science, 17*(3), 275–304.

Deng, J.Y., Walker, G. J., & Swinnerton, G. (2006). A comparison of environmental values and attitudes between Chinese in Canada and Anglo-Canadians. *Environment and Behavior, 38*(1), 22–47.

Donthu, N. & Cherian, J. (1992) Hispanic coupon usage: Impact of strong and weak ethnic identification. *Psychology and Marketing, 9,* 501–510.

D'Souza, C., & Taghian, M. (2005). Green advertising effects on attitude and choice of advertising themes. *Asia Pacific Journal of Marketing and Logistics, 17*(3), 51–66.

Dunlap, R. E., & Van Liere, K. D. (2008). The new environmental paradigm. *Journal of Environmental Education, 40*(1), 19–28.

Greenberg, M. R., & Schneider, D. (1996). *Environmentally devastated neighborhoods: Perceptions, realities, and policies.* New Brunswick, NJ: Rutgers University Press.

Grillo, N., Tokarczyk, J., & Hansen, E. (2008). Green advertising developments in the U.S. forest sector: A follow up. *Forest Products Journal, 58*(5), 40–46.

Grob, A. (1995). A structural model of environmental attitudes and behavior. *Journal of Environmental Psychology, 15,* 209–220.

Grunert, S. C. (1993). Green consumerism in Denmark: Some evidence from the OKO foods-project. *Der Markt, 32*(3), 140–151.

Grunert, S. C., & Kristensen, K. (1994). The green consumer: Some Danish evidence. *Marketing Review, 19*(2), 138–145.

Hines, J. M., Hungerford, H. R., & Tomera, A. N. (1987). Analysis and synthesis of research on responsible environmental behavior: A meta-analysis. *Journal of Environmental Education, 18*(2), 1–8.

Inglehart, R. (1990). *Culture shift in advanced industrial society*. Princeton: Princeton University Press.

Iyer, E.S., & Banerjee, B. (1993). Anatomy of green advertising. *Advances in Consumer Research, 20,* 494–501.

Jain, S. K., & Kaur, G. (2004). Green marketing: An attitudinal and behavioral analysis of Indian consumers. *Global Business Review, 5*(2), 187–205.

Johnson, C. Y., Bowker, J. M., & Cordell, K. H. (2004). Ethnic variation in environmental belief and behavior: An examination of the new ecological paradigm in social psychological context. *Environment and Behavior, 36*(2), 157–186.

Kidd, Q., & Lee, A.-R. (1997). Postmaterialist values and the environment: A critique and reappraisal. *Social Science Quarterly, 78*(1), 1–15.

Korgaonkar, P., Karson, E, & Lund, D. (2000). Hispanics and direct marketing advertising. *Journal of Consumer Marketing, 17,* 100–108.

Lee, W.-N. (1993). Acculturation and advertising communication strategies: A cross cultural study of Chinese and Americans. *Psychology and Marketing, 10*(5), 381–397.

Leung, C., & Rice, J. (2002). Comparison of Chinese-Australian and Anglo-Australian environmental attitudes and behavior. *Social Behavior and Personality, 30*, 251–262.

Lynch, B. D. (1993). The garden and the sea: U.S. Latino environmental discourses and mainstream environmentalism. *Social Problems, 40*(1), 108–124.

Marin, G., & Vanoss, B. (1991). *Research with Hispanic populations*. London: Sage.

McCabe, M. B., & Corona, R. (2011). Marketing to Hispanics: Eco-friendly behavior patterns. Paper presented at the 2011 Barcelona European Academic Conference. http://conferences.cluteonline.com/index.php/IAC/2011SP/paper/view/482/.

Mukherji, J. (2005). Is cultural assimilation related to environmental attitudes and behaviors? *Advances in Consumer Research,* 32, 415–421.

Newell, S.J., Goldsmith, R. E., & Banzhaf, E.J. (1998). The effect of misleading environmental claims on consumer perceptions of advertisements. *Journal of Marketing Theory and Practice, 6*(2), 48–60.

Noe, F. P., & Snow, R. (1990). Hispanic cultural influence on environmental concern. *Journal of Environmental Education, 21,* 27–34.

Ogden, D. T., Ogden, J. R., & Schau, H. J. (2004). Exploring the impact of culture and acculturation on consumer purchase decisions: Toward a microcultural perspective. *Academy of Marketing Science Review, 2004*(1). www.amsreview.org/articles/giese01–2000.pdf.

O'Guinn, T. C., Lee, W.-N., & Faber, R. J. (1986). Acculturation: The impact of divergent paths on buyer behavior. *Advances in Consumer Research, 13,* 579–583.

Pew Research Center (2008). U.S. Population Projections: 2005–2050. http://pewhispanic.org/reports/report.php?ReportID=85/.

Pfeffer, M. J., & Stycos, M. J. (2002). Immigrant environmental behaviors in New York City. *Social Science Quarterly, 83*(1), 64–81.

Roberts, A. J. (1996). Green consumerism in the 1990s: Profile and implications for advertising. *Journal of Business Research, 36*(3), 217–231.

Schahn, J., & Holzer, E. (1990). Studies of individual environmental concern: The role of knowledge, gender, and background variables. *Environment and Behavior, 22*(6), 767–786.

Schlegelmilch, B. B., Bohlen, G. M., & Diamantopoulos, A. (1996). The link between green purchasing decisions and measures of environmental consciousness. *European Journal of Marketing, 30*(5), 35–55.

Schuhwerk, M. E., & Lefkoff-Hagius, R. (1995). Green or non-green? Does type of appeal matter when advertising a green product? *Journal of Advertising, 24*(2), 45–54.
Schultz, P. W., Unipan, J. B., & Gamba, R. J. (2000). Acculturation and ecological worldview among Latino Americans. *Journal of Environmental Education, 31*(2), 22–27.
Simmons, D., & Widmar, R. (1990). Motivations and barriers to recycling: Toward a strategy for public education. *Journal of Environmental Education, 22*(1), 13–18.
Thøgersen, J, (2006). Media attention and the market for green consumer products. *Business Strategy and the Environment, 15*(3), 145–156.
Torres, I., & Briggs, E. (2005). Does Hispanic-targeted advertising work for services? *Journal of Services Marketing, 19*, 150–156.
Ward, C. W. (2001). The A B Cs of acculturation. In D. Matsumoto (Ed.), *The handbook of culture and psychology* (pp. 411–445). Oxford: Oxford University Press.
Watson, R. K., Kilfoyle, F. E., Murphy, M. H., & Moore, S. M. (1999). An opportunistic field experiment in community water conservation. *Population & Environment, 20*(6), 545–560.
Whittaker, R. J., Araújo, M. B., Jepson, P., Ladle, R. J., Watson, J. E. M., & Willis, K. J. (2005). Conservation biogeography: Assessment and prospect. *Diversity and Distributions, 11*, 3–23.
Zuckerman, B. (1999). The Sierra Club immigration debate: National implications. *Population & Environment, 20*(5), 401–412.

8

The Influence of Visual Information on Environmentally Significant Behavior

Jill Mosteller

This chapter explores and discusses literature concerning three overarching aspects related to consumers enacting environmentally significant behavior: the informational context of stimuli presented to inform behavior, mediating/moderating factors that may influence how consumers process and evaluate information presented, and the behavioral responses that may ensue after attending and processing the information. Environmental psychologists conceptualize this process within a stimulus-organism-response (SOR) framework (Mehrabian & Russell, 1974). For the purposes of clarity and flow, but not to the exclusion of other theoretical lenses, I discuss each of these areas separately, starting with consumer response behaviors within the context of environmentally significant behavior, followed by consumer processes that may mediate stimuli perceived. Research highlighting how the visual presentation of stimuli may influence subsequent processes and outcomes follows; I acknowledge that various theoretical linkages may extend from one area to another within the discussion.

The chapter's purpose is to discuss and integrate existing research from diverse disciplines and theoretical perspectives to propose research that may enhance our understanding of consumers and environmentally related behaviors. As noted by many researchers, (for a review, see Jackson [2005]), gaps between consumers' attitudes and behaviors may be due to the complexity of many factors involved (Owens & Driffill, 2008). This chapter attempts to identify some areas for future research that may be beneficial in bridging some of these gaps.

Environmentally Significant Behavior

Environmentally significant behavior (ESB) can be defined as behavior engaged in with the intent to benefit the environment (Stern, 2000). Although the actual impact of the behavior may differ from intent (e.g., only one person recycles in a community), intent may be considered a form of indirect ESB. ESB can also be indirect by shaping the context in which choices are made that directly cause environmental change (Stern, 2000, p. 408). Environmentally related behavior is conceptualized as including socially and environmentally related impacts. Socially related behavioral impacts may include consumers abstaining from acquiring products that foster poor labor practices and working conditions of the people employed in the production of those consumer goods or those willing to pay a price premium for a product (e.g., coffee) because of fair labor practices (e.g., Fair Trade) employed (De Pelsmacker, Driesen, & Rayp, 2005). Through collective diminished demand (or willingness to pay a premium), consumers may signal to producers that the value offered is or is not desirable. For some consumers, purposely boycotting company products that employ poor social or environmental production practices may serve as a means of expressing political and ethical empowerment in the market (Shaw, Newholm, & Dickinson, 2006).

Environmentally related behavior may include consumers favoring products that emit less carbon into the air during the product's production or related to the transportation of the good to the retailer where it is ultimately acquired or consumed. In addition to the acquisition and use of products that may be less environmentally harmful (e.g., energy-saving light bulbs, organic foods), activities like using public transportation, composting, and turning the water off when brushing one's teeth are also considered environmentally friendly behaviors (Thøgersen & Folke, 2002). In terms of disposition, consumers may avoid acquiring products that are packaged in nonrecyclable materials, suggesting that how one will dispose of the product in the future may influence acquisition choices. Consumer demand for information at the point of display and green initiatives were reported to influence retailers' strategies (Coupe, 2010).

How researchers conceptualize and define environmentally related behavior varies. Donation intentions toward social or environmental organizations (De Groot & Steg, 2008), willingness to pay a price premium for public goods or fair-trade products (Kahneman, Ritov, Jacowitz, & Grant, 1993; De Pelsmacker et al., 2005; Onozaka & McFadden, 2011), and self-reports of curbside recycling (Guagnano, Stern, & Dietz, 1995) are just a few examples. Stern's (2000) private-sphere behaviors, one subcategory of pro-environmental behavior, include the purchase, use, and disposal of personal and household products that have an environmental impact. These private sphere behaviors have "direct environmental consequences and can be significant in aggregate when many people independently do the same things" (Stern, 2000, p. 410). In sum, environmentally related consumer behavior may involve any action (or inaction) that results in reduced negative environmental or social impact. One example of consumer inaction is purposely abstaining or limiting the acquisition of material items (i.e., voluntary simplicity), thus continuing to reuse existing products (e.g., clothing or a cell phone) over a longer period. Consumers may wish to pursue a life of voluntary simplicity due to the ecological impacts associated with consumerism and consumption (Huneke, 2005).

Consumer Contextual Factors

Product Contexts

Certain types of goods offered may be associated with unique environmental aspects or social conditions. Technological products (e.g., computers, cell phones) are one example of items whose impact on the environment can be considered significant in terms of hazardous toxins being released into landfills in addition to the nonrecyclable materials contributing to landfill waste (Ongondo, Williams, & Cherrett, 2011). In view of the fact that 82 percent of all U.S. adults are estimated currently to own a cell phone (Smith, 2010), this equates to the use of more than 255 million cell phones in a given year (U.S. Census Bureau, 2009). Assuming that each adult buys a new cell phone every two years, this would suggest that more than 95 million cell phones may be disposed of annually. These estimates exclude technology use by those younger than 18, further compounding the issue, because the under 18 group was not counted in the census but do use cell phones. Thus technology product contexts may be one area for future study.

Cell phones play an integral part in many consumers' lives because they are a person's primary means of connecting with others (Smith, 2010). This suggests that how integral a product is in one's life may influence what attributes may be considered compensatory (i.e., allowing diminished utility of one attribute for increased utility in another attribute) versus noncompensatory. A study in which consumers performed choice-based tasks shows that noncompensatory processing is strongly evident (Hauser, Ding, & Gaskin, 2009). This suggests that understanding where attribute tradeoffs can be made in a product's social and environmental development process could be critical and may vary across product contexts (Onozaka & McFadden, 2011). A person who uses a cell phone for communicating with clients may not consider exchanging voice quality performance for a phone's reduced carbon footprint in production and distribution if an alternative that provides both does not exist. Consumers may employ different types of decision criteria across various products, depending on the relative importance and perceived sacrifice tradeoffs that may be entailed. This is evident in Onozaka and McFadden's (2011) results given each of the standard deviations for the parameter estimates (e.g., certified fair trade, carbon footprint, and certified organic) were significant, indicating preference heterogeneity among respondents. Parameter estimates for apples and tomatoes also varied, with fair trade yielding a negative value for tomatoes (–0.2457) and a positive value for apples (0.8703), suggesting that the characteristics and associated knowledge with each product, despite being in a similar category, may be thought of differently by consumers.

Dilemmas, Values, Ethics, and Beliefs

Consumers considering tradeoffs between attributes that benefit the self versus benefitting others confront social dilemmas. Social dilemmas are characterized as conflicts in choice between one's self-interest and the common good (Karp, 1996). Implicit in a dilemma is conflict. Ecological dilemmas are characterized as conflicts between the self and the natural resources extracted to provide the desired benefit (Axelrod, 1994; Merchant, 1992). The level of tension associated with social or ecological dilemmas may be based upon one's level of conflicting values guiding the decision. Materialism, a value that associates importance with the acquisition of material objects (Richins & Dawson, 1992), was found to create psychological tension with one's collective values (e.g., family and religion), negatively affecting one's well-being (Burroughs & Rindfleisch, 2002). Axelrod's (1994) research specifically tested ecological dilemmas in terms of economic, social, and environmental experimental conditions. One's decision tended to reflect the value orientation of the individual; specifically, those who were universally oriented were more prone to endorse environmentally protective actions and economically oriented individuals were more prone to be influenced by economic shifts. Socially oriented individuals varied, depending on the social justice situation. Social distance may be a moderator in these contexts, suggesting that people may feel more accountable for those closer to them (e.g., local farmers) than those who are far away (e.g., field workers in a foreign country) (Trope & Liberman, 2003). Thus, how or whether a decision creates an ethical dilemma may be contingent on the existence of two competing values and these values emerging within the context of the tradeoff decision.

Merchant (1992) suggested three ethics involved in natural resource dilemmas: egocentric, homocentric, and eco-centric. Egocentric people believe that individuals are entitled to extract or use natural resources to enhance their own lives, limited only by the effects on their neighbors. Homocentric people believe that social good should be maximized and human evil minimized with the greatest good for the greatest number of individuals. Ecocentric individuals believe that all things in the ecosystem have intrinsic value and deserve moral consideration, that everything is connected to everything, and that the whole is greater than the sum of the parts. Ethics are closely related to values in that ethics distinguish what a person intrinsically values and believes deserve moral consideration (De Groot & Steg, 2008). How one perceives one's relationship with others and the natural environment may serve as a guiding principle. The more distinct and separate a person views himself from others and the natural environment, the more egocentric is his orientation, though it is not derived from narcissism or selfishness (Merchant, 1992).

Empirical evidence demonstrates attitudinal and behavioral intentions—which are conceptually similar to the three respective value orientations discussed—vary across individuals who differ in terms of egoistic, altruistic, and biospheric value orientations (De Groot & Steg, 2008). One's environmental concern (operationalized as the New Environmental Paradigm [NEP] scale), attitude toward recycling, and donation intentions toward either humanitarian or environmental organizations represented the outcomes in this cross-sectional study. A longitudinal panel study of Danish consumers suggests that universalism values influence environmentally friendly behavior (Thørgersen & Folke, 2002), testing the directional influence between values and behavior. Universalism is represented by the importance of protecting the environment; unity with nature, social justice, and equality are guiding principles (Schwartz, 1994). Thus the conceptualization of the universalism value integrates both social and environmental aspects. Schwartz's (1994) universalism value has been positively associated with the NEP, reflective of an ecological worldview (Stern, 2000) and associated with good citizen, activist, and healthful behaviors (Karp, 1996).

The NEP is a 15-item scale designed to assess how one views the relationship between humans and the environment (Dunlap, Van Liere, Merig, & Jones, 2000). Sample statements include: "human ingenuity will ensure that we do NOT make the earth unlivable," "humans are meant to rule over the rest of nature," and "if things continue on their present course, we will soon experience a major ecological catastrophe" (Dunlap et al., 2000). Six scale items, ranging from "strongly agree" to "strongly disagree," are used to score responses. Beliefs associated with the NEP and adverse consequence for valued objects (AC) (discussed later) along with values (biospheric, altruistic, and egoistic) accounted for 56 percent of the variance in one's pro-environmental personal norms, considered a general predisposition toward taking pro-environmental action (Stern, 2000).

In sum, values and related moral beliefs concerning the inherent value of self, others, and the natural environment have demonstrated conceptual and predictive distinctiveness in terms of people's attitudes, behavioral intentions, self-reported behaviors, and experimental choices. Factors that may influence why marketplace behaviors do not reflect these values and moral considerations are discussed next.

Choice Context

Many choices that consumers make today may not be characterized as social or ecological dilemmas because product information that informs the consumer of the social or ecological impact is largely invisible (Goleman, 2009). When social or environmental information is presented within a choice context, some value of utility is usually captured and is likely to vary in importance by product and consumer segment (e.g., Kahneman et al., 1993; Onozaka & McFadden, 2011). The way in which choice information is visually presented may influence how a consumer attends and processes the information (Lurie & Mason, 2007). Heuristic decision rules are more likely when there are many products with many features that need to be evaluated and the product is mature; conversely, heuristics are less likely when the product is new with and few features and few alternatives (Hauser et al., 2009). This would suggest that when a new product is introduced with a new feature (e.g., recyclability rating), consumers may initially take the time to process the information more thoroughly than usual, assuming that the information is perceived. The implication is that new information may initially attract attention and processing effort, but the conditions under which the information is persuasive may vary. One study found that consumers valued transparent pricing (i.e., disclosure of allocation of proceeds between agents) over opaque pricing (i.e., no allocation information provided), suggesting that social considerations were elicited within the decision context when the allocation information was presented and also indicated a willingness to pay higher prices when provided more information (Carter & Curry, 2010). This study suggests that the context of information presented at the point of choice influences how consumers may think about the decision.

Visual Information

Next, I discuss three factors related to informational properties that may influence consumer decisions: negative versus positive valenced information, visual versus text information, and concrete versus abstract types of information. These three categories are neither exhaustive nor complete in terms of informational properties that may influence how and what a consumer processes but are selected because they may be particularly relevant in terms of discussing informational contexts that a consumer may encounter in an online or offline retailing environment.

Negative Versus Positive Valenced Information

Prospect theory suggests that incremental losses in utility are experienced with more acuity than are incremental gains (Kahneman & Tversky, 1979). The implication of this is that a loss frame (e.g., diminished performance) may resonate more strongly than a gain frame (e.g., improved performance), suggesting that negative information in terms of losses may be more effective at eliciting behavioral responses, all other conditions being held constant. The initial anchor point one references (e.g., strong performance/three-star rating) may serve to determine how subsequent ratings on alternatives are viewed and may vary by consumer due to heterogeneity of preferences.

One example of a retailer that employs a three star rating system on store shelves is Hannaford, a food retailer based in Maine (2011). More than twenty-five thousand products offered in the stores were scored, with 28 percent receiving a score of one or more stars. One year after the "guiding stars" rating system was introduced, sales data indicated that sales of many products with stars increased and products without stars decreased, varying by product category, with packaged and frozen goods scored with stars seeing the strongest growth (Martin, 2007). According to Hannaford, 81 percent of customers surveyed stated that they were aware of the guiding stars system, and 50 percent reported using it fairly often (Martin, 2007). Although the information that Hannaford reported was selective, and thus no conclusive results can be inferred, the context demonstrates how a retailer, using positive valenced visual imagery, may have reframed attribute considerations at the point of sale. How this information influenced choice at the individual level is indeterminable, but the changes in product choice within a category may provide insight. For example, if a consumer normally purchased brand A and changed to brand B (within the same product category), the difference in star scores could be computed, taking into consideration variation in price and the star-rating starting point of brand A relative to brand B. Results reported by Hannaford suggest that rating information presented at the point of sale, scored by a third party, can influence consumer choice. Nutritional experts composing the advisory panel that created the star guidelines may have contributed to the credibility and trustworthiness of the scoring system, thus enhancing the guiding stars' influence. Consumer trust in the marketing source and attributions of consumer responsibility (AR) were found to be critical in the effectiveness of pro-social positioning strategies; when trust and AR are not present, reverse effects may occur (Osterhus, 1997). Osterhus's study, integrated with Hannaford's findings, suggests that consumers must care about the content and trust the context of the information provided in order for it to influence behavior.

Negative information generally elicits a stronger call to action than positive information, explained in part by the consumer's wanting to alleviate the negative effect (e.g., in some cases an outrage effect) associated with the information (Kahneman et al., 1993). Recent empirical evidence suggests that a person's implicit theory of the world around him may moderate these framed gain or loss effects, with entity theorists less susceptible to framing effects compared to incremental theorists (Jain, Mathur, & Maheswaran, 2009). A consumer with an entity orientation focuses on outcomes and believes that the world is immutable; conversely, an incremental theorist is process-oriented and believes that the world can change, given the right conditions (Levy, Stroessner, & Dweck, 1998). Idealism was found to be a determining factor for ethical behavior (Roozen, De Pelsmacker, & Bostyn, 2001), suggesting that one's view of the world may influence how one responds to environmental information based upon expectations of how actions can lead to impactful change. Empirical evidence discussed suggests that those with a more incremental and idealist view may believe that individual change and impact are possible and thus may be more prone to take environmental action. One who views the world with an entity orientation may be more cynical that people's behavior will change and thus may be less likely to take environmental action.

In Stern's (2000) Values Belief Norm (VBN) theory of environmentalism, a belief in adverse consequences (AC) for valued objects and a perceived ability to reduce the threat (ascription of responsibility [AR]) are postulated as key antecedents and determinants of one's sense of obligation to take pro-environmental action. Further empirical investigation of these two factors (AC & AR) in consumer choice contexts may help to illuminate the attitude–behavior gap between what people say and what they actually do. To illustrate, a consumer may have strong pro-environmental beliefs and support altruistic and biospheric values, but if he or she is unaware of the social or environmental consequences of choosing product A versus product B, then why would these considerations be influential at the point of sale? Assuming that a consumer is aware of the consequences of choosing between two products (e.g., one that is recyclable versus one that is not), if she feels that her choice is inconsequential in terms of externality gains for nature or society (i.e., no one else will do it, so why should I put forth the effort?), the relative importance of that attribute may be diminished, all other factors held constant.

In two pilot studies, one employing a five-star rating system across all four product attributes (excluding the numeric value for price), a second employing a three-level negative, neutral, and positive visual image to communicate social and ecological impacts (five-star rating system for performance and style/design), Mosteller and Wilhelm (2011) found that consumers exposed to the negative and positive visual imagery context scored the environmental impact utility higher (17 percent) compared to the five-star imagery (8.9 percent) in a cell phone conjoint-choice experiment. One plausible explanation is that the distinctiveness of the visual imagery and its related negative valence for the environmental impact attribute may have contributed to the results through salience of consequences or vividness effects. The more time someone spends visually inspecting one alternative compared to another can affect choice (Armel, Beaumel, & Rangel, 2008).

Results from three behavioral experiments suggest that the "appetitive" versus "aversive" valence of the information for food and art posters influences binary choice outcomes differently when consumers are forced to pay attention to the visual information. Specifically, consumers are less likely to choose aversive items under long fixation conditions and are more likely to choose appetitive items under long fixation conditions (Armel et al., 2008). These results could suggest an approach or avoidance response based upon the emotions elicited during the exposure to the stimulus (Mehrabian & Russell, 1974), the underlying explanatory mechanism being associated with the visual consumption experience at the point of choice. An alternative explanation offered is that the actual value of the choice is derived from the anticipated value of consuming the item and thus aversive items would elicit less value than appetitive items (Armel et al., 2008). Combined, these two studies suggest that the valence of information processed (i.e., negative/positive or aversive/appetitive), the perceived impact of the production (environmental), or the present versus anticipated consumption context may influence product evaluations at the point of choice.

Text Versus Pictures or Images

Pictures are generally considered more attention-getting, pleasant, and easier to process than verbal text (Edell & Staelin, 1983, p. 46). Images are regarded as symbolic processes that are linked developmentally to associative experiences involving concrete objects and events (Paivio, 1969, p. 243). Viewed pictorial information is generally recalled with greater recognition than verbal content in an advertising context (Hirschman, 1986; Nelson, Reed, & Walling, 1976), which may be explained by a dual-coding process that more likely occurs for images than for words (Paivio, 1969). The basic assumption of dual-coding theory is that all cognition involves the activity of two functionally independent but interconnected modal systems: a verbal and nonverbal system (Paivio, 2010). When a person views an image of a tree, he/she may encode it visually (image) and semantically (word), thus forming two connection points in memory. If a person reads the word "tree," it may be only semantically encoded, thus providing only one connection point. The more connection points made during the encoding process (i.e., two paths are better than one), the stronger the likelihood that one will be able to retrieve the information from memory at a later time. During the encoding process, recent research suggests when visual images (e.g., a gigantic oak tree with bright green leaves) are constructed from verbal events (e.g., the tree grew on a hill) that accessibility (recall) of the event is improved (Wyer, Hung, & Jiang, 2008). Stated differently, one's personal experiences or exposure to similar stimuli prior to the verbal event exposure may contribute to visual imagery being associated with verbal events during the encoding process, thus potentially enhancing recall fluency. All this suggests that how information is encoded may influence how it is processed and evaluated. The more elaboration (i.e., connection points made and thinking associated with the encoding process) one engages in with the stimulus, the more likely recall and recognition will be elicited at a later time.

Working memory, associated with the simultaneous storage and processing of information, refers to the temporary storage and manipulation of information necessary for cognitive tasks such as comprehension, learning, and reasoning (Baddeley, 1992). Working memory comprises three aspects: first is the central executive associated with attention-controlling; second and third are two slave systems, the visuospatial sketch pad that manipulates visual images and the phonological loops that store and rehearse speech-based information (Baddeley, 1992). In terms of attention to visual information, visual receptors measure the differences in the intensity of signals from the environment and the perceptual system coordinates or differentiates these signals in order to attribute meaning to the information (Janiszewski, 1998, p. 292). As object contrast and size become more prominent, receptor cones become activated and the signal strength grows stronger (Steinman & Levinson, 1990). As objects exhibit more contrast with the surrounding environment, they are more likely to activate a consumer's visual receptors.

Rossiter and Percy (1980) empirically tested how a variation in visual size (large versus small sketch of a mug of beer) and verbally written belief claims (explicit/implicit) in ad copy influenced consumers' product attitudes. Consumers reported the strongest product attitudes toward the ad copy that presented a large visual with explicit belief statements (Rossiter & Percy, 1980). In addition to capturing visual receptor attention, the large visual of the frosty mug of beer (all subjects were beer drinkers) may have elicited experiential imagery associated with previous consumption experiences, which may have in turn elicited a positive effect. As noted by Rossiter and Percy (1980), "we often lose sight of the fact that the reason why beliefs (cognitive) are capable of altering attitude (affective) is because of their own affective connotations" (p. 11). Hirschman (1986) empirically tested how all-visual or all-verbal stimuli presented across several product categories influenced perceptions of products on an aesthetic/emotional and utilitarian/rational basis. Mean deviation scores of emotional and rational indexes were compared between verbal and pictorial treatments. Overall, verbal ads elicited higher utilitarian/rational perceptions and pictorial ads elicited higher deviation means for eliciting aesthetic/emotional perceptions with a few product exceptions (e.g., tea set, hair dryer, sleeping bag) (Hirschman, 1986). These results suggest that despite how an informational stimulus may prime how one processes it, the product category may elicit unique associations by the individual in the process of rendering a judgment. Those who viewed all picture treatments also reported being more familiar with the products than those exposed to the all verbal treatments, suggesting that pictures may elicit verbal and nonverbal cues from memory, thus enhancing familiarity.

In another study, the context being a public service announcement promoting safe tanning, pictures were effective in attracting attention but not effective in enhancing comprehension (Boer, Ter Huurne, & Taal, 2006). The presence or absence of textual arguments and pictures was tested across 159 participants with "Practice safe sun tanning" as the main tag line with a drawing of a smiling sun positioned above it. The sub tag line varied among four protection advices (e.g., use sunscreen on uncovered skin, wear covering clothes, avoid the sun between noon and 3 P.M., and wear sunglasses with ultraviolet protection). The visual imagery varied across copy but represented the consequences of physical damage that the sun can do to organs (e.g., two photographs of discolored skin with dark, irregular lesions); the textual arguments communicated the number of people diagnosed with skin cancer annually, the ease in which it can reoccur to damaged skin, and patients having to get rechecked years after being diagnosed. The textual argument conditions yielded significant main effects on credibility and comprehension. In terms of reflection on Public Service Announcement (PSA) and knowledge of the consequences of excessive sun exposure, those exposed to both pictures and textual arguments yielded higher mean scores (Boer et al., 2006). This study lends support to the argument that negative information can capture attention but the degree of negative effect it elicits may suppress other cognitive comprehensive processes.

In sum, studies vary in the use of pictures or images and textual information treatments, product categories, and outcomes measurements, contributing to mixed results on the effectiveness or superiority claims of one means of visual information over another. From a biological, sensory perspective, visual information that is larger, brighter, or more distinct than other information in its visual environment is more likely to be noticed (Jarvenpaa, 1990). Judgment concerning how (or whether) the information presented is encoded from working to long-term memory (Hastie & Park, 1986) may be subject to individual differences, and one's previous experiences and related thoughts may be elicited during the judgment and decision-making process (Schwarz, 2004). Stated differently, how the information is presented may influence how a person processes it online (e.g., rationally, emotionally, selectively, or comprehensively), which may also be influenced by what comes to mind from memory in response to the stimulus. One final area that may provide additional depth and dimension to the domain of visual information and processing style is abstract versus concrete information.

Abstract Versus Concrete

Although abstract and concrete concepts are generally thought to be processed and remembered differently, the underlying process is not well understood (Huang, Lee, & Federmeier, 2010). Research testing abstract and concrete concepts typically employs words as the informational stimuli treatment (for a review, see Chiarello, Liu, & Shears, 2001). Recent research by Huang and associates (2010) examined neuroimaging scans taken while people were exposed to concrete and abstract adjective nouns ($n_{\text{words pairs}} = 112$) (e.g., green book/engaging book) and varied exposure through one visual half-field (VF) (i.e., left visual field [LVF] = right hemisphere [RH] versus right visual field [RVF] = left hemisphere [LH]). Results indicated that concrete adjective nouns exposed to the right visual field (thus activating the left hemisphere) were easier to process perceptually and semantically, while concrete adjective nouns presented to the left visual field (activating the RH) elicited a "sustained frontal negativity" previously linked to imagery (Huang et al., 2010). Stated differently, results suggest that the RH may be critical in linking language (words) to sensory imagery. Results support the linkage between sensory imagery (i.e., "green" reflecting a visual aspect of a noun) and concreteness effects (Paivio, 1991) while also providing evidence that the brain processes information differently depending on the stimuli type and visual field in which it is perceived.

In another study examining concreteness effects (i.e., why concrete words are easier to remember than abstract words) Parker and Dagnall (2009) employed a static versus dynamic visual noise (snow screen) condition between subjects and then tested subjects' ability to encode and recall abstract and concrete words (within treatment conditions) that were presented orally. Under dynamic visual noise conditions (thus impairing the visual connection component during the encoding process), subjects were less able to recall concrete words than abstract words, producing an abstract (word) superiority effect (Parker & Dagnall, 2009). These results were replicated and expanded in a second study that included additional response outcomes while also controlling for words used in terms of frequency, number of syllables, and word length.

Results suggest that visual working memory acts as an access route for sensory information. One potential implication is the impact other visual sensory stimulation may have on the encoding and recall process for abstract and concrete information in which the task is embedded (e.g., dynamic messaging screens placed on store shelves). Empirical evidence suggests that what is encoded and retained may vary depending on the nature of the information presented and the nature of the environment in which it is encoded. Thus the context of the information (i.e., abstract/concrete) and the context of the environment (other competing visual stimuli and from what visual field it may be encoded) may influence how information is processed and retained. A situational factor that may further moderate these effects is the temporal distance employed in the task.

Construal theory proposes that temporal distance changes people's responses to future events by changing the way in which people mentally represent those events (Trope & Liberman, 2003). In a series of choice experiments, manipulating how people thought about a choice (i.e., low construal/temporally near: write down a goal that they wanted to achieve by the end of the week versus high construal/temporally distant: write down a goal that they wanted to achieve by the end of next year) influenced how they thought about the features under consideration (Khan, Zhu, & Kalra, 2011). Specifically, those in a high-construal condition focused on central features (key, higher-level features) and less on compensatory tradeoffs than those in the low-construal condition. Results suggest that consumers were less likely to use compensatory decision rules in high-construal conditions than in low-construal conditions (Khan et al., 2011). Those in a high-construal-choice condition may engage in higher-level, more-abstract ways of thinking, focusing on key attributes, while those in a lower-construal condition may engage in more detailed, concrete ways of thinking (Trope & Liberman, 2003).

Related research suggests that consumers' recycling intentions may be indirectly influenced through self-efficacy by the processing fluency of the message, which comprises the fit between the construal (abstract or concrete mindset) and the framing of the message (gain/loss). White, MacDonnell, and Dahl's (2011) three experimental studies suggest that activating an abstract mind-set that focuses on higher-level thinking about engaging in a behavior (why do it) is processed more fluently when the message is framed positively in terms of gains than it is when the message is framed in terms of losses. A message is also processed more fluently when a concrete mind-set is activated (e.g., how to recycle) and framed negatively in terms of losses rather than gains. Across the experimental treatments, different visuals were employed and thus no conclusive insights could be made in terms of the effectiveness or influence of the images (e.g., one message depicted a man, woman, and two young boys smiling and looking up at an adjacent recycling bin; the other message employed pictures of products that can be recycled); however, White, MacDonnell, and Dahl's research results do suggest that the fit between the valence (negative/positive) and construal (concrete or abstract) of the imagery may influence processing fluency outcomes.

In sum, empirical evidence suggests that concrete and abstract stimuli are encoded differently, with concrete stimuli being associated with visual as well as verbal connection points during encoding, thus enhancing recall at a later time. When direct dynamic visual noise is introduced to the task environment, the encoding of concrete stimuli becomes impaired and abstract stimuli may encode with similar or slightly superior efficacy. If the visual field is limited or focused on one side (LVF) versus the other (RVF), this also has implications for neurobiological processing. The temporal distance associated with evaluation and choice has been empirically associated with how consumers construe and think about the information presented, with abstract information associated with greater temporal distances. Abstract (concrete) thinking combined with positive (negative) framed messages elicits a more fluent processing of the information, which has empirically been demonstrated to be associated with greater feelings of self-efficacy and behavioral intentions to perform conservation behaviors. Combined empirical evidence suggests that imagery may be particularly persuasive when considering the consumer, the context, and the desired outcome. Processing fluency can be enhanced by asking consumers to think about the future (e.g., long-term positioning/branding strategies) employing abstract imagery and positive message frames. Conversely, processing can be enhanced and may lead to action if consumers are presented with concrete imagery showing the consequences if actions are not taken.

Future Research

The research is vast and the information discussed varies across disciplines. Given space constraints, I discuss only a small sample of relevant research, but this sample highlights opportunities for further exploration. Questions such as how and why a consumer perceives information in a certain way may be key to understanding why some visual strategies may be more effective than others in influencing desired outcomes. How one attends and processes information may be based on a confluence of informational properties, individual values and beliefs, preferred or induced processing styles, and environmental contexts in which the behavior is embedded. The model in Figure 8.1 outlines the overarching concepts discussed. Future research that focuses on aspects covered in each domain in various combinations may illuminate understanding concerning consumers' attitudes and behaviors in relation to environmentally significant behavior.

Although negative valenced visual information may drive behavioral action, one has to consider the environment in which this information will be conveyed. A negative visual (e.g., a photograph of dark water spewing out of a rusted pipe) in a newspaper or on a billboard to convey environmental impact may be used as a viable communications strategy to get people to vote on a community clean water initiative, but presenting a similar visual in a retail food store would not be viable. The context in which the consumer is likely to make the decision should be taken into consideration when choosing the type of visual stimuli to test.

Exploration of different contexts to reframe the decision-making process may also be informative. For example, in terms of temporal construals, do decisions made today about future actions elicit more abstract thinking, influencing consumers to be more likely to consider or value social or environmental externalities? Values are considered higher-level thinking. If the decision context aligns with

Figure 8.1 **Research Framework for Influence of Visual Information on ESB**

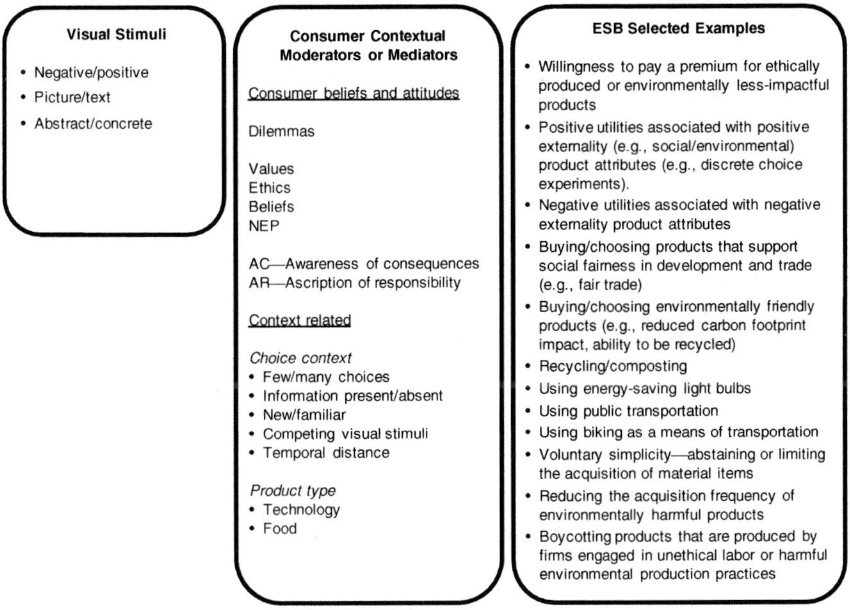

higher-order thinking, do externality impacts shift in importance compared to decisions concerning action taken today or this week? Continuing this reasoning, does visual imagery conveyed in an abstract (conceptually more distant) or concrete (conceptually closer) manner elicit different ways of thinking, thus influencing decision making? Research reviewed typically employed words as the stimulus. How does abstract or concrete imagery, particularly in the context of labeling, influence attention and thought? If the labeling is conveyed online during a consumer search process about a decision to be made in the future, how may the label's effectiveness vary versus being placed on a store shelf with the decision to be made immediately?

Within the consumer domain, awareness of consequences (AC) and ascription of responsibility (AR) are two aspects that appear to be underresearched in the consumer psychology domain. These factors may help to explain some of the variance between consumer attitudes and behaviors, acknowledging that a curvilinear relationship between AC and AR and the desired behavior may exist, particularly when the appeal to act is perceived as high pressure or illegitimate, eliciting a psychological reactance (Schwartz, 1970).

In terms of behaviors, many options are available. One suggestion is to examine consumer behaviors in which the aggregate impact of individual consumers' actions may yield impactful environmentally significant behavior.

References

Armel, K. C., Beaumel, A., & Rangel, A. (2008). Biasing simple choices by manipulating relative visual attention. *Judgment and Decision Making, 3*(5), 396–403.

Axelrod, L. J. (1994). Balancing personal needs with environmental preservation: Identifying the values that guide decisions in ecological dilemmas. *Journal of Social Issues, 50*(3), 85–104.

Baddeley, A. (1992). Working memory. *Science, 255*(5044), 556–559.

Boer, H., Ter Huurne, E., & Taal, E. (2006). Effects of pictures and textual arguments in sun protection public service announcements. *Cancer Detection and Prevention, 30,* 432–438.

Burroughs, J. E., & Rindfleisch, A. (2002). Materialism and well-being: A conflicting values perspective. *Journal of Consumer Research, 29*(3), 348–360.

Carter, R. E., & Curry, D. J. (2010). Transparent pricing: Theory, tests, and implications for marketing practice. *Journal of the Academy of Marketing Sciences, 38,* 759–774.

Chiarello, C., Liu, S., & Shears, C. (2001). Does global context modulate cerebral asymmetries? A review and new evidence on word imageability effects. *Brain and Language, 79*(3), 360–378.

Coupe, K. (2010, February 1). Retailers look to efficiency & effectiveness in 2010. *Morning News Beat.* www.morningnewsbeat.com/News/News_Article_Detail_S.las?A=32895&Date=2010–02–01/.

De Groot, J. I. M., & Steg, L. (2008). Value orientations to explain beliefs related to environmental significant behavior: How to measure egoistic, altruistic, and biospheric value orientations. *Environment and Behavior, 40,* 330–354.

De Pelsmacker, P., Driesen, L., & Rayp, G. (2005). Do consumers care about ethics? Willingness to pay for fair-trade coffee. *Journal of Consumer Affairs, 39,* 363–385.

Dunlap, R. E., Van Liere, K. D., Merig, A. G., & Jones, R. E. (2000). Measuring endorsement of the new ecological paradigm: A revised NEP scale. *Journal of Social Issues, 56*(3), 425–442.

Edell, J. A., & Staelin, R. (1983). The information processing of pictures in print advertisements. *Journal of Consumer Research, 10*(June), 45–61.

Goleman, D. (2009). *Ecological intelligence: How knowing the hidden impacts of what we buy can change everything*. New York: Broadway Books.

Guagnano, G. A., Stern, P.C., & Dietz, T. (1995). Influences on attitude–behavior relationships: A natural experiment with curbside recycling. *Environment and Behavior, 27,* 699–718.

Hannaford (2011). Guiding stars: Nutritious choices made simple. www.hannaford.com/content.jsp?pageName=GuidingStars&leftNavArea=HealthLeftNav/ (accessed May 5, 2011).

Hastie, R., & Park, B. (1986). The relationship between memory and judgment depends on whether the judgment task is memory based or on-line. *Psychological Review, 93*(3), 258–268.

Hauser, J. R., Ding, M., & Gaskin, S. P. (2009). Non-compensatory (and compensatory) models of consideration-set decisions. In *2009 Sawtooth Software Conference Proceedings* (pp. 207–232, Delray Beach, FL). www.sawtoothsoftware.com/download/techpap/2009Proceedings.pdf.

Hirschman, E. C. (1986). The effect of verbal and pictorial advertising stimuli on aesthetic, utilitarian and familiarity perceptions. *Journal of Advertising, 15*(2), 27–34.

Huang, H.-W., Lee, C.-L., & Federmeier, K. D. (2010). Imagine that! ERP's provide evidence for distinct hemispheric contributions to the processing of concrete and abstract concepts. *NeuroImage, 49*(1), 1116–1123.

Huneke, M. E. (2005). The face of the un-consumer: An empirical examination of the

practice of voluntary simplicity in the United States. *Psychology and Marketing, 22*(7), 527–550.
Jackson, T. (2005). *Motivating sustainable consumption: A review of evidence on consumer behaviour and behavioural change*. Report to the Sustainable Development Research Network, United Kingdom. www.sd-research.org.uk/wp-content/uploads/motivating-scfinal_000.pdf.
Jain, S. P., Mathur, P., & Maheswaran, D. (2009). The influence of consumers' lay theories on approach/avoidance motivation. *Journal of Marketing Research, 66*(February), 56–65.
Janiszewski, C. (1998). The influence of display characteristics on visual exploratory search behavior. *Journal of Consumer Research, 25*(December), 290–301.
Jarvenpaa, S. L. (1990). Graphic displays in decision making—The visual salience effect. *Journal of Behavioral Decision Making, 3*(4), 247–262.
Kahneman, D., & Tversky, A. (1979). Prospect theory: An analysis of decision under risk. *Econometrica, 47*(2), 263–292.
Kahneman, D., Ritov, I., Jacowitz, K. E., & Grant, P. (1993). Stated willingness to pay for public goods. *Psychological Science, 4*(5), 310–315.
Karp, D. G. (1996). Values and their effects on pro-environment behavior. *Environment and Behavior, 28,* 111–133.
Khan, U., Zhu, M., & Kalra, A. (2011). When trade-offs matter: The effect of choice construal on context effects. *Journal of Marketing Research, 68*(February), 62–71.
Levy, S. R., Stroessner, S. J., & Dweck, C. S. (1998). Stereotype formation and endorsement: The role of implicit theories. *Journal of Personality and Social Psychology, 74*(6), 1421–1436.
Lurie, N., & Mason, C. (2007). Visual representation: Implications for decision making. *Journal of Marketing, 71*(1), 160–177.
Martin, A. (2007, September 6). Store chain's test concludes that nutrition sells. *New York Times,* p. C3.
Mehrabian, A., & Russell, J. A. (1974). *An approach to environmental psychology.* Cambridge: MIT Press.
Merchant, C. (1992). *Radical ecology: The search for a livable world.* New York: Routledge.
Mosteller, J., & Wilhelm, W. (2011). The influence of visual imagery on environmentally significant behavior. Paper presented at the Annual Advertising and Consumer Psychology Conference, University of Oregon, Eugene, Oregon, May 5–6.
Nelson, D., Reed, V., & Walling, J. (1976). Pictorial superiority effect. *Journal of Experimental Psychology: Human Learning and Memory, 2,* 523–528.
Ongondo, F. O., Williams, I. D., & Cherrett, T. J. (2011). How are WEEE doing? A global review of the management of electrical and electronic wastes. *Waste Management, 31*(4), 714–730.
Onozaka, Y., & McFadden, D. T. (2011). Does local labeling complement or compete with other sustainable labels? A conjoint analysis of direct and joint values for fresh produce claims. *American Journal of Agricultural Economics, 93*(3), 693–706.
Osterhus, T. (1997). Pro-social consumer influence strategies: When and how do they work? *Journal of Marketing, 61*(October), 16–29.
Owens, S., & Driffill, L. (2008). How to change attitudes and behavior in the context of energy. *Energy Policy, 36,* 4412–4418.
Paivio, A. (1969). Mental imagery in associative learning and memory. *Psychological Review, 76*(May), 241–263.
Paivio, A. (1991). Dual coding theory: Retrospect and current status. *Canadian Journal of Psychology, 45,* 255–287.
Paivio, A. (2010). Dual coding theory and the mental lexicon. *Mental Lexicon, 5*(2), 205–230.

Parker, A., & Dagnall, N. (2009). Concreteness effects revisited: The influence of dynamic visual noise on memory for concrete and abstract words. *Memory, 17*(4), 397–410.
Richins, M., & Dawson, S. (1992). A consumer values orientation for materialism and its measurement: Scale development and validation. *Journal of Consumer Research, 19*(3), 303–316.
Roozen, I., De Pelsmacker, P., & Bostyn, F. (2001). The ethical dimensions of decision processes of employees. *Journal of Business Ethics, 33*(2), 87–99.
Rossiter, J. R., & Percy, L. (1980). Attitude change through visual imagery in advertising. *Journal of Advertising, 9*(2), 10–16.
Schwartz, S. H. (1970). Elicitation of moral obligation and self-sacrificing behavior: An experimental study of volunteering to be a bone marrow donor. *Journal of Personality and Social Psychology, 15*(4), 283–293.
Schwartz, S. H. (1994). Are there universal values in the structure and contents of human values? *Journal of Social Issues, 50*(4), 19–35.
Shaw, D., Newholm, T., & Dickinson, R. (2006). Consumption as voting: An exploration of consumer empowerment. *European Journal of Marketing, 40*(9/10), 1049–1067.
Smith, A. (2010). *Mobile access 2010.* Pew Internet and American Life Project, July 7. http://pewinternet.org/Reports/2010/Mobile-Access-2010.axpx.
Steinman, R., & Levinson, J. (1990). The role of eye movement in the detection of contrast and spatial detail. In E. Knowler (Ed.), *Eye movements and their role in visual and cognitive processes* (pp. 115–160). New York: Elsevier.
Stern, P. C. (2000). Toward a coherent theory of environmentally significant behavior. *Journal of Social Issues, 56*(3), 407–424.
Thøgersen, J., & Folke, O. (2002). Human values and emergence of a sustainable consumption pattern: A panel study. *Journal of Economic Psychology, 23,* 605–630.
Trope, Y., & Liberman, N. (2003). Temporal construal. *Psychological Review, 110*(3), 403–421.
U.S. Census Bureau. (2009). S0201: Selected population profile in the United States. American Community Survey. http://factfinder.census.gov.
White, K., MacDonnell, R., and Dahl, D. W. (2011). It's the mind-set that matters: The role of construal level and message framing in influencing consumer efficacy and conservation behaviors. *Journal of Marketing Research, 68*(June), 472–485.
Wyer, R. S., Hung, I. W., & Jiang, Y.-W. (2008). Visual and verbal processing strategies in comprehension and judgment. *Journal of Consumer Psychology, 18*(October), 244–257.

Part III

Increasing Sustainable Consumption Conceptual Frameworks

Although environmental sustainability issues have gained importance and popularity over the years, many consumers are still reluctant to engage in sustainable consumption. To deal with this problem, the chapters in this section introduce conceptual frameworks that may be used to increase sustainable consumption.

Xie, Cavallero, and Cheng connect two streams of research, green advertising and persuasion knowledge, to understand the mechanisms responsible for consumer resistance against green advertising. Specifically, the authors discuss three issues (i.e., information processing, construal level, and perceived efficacy) related to the green persuasion knowledge that can have important theoretical, practical, and public policy implications. They suggest that, for information processing, the integration of the green persuasion knowledge with dual or tri-process models can enhance the effectiveness of the study of persuasion knowledge. Similarly, the green persuasion knowledge studies and the construal level studies should be integrated as the types and frames of green claims can interact with the construal level when consumers assess those green claims. Finally, Xie, Cavallero, and Cheng propose that the perceptions of self-efficacy (how green tactics influence oneself) and other-efficacy (how green tactic influence other people) may be important factors when studying green persuasion knowledge.

Han, Yu, and Teng proposes a model of message framing to address the communication problems related to promoting the low-carbon policy (LCP) to the public. Based on a hierarchical order of promotional goals from awareness to action, this model considers the impact of various moderators on the relationship between message framing and LCP promotional goals. In a way, the moderators included in this model construct the communication situation for the promotional campaign. Accordingly, marketers and public policy makers can use these moderators to perform situational analyses and choose appropriate message framing strategies. The use of these message-framing strategies, in turn, can help marketers and public policy makers convince the public on the necessity of the LCP and lead people to take action to decrease their footprint.

Yang, Bublitz, Wang, and Peracchio integrate the research on environmental sustainability and creativity and discuss how consumer creativity can encourage sustainable consumption. In other words, the authors suggest that consumer creativity can be used to shift consumers toward innovations in sustainable consumption. Various factors (e.g., making consumers adopt a creative mindset) that may promote creative solutions to environmental concerns are discussed in this chapter. They also provide suggestions to identify factors that would lead consumers to convert their creative environmental ideas into actions as well as to use creative advertising (by marketers and public policy makers) to promote environmentally conscious behaviors.

Jones, Owen, and Kahle examine the Germany's Green Dot (GD) program and its impact on the progress toward sustainable development in Germany and the rest of Europe. More specifically, the authors discuss both the criticisms (e.g., not giving enough attention to avoiding waste in the first place, not promoting refillable bottles, misleading the public with the GD symbol, and being perceived as a barrier to trade) and the successes of the GD program in detail. They conclude this chapter by identifying several factors (e.g., resistance from municipal and state governments, industry cooperation in the venture, consumer attitudes toward recycling, and recycling capacities and technologies currently available) that might affect the success of the program in the United States.

9

Reluctant for a Reason?

A Persuasion Knowledge Perspective on Green Advertising

Guang-Xin Xie, Alex Cavallero, and Meng Cheng

Since the 1990s, as sustainability has gained increasing importance on the business and public affairs agenda, the notion of "green growth" has gained greater visibility in advertising (Kotler, 2011). Despite the popularity of this notion, consumers appear to be reluctant to accept green advertisements as a trustworthy source of information (Zinkhan & Carlson, 1995). In fact, green advertising can be ambiguous and even misleading at times—for example, a package label that reads "50 percent more recycled content than before." The claim suggests an increase in recycled goods by half; however, the manufacturer's total increase in recycled content has only improved by a small percentage. Although the message is technically true, the Federal Trade Commission (FTC, 2011) rules the advertisement deceptive because it can create a false impression.

Over the past four decades, extant research has examined a variety of claims and consumer characteristics that make green advertising more or less effective (e.g., Chan, 2000; Easterling, Kenworthy, & Nemzoff, 1996; Kilbourne, 1995; Kinnear, Taylor, & Ahmed, 1974; Obermiller, 1995; Schuhwerk & Lefkoff-Hagius, 1995). Although researchers are aware that consumers can be skeptical about advertising, an implicit assumption is that they retain some trust in green claims of product/service attributes. This assumption does not always hold: Under what circumstances do consumers tend to question green advertising as a guileful persuasion tactic, rather than a genuine pro-social action? Specifically, what kind of consumers are more skeptical? Under what conditions do consumers think a green claim is not trustworthy? What are the psychological mechanisms and behavioral consequences? How do green advertisers respond to consumer reactions?

The Persuasion Knowledge Model (PKM) (Friestad & Wright, 1994) provides a theoretical framework to organize research in exploring these questions. Persuasion knowledge is personal knowledge that individuals develop about the motives and tactics in persuasion attempts. The use of persuasion knowledge involves a set of cognitive structures and procedures beyond thinking about product/service attributes. The literature has documented that persuasion knowledge can induce more or less acceptance of an external influence, depending upon a number of individual and situational difference factors (e.g., Campbell & Kirmani, 2000; Kirmani & Campbell, 2004; Kirmani & Wright, 1989; Kirmani & Zhu, 2007; Mita, Bettman, & Sujan, 1986). Once information is accessible and diagnostic, persuasion knowledge can affect how people detect, interpret, and cope with persuasion attempts (Campbell & Kirmani, 2008).

The PKM is particularly useful in understanding the mechanisms responsible for consumer resistance to green advertising. Many consumers are aware of broad environmental concerns, but they may not fully understand issue-specific claims, jargon, or terminology (Kangun & Polonsky, 1995). Even if they are able to overcome the comprehension barriers, green claims sometimes deal with environmental issues about which ordinary consumers may lack sufficient expertise. Consumers often cannot verify the green claims (in contrast to typical household product advertisements) through first-hand experience. As a result, they sometimes use persuasion knowledge as a basis for evaluating green advertising.

This chapter is intended to connect two streams of research: green advertising and persuasion knowledge. The purpose is to formulate a research agenda on green advertising from a perspective that has not yet been fully addressed. This chapter begins with a conceptual overview of green advertising. Next, the persuasion knowledge research is introduced with a focus on its theoretical relevance to green advertising. The following section discusses consumers' use of persuasion knowledge in response to green advertising. This chapter concludes with a set of recommendations for future research. Note that this chapter focuses on verbal claims in broadcast and print commercial advertisements targeting adult consumers.

Green Advertising

Green advertising is part of a sustainable marketing strategy for organizations that are dedicated to improving public perceptions of the organizations as a whole or their counterparts (Chabowski, Mena, & Gonzalez-Padron, 2011; Iyer & Zinkhan, 1994). The American Marketing Association (AMA) identifies three core functions of "green marketing." First, as a retailing function, it refers to marketing of products/services that are presumed to be environmentally safe. Second, as a social marketing function, it can be defined as the development and marketing of products/services designed to minimize negative effects on the physical environment or to improve its quality. Third, as an environmental function, it suggests that the efforts by organizations to produce, promote, package, and reclaim products/services are occurring in a manner that is sensitive or responsive to ecological concerns (AMA, 2008).

Over the past four decades, green advertising research has evolved from categorizing green claims and profiling target consumers (e.g., Kinnear et al., 1974; Murphy, Kangun, & Locander, 1978; Stafford, Stafford, & Chowdhury, 1996) to a comprehensive approach that integrates individual consumer responses with the organizational goals (Kilbourne & Beckmann, 1998; Montoro-Rios, Luque-Martínez, & Rodríguez-Molina, 2008; Schuhwerk & Lefkoff-Hagius, 1995; Sheth, Sethia, & Srinivas, 2011). Specifically, green advertising usually has at least one of the following traits: (1) it explicitly or implicitly addresses the relationship between a product/service and the biophysical environment; (2) it promotes a green lifestyle with or without highlighting a product/service; and (3) it presents a corporate image of environmental responsibility (Banerjee, Gulas, & Iyer, 1995, p. 22).

Green Typologies

Green claims can be categorized by the stage of the product life cycle: production, consumption, or disposal (Scammon & Mayer, 1995). Organizations frequently launch advertisements linking their products/services to one or more of these stages according to when the pro-environmental measures are implemented. Production focuses on the amount of recycled materials used in the manufacturing processes and the amount of resource reduction. Consumption addresses the reduced effects on the natural environment regarding energy efficiency of a product/service that is consumed. Disposal entails the level of product degradability, recyclability, and compostability after consumption.

With respect to the information content, Hartmann and Apaolaza-Ibáñez (2009) proposed two broad categories: substantive and associative claims. Substantive claims "present concrete, tangible benefits and reflect intent to maintain or enhance consumers' perception of an organization as environmentally responsible or of a product as environmentally sound" (p. 718). In contrast, associative claims are intangible presentations that are "image related or present environmental facts" (p. 718). More specifically, Carlson, Grove, and Kangun (1993, p. 31) divided environmental advertising claims into five types: (1) product orientation—the claim focuses on the environmentally friendly attributes that a product possesses; (2) process orientation—the claim deals with an organization's internal technology, production technique, or disposal method that yields environmental benefits; (3) image orientation—the claim associates an organization with an environmental cause or activity for which there is broad-based public support; (4) environmental fact—the claim involves an independent statement that is ostensibly factual in nature from an organization about the environment at large, and (5) combination—the claim appears to have multiple facets. Note that these typologies mainly address the message characteristics in green advertising, and much remains to be learned about how to categorize visual presentations.

Green Lifestyle

Green advertising typologies have been adjusted over time in relation to the notion of "green lifestyle." The concept of lifestyle is an integrated system of attitudes, values, opinions, and interests as well as overt behaviors (Anderson & Golden, 1984; Berkman & Gilson, 1978). A green lifestyle is circumstantial depending on multiple pro-environmental life dimensions and the level of importance that people assign to each dimension. A green lifestyle reflects an environmental value that people uphold to reduce or eliminate human society's negative effects on the natural environment and to increase positive implications through specific actions. In particular, a green lifestyle may include everyday activities that (1) reduce the consumption of natural resources and energy, (2) recycle or reuse resources and materials, (3) support technological development to pursue renewable energy, and (4) involve actions that restore the natural environments that have been adversely affected by human behaviors (Kilbourne, 1995).

Persuasion Knowledge

Green advertising is one form of marketing persuasion. It is often planned strategically to influence the targets' perceptions, viewpoints, intentions, and behaviors. Wright (1986) first introduced the concept of "schemer schema," arguing that individual consumers develop lay theories about why and how marketers use strategies, tactics, and maneuvers to achieve their persuasive goals. This idea was formally theorized in the PKM (Friestad & Wright, 1994). The theory posits that consumers have three types of knowledge structures that interact in shaping the outcomes of a persuasion attempt: (1) agent knowledge—consumer thoughts/beliefs about the traits, competencies, and goals of a persuasion agent, (2) topic knowledge—consumer thoughts/beliefs about the topic of the persuasion messages, and (3) persuasion knowledge—consumer thoughts/beliefs about a persuasion agent's motives and tactics (Figure 9.1). Specifically, persuasion knowledge addresses a wide variety of subtopics, including "beliefs about marketers' motives, strategies, and tactics; effectiveness and appropriateness of persuasion tactics; psychological mediators of tactic effectiveness; and ways of coping with persuasion attempts" (Campbell & Kirmani, 2000, p. 69).

Conceptual Background

The PKM postulates that these three types of knowledge are functionally independent cognitive schemata. For example, a consumer may know little about the technical ingredients in a new cosmetics product advertised in a commercial, but his or her agent knowledge (e.g., brand awareness), topic knowledge (e.g., experience with fragrances), and persuasion knowledge (e.g., advertisers' intentions and tactics) can all operate as signals about the product quality to some degree (Kirmani & Rao, 2000). The effect of persuasion knowledge can be salient when consumers lack valid and relevant agent or topic knowledge (Boulding & Kirmani, 1993; Burke, DeSarbo, Oliver, & Robertson, 1988; Kirmani & Wright, 1989). Activated persuasion knowledge can change the cognitive processing

Figure 9.1 **Persuasion Knowledge Model**

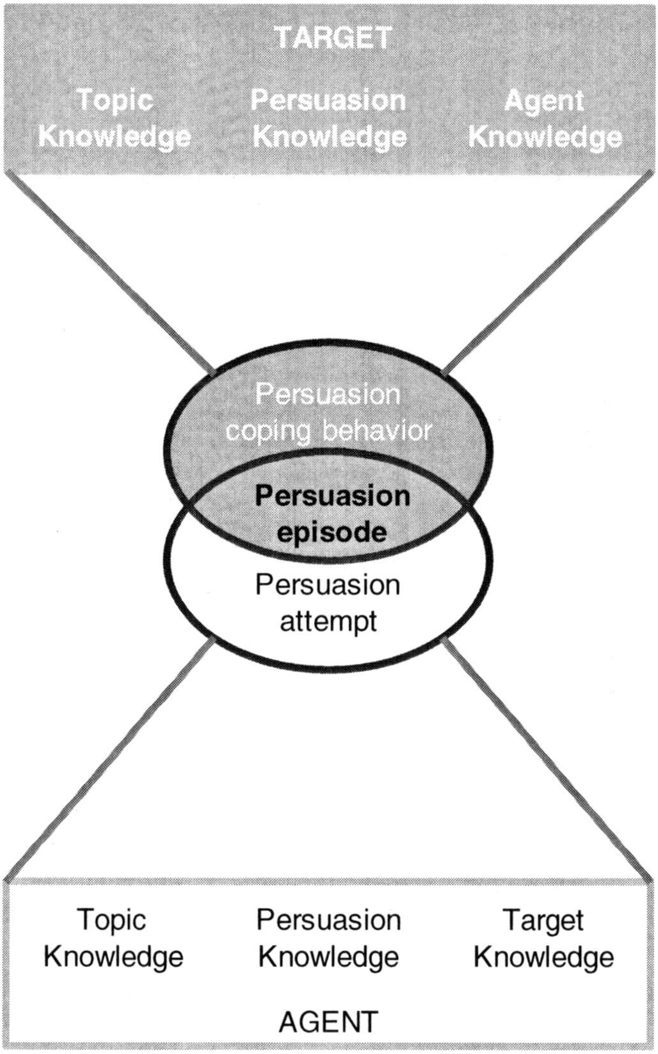

Source: Friestad and Wright 1994.

foci from the explicit messages to the implicit motives and tactics (Friestad & Wright, 1994).

The PKM specifies the nature of a set of cognitive structures and mechanisms used when consumers respond to persuasion attempts. It highlights the importance of certain types of knowledge that can elicit "the change of meanings": Consumer mindsets can shift from message-centric to motive- or tactic-centric. As a theoretical framework, the PKM addresses focus dependence, rather than path dependence, when consumers process the information in a persuasion attempt. In that sense, the PKM is distinct from the classic persuasion models such as the Elaboration Likelihood Model (ELM; Petty & Cacioppo, 1986) and the Heuristic-Systematic Model (HSM; Chaiken, Liberman, & Eagly, 1989) that emphasize the different processing routes during attitude formation and change.

Recent research suggests that persuasion knowledge is often intertwined with agent and topic knowledge when consumers encounter a persuasion attempt. A number of studies suggest that certain agent or topic knowledge sometimes activate persuasion knowledge in a relatively automatic process (e.g., DeCarlo, 2005; Forehand & Grier, 2003). For example, when a salesperson in a department store makes a positive comment on a consumer's choice of clothing prior to the purchase decision, the consumer may consider the flattery a sales pitch rather than a sincere recommendation (Campbell & Kirmani, 2000). When the persuasion agent is a friend or family member, suspicion of the ulterior selling motives significantly declines (Main, Dahl, & Darke, 2007). To date, however, the structural interdependency of the three types of knowledge has not been fully examined at the neuropsychological level.

Current Status of PKM Research

The PKM is an influential theory that leads to a stream of fruitful research. During the past two decades, it has been well documented that cognitive schemata about marketers' persuasion motives and tactics can influence consumer perceptions, attitudes, and behaviors. Researchers have examined the role of persuasion knowledge in the following five main domains: (1) the effect of suspicion on consequential attitudes and behaviors (e.g., Campbell & Kirmani, 2000; Kirmani & Campbell, 2004; Kirmani & Zhu, 2007; Williams, Fitzsimons, & Block, 2004); (2) the interactions between persuasion knowledge and persuasion messages (e.g., Ahluwalia & Burnkrant, 2004); (3) persuasion knowledge as an individual difference in consumer self-confidence or a stable mental state against marketing persuasion (e.g., Bearden, Hardesty, & Rose, 2001; Obermiller & Spangenberg, 1998); (4) context-specific forms and functions of persuasion knowledge (e.g., Darke & Ritchie, 2007; Kirmani, 1990); and (5) the nature and structure of persuasion knowledge across developmental stages (e.g., Boush, Friestad, & Rose, 1994; Friestad & Wright, 1995; Williams & Drolet, 2005). In essence, the literature suggests that persuasion knowledge can function as either an individual or a situational difference variable.

The literature suggests that both positive and negative outcomes are possible when persuasion knowledge is in use (Campbell & Kirmani 2008). It is intuitive that persuasion knowledge (PK) can lead to less favorable perceptions of a persuasion agent (e.g., Campbell & Kirmani, 2000), more negative attitude toward the brand or firm (e.g., Ahluwalia & Burnkrant, 2004; Jain & Posavac, 2004), and lower purchase intention (e.g., Brown & Krishna, 2004), compared to situations when persuasion knowledge is not used. However, it is also evident that activation of persuasion knowledge can generate positive responses toward a persuasion agent (e.g., Boulding & Kirmani, 1993; Morales, 2005; Warlop & Alba, 2004). Although consumers tend to hold less favorable attitudes toward persuasion attempts when PK is activated than otherwise, they sometimes do recognize and appreciate a smart, creative, or socially responsible persuasion attempt. In other words, the negative effect of PK-induced cognition on consumer attitudes and behaviors can be attenuated or moderated.

Consumers can also use persuasion knowledge for self-benefits. For instance, Kirmani and Campbell (2004) demonstrated that consumers not only react negatively against marketers but also adaptively use persuasion knowledge to achieve their own goals. They speculated that consumers high on assertiveness (Richins, 1983) and self-confidence (Bearden et al., 2001) are more likely to actively engage, for example, by using the persuasion to obtain personal goals, rather than to simply resist persuasion attempts. Only a few studies have systematically integrated the conditional variations with individual differences in persuasion knowledge (e.g., Ahluwalia & Burnkrant, 2004; Shrum & Lowrey, 1995). For example, Shrum and Lowrey (1995) found that green consumers tend to be more skeptical about advertising, a counterintuitive phenomenon that calls for more in-depth research. Much remains to be learned about the extent to which high-persuasion knowledge and low-persuasion knowledge consumers react differently in relation to the types and nature of green claims.

Green Persuasion Knowledge

Green persuasion knowledge is a subset of persuasion knowledge. It reflects consumers' context-specific abilities in detecting, interpreting, and coping with environmental advertising effectively. Consumers develop green persuasion knowledge mainly from social learning and accumulated experiences during the socialization process (for a review on consumer socialization, see John, 1999). It consists of two main cognitive schemata: why green advertising is used (i.e., motives) and how it can be effective (i.e., tactics). Specifically, green persuasion knowledge represents subjective judgments about the mechanisms of persuading people to adopt certain beliefs, ideas, or behaviors by leveraging environmental concerns. Like other types of context-specific knowledge, green persuasion knowledge can comprise simple heuristics and naive beliefs. Over the course of socialization, such kinds of knowledge can become more systematic, in-depth, and sophisticated.

Green persuasion knowledge can regulate consumer reactions to green advertising. Intuitively, a minimal level of basic cognitive abilities is necessary to process any environmental messages to interpret related contextual cues, develop response strategies, and execute intended behaviors. In a more complicated situ-

Figure 9.2 **A Conceptual Framework of the Use of Persuasion Knowledge**

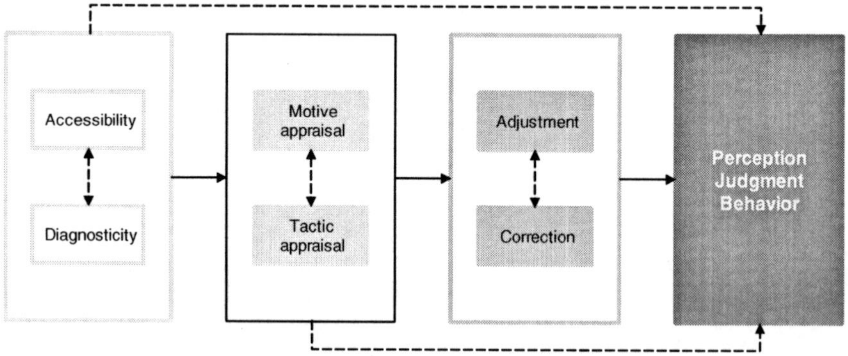

ation, multiple abilities are needed to think and react effectively. These abilities may include short-term and long-term memory, attention span, cognitive capacity, perceptual accuracy, deductive and inductive reasoning, and logical coherence. This chapter addresses three key issues in the use of green persuasion knowledge from the perspective of processing: accessibility and diagnosticity, motives and tactics appraisals, adjustment and corrections (see Figure 9.2). It is important to note that each process may function independently to influence consumer perception, judgment, and behavior. Consumers do not necessarily go through the entire linear procedure.

Accessibility and Diagnosticity

When consumers are exposed to a green claim, they may or may not activate any persuasion knowledge. As the accessibility-diagnosticity model suggests (Feldman & Lynch, 1988), cognitive thinking must be salient and relevant in order to influence the subsequent reactions in the appraisal process. Accessibility is higher when the contexts make certain schemata more likely to be used. Campbell and Kirmani (2000) found that activation of persuasion knowledge depends on the situational salience and cognitive busyness. A salesperson's flattery is more likely to trigger suspicion of ulterior sales motive before the purchase than after the purchase. The accessibility is subject to the available cognitive resources at the moment: Cognitively busier consumers are less likely to infer a salesperson's sales motives than those who are less busy. With regard to green advertising, consumers may have a default positive impression of an organization's eco-friendly efforts. As a result, the accessibility of persuasion knowledge in response to green advertising may be lower than that in response to typical nongreen advertising, all other things being equal. Researchers may explore the mechanisms through which accessibility can be enhanced. Typical red flags may include low source credibility, message ambiguity, and product category-brand image inconsistency.

Accessible schemata may or may not be diagnostic to a specific persuasion task. Diagnosticity is higher when the use of persuasion knowledge is perceived as relevant for consumers to understand and cope with a particular situation. Main et al. (2007) found that when the persuasion agent is a family relative or a friend, consumers are much less likely to infer the sales motive than when the agent is a salesperson. Consumers' motivational mindset can also regulate the relevance of persuasion knowledge. Kirmani and Zhu (2007) show that the use of defensive persuasion knowledge is in line with a protective mindset to avoid negative outcomes. With regard to green advertising, consumers may lack solid knowledge background to question the tactics. A general suspicion may not be strong enough to hold against potential counterarguments. It will be interesting to explore the differential effects of accessible/diagnostic vs. accessible/not diagnostic green persuasion knowledge.

Motive and Tactic Appraisal

Resistance to green advertising can be elicited by a simple belief that marketers intend to influence consumers to make profits. Friestad and Wright (1994) argue that motive-based attributions can account for this phenomenon. For example, DeCarlo (2005) found that suspicion of ulterior sales motives leads to a change in attribution from product-focused to agent-focused. Suspicious consumers are likely to see a discrepancy between what appears to be true and the "real truth" behind what they are told. Consumer may believe that organizations or individuals are motivated to seek self-centric benefits such as social acceptance, higher profitability, and positive images. The notion of green is considered instrumental in gaining self-benefits rather than social well-being as advertised. Note that green advertising can be also ascribed to truly altruistic or mixed motives.

Another dimension is the appraisal of green tactics. Friestad and Wright (1994) argue that consumer judgments of a persuasion agent depend upon the perceived appropriateness and effectiveness, specifically the beliefs about the "fairness and manipulativeness" (p. 5) as well as whether the tactics are "moral or normatively acceptable (i.e., within the boundaries or 'rules of the game')" (p. 10). A number of studies have examined the perceived manipulativeness in green advertising (e.g., Kangun & Polonsky, 1995; Shrum & Lowrey, 1995). In contrast, only a few studies have addressed how the perceived effectiveness of green tactics influences consumer acceptance (e.g., Berger & Corbin, 1992; Ellen, Wiener, & Cobb-Walgren, 1991).

One of the most critical issues of green claims is the potential deceptiveness in "greenwashing" (Carlson et al., 1993; Kangun, Carlson, & Grove, 1991; Polonsky et al., 1998). Deception has been a focal concern for public policy makers and advertising scholars (for a review, see Xie & Boush, 2011). According to Grice's cooperative principles in conversations (1975), persuaders should attempt to present only a sufficient amount of truthful, valid, and relevant information in a clear manner. Any intentional and unilateral violation of one or more of these maxims can mislead the recipients to acquire false beliefs or draw erroneous inferences (McCornack, 1992). Any violation of the cooperative principles in green advertising can be potentially deceptive, and the consequences may partially depend upon the types and the magnitude of violations. For example, if green claims contain ambiguous information but not necessarily false, consumers use their persuasion knowledge and conclude that advertisers use a tactic intentionally. As a result, some consumers may consider this green advertisement less honest and more deceptive.

Adjustment and Correction

Cialdini (2001) described a personal experience of how people may cope with a seemingly persuasive attempt. A 10-year old girl was giving a flower to each visitor who entered the school grounds when the children of her class were hosting an open house for their grandparents. The first man she approached with a flower growled at her, "Keep it." Not knowing what to do, she extended it toward him again. The man asked what she wanted in return. "When she replied weakly, 'Nothing, it's a gift,' he fixed her with a disbelieving glare, insisting that he recognized 'her game,' and brushed on past" (p. 47). This is an example of how the use of persuasion knowledge can turn out to be a false alarm. Cialdini (2001) ascribed it to the "insensitiveness" of the man in the scenario. If the man had taken a little more time to ask the girl why she was giving gifts, considered his presumption about "her game," or accepted the flower to see what was next, would his attitude have been different? This raises an important question about the potential adjustment and correction of persuasion knowledge-based judgments.

According to Meyers-Levy and Malaviya's (1999), "people generally are included to correct their judgments because they prefer to hold views that are reasonably accurate and free from bias" (p. 53). The initial judgments and reactions due to the use of green persuasion knowledge can be relatively positive, negative, or mixed. However, consumers can correct the initial product judgment when the following three conditions are met: (1) they are aware of biases, (2) they are able to identify why biases or inappropriateness occur, and (3) they are able to allocate adequate cognitive resources to engage in the correction process. Otherwise, the initial judgment becomes final (Meyers-Levy & Malaviya, 1999).

The green advertising literature suggests some interesting clues about potential corrections. A number of studies suggest that green attributes of a product/service can have positive impacts on other attributes and the overall judgment of the advertised brand (e.g., Luchs, Naylor, Irwin, & Raghunathan, 2010; Sen & Bhattachara, 2001; Trudel & Cotte, 2008). This is the "halo effect," when positive responses to a green attribute carry over to other attributes. However, the halo effect can be mitigated due to thinking about the cost of going green in the "tradeoff" effect (Chernev

& Carpenter, 2001). That is, a superior green attribute can be associated with the other relatively "inferior" attributes, because consumers infer that companies are resource-limited but remain profit-oriented. The more resources are allocated to the green attributes, the less can be used for the other attributes. In that sense, the initial positive judgments can be modified or corrected if consumers think about the why and how the company is "going green."

Future Research

Extant research has convincingly demonstrated the effect of persuasion knowledge on consumer perceptions, attitudes, and coping behaviors with persuasion attempts. Green advertising is a unique context in which the theory of persuasion knowledge can be applied. It is predicted that the effectiveness of green advertising depends partially upon the accessibility and diagnosticity, motive and tactic appraisals, adjustment and correction when consumer persuasion knowledge is in use. This section discusses three emerging issues that may lead to more interesting research: (1) information processing, (2) construal level, and (3) perceived efficacy. Future research along these lines has the potential to add important theoretical, practical, and public policy implications.

Information Processing

The study of persuasion knowledge can be further enhanced by integrating with the theories of dual- or triprocess models. The basic notion of route-based processing theories is that source, message, individual, and situational variables all have an impact on judgment and attitude through a finite number of processing pathways. The outcomes may vary in terms of the attitude valence, certainty, and magnitude. For instance, the classic ELM proposed two distinct processes (e.g., central and peripheral) depending on an individual's motivation and ability to process target information (Petty & Cacioppo, 1986). Meyers-Levy and Malaviya (1999) added an experiential process to include an automatic, affective, and subconscious processing. In their model, a systematic, a heuristic, or an experiential process will dominate how the cognitive tasks are performed. In the more recent Multiple Pathway Anchoring and Adjustment (MPAA) model of attitude generation and recruitment, Cohen and Reed (2006) further differentiated the paths between constructing attitudes "online" from available information and accessing prior attitudes in the form of memory-based nodes. This notion is essentially compatible with experiential information processing when minimal cognitive resources are allocated to make a judgment (Petty, 2006).

The use of green persuasion knowledge can occur via either a relatively systematic or heuristic process, in which both the width and depth of processing modes may influence the consequential responses. Previous studies have documented that after consumers recognize the potentially deceptive tactics in advertising, they tend to process the embedded information in a heuristic manner because of the defensive suspicion (Darke & Ritchie, 2007). Main et al. (2007) also suggested that consumer reactions can be relatively automatic and are prone to misattribution. With respect to green advertising, some consumers may consider green advertising a marketing tactic without much thinking, while others may take multiple cues into consideration. As a result, the consequential attitude or judgments may differ in valence and strength.

At the same time, a number of studies have suggested that the use of persuasion knowledge can be systematic, deliberate, and effortful, especially when consumers are motivated to achieve certain goals (Kirmani & Campbell, 2004). It will be interesting to explore the situations when persuasion knowledge is processed along the line suggested by the dual-process models, such as systematic vs. heuristic (Chaiken et al., 1989), central vs. peripheral (Petty & Cacioppo, 1986), analytic vs. holistic (Nisbett, Peng, Choi, & Norenzayan, 2001), and associative vs. propositional (Gawronski & Bodenhausen, 2006). Meanwhile, researchers should be cautious about the potential overlap between these models, avoiding repetitive studies at both theoretical and empirical levels.

Construal Level

Persuasion knowledge varies in the level of construal: abstract or concrete. According to the Construal Level Theory (CLT) (Trope, Liberman, & Wakslak, 2007), the low-level construal is relatively concrete, unstructured, and contextualized. The high-level construal is abstract, schematic, and decontextualized. With regard to green advertising, some consumers tend to distrust advertising in general or certain types of advertising. Such abstract beliefs may carry over to the green claims. As a result, they may consider "green" another marketing tactic and thus less trustworthy. In comparison, consumers may rely on more concrete thinking about specific cues such as the type of claims, product category, and source credibility. Future research may integrate persuasion knowledge with construal level. The types (e.g., substantive vs. associative) and the frames (e.g., gain vs. loss) of green claims may interact with the construal level of persuasion knowledge in terms of consumers' perceptions, judgments, and behavioral intentions.

Perceived Efficacy

Persuasion knowledge can be a subjective belief that reflects self-efficacy and other efficacy in related abilities in response to green advertising. It is possible that self-efficacy is biased toward maintaining positive self-perception. For example, some consumers would like to believe that they are good at coping with persuasion tactics, but in fact they may not be very good. The outcomes of inflated self-efficacy in persuasion knowledge can be error prone. The consequences of such inadequacy may include biases and misperceptions. For example, some consumers can be cynical and skeptical toward advertising despite the actual validity of the claims. Cialdini (2001) suggests that in some situations, people can mistakenly interpret a social encounter and overreact to a persuasion agent who does not have any malicious or manipulative intentions. To date, the extent to which high self-efficacy in persuasion knowledge can actually backfire is largely unknown.

Another direction is the perceived efficacy of others in persuasion knowledge. The magnitude of environmental problems is often overwhelming and requires the collective reactions of many people. One's judgment of how effective a green claim is may partially depend on the expected effectiveness on others. This is consistent with the notion of the materiality of advertising (see Richards & Preston, 1992)—the degree to which the effect of an advertisement is significant. For example, a green advertisement may take on an extremely difficult task and the advocated actions may sound impractical, if most people do not react. As a result, to what extent consumers think this tactic is effective can be contingent upon their perceptions of how green tactics influence others.

Conclusion

This chapter aims to provide a persuasion knowledge perspective on green advertising. It speculates that consumer knowledge about persuasion motives and tactics may play an important role in influencing consumer acceptance of green advertising. This article highlights three areas of persuasion knowledge theory that are congruent with the green advertising research: accessibility and diagnosticity, motive and tactic appraisals, and adjustment and correction. The purpose is not to offer a comprehensive review of either the green advertising or the persuasion knowledge literature. Instead, this chapter plays a role in advocacy for applying the persuasion knowledge theory in the green advertising context.

References

Ahluwalia, R., & Burnkrant, R. E. (2004). Answering questions about questions: A persuasion knowledge perspective for understanding the effects of rhetorical questions. *Journal of Consumer Research, 31*(1), 26–42.

American Marketing Association (AMA). (2008). Dictionary: Green marketing. www.marketingpower.com/_layouts/Dictionary.aspx?dLetter=G/ (accessed August 1, 2011).

Anderson, W. T., Jr., & Golden, L. L. (1984). Lifestyle and psychographics: A critical review and recommendation. *Advances in Consumer Research, 11*(1), 405–411.

Banerjee, S., Gulas, C. S., & Iyer, E. (1995). Shades of green: A multidimensional analysis of environmental advertising. *Journal of Advertising, 24*(2), 21–31.

Bearden, W. O., Hardesty, D. M., & Rose, R. L. (2001). Consumer self-confidence: Refinements in conceptualization and measurement. *Journal of Consumer Research, 28*(1), 121–133.

Berger, I. E., & Corbin, R. M. (1992). Perceived consumer effectiveness and faith in others as moderators of environmentally responsible behaviors. *Journal of Public Policy & Marketing, 11*(2), 79–89.

Berkman, H. W., & Gilson, C. C. (1978). *Consumer behavior: Concepts and strategies.* Encino, CA: Dickenson.

Boulding, W., & Kirmani, A. (1993). A consumer-side experimental examination of signaling theory. *Journal of Consumer Research, 20*(1), 111–123.

Boush, D. M., Friestad, M., & Rose, G. M. (1994). Adolescent skepticism toward TV advertising and knowledge of advertiser tactics. *Journal of Consumer Research, 21*(1), 165–174.

Brown, C. L., & Krishna, A. (2004). The skeptical shopper: A metacognitive account for the effects of default options on choice. *Journal of Consumer Research, 31*(3), 529–539.

Burke, R. R., DeSarbo, W. S., Oliver, R. L., & Robertson, T. S. (1988). Deception by implication: An experimental investigation. *Journal of Consumer Research, 14*(4), 483–494.

Campbell, M. C., & Kirmani, A. (2000). Consumers' use of persuasion knowledge: The effects of accessibility and cognitive capacity on perceptions of an influence agent. *Journal of Consumer Research, 27*(1), 69–83.

Campbell, M. C., & Kirmani, A. (2008). I know what you're doing and why you're doing it: The use of persuasion knowledge model in consumer research. In C. P. Haugtvedt, P. M. Herr, & F. R. Kardes (Eds.), *Handbook of consumer psychology* (pp. 549–574). New York: Taylor & Francis Group.

Carlson, L., Grove, S. J., & Kangun, N. (1993). A content analysis of environmental advertising claims: A matrix method approach. *Journal of Advertising, 22*(3), 27–39.

Chabowski, B. R., Mena, J.A., & Gonzalez-Padron, T.L. (2011). The structure of sustainability research in marketing, 1958–2008: A basis for future research opportunities. *Journal of the Academy of Marketing Science, 39*(1), 55–70.

Chaiken, S., Liberman, A., & Eagly, A. H. (1989). Heuristic and systematic information processing within and beyond the persuasion context. In J. S. Uleman and J. A. Bargh (Eds.), *Unintended thought* (pp. 212–252). New York: Guilford Press.

Chan, R. Y. K. (2000). The effectiveness of environmental advertising: The role of claim type and the source country green image. *International Journal of Advertising, 19*(3), 349–375.

Chernev, A., & Carpenter, G. S. (2001). The role of market efficiency institutions in consumer choice: A case of compensatory inferences. *Journal of Marketing Research, 38*(3), 349–361.

Cialdini, R. B. (2001). *Influence: Science and practice.* Needham Heights, MA: Allyn and Bacon.

Cohen, J. B., & Reed, A., II (2006). A multiple pathway anchoring and adjustment (MPAA) model of attitude generation and recruitment. *Journal of Consumer Research, 33*(1), 1–15.

Darke, P. R., & Ritchie, R. J. B. (2007). The defensive consumer: Advertising deception, defensive processing, and distrust. *Journal of Marketing Research, 44*(1), 114–127.

DeCarlo, T. (2005). The effects of sales message and suspicion of ulterior motives on salesperson evaluation. *Journal of Consumer Psychology, 15*(3), 238–249.

Easterling, D., Kenworthy A., & Nemzoff, R. (1996). The greening of advertising: A twenty-five-year look at environmental advertising. *Journal of Marketing Theory and Practice, 4,* 20–34.

Ellen, P. S., Wiener, J. L., & Cobb-Walgren, C. (1991). The role of perceived consumer effectiveness in motivating environmentally conscious behaviors. *Journal of Public Policy & Marketing, 10*(2), 102–117.

Federal Trade Commission (FTC). (2011). *Guides for the use of environmental marketing claims.* www.ftc.gov/bcp/grnrule/guides980427.htm (accessed August 1, 2011).

Feldman, J. M., & Lynch, J. G., Jr. (1988). Self-generated validity and other effects of measurement on belief, attitude, intention, and behavior. *Journal of Applied Psychology, 73*(3), 421–435.

Forehand, M. R., & Grier, S. (2003). When is honesty the best policy? The effect of stated company intent on consumer skepticism. *Journal of Consumer Psychology, 13*(3), 349–356.

Friestad, M., & Wright, P. (1994). The persuasion knowledge model: How people cope with persuasion attempts. *Journal of Consumer Research, 21*(1), 1–31.

Friestad, M., & Wright, P. (1995). Persuasion knowledge: Lay people's and researchers' beliefs about the psychology of persuasion. *Journal of Consumer Research, 21*(1), 62–74.

Gawronski, B., & Bodenhausen, G. V. (2006). Associative and propositional processes in evaluation: An integrative review of implicit and explicit attitude change. *Psychological Bulletin, 132*(5), 692–731.

Grice, H. P. (1975). Logic and conversation. In P. Cole and J. L. Morgan (Eds.), *Syntax and semantics* (Vol. 3, pp. 41–58). New York: Academic Press.

Hartmann, P., & Apaolaza-Ibáñez, V. (2009). Green advertising revisited. *International Journal of Advertising, 28*(4), 715–739.

Iyer, E., & Zinkhan, G. M. (1994). Environmental marketing: Positive strategies for reaching the green consumer/green marketing: Challenges and opportunities for the new marketing age. *Journal of Marketing, 58*(2), 127–129.

Jain, S. P., & Posavac, S. S. (2004). Valenced comparisons. *Journal of Marketing Research, 41*(1), 46–58.

John, D. R. (1999). Consumer socialization of children: A retrospective look at twenty-five years of research. *Journal of Consumer Research, 26*(3), 183–213.

Kangun, N., Carlson, L., & Grove, S. J. (1991). Environmental advertising claims: A preliminary investigation. *Journal of Public Policy & Marketing, 10*(2), 47–58.

Kangun, N., & Polonsky, M. J. (1995). Regulation of environmental marketing claims: A comparative perspective. *International Journal of Advertising, 14*(1), 1–24.

Kilbourne, W. E. (1995). Green advertising: Salvation or oxymoron? *Journal of Advertising, 24*(2), 7–20.

Kilbourne, W. E., & Beckmann, S. C. (1998). Review and critical assessment of research on marketing and the environment. *Journal of Marketing Management, 14*(6), 513–532.

Kinnear, T. C., Taylor, J. R., & Ahmed, S. A. (1974). Ecologically concerned consumers: Who are they? *Journal of Marketing, 38*(2), 20–24.

Kirmani, A. (1990). The effect of perceived advertising costs on brand perceptions. *Journal of Consumer Research, 17*(September), 160–17.

Kirmani, A., & Campbell, M. C. (2004). Goal seeker and persuasion sentry: How consumer targets respond to interpersonal marketing persuasion. *Journal of Consumer Research, 31*(3), 573–582.

Kirmani, A., & Rao, A. R. (2000). No pain, no gain: A critical review of the literature on signaling unobservable product quality. *Journal of Marketing, 64*(2), 66–79.

Kirmani, A., & Wright, P. (1989). Money talks: Perceived advertising expense and expected product quality. *Journal of Consumer Research, 16*(3), 344–353.

Kirmani, A., & Zhu, R. (Juliet) (2007). Vigilant against manipulation: The effect of regulatory focus on the use of persuasion knowledge. *Journal of Marketing Research, 44*(4), 688–701.

Kotler, P. (2011). Reinventing marketing to manage the environmental imperative. *Journal of Marketing, 75*(4), 132–135.

Luchs, M. G., Naylor, R. W., Irwin, J. R., & Raghunathan, R. (2010). The sustainability liability: Potential negative effects of ethicality on product preference. *Journal of Marketing, 74*(5), 18–31.

Main, K. J., Dahl, D. W., & Darke, P. R. (2007). Deliberative and automatic bases of suspicion: Empirical evidence of the sinister attribution error. *Journal of Consumer Psychology, 17*(1), 59–69.

McCornack, S. A. (1992). Information manipulation theory. *Communication Monographs, 59*(1), 1–16.
Meyers-Levy, J., & Malaviya, P. (1999). Consumers' processing of persuasive advertisements: An integrative framework of persuasion theories. *Journal of Marketing, 63*(4), 45–60.
Mita, S., Bettman, J. R., & Sujan, H. (1986). Effects of consumer expectations on information processing in selling encounters. *Journal of Marketing Research, 23*(4), 346–353.
Montoro-Rios, F. J., Luque-Martínez, T., & Rodríguez-Molina, M.-A. (2008). How green should you be: Can environmental associations enhance brand performance? *Journal of Advertising Research, 48*(4), 547–563.
Morales, A. C. (2005). Giving firms an E for effort: Consumer responses to high-effort firms. *Journal of Consumer Research, 31*(4), 806–812.
Murphy, P. E., Kangun, N., & Locander, W. B. (1978). Environmentally concerned consumers—Racial variations. *Journal of Marketing, 42*(4), 61–66.
Nisbett, R. E., Peng, K.P., Choi, I.C., & Norenzayan, A. (2001). Culture and systems of thought: Holistic versus analytic cognition. *Psychological Review, 108*(2), 291–310.
Obermiller, C. (1995). The baby is sick/the baby is well: A test of environmental communication appeals. *Journal of Advertising, 24*(2), 55–70.
Obermiller, C., & Spangenberg, E. R. (1998). Development of a scale to measure consumer skepticism toward advertising. *Journal of Consumer Psychology, 7*(2), 159–186.
Petty, R. E. (2006). A metacognitive model of attitudes. *Journal of Consumer Research, 33*(1), 22–24.
Petty, R. E. & Cacioppo, J. T. (1986). *Communication and persuasion: Central and peripheral routes to attitude change.* New York: Springer.
Polonsky, M. J., Bailey, J., Baker, H., Basche, C., Jepson, C., & Neath, L. (1998). Communicating environmental information: Are marketing claims on packaging misleading? *Journal of Business Ethics, 17*(3), 281–294.
Richards, J. I., & Preston, I. L. (1992). Proving and disproving materiality of deceptive advertising claims. *Journal of Public Policy & Marketing, 11*(2), 45–56.
Richins, M. L. (1983). An analysis of consumer interaction styles in the marketplace. *Journal of Consumer Research, 10*(1), 73–82.
Scammon, D. L., & Mayer, R. N. (1995). Agency review of environmental marketing claims: Case-by-case decomposition of the issues. *Journal of Advertising, 24*(2), 33–43.
Schuhwerk, M. E., & Lefkoff-Hagius, R. (1995). Green or non-green? Does type of appeal matter when advertising a green product? *Journal of Advertising, 24*(2), 45–54.
Sen, S., & Bhattacharya, C. B. (2001). Does doing good always lead to doing better? Consumer reactions to corporate social responsibility. *Journal of Marketing Research, 38*(2), 225–243.
Sheth, J., Sethia, N.K., & Srinivas, S. (2011). Mindful consumption: A customer-centric approach to sustainability. *Journal of the Academy of Marketing Science, 39*(1), 21–39.
Shrum, L., & Lowrey, T. (1995). Applying social and traditional marketing principles to the reduction of household waste: Turning research into action. *American Behavioral Scientist, 38*, 646–657.
Shrum, L. J., McCarty, J. A. & Lowrey, Tina M. (1995). Buyer characteristics of the green consumer and their implications for advertising strategy. *Journal of Advertising, 24*(2), 71–82.
Stafford, M. R., Stafford, T. F., & Chowdhury, J. (1996). Predispositions toward green issues: The potential efficacy of advertising appeals. *Journal of Current Issues & Research in Advertising, 18*(1), 67–79.
Trope, Y., Liberman, N., & Wakslak, C. (2007). Construal levels and psychological distance: Effects on representation, prediction, evaluation, and behavior. *Journal of Consumer Psychology*, 17(2), 83–95.

Trudel, R., & Cotte, J. (2008, May 12). Does being ethical pay? *MIT Sloan Management Review, 50*(2), 61–69. http://sloanreview.mit.edu/executive-adviser/2008–2/5028/does-being-ethical-pay/.

Warlop, L., & Alba, J. W. (2004). Sincere flattery: Trade-dress imitation and consumer choice. *Journal of Consumer Psychology, 14*(1/2), 21–27.

Williams, P., & Drolet, A. (2005). Age-related differences in responses to emotional advertisements. *Journal of Consumer Research, 32*(3), 343–354.

Williams, P., Fitzsimons, G. J., & Block, L. G. (2004). When consumers do not recognize benign intention questions as persuasion attempts. *Journal of Consumer Research, 31*(3), 540–550.

Wright, P. (1986). Schemer schema: Consumers' intuitive theories about marketers' influence tactics. In Lutz, R. J. (Ed.), *Advances in Consumer Research* (Vol. 13, pp. 1–3). Provo, UT.

Xie, G.-X., & Boush, D. M. (2011). How susceptible are consumers to deceptive advertising claims? A retrospective look at the experimental research literature. *Marketing Review, 11*(3), 293–314.

Zinkhan, G. M., & Carlson, L. (1995). Green advertising and the reluctant consumer. *Journal of Advertising, 24*(2), 1–6.

10

Promoting Low-Carbon Policy to the Public

Message Framing Matters

Sidney Su Han, Ying Yu, and Lefa Teng

On July 1, 2008, the province of British Columbia (B.C.), Canada, embarked on an ambitious climate policy path when it implemented North America's first carbon tax law. B.C.'s carbon tax aimed to reduce carbon emissions and was praised by environmentalists and economists (Elgie, Rivers, & Olewiler, 2010). However, two years after implementation, when the preliminary assessment was conducted, a number of concerns were raised regarding the policy's effectiveness. Although thousands of variables affected the results of the evaluation, one factor cannot be ignored: effective communication with the public. The government should take responsibility for promoting the public policy among its citizens using effective communication strategies, rather than merely passing legislation to constrain people's behavior. For more than a decade, climate change has been widely recognized as a threat to sustainable development as well as the safety of human beings. The urgency of developing solutions to the climate change problem and the need for the rapid introduction of new, more sustainable approaches for businesses and industries have become more severe than ever (Scrase & Ockwell, 2009). Many governments, like B.C.'s, have established policies to prepare their citizens for the transition to a low-carbon energy system and society. However, according to a climate report by Van de Velde, Verbeke, Popp, and Van Huylenbroeck (2010), global carbon emissions continue to increase at an alarming rate, and the researchers claim that industry's practices under current energy policies are a long way from the kind of sustainable best practices proposed by the policies. Among the factors influencing the outcome of these policies, communication strategies for exposing the public to the low-carbon policy (LCP) have been receiving increased attention (Scrase & Ockwell, 2009).

Four main issues hinder the communication with the public and promotion of the LCP. First, the public in some regions is not sufficiently aware of the threat that climate change poses to human beings and the environment in which we live. Second, some citizens have not developed a positive attitude toward reducing carbon emissions and using new types of energy. Third, the public's knowledge of climate change and energy conservation is relatively limited (Van de Velde et al., 2010). Fourth, especially in developed countries, although a majority of citizens express concern about climate change and environmental protection, this concern does not translate into environmentally responsible behaviors, such as using public transportation, conserving energy, and using new, alternative sources of energies. Therefore, Davis (1995) argues that the challenges facing marketers who wish to change behavior for public good, are to identify specific approaches that motivate individuals to act on their concerns and take immediate action, while continuing to raise public awareness and aid in the development of positive cognitive and affective attitudes toward low-carbon and new energy policies.

This chapter addresses the communication issues faced by social marketers trying to promote LCP among the public in an effective and efficient manner. The theories of message-framing effects (Aaker & Lee, 2001; Higgins, Friedman, & Shah, 1997; Maheswaran & Meyers-Levy, 1990) act as the conceptual foundation, providing a theoretical base. A conceptual model of message framing is created in order to address two unsolved issues regarding LCP promotion: the formation of promotion goals that entail moving from awareness to action and interventional factors that affect message framing's effects on promotional goals. The model offers an integrated framework for solving communication problems systematically; for example, from building awareness, facilitating creation of implicit and explicit memories, changing cognitive and affective attitudes, and enhancing behavior intentions, to promoting specific actions and behaviors. The goal of the policy makers is not only to let people know about LCP (awareness and memory) and encourage them to like or accept it (attitude), but to also encourage them to take immediate action. Using this framework, public marketers can find ways to solve various communication problems and thereby accomplish this goal.

Conceptual Background (I): The Theory of Message-Framing Effects

In this section, the theory of message-framing effects is critically and systematically reviewed and analyzed in order to create a conceptual framework, facilitating its application to the promotion of LCP, which is discussed below. In this section, message framing is defined, then the main effects of message framing are investigated, and, finally, major influences on the message framing effects are explained.

Message Framing

Message framing is defined in many different ways. Similar messages (equivalent property of information) can be phrased using either a positive or negative approach. Message framing is widely studied as a way to emphasize the pursuit of a promotion focus (positive outcome) and the avoidance of a prevention focus (negative

Table 10.1

Summary of Different Message Framing Approaches

	Outcome focus (anchor)	
	Loss end-state	Gain end-state
Achievement/Promotion		
Negative valence	Presence of loss outcome (loss)	Absence of gain outcome (nongain)
Positive valence	Absence of loss outcome (nonloss)	Presence of gain outcome (gain)
Security/Prevention		
Negative valence	Presence of loss outcome (loss)	Absence of gain outcome (nongain)
Positive valence	Absence of loss outcome (nonloss)	Presence of gain outcome (gain)

Sources: Modified from Yi and Baumgartner (2008, 2009).

outcome) (Aaker & Lee, 2006; Yi & Baumgartner, 2008). Promotion message framing stresses the achievement of a desirable outcome, whereas prevention message framing highlights the motivation to avoid undesirable outcomes.

Yi and Baumgartner (2008, 2009) reviewed prior studies of message framing and concluded that message framing may be phrased using one of at least three approaches: (1) the message is phrased from the perspective of the outcome focus of the message, such as gains or losses framing; (2) the message is phrased from the perspective of the overall valence of the message, such as a positive or negative valence; and (3) the message is phrased from the perspective of the potential benefit or harm that is emphasized, such as achievement and security. The different framing approaches are summarized in Table 10.1.

Message-Framing Effects

Messages can be phrased within different frames, and different message framing approaches can produce different impacts on viewers' responses to the messages. The message-framing effect has been investigated in many disciplines, including psychology (Berry & Carson, 2010), communications (Davis, 1995), marketing (Chang, 2007), and consumer behavior (Aaker & Lee, 2001). It is generally accepted that message framing can affect the cognitive and affective processing of a message (Lee & Aaker, 2004), attitude and behavior (Levin & Gaeth, 1988), and judgment and decision making (McClure, White, & Sibley, 2009). In this section, message framing is discussed in terms of its main effects on five dependent variables: awareness, memory, attitude, behavior, judgment, and choice. These variables have been chosen for discussion and examination because each is part of the process of promoting LCP among the public, from raising awareness to stimulating action and behavior.

Awareness

Message framing can help raise awareness. Differently framed messages can have different impacts in terms of raising people's awareness of a certain issue. O'Connor, Warttig, Conner, and Lawton (2009) conducted a study exploring the efficacy of a Web-based intervention aimed at raising awareness concerning the risks associated with high blood pressure and hypertension. The study shows that a prevention-framed message was more effective in raising people's awareness of the target issue than a promotion-framed message, even though this effect was moderated by another variable: consideration of future consequences. The underlying reason for this effect was that the prevention-framed message drew more of the audience's attention to the message in this context, resulting in stronger awareness of the message, whereas the promotion-framed message was not as attractive as the prevention-framed one, and thus it was less effective in raising awareness. This effect could be used to build the public's awareness of LCP, through applying proper message framing to LCP promotional campaigns.

Memory

Message framing also affects cognitive responses to messages by influencing memory differently according to how a message's content or information is framed. Aaker and Lee (2001) found that Americans are likely to recall more after viewing a promotion-framed advertising message than after viewing a prevention-framed adverting message. Meyerowitz and Chaiken (1987) examined subjects' responses to two pamphlets that used either gain or loss framing. However, they concluded that the pamphlet with negative framing (prevention) generated a better memory of the contents than the pamphlet with positive framing (promotion). They explain that the underlying reason the prevention-framed message could have led to a stronger memory was that participants likely processed the prevention-framed message for longer than the promotion-framed message. It is unclear, however, why framing's effects on memory are inconsistent between studies. The effect of message framing on memory is very important for social marketers to consider when they intend to educate the public about low-carbon facts and policy. Marketers could use the message-framing effect to provide people with knowledge of the LCP in an effective manner, such as letting the public know about the threat of climate change, the benefits of LCP, and which everyday behaviors can be adopted to reduce carbon emissions.

Attitude and Behavior

Different message-framing strategies can influence viewers' attitudes and behaviors in very different ways. Davis (1995) conducted a study exploring the effect of message framing on people's responses to communications about the environment.

Through a three-factor design experimental study, it was found that people establish the most positive attitudes about being environmentally responsible and build the greatest intention to participate in environmentally friendly behaviors (such as recycling) after viewing the communication that discussed losses to the current generation (negative framing), compared to the positive framing strategy (Davis, 1995). Meyerowitz and Chaiken (1987), in their research concerning the effect of message framing on attitudes and behaviors surrounding breast self-examination, claim that subjects who read a pamphlet with an argument framed in loss language manifested more positive attitudes and behaviors about breast self-examination than those who were exposed to the gain message. In the case of promoting LCP among the public, shaping the public's positive attitude toward LCP and encouraging them to behave in a pro-LCP manner are two major communication goals for promotional campaigns, so studying how to use appropriate message framing will help marketers inspire the attitudes and behaviors that they want people to adopt.

Judgments and Choices

Message framing can also influence judgment and choice. Kahneman (2003), after reviewing earlier studies of intuitive judgment and decision making, defines "accessibility" as the ease with which thoughts come to mind; intuitive thoughts, like percepts, are highly accessible. The researcher investigates how different approaches to message framing could affect judgment and choice by influencing a message's accessibility: The same property might be highly accessible in one message, framed a certain way, but not in another that is framed differently, even though both messages contain the same information (Kahneman, 2003). Furthermore, the study claims that framing effects could affect decision making as well. In promoting LCP among the public, influencing the public's judgment of how LCP will affect their lives and the public's choices concerning LCP-related behaviors are also important for communication and promotional campaigns. Employing appropriate message framing in LCP promotional campaigns will definitely help social marketers influence the public's judgments and choices.

Influential Factors

An analysis of the results of previous research on message framing indicates that message-framing effects can be inconsistent and contradictory. For example, some studies indicate that a promotion-framed message is more persuasive than a prevention-framed one, whereas other studies show the reverse. Ignoring some moderating factors, which can influence the message-framing effects, may yield these controversial research results. Therefore, message-framing researchers have identified various moderators, which can influence the effects of message framing. In this section, we discuss the most commonly considered moderators of message-framing effects.

Self-regulatory goals play a significant role in moderating the effect of message framing on an individual's response to a message. Several studies (Aaker & Lee, 2001, 2006; Higgins, Shah, & Friedman, 1997; Kim, 2006; Lee & Aaker, 2004) report that a strong fit between the self-regulatory goal and message framing enhances processing fluency and persuasion, which consequently improves the message-framing effects. For example, a message presented within a gain/promotion frame is more persuasive to an individual who has a promotion self-regulatory focus, whereas a message presented within a loss/prevention frame is more persuasive to an individual with a prevention self-regulatory focus. However, researchers find that in a situation in which message framing does not match a viewer's self-regulatory focus, the effect of message framing will be compromised or may even disappear. For example, when an individual with a promotional self-regulatory goal views a prevention/loss-framed message, the framed message may not affect the viewer's response to the message, so persuasion may not occur in this situation due to a poor fit. In the LCP promotion context, marketers should learn what style of self-regulation is dominant among members of their target audience and frame their messages accordingly, in order to maximize the communication effects by creating a strong fit between viewers' self-regulatory goals and how messages are framed.

Involvement is another important moderator that explains the inconsistencies among several studies concerning message-framing effects, although the results are mixed. Maheswaran and Meyers-Levy (1990) report that positively framed messages may be more persuasive when relatively little emphasis is placed on the details in the message (low involvement), but negatively framed messages may be more persuasive when the processing of details is emphasized (high involvement). Another study (Durairaj & Meyers-Levy, 1990) also reported finding that a promotion-framed message is more effective in low-involvement situations whereas a prevention-framed message is more effective in a high-involvement situation. However, the study conducted by Aaker and Lee (2006) claims that in the low-involvement condition, a prevention-framed message usually generated more powerful impacts than a promotion-framed message, while in the high-involvement condition message framing did not affect individual cognitive processing and persuasion. In the context of LCP promotion, marketers should understand the public's level of involvement with LCP-related issues and then decide which framing strategy should be employed in a promotional campaign because, as explained above, the level of involvement could affect the message-framing effects.

Message-framing effects can also be moderated by subjective product knowledge and information (Cox, Cox, & Zimet, 2006). When Kim and Park (2010) studied the effect of message framing on the effectiveness of direct-to-consumer advertising concerning the use of prescription medicine, they found that drug use intentions were significantly related to the interaction between message frame and subjective knowledge. Their results indicate that when individuals have low knowledge of the target product, negatively framed messages have a greater impact on their intention to use the drug. In contrast, when individuals have more knowledge of the target product, both frames equally influence their intentions. Some researchers argue that subjective knowledge could mediate processing of the target message as well as influence the involvement of an individual's information processing (Kim & Park, 2010). Therefore, the public's knowledge of LCP should be investigated before promotional campaigns are planned and conducted, because the public's knowledge level will influence the effect of different message-framing strategies, and marketers can set up different communication goals based on their knowledge of the public's current level of knowledge concerning LCP.

Culture also influences message-framing effects, as indicated by several studies focused on framing (Chen, Ng, & Rao, 2005; Orth, Oppenheim, & Firbasova, 2005). In a study of consumer impatience conducted by Chen et al. (2005), results showed a clear interaction between message framing and culture. They found that a promotion-framed message affects individuals from Western cultures more than a prevention-framed message does, while the latter will have a greater impact on individuals from Eastern cultures. Clearly, the impact that message framing has on the cognitive and affective responses of individuals depends on their cultural background. Cross-cultural variations in how people perceive different message frames influence message-framing effects. In the context of promoting LCP among the public, understanding the dominant cultural backgrounds of the target audience will be important for planning message-framing strategies, especially in mixed-culture regions and cross-cultural campaigns.

Another influential factor that could affect message-framing effects is the compatibility or conflict between a target message's goal (promotion or prevention) and prior advertising messages for related products. Labroo and Lee (2006) identify this moderator in their study evaluating the effect of advertising message goals on attitudes toward brands when participants are exposed sequentially to advertisements for two products (prime and target). The researchers claim that the target advertising message will have a more powerful impact on brand evaluation only if the two advertisement messages are compatible with each other in their message framing. The study also explores how goal fluency mediates the moderation of goal compatibility on framing effect, since participants will be more influenced by the target advertising message, due to experiencing goal fluency, if the prime advertising message is framed in a manner that is compatible with the target advertising message. In the context of promoting LCP among the public, when conducting media planning or scheduling promotional activities (such as mass media advertisements), marketers should consider the compatibility of message framing between the LCP advertisement and prior advertisements or media characteristics (positive or negative frame based) in order to maximize communication's message-framing effect.

Conceptual Background (II): Low-Carbon Policy (LCP)

It is generally accepted by respected scientists that human activity is altering the climate. Due to a century and a half of increasing fossil fuel consumption by humans, the level of carbon dioxide in the atmosphere is now 35 percent higher than it was in the preindustrial era (Lewis, 2009). This increase has arguably caused extreme weather events (e.g., hurricanes and tornados), changed weather patterns, and natural disasters (e.g., floods, droughts, and wildfires). In addition, the increase in carbon dioxide emissions has led glacial, Arctic, and Antarctic ice to melt, causing sea levels to rise and generating a significant threat to biodiversity and human security (Greer, Ng, & Fishman, 2008). In addition, climate change poses substantial risks to human health and has been found to be a major cause of some public health problems, for example, heat stroke and mosquito-borne infections (Diaz, 2006). Scientists predict that even if all emissions were to stop today, the carbon dioxide that has already accumulated in the atmosphere would remain there for decades, resulting in further climate change and future impacts (Lewis, 2009).

Within the context of global climate change, the notion of a low-carbon economy has become an increasing topic of discussion around the world. A "low-carbon economy" refers to an economy based on three criteria: low power consumption, low pollution, and low emissions (Chi, Zhang, Song, & Chi, 2010). In a low-carbon economy, human development and carbon production can be balanced at a certain level, realizing the vision of controlling carbon dioxide emissions. Clearly, it is urgent for the carbon dioxide emissions created through economic and industrial activity to be reduced. According to Chi et al. (2010), the current approach to controlling international carbon emissions includes three options: improving energy conservation and energy efficiency (e.g., reducing consumption of fossil-fuel-based energy); adjusting energy structures and developing low-carbon economies (e.g., reducing coal-dominant and oil-dominant energy generation and increasing wind and solar power generation); and capturing and storing carbon.

Because climate change is both a global and a local issue, LCPs have been established, or attempts have been made to establish them, at multiple levels in order to control and reduce carbon emissions and address climate change. Internationally, several treaties and agreements have been signed by the United Nations (UN) and its members, for example, the UN Framework Convention on Climate Change (UNFCCC) (1994), the Kyoto Protocol (1997), and the Copenhagen Accord (2009). Even though their efficacy is arguable, these treaties at least provide frameworks within which global emission-reduction targets can be negotiated. At the national level, early in 2005 the Japanese government instituted an environmental tax program, providing tax breaks for environmentally responsible households. For example, drivers of high-emission vehicle were able to reduce their tax by 50 percent to 60 percent by trading in their vehicle for a low-emission one. In 2009, the U.S. government announced that it would provide $41 billion in tax incentives to encourage the use of renewable energy and efficient energy technologies, such as hybrid and fuel-cell vehicles, solar- and gas-powered water-heating systems, wind power, and biomass and gas cogeneration systems (Chi et al., 2010). The Canadian government set a target of reducing total carbon emissions in Canada by 20 percent by 2020, beginning in 2006 (Environment Canada, 2009). Furthermore, it announced the regulation of fuel standards for vehicles and funded activities across the country for projects aimed at the development of biofuels (Environment Canada, 2013).

Although governments have implemented regulations and passed policies in an attempt to reduce carbon emissions, many of these policies have not succeeded in realizing their goals. The barriers to the effective implementation of policies are likely many. One major barrier is related to policy itself. A policy cannot be successful if it does not take into account the triple-bottom-line: balancing environmental focus, social equity, and economic viability. The policy must include good trade-offs for society, industry, and individuals (Coffman & Umemoto, 2010). Moreover, the influence of discourse and linguistic-framing effects can be crucial for sustaining the dominance of existing policy positions (Scrase & Ockwell, 2009). Burch (2010) studied three cities in B.C. and their residents to investigate the sociocultural and institutional barriers to undertaking actions at the local level to prevent climate change. At the organizational level, incentives are one of the biggest barriers to implementing LCP, whereas at the individual level, a lack of publicity related to LCP is blocking the policy's execution. Brick and Visser (2010) found that communication between policy makers and the public can significantly increase individuals' cooperation with policy implementation.

Conceptual Framework: A Model of Message Framing for LCP Promotion

The effective promotion of LCP among the public is crucial for its success. According to policy research, any public policy needs to be communicated to the public in order for it to be effective. Without sufficient publicity, public policy will not be successful (Scrase & Ockwell, 2010). If a policy is effectively communicated to the public, residents will have knowledge about it, they can develop an attitude toward the policy, and they can also take appropriate action.

As explained above, policy makers and public marketers face some challenges when launching LCP promotional campaigns targeting the public. The first challenge is that in some regions, especially in some developing countries, awareness of the threat of climate change to humans and the environment is relatively low. Second, a positive attitude toward reducing carbon emissions and using new types of energy has not been fostered. For example, the majority of the population in Belgium believes that the climate problem is exaggerated (Van de Velde et al., 2010). Also, the public's knowledge of climate change and energy conservation is generally limited. For example, not many people know about new types of fuels and vehicles (Van de Velde et al., 2010). Moreover, especially in developed countries, even though a majority of citizens express concern about climate change and environmental protection, such attitudes do not translate into environmentally responsible behaviors, such as conserving energy, using new energy, and using public transportation. Therefore, Davis (1995) argues that the challenges that social marketers face are identifying specific approaches that motivate individuals to act on their concerns immediately and producing awareness and positive cognitive and affective attitudes about low-carbon and new energy policies.

Although many factors affect the communication results of LCP, message-framing strategies significantly influence the effectiveness of LCP promotion. According to communication theory, the success of a communication depends on how a sender encodes a message and how a receiver decodes it, as well as the message channel. In this process, message framing plays an important role in communication effectiveness, because it affects how receivers decode the message and what information and impressions they gain. This is the case with any kind of message, including those related to environmental responsibility. For example, Joutsenvirta (2009) beneficially analyzed the language managers and other societal actors, such as Greenpeace, use to describe and explain environmental and social problems. Therefore, the proper use of message-framing strategies is important for effective communication of LCP to the public.

To the author's knowledge, message framing's effect on LCP promotion has not been previously investigated, although some studies have focused on the effects of message framing on general pro-environmental promotion (Davis, 1995; Van de Velde, et al 2010). However, the majority of earlier studies of pro-environmental promotion focus on the main effects of message framing without considering the interactional functions of some moderator factors, that is, only studying which effects could be created by using different message frames (promotion versus prevention). For example, Van de Velde et al. (2010) conducted a study on the importance of message framing for providing information about sustainability and environmental aspects of energy, and they claim that individuals' attitudes and behavioral intentions can be significantly influenced by the choice of message frame. The study, however, ignores any psychological or situational variables that could moderate message framing's effect on attitude and behavioral intention. Therefore, if we use the results of that research to conduct a promotional campaign for LCP, the promotion may not work optimally due to the study's insufficiencies.

Another limitation of some previous studies of message framing for pro-environmental promotion is that they concentrate on only one or a few effects of message framing without considering the integration of the effects. As we know, the final goal of the policy is to encourage people to take action (behavior), but in order to achieve such a goal, individuals must go through the whole cognitive process, including building awareness, establishing a positive attitude, remembering the information, developing strong behavioral intentions, and, finally, taking action. Few previous studies have considered how the effects of message framing could work within this dynamic process, from one step to the next. For example, Davis (1995) studies the effect of message framing on responses to environmental

Figure 10.1 **The Conceptual Model of Message Framing for Low-Carbon Policy (LCP) Promotion**

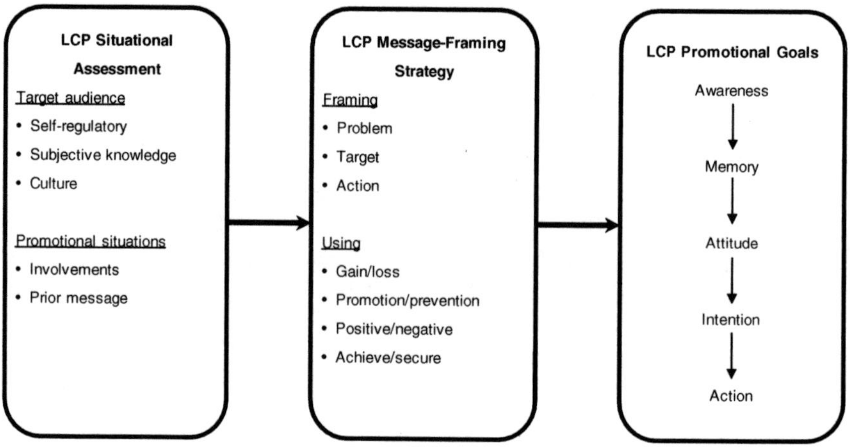

communications, and the major dependent variable in this study is the responder's level of intention to adopt environmentally responsible behaviors. Without considering the communication goals as being achieved through a process that moves from awareness to action, promotional activities cannot maximize their effectiveness and efficiency.

In order to solve the communication problems of the LCP promotion, a new model needs to be created and applied in practice. Based on the theory of message-framing effects, we developed a model of message framing for LCP promotion, taking into account the features of LCP promotion and the limitations of prior studies of message framing's effects on pro-environmental promotion (see Figure 10.1). This model not only provides a theoretical framework for applying message framing theory to LCP promotion, but also offers practical guidelines for social marketers who wish to apply message-framing theory to the promotion of LCP to the public.

This is the first conceptual model to be developed about message framing for LCP promotion, and it is unique compared to other theoretical frameworks for message framing's effects on promotion. First, the model considers the achievement of LCP promotional goals as an integrated process of cognitive and behavioral responses to message framing, rather than as a response to one or more message-framing effects. Second, the model addresses the several moderators that influence the effect of message framing on LCP promotional goals, such as the target audience's self-regulation, culture, and level of involvement. If these factors are not understood before message frames are designed for promotional activities, uncertainty about reaching effective communication results can be greater.

The Application of the Model of Message Framing for LCP Promotion

Because message-framing theory thoroughly explains the effectiveness of the communication strategy of different framings in various conditions, it has been widely studied for its applications in many fields, such as environmental communications (Davis, 1995), promoting new energy (Scrase & Ockwell, 2010; Van de Velde et al., 2010), disaster preparation (McClure et al., 2009); and healthy behavior communications (Meyerowitz & Chaiken, 1987; Rothman, Bartels, Wlaschin, & Salovey, 2006). The model of message framing for LCP promotion extends the application of message-framing theory to the promotion of LCP to the public. In this section, a variety of communication strategies and issues related to promoting LCP based on the model is discussed.

Understanding the communication situation is the first important and necessary step for any effective promotional campaign or activity. Public marketers usually feel challenged when analyzing situations because they lack clear and solid guidelines for strong situational analyses. The model for message framing for LCP promotion could guide public marketers in performing situational analyses before they plan promotional campaigns to promote LCP to the public.

According to the model, understanding the target audience's demographic and psychographic information (self-regulation, subjective knowledge, and culture) will help public marketers develop message-framing strategies. According to the theory of message-framing effects, a particular message-framing strategy could have different impacts on individuals in different situations. For example, a promotion- and gain-framed message may be more effective for individuals with a fitting self-regulatory goal (promotion) who are from a Western culture, whereas a prevention- and loss-framed message may be more effective for those with a prevention self-regulatory goal who are from an Eastern culture. Therefore, it is best to conduct thorough research on the cultural background, self-regulation, and subjective knowledge about LCP of the target population before such messages are planned. Marketers would be well advised to discover general patterns for any or all of these factors as they will be helpful in an effective framing strategy for the communication of LCP promotion.

Based on analysis of the situation, messages can be planned and developed by choosing appropriate message-framing strategies. The first step is determining a clear and solid communication objective, which plays a crucial role in message planning. According to the model, several other steps in a cognitive process must take place in order for the final goal (action or behavior) to be achieved. For example, a promotional campaign might aim first to build awareness, followed by shaping attitudes, and finally encouraging behavior. According to the model of message framing for LCP promotion, the employment of different framing strategies will help achieve different communication goals. It is important that public marketers understand what specific goals to achieve (and at what stage of the process) before designing their message-framing strategy.

Which message-framing strategies should be selected in the promotion of LCP? Based on the environmental message-framing theory developed by Davis (1995), the model of message framing for LCP promotion proposes that three issues (problems, targets, and actions) can be framed using four different strategies: gain versus loss, promotion versus prevention, positive versus negative, and achieve versus secure.

First, climate change and environmental problems can be framed using either a gains or a losses message-framing strategy, emphasizing either positive or negative information in the communication. One example of a gain framing message is, "Use public transit: conserve energy and resources, and slow climate change," while an example of a loss framing message is, "By not using public transit, you waste energy and resources and worsen climate change." Next, communication messages can frame the communication target as one affecting either current or future generations. Climate change issues may be framed in a short-term (current generation) or long-term (future generations) context. For example, a message can be framed in four different ways using the problem and target axis: gain for current or future generations versus loss for current or future generations. The last approach is to frame action according to a strategy of either taking less (e.g., driving your own car less) or doing more (e.g., using public transit more). Although message-framing theory does not suggest which strategy is more likely to be persuasive, it will be very helpful for public marketers to consider the moderating factors of message-framing effects when determining which strategy should be used.

After message planning is complete, message execution and implementation are prepared for. One relevant issue related to application of the model for LCP promotion is media selection, specifically for campaigns using mass media. According to the theoretical model, one variable (prior message framing) will affect the audience's processing fluency of the target message. If two consequential advertisements have fitting message framing (promotion to promotion), the audience will be more likely to respond positively to the second advertisement. However, if the message framing between two advertisements is not a good fit, the audience will not experience a smooth processing of messages, which will lead to ineffective message communication. Therefore, when media are purchased, unfit message framing with the target message should be strictly avoided so as not to compromise the effectiveness of the communication. The last issue that public marketers should keep in mind is that, when planning and implementing message framing strategies, they should take into account other message and communication strategies used in the promotion, even though the model does not include these factors and variables.

Conclusion

Climate change threatens the security of humans and our living environment, and LCP will help reduce carbon emissions and protect our environment. In order to promote LCP to the public, an effective communication strategy should be employed by public marketers. This paper uses the theory of message-framing effects as a conceptual framework to create a model of message framing for LCP promotion (Figure 10.1), and the model also takes into account the features of LCP promotion and the limitations of current models of message framing for pro-environmental promotions. The model is the first conceptual framework to explain the effect of message framing for LCP promotion, extending message-framing theory to LCP promotion and sustainability literature. Practically speaking, the model provides a guide for public marketers promoting LCP to the public, offering an integrated approach to solving communication problems related to LCP promotion. Applying the model of message framing for LCP promotion into practice could help increase the communication effectiveness and efficiency of LCP promotion, maximizing the impact of message-framing effects. Due to limited resources, the current paper focuses only on conceptual discussions and development, without providing sufficient empirical evidence to show the efficacy of the theoretical framework, which could be explored in future research. Also, the model covers only a few variables that influence the effects of message framing, and future research could reveal more factors to investigate in relation to message framing's effects on LCP promotion.

References

Aaker, J.L., & Lee, A.Y. (2001). "I" seek pleasures and "we" avoid pains: The role of self-regulatory goals in information processing and persuasion. *Journal of Consumer Research, 28*(1), 33–49.

Aaker, J.L., & Lee, A.Y. (2006). Understanding regulatory fit. *Journal of Marketing Research, 43*(1), 15–19.

Berry, T.R., & Carson, V. (2010). Ease of imagination, message framing, and physical activity messages. *British Journal of Health Psychology, 15*(1), 197–211.

Brick, K., & Visser, M. (2010). Meeting a national emission reduction target in an experimental setting. *Climate Policy, 10,* 543–559.

Burch, S. (2010). In pursuit of resilient, low carbon communities: An examination of barriers to actions in three Canadian cities. *Energy Policy, 38*(12), 7575–7585.

Chang, C. (2007). Interactive effects of message framing, product perceived risk, and mood. The case of travel healthcare product advertising. *Journal of Advertising Research, 47*(1), 51–65.

Chen, H., Ng, S., & Rao, A.R. (2005). Cultural differences in consumer impatience. *Journal of Marketing Research, 42*(3), 291–301.

Chi, Y.Y., Zhang, L.J., Song, Y., & Chi, Y.Q. (2010). The revelation of foreign carbon emission policies for developing China low-carbon economy. *Canadian Social Science, 6*(2), 44–52.

Coffman, M., & Umemoto, K. (2010). The triple-bottom-line: Framing of trade-offs in sustainability planning practice. *Environment, Development, Sustainability, 12,* 597–610.

Cox, A.D., Cox, D., & Zimet, G. (2006). Understanding consumer responses to product risk information. *Journal of Marketing, 70*(1), 79–91.

Davis, J.J. (1995). The effects of message framing on response to environmental communications. *Journalism and Mass Communication Quarterly, 72*(2), 285–299.

Diaz, H.J. (2006). Global climate changes, natural disasters and travel health risks. *Journal of Travel Medicine, 13*(6), 361–372.

Durairaj, M., & Meyers-Levy, J. (1990). Influence of message framing and issue involvement. *Journal of Marketing Research, 27*(3), 361–367.

Elgie, S., Rivers, N., & Olewiler, N. (2010, July 28). B.C. carbon-tax risk paying off. *Edmonton Journal.*

Environment Canada. (2009–2010). Report on Plans and Priorities for Environment Canada. http://www.tbs-sct.gc.ca/rpp/2009–2010/inst/doe/doe-eng.pdf (accessed July 25, 2013).

Environment Canada Fuel Regulations. 2013. http://www.ec.gc.ca/energie-energy/default.asp?lang=En&n=EE068DA8–1 (accessed July 25, 2013).

Greer, A., Ng, V. & Fishman, D. (2008). Climate change and infectious diseases in North American: The road ahead. *Canadian Medical Association Journal, 178*(6), 715–722.

Higgins, E. T., Friedman, R.S., & Shah, J. (1997). Emotional responses to goal attainment: Strength of regulatory focus as moderator. *Journal of Personality and Social Psychology, 72*(3), 515–525.

Joutsenvirta, M. (2009). A language perspective to environmental management and corporate responsibility. *Business Strategy and the Environment, 7*(18), 240–253.

Kahneman, D. (2003). A perspective on judgment and choice mapping bounded rationality. *American Psychologist, 58*(9), 672–720.

Kim, K., & Park, J. (2010). Message framing and the effectiveness of DTC advertising: The moderating role of subjective product knowledge. *Journal of Medical Marketing, 10*(2), 165–176.

Kim, Y. (2006). The role of regulatory focus in message framing in antismoking advertisements for adolescents. *Journal of Advertising, 35*(1), 143–151.

Labroo, A.A., & Lee, A.Y. (2006). Between two brands: A goal fluency account of brand evaluation. *Journal of Marketing Research, 43*(3), 374–385.

Lee, A.Y., & Aaker, J.L. (2004). Bringing the frame into focus: The influence of regulatory fit on processing fluency and persuasion. *Journal of Personality and Social Psychology, 86*(2), 205–218.

Levin, I.P., & Gaeth, G.J. (1988). How consumers are affected by the framing of attribute information before and after consuming the product. *Journal of Consumer Research, 15*(3), 374–378.

Lewis, J.I. (2009). Climate change and security. *International Affairs, 85*(6), 1195–1213.

Maheswaran, D., & Meyers-Levy, J. (1990). The influence of message framing and issue involvement. *Journal of Marketing Research, 27*(3), 361–367.

McClure, J., White, J., & Sibley, C.G. (2009). Framing effects on preparation intentions: Distinguishing actions and outcomes. *Disaster Prevention and Management, 18*(2), 187–199.

Meyerowitz, B.E., & Chaiken, S. (1987). The effect of message framing on breast self-examination attitudes, intentions, and behavior. *Journal of Personality and Social Psychology, 52*(3), 500–510.

O'Connor, D.B., Warttig, S., Conner, M., & Lawton, R. (2009). Raising awareness of hypertension risk through a web-based framing intervention: Does consideration of future consequence make a difference? *Psychology, Health and Medicine, 14*(2), 213–219.

Orth, U.R., Oppenheim, P.P., & Firbasova, Z. (2005). Measuring message framing effects across Europe. *Journal of Targeting, Measurement and Analysis for Marketing, 13*(4), 313–326.

Rothman, A.J., Bartels, R.D., Wlaschin, J., & Salovey, P. (2006). The strategic use of gain- and loss- framed messages to promote healthy behavior: How theory can inform practice. *Journal of Communication, 56,* S202–S220.

Scrase, J., & Ockwell, D. (2009). Energy issues: Framing and policy change in energy for the future, a new agenda. Basingstoke: Palgrave Macmillan.

Scrase, J., & Ockwell, D. (2010). The role of discourse and linguistic framing effects in sustaining high carbon energy policy—An accessible introduction. *Energy Policy, 38*(5), 2225–2233.

Van de Velde, L., Verbeke, W., Popp, M., & Van Huylenbroeck, G. (2010). The importance of message framing for providing information about sustainability and environmental aspects of energy. *Energy Policy, 38*(10), 5541–5549.

Yi, S., & Baumgartner, H. (2008). Motivational compatibility and the role of anticipated feelings in positively valenced persuasive message framing. *Psychology & Marketing, 25*(11), 1007–1026.

Yi, S., & Baumgartner, H. (2009). Regulatory focus and message framing: A test of three accounts. *Motivation and Emotion, 33*(4), 435–443.

11

Consumer Creativity and Its Implications for Sustainability Marketing

Xiaojing Yang, Melissa G. Bublitz, Kai-Yu Wang, and Laura A. Peracchio

Time is of the essence. Now is the time to encourage policymakers and consumers alike to adopt a creative mindset, allowing them to envision innovative ways of engaging in environmentally responsible consumption. Why seek more creative problem-solving approaches in the area of environmental sustainability? Despite the best efforts of environmental advocates, educators, and policymakers to encourage sustainable behavior, many parts of the United States struggle to meet their environmental goals. As an example, New York City "recycles about 16 percent of its residential trash, falling short of the 25 percent goal specified in its recycling law" (Navarro, 2009). The total amount of municipal solid waste discarded in landfill in the United States, after accounting for recycling efforts, was virtually the same in 2007 as it was 1960, approximately 2.5 pounds per person a day (EPA, 2007). Although the United States recycles more trash today than 50 years ago, more household waste is sent to landfill than in 1960 due to population growth and greater consumption. Experts and researchers alike believe "the seriousness of environmental degradation, the clear depletion of and constraints to natural resources" urgently require change (Press & Arnould, 2009).

In this chapter, we build a case for encouraging more creative thinking to develop environmental solutions and encourage future generations of consumers to engage in environmentally conscious consumption. First, we review the literature on environmentally conscious consumption. Second, we look at how research on consumer creativity may be used to cultivate new environmental ideas and solutions as well as to promote environmentally responsible behavior. Finally, we examine how creative advertising can help promote environmental consciousness and responsible consumption behaviors.

Environmentally Conscious Consumption

Early research on consumption activities painted a picture of the environmentally conscious consumer as young, affluent, and highly educated (for a review, see

Granzin & Olsen, 1991). However, Kinnear, Taylor, and Ahmed (1974) dispelled the notion that demographic variables were the main predictor of which consumers were more likely to engage in environmentally conscious consumption and shifted the focus to personality traits. Personal values such as altruism and frugality, in addition to a desire for personal satisfaction from helping the environment, were found to motivate consumers to engage in recycling and other environmentally conscious behaviors (Granzin & Olsen, 1991). When consumers believe that their individual actions in recycling directly improve the environment (Berger & Corbin, 1992; Ellen, Wiener, & Cobb-Walgren, 1991), recycling efforts are strengthened. However, understanding the characteristics of consumers who engage in environmental behaviors is only the first step in increasing socially responsible consumption.

As marketers and public policy officials began to seek opportunities beyond identifying individual characteristics of those who conserve and recycle, research shifted to investigating how policymakers can encourage environmentally responsible consumer behavior. Investigating attitudes toward waste reduction revealed that social appeals may be more effective than personal appeals (Taylor & Todd, 1995). In addition, researchers found that education to enhance consumers' perceptions about their individual ability to engage in waste reduction as well as simplifying steps toward waste reduction were critical to influencing recycling compliance (Taylor & Todd, 1995).

Not all consumers are motivated in the same way. Some consumers are intrinsically motivated to engage in environmentally responsible behaviors that satisfy psychological and altruistic needs and create personal satisfaction. However, other consumers are motivated to engage in environmentally conscious behaviors when provided with some extrinsic motivation such as a reward for doing so or a punishment for noncompliance. It is important to understand whether the underlying motivation for environmental behaviors stems from intrinsic or extrinsic goals since goal source influences the staying power of behavioral change. Specifically, intrinsic motivation may prompt more persistence and a sustained commitment to pro-social goals (Grant, 2008). As an added benefit, consumers who are intrinsically motivated to engage in environmentally responsible behaviors report higher confidence in their ability to perform recycling, set more rigorous environmental goals, and derive more personal satisfaction from fulfilling those goals (Tabernero & Hernández, 2011). Further, environmentally conscious behaviors resulting from extrinsic motivation such as financial incentives or punishment may not result in lasting or long-term changes after incentives or rewards are removed (Porter, Leeming, & Dwyer, 1995). Finding ways to motivate environmental behaviors by consumers, encouraging them to internalize attitudes and environmental consumption goals, may result in permanent and lasting behavioral change.

One way to shift attitudes toward environmentally responsible behavior comes from exposure to environmental literature and education that increases environmental sensitivity. For example, consumers who read classical environmental literature such as *A Sand County Almanac, Walden,* and *Silent Spring* were more likely to engage in environmentally responsible behavior (Mobley, Vagias, & DeWard, 2010). These researchers suggest that incorporating environmental sensitivity and knowledge into formative educational efforts can positively influence environmental attitudes as well as encourage behavioral changes. Further, an examination of the environmental attitude shift among adolescents reveals that when young consumers believe that resources are scarce, environmentally responsible consumption increases (Wray-Lake, Flanagan, & Osgood, 2010). However, as materialism among young consumers increases, environmentally conscious behavior decreases (Mobley et al., 2010). These findings point to opportunities to educate and sensitize young consumers to the importance of and need for environmentally responsible consumption.

A deeper motivation for environmental responsibility may help to expand the range of sustainable behaviors displayed by consumers. For example, reducing waste and recycling or reusing products is one way that consumers can change their consumption patterns to advance environmental goals. Conserving energy is another. Still another way is taking the environmental impact of the available modes of transportation into account. Once again, deeper internal motivations, such as feeling a sense of moral responsibility, combined with demographic and socioeconomic factors, push consumers to reduce driving and to choose public transportation or nonmotorized alternatives (Hunecke, Haustein, Böhler, & Grischkat, 2010). Social norms may apply positive peer pressure to encourage environmentally sustainable consumption. For example, researchers found that hotel patrons who were informed that the majority of guests who had previously stayed in their room participated in a towel reuse program were more likely to participate than were those presented with more generic messages designed to promote the environmentally conscious choice (Goldstein, Cialdini, & Griskevicius, 2008). A similar approach may be used to promote a variety of sustainable behaviors. Marketing campaigns that show how others in a social group similar to a specific target audience choose public transportation may increase usage within that group. Social norms that activate a personal connection to a similar social group as well as a situational factor that triggers sustainable behavior may be more effective at encouraging consumers to make an environmentally conscious choice (Biel & Thøgersen, 2007). Creative promotion of the social acceptance of sustainable choices provides opportunities to change consumption norms.

Consumers believe that they are more motivated but less able to recycle than public entities such as governments, agriculture, and industry (Pieters, Bijmolt, van Raaij, & de Kruijk, 1998). This may mean that consumers underestimate their ability to contribute ideas that advance recycling efforts beyond the traditional solutions. However, as consumers see the organizations for which they work engaging in environmentally responsible behavior, they may gain confidence in their ability to effect change. In this way, organizations that make their environmental contributions visible to their employees can make both a direct and an indirect contribution to sustainability efforts. Research demonstrates that consumers who engage in environmentally conscious behaviors at work are more likely to make environmentally conscious choices in their own consumption (Berger & Kanetkar, 1995). As organizations and communities participate in and promote environmental initiatives, spillover between the public and the private can mobilize citizens to engage in environmentally responsible consumption (Prothero et al., 2011).

Much of the extant research on environmental behavior focuses on the consumer in a passive role and seeks to expand our understanding of how to educate, facilitate, and motivate consumers to engage in pro-environmental behavior. However, recent work on stakeholder marketing demonstrates that active engagement by consumers in the design of products (Dahl & Moreau, 2007) or through social media makes consumers feel connected to the brand or organization (Chakravorti, 2010). In this way, involvement in the creation of environmental solutions can help consumers become more engaged in conservation efforts. Behaviors that promote environmental efforts extend beyond participation in programs to reduce, reuse, and recycle to include activities such as political activism and encouraging employees to push for environmental behaviors in their workplace (Stern, 2000). Next, we explore how creative processes can encourage environmentally responsible consumption. Transitioning consumers to the role of active idea generator may lead to more creativity in the environmental domain.

The Role of Consumer Creativity in Environmentally Conscious Behaviors

In a marketing context, "consumer creativity" means consumption practices or solutions for consumer problems that represent a departure from convention and exhibit novel yet functional methods or elements (Burroughs & Mick, 2004; Dahl, Chattopadhyay, & Gorn, 1999; Moreau & Dahl, 2005). Creativity is a result of two cognitive production systems: divergent and convergent thinking (Guilford, 1956). In this section, we analyze how these parallel yet opposing cognitive frames underscore creative thinking.

Guilford (1967, 1968) posited that the key to creativity is divergent thinking, a thinking process that produces multiple unusual and novel solutions to a single problem. When such a process is in operation, consumers break away from existing mental frameworks (Burroughs & Mick, 2004; Smith & Yang, 2004). According to Guilford's "Structure of Intellect Model," regarded as one of the pioneering works to acknowledge the importance of human creativity, a crucial function of human cognition is divergent thinking, suggesting that all consumers have the potential to engage in creative behavior and respond favorably to creative stimuli.

Convergent thinking, by contrast, is the ability to follow a set of predetermined rules or logic to arrive at a single correct solution (Guilford, 1967, 1968). In a marketing context, convergent thinking is also important because after a divergent idea is produced, it must be shaped in a manner so as to make it relevant (i.e., solve a problem or achieve a goal). This second dimension of creativity, referred to as "relevance" (Smith & Yang, 2004), or functionality (Burroughs & Mick, 2004), is widely acknowledged in the creativity literature.

Creative problem solving, then, might examine ideas that diverge from traditional solutions but present optimal outcomes directly relevant to the problem. Both divergence and relevance are needed to explain how creative thinking might encourage environmentally conscious behaviors. As previously stated, significant evidence indicates that our current patterns of resource consumption are not sustainable. Creativity research can shed light on how to encourage ideas that will promote environmentally conscious behaviors.

Creativity as a Syndrome

Following Guilford's seminal model of creativity, research suggests that the initial view of creativity as an inherent human trait or a mental ability cannot fully predict the situations in which people are more or less creative. Summarizing findings across multiple creativity studies, Mumford and Gustafson (1988) maintained that creativity is likely to be determined by a complex interaction between the attributes of the individual and environmental factors (see also Burroughs & Mick, 2004). Based on this integrated view, creativity is conceptualized as a syndrome that comprises a number of different elements (Mumford & Gustafson, 1988, p. 28):

a. The processes underlying an individual's capacity to generate new ideas or understandings;
b. The characteristics of the individual's facilitating process operation;
c. The characteristics of the individual's facilitating the translation of these ideas into action;
d. The attributes of the situation conditioning the individual's willingness to engage in creative behavior; and
e. The attributes of the situation influencing evaluation of the individual's productive efforts.

Next, we summarize findings from creativity research and discuss implications for facilitating environmentally conscious behavior.

Creative Processes

A considerable amount of research has shown that the generation of creative ideas involves the retrieval and novel combination of fragments of knowledge from different segments of the associative network in memory (Burroughs, Moreau, & Mick, 2008; Smith, 1995). Most individuals access associations that are closely linked within their own cognitive structure, resulting in less creative ideas (Martindale, 1995). Divergent thinking promotes a broad information search of an individual's associative networks (Burroughs et al., 2008). By processing a larger working set of associative networks (Finke, Ward, &, Smith, 1992; Smith, 1995) that contain both commonly associated and uncommonly associated nodes, it becomes easier for individuals to make new internal connections between distally located constructs, which in turn permits them to represent and evaluate the external world in a more novel and creative manner (Burroughs et al., 2008). In this way, promoting creative ideas in the environmental domain may result in nontraditional solutions to old environmental problems.

In a similar vein, some research findings demonstrate that the integration and reorganization of cognitive structures is likely to underlie major creative contributions and the application of existing cognitive structures is likely to underlie relatively minor contributions (Mumford & Gustafson, 1988). For instance, Kuhn (1993) concluded that major scientific breakthroughs often stem from a person's willingness to redefine and reorganize concepts learned in the past when they cannot apply existing knowledge to account for the counterintuitive findings encountered. The first and most essential element of creativity is divergence, which ultimately stems from the divergent production system. When a divergent idea is produced, individuals must ensure that the divergent idea is relevant. The idea must be able to solve the problem at hand or help achieve consumers' needs and desires. This secondary stage of creativity is driven by the convergent production system in Guilford's Model (1956).

Individual Factors That Facilitate Creativity

Researchers have investigated the relationship between personality traits and creativity. For instance, Hirschman (1980) found that consumer creativity is correlated with modernity, cognitive complexity, and seeking new experiences. In a subsequent study, Hirschman (1983) demonstrated that consumer creativity is correlated positively with active memory capacity and phenotypic intelligence (the ability to acquire and use knowledge to solve problems). Two sets of core personality traits have been found to predict individuals' creative achievement (Mumford & Gustafson, 1988). The first set of core personality traits (e.g., broad interests, intellectual and artistic values, a preference for complexity, and a tolerance for ambiguity) are important because they foster the creation of new understanding as people integrate and reorganize their existing knowledge structures (Mumford & Gustafson, 1988). The second set of core personality traits (i.e., autonomy, independence, self-confidence, and a willingness to work) are also crucial to creative accomplishment as people translate their creative ideas into actions by forgoing other activities to ensure that the creative idea comes to fruition.

In a meta-analysis, Feist (1998) found that individuals' personality characteristics—such as openness, conscientiousness, self-acceptance, hostility, and impulsivity—have the greatest impact on creativity. By examining one group of consumers who are passionate about environmental sustainability, it is easy to see how a similar set of personality traits both fuel creative thinking and strengthen their desire to reject materialism. Voluntary simplifiers are consumers who, by their own free will, strive to consider the "ethical, resource, waste, and community implications" of each purchase they make (McDonald, Oates, Young, & Hwang, 2006, p. 516). One source of creative environmentally conscious consumption ideas may stem from research designed to examine how and why consumers make nontraditional choices that run counter to materialistic consumption norms in an effort to live a sustainable life.

Situational Factors That Facilitate Creativity

Researchers have also acknowledged that personality by itself cannot fully account for creativity. Over the years, research has been conducted to investigate situational factors that facilitate or inhibit creativity. For instance, Burroughs and Mick (2004) used a person–by-situation approach to investigate the antecedents and consequences of consumer creativity. The authors found that person-level factors (metaphoric thinking and locus of control) and situational factors (situational involvement and time constraints) interact to affect consumer creativity. The influence of situational involvement on creativity was larger when time constraints were present (vs. absent). However, the presence of time constraints led to greater creativity only when the respondent had an internal locus of control. In an examination of recycling behaviors, perceived behavioral control or one's perceptions of their ability to engage in recycling programs was positively correlated with participation in recycling initiatives (Oom Do Valle, Rebelo, Reis, & Menezes, 2005). However, these same researchers found that perceptions of control over their ability to recycle were determined in part by situational factors such as convenience and logistics of the collection program (Oom Do Valle et al., 2005). Similarly, in promoting creative solutions, policy officials and advocates must consider both personal and situational variables that will not only encourage environmentally responsible consumption but may also inhibit the implementation of new ideas.

How creative ideas evolve may also influence how much they diverge from traditional ideas that promote environmentally responsible consumption. Moreau and Dahl (2005) distinguished two types of creative cognitions: the top-down generative creative process and the bottom-up explorative creative process. They found that participant's tendency to follow the path of least resistance (i.e., the top-down, generative creative process) is quite robust. Only when participants were constrained in terms of input would they abandon the top-down, exemplar-driven approach in exchange for a more constructive, creative process. In an environmental sustainability context, engaging in top-down, generative creative processes means consumers' existing knowledge structures and current habits (usually less environmentally conscious) tend to be highly salient and negatively influence environmental behaviors. For instance, consumers might not be motivated to sort their trash, might be unwilling to switch to energy-efficient appliances, and might be less mindful of the negative implications of their behavior on the environment.

However, involvement in a bottom-up, explorative creative process encourages consumers to explore more alternatives and seek out environmentally friendly approaches to consumption. Moreau and Dahl's (2005) research has implications for policymakers in that consumers often will adhere to the path of least resistance when it comes to environmentally conscious behavior. Unless they face constraints, it may be difficult for consumers to abandon their old ways and explore nontraditional or creative consumption that is more environmentally conscious. Thus, it may be more effective for policymakers to encourage explorative creative processes by directing consumer attention to the environmental constraints both individuals and society face (e.g., a limited energy or resource).

Consumer Creativity and Its Implications for Environmentally Conscious Behavior

It is important to note that creativity is defined as ideas that diverge from traditional solutions yet are relevant in solving the problem at hand (Smith & Yang, 2004). Therefore, we must consider how new ideas relate to the broader domain of environmental consciousness. While thinking at an abstract level invites access to associations that are more remotely related to the task, thinking at a concrete level leads consumers to focus on the associations readily available in their memory. Thus creative consumers are likely to consider the broader issues and generate ideas that not only diverge from traditional environmental solutions but also may relate more broadly to the purpose of sustainability and conservation. Therefore, consumers who adopt a creative mindset will likely generate more ideas that reflect a broader sense of environmental consciousness (e.g., energy conservation) when thinking about solutions to everyday problems such as recycling. But individuals who adopt a less creative mindset are more likely to be restrained to close associations stored in memory and thus are more likely to generate ideas that reflect traditional solutions, as opposed to consumption behaviors that are more environmentally friendly. Future research should explore how different creative mindsets lead to different types of environmental solutions. As a variety of variables influence environmentally conscious behaviors, creative approaches are required to drive behavioral changes (Stern, 2005).

Creativity researchers (e.g., Finke, 1995; Ward, 1995) demonstrate that information processing at an abstract, higher level is more likely to promote creativity. Thinking at an abstract, higher level enables consumers to access associations that are more remotely connected within their cognitive structure, leading to the generation of creative ideas (Förster, Friedman, & Liberman, 2004). Thus factors that prompt consumers to think at an abstract level might promote creative solutions to environmental concerns. One example shown to promote abstract thinking is temporal distance. Trope and Liberman (2003) find that when consumers think about events that will occur in the near future, they are likely to focus on the concrete details of the task. By contrast, thinking about an event in the distant or far future triggers consumers to think about more abstract or holistic features of the event (Trope & Liberman, 2003). Shifting temporal construal of the task from the near to the distant future may result in a parallel shift from thinking about environmental problems in concrete terms to thinking about the problem in a holistic way. Such a shift in how we approach the problem may result in the development of creative solutions.

Another approach that may promote creativity involves inducing a visual processing style among consumers. Certain groups of consumers may be predisposed to engage in visual processing, spontaneously generating vivid visual images when they encounter information (Childers, Houston, & Heckler, 1985). By contrast, other consumers demonstrate a preference for verbal processing. Research in consumer psychology contends that consumers with a visual processing style tend to process information at a holistic level (MacInnis & Price, 1987; Wyer, Hung, & Jiang, 2008) and focus on abstract, higher-level information when generating solutions to a problem. By comparison, consumers who rely on verbal processing are detail-oriented and process information at a concrete level when thinking about solutions (MacInnis & Price, 1987; Wyer et al., 2008). By understanding how processing style may encourage thinking at an abstract versus concrete level, we may be able to set the stage for more creative idea generation as consumers envision the environmental solutions of tomorrow.

Future research should also investigate factors that lead consumers to convert their creative environmental ideas into action. As discussed earlier, the personality traits that facilitate creative idea generation and creative behavior engagement are not necessarily the same. Burroughs and Mick (2004) demonstrated that consumers with creative responses possess a higher level of positive affect (i.e., satisfaction, pride, and accomplishment). In addition, some consumers derive personal satisfaction from taking altruistic actions that they believe advance broader social initiatives (Tabernero & Hernández, 2011). This may mean that encouraging creativity in the environmental domain creates a positive feedback loop for some consumers who draw upon the positive affect that they experience when engaging in pro-social behavior to fuel their own creativity in generating new ideas. However, for other consumers, abstract thinking may not provide the specificity they need to turn creative thought into specific environmentally conscious consumption. Thus it might be fruitful to examine the factors (1) that foster or inhibit creativity ideation and engagement at the same time and (2) that facilitate one stage but have no (or even adverse) effect on the implementation of environmentally conscious behaviors. Drawing upon the research on creativity may help policymakers as well as organizational and community leaders activate a creative mindset that enables consumers to generate innovative environmentally responsible consumption ideas. However, generating ideas is only the first step. For new ideas to have a meaningful impact on sustainability efforts, consumers must be persuaded to adopt these ideas as part of their daily habits and routines.

Using Creative Advertising to Promote Environmentally Conscious Behaviors

In the same way that creative thinking stems from the dimensions of divergence and relevance, ad creativity is also defined as a function of these two traits (Smith & Yang, 2004; Smith, Chen, & Yang, 2008, Tellis, 1998; Thorson & Zhao, 1997). Divergence refers to the extent to which an ad contains elements that are novel and unusual (Smith & Yang, 2004; Till & Baack, 2005). Smith et al. (2007) identified five formative factors that account for the various ways in which divergence could be achieved in an advertisement:

a. Originality—ads that contain elements that are rare, surprising, or move away from the obvious and commonplace;
b. Flexibility—ads that contain different ideas or switch from one perspective to another;
c. Elaboration—ads that contain unexpected details or finish and extend basic ideas so they become more intricate, complicated, or sophisticated;
d. Synthesis—ads that combine, connect, or blend normally unrelated objects or ideas;
e. Artistic value—ads that contain artistic verbal impressions or attractive colors or shapes.

Ads that diverge on one or more dimensions may be more successful at capturing the attention of the intended target audience. This important first step in the communication process not only provides an opportunity to cut through the advertising clutter of today's marketing landscape but may also begin to build source credibility by commanding attention. After an ad has captured the attention of its intended audience, it must convey a reason for the audience to remain connected long enough for it to transmit its intended message. At this point, only ads that the receiver deems personally relevant are likely to maintain the audience's attention. Relevance refers to the extent to which the ad contains elements that are meaningful, appropriate, or valuable to the audience. These elements may be brand related (e.g., new information on salient attributes) or ad related (e.g., meaningful images and music). Creative marketing communications are an important piece of the puzzle that policymakers, advocates, and communities need to promote environmentally responsible behaviors.

Recent research in creative advertising might shed some insights as to how policymakers and advocates can use creative ads to promote environmentally conscious behaviors. Early research in advertising creativity examined the effect of creative ads on variables such as recall, evaluations, and behavioral intentions. For instance, Pieters, Warlop, and Wedel (2002) studied the impact of originality and familiarity on brand attention, as reflected by attention to the brand, text, and picture as well as memory for the advertised brand. They found that original ads brought more attention to the advertised brand. Ads that were both original and familiar drew the most attention to the advertised brand, which in turn improved brand memory. In another study, Till and Baack (2005) examined the effect of creative ads versus noncreative ads on recall (aided vs. unaided) and persuasion measures (brand attitudes and purchase intentions). They found that creative ads improved unaided recall of both brand names and commercials. From this research, we can infer that creative ads used to promote environmental issues will be more likely to attract attention, communicate their message, and persuade consumers.

In recent years, there has been growing interest in the psychological mechanisms underlying the effect of creative ads. For example, Smith and colleagues (2008) studied the effect of creative advertising on consumer processing and responses. Specifically, they investigated how creative advertising influences attention, motivation to process, depth of processing, evaluations of the advertisement, and purchase intentions. They found that divergence and relevance (two dimensions of advertising creativity) interact to affect consumer processing and response to these variables. To successfully promote creative ideas designed to encourage environmental responsibility and foster the conversion of these concepts into consumers' daily lives, creative marketing and advertising strategies will be needed to communicate these ideas and persuade consumers to act.

As another example, Yang and Smith (2009) identified the "desire to postpone closure" as the key mechanism explaining the effect of creative advertising. Cognitive closure refers to an individual's desire for a firm answer to a question and an aversion for ambiguity (Kardes, Cronley, Kellaris, & Posavac, 2004; Kruglanski & Webster, 1996). Thus, there is a continuum anchored at one end by a high need for cognitive closure and at the other end by a high desire to postpone closure. If consumers have a high need for closure, they are unlikely to consider new and novel information regarding the brand and may be more likely to stick to their original opinions of the advertised brand. The authors found that exposure to creative ads makes consumers more open minded with regard to the advertised brand, eliciting curiosity among consumers and increasing a tendency to postpone judgment (i.e., lowering the tendency to make a quick judgment). As previously discussed, it is difficult for consumers to break away from the old ways of doing things (i.e., following the path of least resistance) and embrace environmentally conscious consumptions. Open-mindedness toward the message may be an essential piece of the communication strategy as new sustainable behaviors are encouraged.

Another set of researchers examined the effect of a creative mindset on consumers' processing of a subsequently encountered, unrelated persuasive message (Yang, Ringberg, Mao, & Peracchio, 2011). In two experiments, the authors primed a creative mindset by exposing consumers to a set of three award-wining, creative ads versus three randomly chosen, less-creative ads. Much of the extant research suggests that ad messages that are compatible with consumers' mental construal (i.e., the level of abstraction at which a target is represented in consumers' mind) are more persuasive. The authors showed that only when consumers have a less-creative mindset will this compatibility effect be observed. When consumers have a creative mindset (i.e., after watching creative TV commercials), messages that are incompatible with their mental construal were more appealing; this finding is contrary to the extant literature. That is, individuals with an abstract (concrete) construal mindset are susceptible to advertising appeals featuring concrete (abstract) features. The authors also identified a psychological explanation for these observed findings. Driven by a motive to break away from their existing mental framework, consumers with a creative mindset are more likely to search for information that is remotely associated with their mental construal (Yang et al., 2011). This research demonstrates the incidental effect of creative advertising such that exposure to creative ads will affect consumers' subsequent judgment and decision making in such a way that consumers will break away from convention. The implication of these findings for policymakers would be to place environmentally conscious messages that challenge conventional consumption behaviors in a creative context (e.g., in a TV program that encourages a creative mindset) so that their messages are better received by viewers.

Advertising Creativity and Its Implications for Environmentally Conscious Behaviors

The findings reviewed earlier suggest that creative advertising makes consumers more open minded, more curious, less likely to apply their existing judgments without considering new information, and more likely to prefer persuasive messages that are counter to their own mental representation. These findings reveal that creative advertising might be a fruitful tool for promoting environmentally conscious behaviors. As discussed earlier, adopting environmentally conscious behaviors often requires consumers to break away from their old way of thinking. As an example, the most common way to dispose of personal belongings is to throw them away. However, recycling will be more likely to come to mind if consumers are able to construe the behavior at a broader, abstract level (e.g., as a way to protect the environment). In addition, alternatives to traditional recycling may become more plausible as consumers adopt a creative mindset. For example, consumers who adopt a creative mindset have been shown to generate more alternative uses for products (Burroughs & Mick, 2004). Consumers may also think of creative alternatives such as a shared use of some products as opposed to individual ownership. As an example, a growing number of consumers participate in car-sharing arrangements, such as Zipcars, in large cities; similar types of shared-use models may be solutions for the future in suburban neighborhoods. Shared-use models like these may work for large pieces of household equipment that are used regularly but not daily, such as lawn mowers and vacuum cleaners. To advance environmental initiatives, more creative solutions to familiar problems are needed.

If creative ads make consumers more open minded and more curious and allow them to consider more information before making a decision or judgment, using creative ads to promote environmentally conscious behaviors will be a very effective way to encourage consumers to accept and adopt these behaviors. This is because a creative mindset steers consumers away from the most common behaviors and directs them, instead, to remote associations. Associations with broad appeal (e.g., environmentally conscious behaviors and environmental sustainability) will thus be viewed as more desirable by consumers with a creative mindset. By contrast, less-creative ads will not activate a creative mindset among consumers and are likely to restrain consumers to close associations. Consequently, consumers are more likely to adhere to old behaviors (e.g., throwing things away) and persuasive messages promoting environmentally conscious behaviors will appear less appealing. Research shows that one of the most common reasons consumers do not engage in environmentally responsible consumption is because they are not in the habit of doing so (Knussen & Yule, 2008). Transferring creative solutions from a novelty to a habitual set of environmentally responsible behaviors will require consumers to open their minds to new patterns of consumption.

General Discussion

In this chapter, we explore how to harness creative thought and encourage consumers and policymakers to think creatively about new ways to promote environmentally responsible behaviors. Drawing upon research on environmental consciousness, creativity, and marketing communications, we demonstrate how creative thought may invigorate the discussion of environmentally responsible consumption.

Over the past 20 years, researchers have moved beyond viewing environmentally conscious consumption as a function of demographics and personal values (Granzin & Olsen, 1991). Attitudes and perceived behavioral control (Taylor & Todd, 1995), affect and subjective norms (Biswas et al., 2000), as well as locus of control and collectivism (McCarty & Shrum, 2001) influence pro-environmental behaviors. As the world of marketing communications continues to evolve, encouraging a creative mindset may engage consumers in designing the environmental solutions of tomorrow (Chakravorti, 2010; Ferrell, Gonzalez-Padron, Hult, & Maignan, 2010). Accordingly, it is increasingly important for consumers to actively participate in creating solutions to the environmental challenges that we face. More work is needed to understand how engaging consumers in the design of creative solutions will influence attitudes toward and adoption of sustainable consumption.

We believe that policymakers interested in increasing the environmental consciousness of society could benefit from considering creativity as a tool to move individuals toward more active and thoughtful solutions for the resource problems that our society faces. Some individuals already exhibit this type of creativity in the sustainable consumption domain. Entrepreneurial individuals create and sell recycled products such as rugs made completely of recycled plastic shopping bags or aluminum cans and tabs turned into handbags or eco-art. Other alternative-use solutions to waste problems are also gaining attention. Nike produced World Cup Soccer jerseys made from plastic bottles removed from landfills (Yoneda, 2010). Taiwan used 1.5 million Polyethylene terephthalate PET bottles as the base of a structure for a massive new building project (Messenger, 2010). To address waste problems, educators and policymakers at all levels should encourage more people to creatively recycle the products that they use and reduce their waste output. Researchers are also investigating creative solutions for increasing consumer awareness of their own waste production via mobile phone applications that track the environmental impact of products and packaging at the point of purchase (Walker, 2010). Similarly, encouraging creativity may ignite more active involvement in environmental efforts as we look for a sustainable model for the future.

References

Berger, I. E., & Corbin, R. M. (1992). Perceived consumer effectiveness and faith in others as moderators of environmentally responsible behaviors. *Journal of Public Policy & Marketing, 11*(2), 79–89.

Berger, I. E., & Kanetkar, V. (1995). Increasing environmental sensitivity via workplace experiences. *Journal of Public Policy & Marketing, 14*(2), 205–215.

Biel, A., & Thøgersen, J. (2007). Activation of social norms in social dilemmas: A review of the evidence and reflections on the implications for environmental behavior. *Journal of Economic Psychology, 28*(1), 93–112.

Biswas, A., Licata, J. W., McKee, D., Pullig, C., & Daughtridge, C. (2000). The recycling cycle: An empirical examination of consumer waste recycling and recycling shopping behaviors. *Journal of Public Policy & Marketing, 19*(1), 93–105.

Burroughs, J. E., & Mick, D. G. (2004). Exploring antecedents and consequences of consumer creativity in a problem-solving context. *Journal of Consumer Research, 31*(2), 402–411.

Burroughs, J. E., Moreau, C. P., & Mick, D. G. (2008). Toward a psychology of consumer creativity. In C. P. Haugtvedt, P. M. Herr & F. R. Kardes (Eds.), *Handbook of consumer psychology* (pp. 1011–1038). New York: Lawrence Erlbaum.

Chakravorti, B. (2010) Stakeholder marketing 2.0. *Journal of Public Policy & Marketing, 29*(1), 97–102.

Childers, T. L., Houston, M. J., & Heckler, S. E. (1985). Measurement of individual differences in visual versus verbal information processing. *Journal of Consumer Research, 12*(2), 125–134.

Dahl, D. W., & Moreau, C. P. (2007). Thinking inside the box: why consumers enjoy constrained creative experiences. *Journal of Marketing Research, 44*(3), 357–369.

Dahl, D. W., Chattopadhyay, A., & Gorn, G. J. (1999). The use of visual mental imagery in new product design. *Journal of Marketing Research, 36*(1), 18–28.

Ellen, P. S., Wiener, J. L., & Cobb-Walgren, C. (1991). The Role of Perceived Consumer Effectiveness in Motivating Environmentally Conscious Behaviors. *Journal of Public Policy & Marketing, 10*(2), 102–117.

EPA (2007, November). Municipal solid waste in the United States. Report EPA530-R-08–010 www.epa.gov/wastes/nonhaz/municipal/pubs/msw07-rpt.pdf (accessed November 29, 2010).

Feist, G. J. (1998). A meta-analysis of personality in scientific and artistic creativity. *Personality and Social Psychology Review, 2*(4), 290–309.

Ferrell, O. C., Gonzalez-Padron, T. L., Hult, G. T. M., & Maignan, I. (2010). From market orientation to stakeholder orientation. *Journal of Public Policy & Marketing, 29*(1), 93–96.

Finke, R. A. (1995). Creative insight and preinventive forms. In R. J Stenberg & J. E. Davidson (Eds.), *The nature of insight* (pp. 255–280). Cambridge: MIT Press.

Finke, R., Ward, T. B., & Smith, S. M. (1992). *Creative cognition: Theory, research, and applications.* Cambridge: MIT Press.

Förster, J., Friedman, R. S., & Liberman, N. (2004). Temporal construal effects on abstract and concrete thinking: Consequences for insight and creative cognition. *Journal of Personality & Social Psychology, 87*(2), 177–189.

Goldstein, N. J., Cialdini, R. B., & Griskevicius, V. (2008). A room with a viewpoint: Using social norms to motivate environmental conservation in hotels. *Journal of Consumer Research, 35*(3), 472–482.

Grant, A. M. (2008). Does intrinsic motivation fuel the prosocial fire? Motivational synergy in predicting persistence, performance, and productivity. *Journal of Applied Psychology, 93*(1), 48–58.

Granzin, K. L., & Olsen, J. E. (1991). Characterizing participants in activities protecting the environment: A focus on donating, recycling, and conservation behaviors. *Journal of Public Policy & Marketing, 10*(2), 1–27.

Guilford, J. P. (1956). The structure of intellect. *Psychological Bulletin, 53,* 267–293.

Guilford, J. P. (1967). *The nature of human intelligence*. New York: McGraw-Hill.

Guilford, J. P. (1968). Intelligence has three facets. *Science, 160*(3828), 615–620.

Hirschman, E. C. (1980). Innovativeness, novelty seeking and consumer creativity. *Journal of Consumer Research, 7*(3), 283–295.

Hirschman, E. C. (1983). Consumer intelligence, creativity, and consciousness: Implications for consumer protection and education. *Journal of Public Policy & Marketing, 2*(1), 153–170.

Hunecke, M., Haustein, S., Böhler, S., & Grischkat, S. (2010). Attitude-based target groups to reduce the ecological impact of daily mobility behavior. *Environmental and Behavior, 42*(1), 3–43.

Kardes, F. R., Cronley, M. L., Kellaris, J. J., & Posavac, S. S. (2004). The Role of selective information processing in price-quality inference. *Journal of Consumer Research, 31*(2), 368–374.

Kinnear, T. C., Taylor, J. R., & Ahmed, S. A. (1974). Ecologically concerned consumers: Who are they? *Journal of Marketing, 38*(2), 20–24.

Knussen, C., & Yule, F. (2008). "I'm not in the habit of recycling." *Environment and Behavior, 40*(5), 683–702.

Kruglanski, A. W., & Webster, D. M. (1996). Motivated closing of the mind: "Seizing" and "Freezing." *Psychological Review, 103*(2), 263–283.

Kuhn, D. (1993). Science as argument: Implications for teaching and learning scientific thinking. *Science Education, 77*(3), 319–337.

MacInnis, D. J., & Price, L. L. (1987). The role of imagery in information processing: Review and extensions. *Journal of Consumer Research, 13*(4), 473–491.

Martindale, C. (1995). Creativity and connectionism. In S. M. Smith, T. B. Ward, & R. A. Finke (Eds.), *The creative cognition approach* (pp. 248–268). Cambridge: MIT Press.

McCarty, J. A., & Shrum, L. J. (2001). The influence of individualism, collectivism, and locus of control on environmental beliefs and behavior. *Journal of Public Policy & Marketing, 20*(1), 93–104.

McDonald, S., Oates, C. J., Young, C. W., & Hwang, K. (2006). Toward sustainable consumption: Researching voluntary simplifiers. *Psychology & Marketing, 23*(6), 515–534.

Messenger, S. (2010, April 14). Massive plastic bottle building unveiled in Taiwan. Tree-

Hugger.com. www.treehugger.com/sustainable-product-design/massive-plastic-bottle-building-unveiled-in-taiwan.html (accessed November 29, 2010).

Mobley, C., Vagias, W. M., & DeWard, S. L. (2010). Exploring additional determinants of environmentally responsible behavior: The influence of environmental literature and environmental attitudes. *Environment and Behavior, 42*(4), 420–447.

Moreau, C. P., & Dahl, D. W. (2005). Designing the solution: The impact of constraints on consumers' creativity. *Journal of Consumer Research, 32*(1), 13–22.

Mumford, M. D., & Gustafson, S. B. (1988). Creativity syndrome: Integration, application, and innovation. *Psychological Bulletin, 103*(1), 27–43.

Navarro, M. (2009, October 23). Mayor's environmental record: Grand plans and small steps forward. *New York Times,* p. A32. www.nytimes.com/2009/10/23/nyregion/23green.html?scp=2&sq=navarro%20and%20%20mayor%E2%80%99s%20environmental&st=cse/ (accessed November 29, 2010).

Oom Do Valle, P., Rebelo, E., Reis, E., & Menezes, J. (2005). Combining behavioral theories to predict recycling involvement. *Environment and Behavior, 37*(3), 364–396.

Pieters, R., Warlop, L., & Wedel, M. (2002). Breaking through the clutter: Benefits of advertisement originality and familiarity for brand attention and memory. *Management Science, 48*(6), 765–781.

Pieters, R., Bijmolt, T., van Raaij, F., & de Kruijk, M. (1998). Consumers' attributions of proenvironmental behavior, motivation, and ability to self and others. *Journal of Public Policy & Marketing, 17*(2), 215–225.

Porter, B. E., Leeming, F. C., & Dwyer, W. O. (1995). Solid waste recovery: A review of behavioral programs to increase recycling. *Environment and Behavior, 27*(2), 122–152.

Press, M., & Arnould, E. J. (2009). Constraints on sustainable energy consumption: Market system and public policy challenges and opportunities. *Journal of Public Policy & Marketing, 28*(1), 102–113.

Prothero, A., Dobscha, S., Freund, J., Kilbourne, W. E., Luchs, M. G., Ozanne, L. K., & Thøgersen, J. (2011). Sustainable consumption: Opportunities for consumer research and public policy. *Journal of Public Policy & Marketing, 30*(1), 31–38.

Smith, R. E., & Yang, S. (2004). Toward a general theory of creativity in advertising: Examining the role of divergence. *Marketing Theory, 4*(1/2), 29–55.

Smith, R. E., Chen, J., & Yang, X. (2008). The impact of advertising creativity on the hierarchy-of-effects. *Journal of Advertising, 37*(Winter), 47–61.

Smith, R. E., MacKenzie, S. B., Yang, X., Buchholz, L., & Darley, W. K. (2007). Modeling the determinants and effects of creativity in advertising. *Marketing Science, 26*(6), 819–833.

Smith, S. M. (1995). Fixation, incubation and insight in memory and creative thinking. In S. M. Smith, T. B. Ward, & R. A. Finke (Eds.), *The creative cognition approach* (pp. 135–156). Cambridge: MIT Press.

Stern, P. C. (2000). Toward a coherent theory of environmentally significant behavior. *Journal of Social Issues, 56,* 409–412.

Stern, P. C. (2005). Understanding individuals' environmentally significant behavior. *Environmental Law Reporter, 35*(11), 10785–10790.

Tabernero, C., & B. Hernández (2011). Self-efficacy and intrinsic motivation guiding environmental behavior. *Environment and Behavior, 43*(5), 658–675.

Taylor, S., & Todd, P. (1995). Understanding household garbage reduction behavior: A test of an integrated model. *Journal of Public Policy & Marketing, 14*(2), 192–204.

Tellis, G. J. (1998). *Advertising and sales promotion strategy.* Reading, MA: Addison-Wesley.

Thorson, E., & Zhao, X. (1997). Television viewing behavior as an indicator of commercial effectiveness. In W. D. Wells (Ed.), *Measuring advertising effectiveness* (pp. 221–237). Mahwah, NJ: Lawrence Erlbaum.

Till, B. D., & Baack, D. W. (2005). Recall and persuasion: Does creativity matter? *Journal of Advertising, 34*(3), 47–57.

Trope, Y., & Liberman, N. (2003). Temporal construal. *Psychological Review, 110*(3), 403–421.

Walker, R. (2010, December 5). Wasted data. *New York Times*, p. MM20. www.nytimes.com/2010/12/05/magazine/05FOB-Consumed-t.html?scp=1&sq=&st=nyt&_r=0/ (accessed December 15, 2010).

Ward, T. B. (1995). What's old about new ideas? In S. M. Smith, T. B. Ward, & R. A. Finke (Eds.), *The creative cognition approach* (pp. 157–178). Cambridge: MIT Press.

Wray-Lake, L., Flanagan, C. A., & Osgood, D. W. (2010). Examining trends in adolescent environmental attitudes, beliefs, and behaviors across three decades. *Environment and Behavior, 42*(1), 61–85.

Wyer, R. S., Jr., Hung, I. R., & Jiang, Y. (2008). Visual and verbal processing strategies in comprehension and judgment. *Journal of Consumer Psychology, 18*(4), 244–257.

Yang, X., & Smith, R. E. (2009). Beyond attention effects: Modeling the persuasive and emotional effect of advertising creativity. *Marketing Science, 28*(5), 935–949.

Yang, X., Ringberg, T., Mao, H., & Peracchio, L. A. (2011). The construal (in)compatibility effect: The moderating role of a creative mindset. *Journal of Consumer Research, 38*(4), 681–696.

Yoneda, Y. (2010, March 7). Nike unveils World Cup soccer jerseys made from recycled plastic bottles. Inhabitat.com. http://inhabitat.com/nike-unveils-world-cup-soccer-jerseys-made-from-recycled-plastic-bottles/ (accessed November 29, 2010).

12

Consequences of Legislating Packaging Behavior

Germany's Green Dot Program and Its Communications

Lukas Jones, Scott Owen, and Lynn R. Kahle

Many companies regard environmental issues as one of their primary brand positioning objectives and target a market of environmentally conscious consumers. The majority, however, adopt a more moderate stance, taking actions that are both environmentally friendly and economically responsible—that is, actions often referred to as the "low-hanging fruit" in this area. Unless government intervenes and defines higher minimum standards, many companies are reluctant to leap into costly eco-friendly programs.

The average American contributes more trash to landfill than any other people in the world, about 4.6 pounds of trash per person per day (Kaufman, 2009). Many cities are beginning to implement restrictions on what can be thrown away based on practices in countries where stricter environmental laws are in place. About one-third of American waste is from packaging, which comprises about 43 percent of the packaging recycled in the United States (Gettelman, 2009). Germany is a prime example of a country where environmental laws have changed the ways in which marketers package their products and is thus worthy of study.

Packaging from consumer products constitutes a surprisingly large percentage of overall post-consumer solid waste in many countries, including Germany, where the government has taken the initiative by defining corporations' environmental responsibility in such activities as packaging. Germany was the first country in Europe to create a government-controlled environmental certification label, known as the Blue Angel seal (Fuller, 1999). It comes as no surprise, then, that a program called Der Grüne Punkt (The Green Dot)was developed as a result of the German law requiring manufacturers to develop or participate in a package recycling program. Green Dot (GD) requires manufacturers to take back post-consumer packaging waste from the products that they produce and recycle it (Fishbein, 1994; Fuller, 1999). In this way, manufacturers take responsibility for the disposal costs of the packaging waste that they generate. In the United States, only some industries, such as soft drinks through deposits regulated by "bottle bills," are required to recycle their packaging (Kahle & Beatty, 1987).

The term "packaging waste," as it is used in Germany, means post-consumer packaging waste that is not contaminated by hazardous materials (Fishbein, 1994). The German program does not include waste involved in the creation of packaging materials, such as factory pollution, or other waste from manufacturing processes. It also does not deal with packaging that may have been in contact with any type of hazardous materials. The packaging that is reduced under the program is solely that which consumer products require for transport, display, and protection of the product itself.

GD is based on the "polluter pays" principle, which many countries have experimented with in various ways (Fuller, 1999). The system allows manufacturers to pay fees, based on the amount of packaging that they produce, to an industry-run organization, which then collects all the packaging waste on behalf of the industry. Packaging from consumer products constitutes a surprisingly large percentage of overall post-consumer solid waste in many countries, including Germany. The packaging is collected in both household waste containers and collection bins that are located in high-traffic areas (Fishbein, 1994). After collection, the packaging waste is sorted and recycled by the industry-run organization.

The program's goals are to encourage a higher recycling rate of existing waste and innovative packaging design to create less waste. The theory is that if manufacturers see these resource recovery costs reflected in the bottom line, they will be motivated to find ways to reduce the amount of unnecessary packaging that they produce (DSD, 2008). In any case, the level of materials recycled will increase and attitudes about environmental responsibility might change. The GD program has been successful since its inception in 1993. In recent years, it has been adopted in some form by 26 European countries. In 2009, 32 million tons of packaging were recycled, equivalent to an approximate reduction of 25 million tons of carbon dioxide greenhouse gases.

Because our planet's ecosystems have reached a precarious condition, much will need to be done in the coming years to slow and, ideally, reverse, the damage that human consumption has caused to the environment to date. We have reached "the tragedy of the commons," and a free-rider mentality has reached its apex, to the detriment of collective humanity. The business sector can be a key component in altering this path, because therein lies the capital and the power necessary to enact real change. The kind of change necessary must be mandated by the government, as in Germany with the GD program or in the United States with outlawing leaded gasoline, so that businesses compete with one another on a level playing field by the same rules.

In this paper, we examine the GD program in Germany and Europe and evaluate its contribution to the goal of sustainable development. We review what both proponents and skeptics say about the program. Using this information, we explore whether this program could be applied successfully in the United States or, at least, under what circumstances the program might succeed or fail. The GD program has been a success in Germany and Europe but not without problems, and it remains to be seen whether this program is appropriate for use outside Europe.

The Emergence of the GD

The GD program developed out of a 1991 Ordinance on Packaging Waste (the *Verpackungsverordnung*), which the German legislature passed in order to address the increasing levels of packaging waste generated by industry (DSD, 2007). The ordinance legally requires companies to be responsible for the recycling and disposal of packaging materials related to their products. Manufacturers could be exempted from collecting the waste themselves, as long as they were able to collectively deal with the waste, so they pooled their funds to create the "Dual System" under the direction of the DSD (Dueles System Deutschland) (DSD, 2008). Manufacturers are not required to join the program, but were required to collect their waste; hence the dual system of developing an individual recycling program or joining the DSD.

GD was developed as a result of the Dueles System Deutschland as a way to consolidate business efforts to comply with the ordinance. The DSD is a not-for-profit that offers participating firms a label under license from the DSD on a per-use basis. This label certifies to the consumer that the product packaging will be dealt with in an ecologically responsible manner. For the most part, this guarantee is valid, but in other cases, the recycling capacity required is simply not available (Fishbein, 1994)—an issue addressed in detail later.

Although similar in nature to the packaging laws of other European countries, the *Verpackungsverordnung* was the strictest initiative of its time. This strictness was due in part to the lack of proper landfill sites in heavily populated Germany. At the time, other countries, such as France, the Netherlands, Sweden, and the UK had their own laws concerning landfill waste and recycling measures, but none had guidelines as strict as the *Verpackungsverordnung*. The European Community was then discussing the idea of a universal packaging ordinance, but it was not developed until 1995 (PRO Europe, 2007).

Types of Packaging Waste

The *Verpackungsverordnung* focuses on three distinct areas of packaging to be reduced: packaging for transport, secondary packaging, and primary packaging (Fishbein, 1994). Packaging for transport, including pallets, corrugated cardboard boxes, and shrinkwrap, is used in the actual transportation of the product from the manufacturer to the retailer; in 1991 it comprised approximately one-third of the packaging waste in Germany (Fishbein, 1994).

The *Verpackungsverordnung* required that major steps be taken immediately to reduce the amount of transport packaging being wasted or sent to landfill. It required, at the very least, that transport packaging be recycled. More important, it emphasized the use of reusable packaging over single-use packaging. Reusable transport packaging has shown up in a variety of ways, such as the plastic boxes that have begun to replace cardboard boxes for shipping products to retailers (Fuller, 1999). These boxes can be reused hundreds of times before they begin to break down, and when they do eventually need to be replaced, they are easily recyclable and the plastic is reused in new applications. Transport packaging norms were drastically redesigned from single- to multiple-use containers so that overall packaging waste was reduced.

Secondary packaging, which is packaging that is essentially unnecessary to the protection or use of the product, was a topic of major concern when the *Verpackungsverordnung* was first initiated. An example of secondary packaging is the box that surrounds a tube of toothpaste or a decorative case for an expensive bottle of wine. Secondary packaging only constituted about 0.5 percent of total packaging waste, but because it is unnecessary, it was to be all but eliminated. This change was of particular concern to marketers, as secondary packaging can play a large role in the appeal of products in the retail environment. This issue is examined later in our criticisms of the GD program.

The *Verpackungsverordnung* required that retail stores put in place bins to recover secondary packaging at the time of purchase. Before the DSD was formed, this particular provision put tremendous strain on manufacturers to recover their secondary packaging, leading to a sharp reduction in compliance from 1991 to 1993 (Fishbein, 1994). During that period, products were increasingly being sold in just their primary packaging. This trend continues, though the DSD's efficient collection services have allowed some of this packaging use to return.

Primary packaging is that which protects the product from contamination or is necessary for using the product. Examples of primary packaging include wrappers on soap and candy bars, and spray bottles for household cleaners. Primary packaging made up approximately two-thirds of the total packaging waste in pre-*Verpackungsverordnung* Germany. This type of packaging is perhaps the most difficult to reduce, and changes in materials were often the best solution.

Reducing the amount of primary packaging often requires that manufacturers look to the product itself. Making this change could be as simple as increasing the concentration of a product so that a smaller container can be used. Another method might be to increase the quantity of product in each package, so that less waste goes into extraneous components of the package such as bottlecaps or handles, and the consumer buys it less frequently. One could also switch the type of materials used in the primary packaging to ones that are more easily recyclable and, therefore, accumulate less in GD fees.

Environmental Costs

Many green business advocates speak of environmental costs as an important factor in the development of sustainable products. However, "environmentally friendly" products sometimes have difficulty competing in the marketplace because of higher manufacturing costs; but if we truly evaluate the impact on the environment from conventional products, we often find that the more environmentally friendly products actually have lower overall costs (Fuller, 1999). If the costs of conventional products are adequately evaluated, taking into account the strain that they place on the environment and the amount of waste that they produce, their true cost will be determined and they will no longer benefit from "subsidies" due to discounting those factors. Dealing with waste is expensive, and the costs of doing so must be taken into account somehow when comparing the two types of products or materials. The more that companies are able to reduce their packaging, the less that they will have to pay in fees to the GD program. The more they waste, the higher their costs (Fishbein 1994; Fuller 1999).

Dueles System Deutschland

The organization that has facilitated the GD efforts in Germany since 1993 is known as Dueles System Deutschland (DSD) (Fishbein, 1994). By acting in partnership with waste collection services nationwide, DSD makes the collection and recycling of packaging materials more efficient. DSD is vital to the success of the whole enterprise because it is far too complex for companies to organize collection efforts individually. Companies pay both a membership fee and a usage fee to DSD for its services (DSD, 2008). This process also allows companies to use the GD logo on their products, showing consumers that they contribute to the recycling efforts of the GD program.

DSD quickly became the subject of criticism, as most people did not trust that it would ever be able to establish itself fully. The *Verpackungsverordnung* had been in effect for about two years, and resistance to the ordinance was already strong. The creation of DSD contributed to the success of the entire endeavor, but much criticism had to be overcome for it to take root. The first step in creating the organization was gaining approval from all seventeen German states (*länder*). Moreover, at the local level there was also resistance from municipal garbage collectors.

Many of these smaller parties viewed DSD as an intruder that would cut into their business (Fishbein, 1994). DSD representatives had to broker countless deals with organizations at this level about how the collection business would be conducted. It soon became clear that, for the most part, the municipal garbage organizations had gotten the better end of these deals (Fishbein, 1994). Problems with these initial contracts led to a severe financial crisis for DSD in its first year, the resolution of which is explained in detail below.

Independent Collection Efforts

At present, only a few small companies still organize their own collection efforts, and the GD program is used otherwise almost universally. If a company has only limited geographical distribution, then it may make sense for it to collect its own packaging waste on regular rounds. On a larger scale, it becomes nearly impossible and much too expensive. Also, many larger stores will refuse to carry products that do not bear the seal, because it leads to greater problems for them in the long run (Fishbein, 1994).

Occasionally, manufacturers who sell directly to the consumer will not put the GD logo on their products, because it brings consumers back into their stores to return the packaging. This twist gives the store another opportunity to sell to the consumer. Apple Computers encountered this situation with a number of its smaller venders in Germany. It decided not to put the logo on packaging destined for these smaller shops, so that repeat business could flourish (Fuller, 1999); however, many larger stores required the logo. Thus, Apple was forced to pay the DSD fees if the larger electronics retailers carried its products.

Packaging Recovery Organization (Pro) Europe

Today, the DSD is only a subsidiary organization of a much larger entity known as Packaging Recovery Organization (PRO) Europe. PRO Europe was founded in 1995 in response to the European Community Initiative on Packaging Waste. It adopted the GD as its symbol of manufacturer responsibility, which it now licenses to all its subsidiary organizations. PRO Europe is the umbrella organization for packaging recovery schemes, such as the DSD, that are now present in twenty-two European countries and three others outside the EU (PRO Europe, 2008). Its main role is currently to monitor and license the GD trademark. It also acts as the common and authoritative voice for the various packaging recovery organizations across Europe.

The PRO Europe Web site states that "the GD has evolved into a proven concept of how implementation of producer responsibility for waste can be achieved" (PRO Europe, 2008). The PRO Europe member organizations are committed to the recycling of used packaging both in Europe and abroad. Programs in Canada (Corporate Social Responsibility), Iceland (Iceland Responsible Fisheries), and the Ukraine (Ukrainian Packaging and Ecological Coalition) all have agreements with PRO Europe to use the GD trademark. All ten countries that became members of the European Union in May 2004 chose to "adopt producer responsibility schemes that utilized PRO Europe's services" (PRO Europe, 2007, p. 2). PRO Europe and its subsidiaries view packaging recycling as a necessary step on the path toward sustainable development.

PRO Europe's mission is to "help national recovery organizations to be able to offer the best possible service for the lowest sustainable costs to their client companies" (PRO Europe, 2008). PRO Europe promotes the GD as an international symbol of producer responsibility and encourages the development and sustainability of markets for recycled materials. Essentially, PRO Europe works to overcome the differences that various countries may have in their recycling policies and create a unified front on behalf of industry throughout Europe.

Criticisms of the GD Program

Throughout the early history of the program, a number of issues arose that later had to be resolved. The issues generally relate to public perceptions of the GD, resistance from certain parties in industry, logistical difficulties with recycling quotas versus capacity, and financial problems. It soon became clear, however, that the GD program would be able to address these problems and succeed.

In 1992, INFORM conducted interviews with public and private organizations that revealed great support for the *Verpackungsverordnung* and its underlying principles (Fishbein, 1994). Among industry representatives, there was great support for allowing the private sector to create its own system of dealing with packaging waste, rather than having too much government involvement. However, in spite of these rather positive reviews from the INFORM study, many other parties criticized the *Verpackungsverordnung* for not having strong enough regulations. Others criticized the DSD itself, saying that it was "protecting the packaging industry rather than the environment" (Europe Information Service, 1993, p. II).

According to Bette Fishbein, author of the INFORM study, the four main criticisms of the GD program in its earlier stages were:

1. It did not pay enough attention to avoiding waste,
2. It did not promote refillable bottles,
3. It misled the public with the GD symbol, and
4. Internationally, it was viewed as a barrier to trade and a form of "green protectionism" (Fishbein, 1994, p. 114).

These criticisms, and others, are discussed in the following sections.

Waste Avoidance at the Source

The *Verpackungsverordnung* did not directly address waste avoidance, also called source reduction, which led to the widespread belief that DSD's focus on recycling could actually undermine waste reduction efforts (Fishbein, 1994). This problem is of particular concern to people who believe that source reduction is the most important issue to be addressed. While the overall aim of the *Verpackungsverordnung* was to make industry accountable for its waste, the underlying objective was obviously to force industry to reduce waste from the start. Early DSD advertisements focused primarily on the benefits of recycling and DSD's contribution toward achieving this goal. Due to the favorable public perceptions of source reduction, DSD has since begun to include it as a primary theme in its advertising (Fishbein, 1994).

Environmental groups across Europe continue to demand that source reduction be the top priority of waste initiatives (Fuller, 1999; Mintu-Wimsatt & Lozada, 1996). These environmental advocates believe that the GD program does not do enough to promote the reduction of packaging waste at the source (McGlade, 2004).

These advocates believe that further reduction of packaging waste should be done at multiple levels, from prevention, reuse, recycling, incineration with energy recovery, incineration without energy recovery, and landfilling (Fishbein, 1994).

Refillable Containers Not Prioritized

Germans have long been attached to paying a *pfand* (deposit) on containers, and many believe strongly in the concept of refillable and reusable containers. Thus, when the *Verpackungsverordnung* was developed and emphasized the importance of recycling, many were concerned that refillable containers would take second place to single-use packaging. A great deal of resistance came from states that had already established strict refillable container requirements. They saw the promotion of single-use containers without a deposit as a threat to the continued use of refillable containers, which often had deposits of the Euro equivalent of $0.30 or more (Fishbein, 1994). They feared that consumers would become less likely to purchase the refillable containers, as they would be harder to dispose and more expensive.

To solve this problem, the Bundesrat (the German upper house of parliament) passed the *Verpackungsverordnung* in conjunction with a separate ordinance on refillable containers, mandating higher refill rates (Fishbein, 1994). The ordinance required that the use of refillable containers would not decline due to the GD program, and in the majority of cases this has held true. This process of reuse rather than recycling saves a great deal of energy (Fuller, 1999).

Most drink containers still carry a deposit, which is generally still quite high, ranging from the U.S. equivalent of $ 0.15 to $1.50 each depending on the size and brand of beverage. Apparently, these containers are then reused time and again, usually employing a system of laser marking around the neck of the bottle. The system tracks how many times each container is refilled and then removes the container from the market after a certain limit has been reached.

The GD Misleads Consumers

One valid critique of the GD system is that it leads consumers to believe that a package is environmentally friendly, when in fact it may be quite the opposite. The GD is a symbol used only on single-use packaging, but it invokes the image of a sustainable package (Fishbein, 1994). A single-use package with the GD is likely more harmful to the environment than a refillable package without the symbol, but typical consumers might think the opposite is true. This was one of the main reasons that the Bundesrat required the separate ordinance on refillable containers.

Another way in which the logo misleads consumers is related to collection quotas versus recycling capacity. The GD label is supposed to be a guarantee that the package will be recycled, even though in 1993 recycling capacity was not nearly large enough to process all the packaging waste collected under the DSD system. Because the number of GDs given out far outpaced the amount recycled, many containers with the GD logo ended up in landfill and incinerators. This issue was one cause of credibility problems that the GD faced in its early years (Fishbein, 1994).

International Considerations

The *Verpackungsverordnung* was sometimes portrayed as a barrier to free trade in what was then the European Community (Fishbein, 1994). This portrayal raised questions that affect countries worldwide, such as: How should conflicts between trade and environmental policy be resolved? The *Verpackungsverordnung* has forced companies that wish to do business in Germany, and other GD member states, to modify and reduce their packaging, as well as pay fees for recovery of that packaging waste (Fuller, 1999). Because of the larger distances traveled by imported products, waste from transport packaging is of particular concern to international firms wanting to do business there. Technically, the GD gives German products, which must only travel short distances and are therefore at less risk of damage, cost advantages in fees and a price advantage in the market.

The United Kingdom was perhaps the most vocal opponent of the *Verpackungsverordnung* during its early stages. The UK argued that member states should be restricted from going "further or faster" than the proposed European Community Directive on Packaging Waste (Environmental Data Services, 1993, pp. 40–41). The German system initially conflicted with the European Directive because of its emphasis on recycling over source reduction. The recycling quotas under the *Verpackungsverordnung* were also much higher than those of the proposed European Directive, and they had to be met much sooner.

The issue of whether the *Verpackungsverordnung* is a form of "green protectionism" has been somewhat resolved by the passing of the European Union Directive on Packaging Waste, as well as the success of PRO Europe in other European countries. There does not seem to be nearly the amount of resistance to environmental directives like the *Verpackungsverordnung* now as in the early 1990s. The European Union Directive on Packaging Waste aims to reduce packaging waste destined for final disposal systems, such as landfill and incinerators. It also aims to create a common policy for EU member states to avoid restraints on trade and the need to contend with different regulations in each country (Fishbein, 1994). While this has been somewhat successful in mitigating the differences between countries, some still maintain higher standards than others, especially when comparing Eastern and Western European countries. It is only a matter of time, however, before the newer EU entrants expand their collection and recycling capacity to the level of earlier members such as Germany and the Netherlands (McGlade, 2004).

Flow of Packaging Waste Across Borders

Another international problem that DSD encountered was the lack of recycling capacity in Germany. Early in the program too much waste was coming into the system, and there was insufficient capacity to recycle the materials. This issue was especially problematic with plastics, which were prohibitively expensive to recycle and whose end product had little demand (Fishbein, 1994). At the time, it was still easier to purchase nonrecycled materials for use in new products, thus many companies were hesitant to use recycled materials. The waste often had to be transported abroad for recycling by other countries. Sometimes, waste was stored in facilities until capacity became available, a practice that was viewed as potentially dangerous and prone to accidents.

Certain environmental groups were skeptical about this state of affairs, with some claiming that DSD was simply shipping waste elsewhere to be put into landfill. For this reason, DSD was made to enlist the aid of various technical watchdog agencies (Technischer Überwachungs-Verein), that would oversee the actions of recyclers both in Germany and abroad wherever German recycling was to be sent (Fishbein, 1994). This policy helped to ease some of the controversy, but certain problems remained. Occasionally, large shipments of GD collectables are found in landfill.

Some resistance also arose in the early 1990s from other countries' recycling industries. Germany was suddenly flooding the international market with materials for recycling (Fuller, 1999). This glut lowered the value of recycled materials drastically around Europe. Laws were proposed to limit the flow of waste across Europe, including materials for recycling, because of the effects of Germany's GD. In many cases, these laws became moot as the European Community Directive on Packaging Waste took effect across Europe (Fishbein, 1994).

DSD Financial Crisis Averted

DSD faced a severe financial crisis in May 1993, soon after the official launch of the program. Officials announced that DSD would experience a shortfall of approximately $300 million for the remainder of the year (Fishbein, 1994). Causes of this financial crisis were said to be delinquency in fee payment, freeloading on the GD system, and high overhead costs. Something had to be done if the GD was to succeed. Industry placed a great deal of importance on DSD because in its absence it would have to collect packaging on its own. Therefore, it agreed to help make up the shortfall for DSD. Retailers, afraid of losing valuable space in their shops to store returned packaging, contributed $120 million to the effort. Waste management industries that work under DSD contracts agreed to contribute $108 million. The rest was made up by asking users of the GD to pay their fees two months in advance.

DSD instituted a severe cost-cutting measure of $144 million in June 1993 to reduce overall costs for the remaining six months (Fishbein, 1994). As part of the plan, DSD renegotiated contracts with local waste management firms and conducted research to determine what percentage of waste placed in the household bins actually carried the GD logo. Efficiencies were designed to reduce overhead as much as possible. Finally, a new fee system was set up to better fund the program for the following year.

The new fee schedule, introduced in 1994, was designed to better estimate the costs of actually handling and recycling the various packaging materials (DSD, 2007). Whereas the original fees were based on the volume of the package, with all materials charged the same rate, the new fee schedule was based on weight and differentiated by material. This new schedule effectively doubled the fees collected in its first year and gave industry the incentive to switch packaging materials to those that were most easily recyclable (Fishbein, 1994).

Industry Criticisms

After these initial implementation and logistical problems were resolved, DSD seemed prepared to overcome any obstacle. Criticisms of the *Verpackungsverordnung* remain, however, especially among industry parties. While industry is in favor of a private plan to recycle packaging waste, it naturally opposes some of the stricter aspects of the *Verpackungsverordnung* (Fishbein, 1994). The plan has increased prices for consumer products across the board, and there is not much that industry can do about it. Also, while GD fees, once adjusted for inflation, are lower now than ever before in Germany, they still create a burden for companies that must eventually pass these costs on to the consumer (PRO Europe, 2007).

Another main concern that industry, especially marketers, has with the *Verpackungsverordnung* is the stress that it places on eliminating secondary packaging waste. Secondary packaging often creates an image in the consumer's mind that could mean the difference between average and extraordinary for a bottle of alcohol, package of cheese, or the latest children's toys (Fuller, 1999). It could be the one thing that differentiates a product from its competitors at the point of purchase, and it provides a convenient location for marketers to build brand recognition and recall. Without secondary packaging, marketers are limited to what they can put on the primary packaging, reducing the potential for brand enhancement.

Successes of the GD

The GD has succeeded as a symbol of environmental responsibility throughout Europe. It is still very much alive today as the primary contributor to the reduction of packaging waste and the promotion of recycling efforts in the EU. DSD continues to lead packaging waste reduction efforts in Germany with great success, despite the arrival of various competitors in the field since it was permitted in 2003. GD fees in Germany are lower than ever before, thanks to innovative processes and technologies developed by DSD (PRO Europe, 2007). The program also enjoys tremendous support from German citizens, who participate in the program daily.

Statistical Successes

In Germany alone, DSD has collected more than 65 million metric tons for recycling, significantly reducing the amount of waste headed for landfills and incinerators

Table 12.1

Recycling Targets and Recovery Percentage by Material

Packaging Material Type	Statutory Recovery Target (%)	Recovery Target Achieved in 2005 (%)*
Aluminum	60	157
Plastics	60	75
Composites	60	64
Paper/Cardboard	70	117
Tinplate	70	100
Glass	75	97

Source: PRO Europe, 2007, p. 14.

Note: *Recovery targets over 100 percent show that DSD has recovered more material than was licensed by the company.

(PRO Europe, 2007, p. 15). This change, in turn, has made significant contributions to the overarching goals of climate protection and resource conservation. In 2005, DSD saved an estimated 71 billion megajoules of primary energy by recovering packaging waste for recycling. The recycling conducted by DSD in that year saved 1.7 million metric tons of carbon dioxide emissions from going into the atmosphere (DSD, 2007, p. 21). This is the equivalent of 3.6 million airline passengers flying from Cologne to the Canary Islands and back again. Recycling targets set by the packaging ordinance amendment of January 7, 2006, and the actual percentages collected by DSD in 2005 are shown in Table 12.1.

These statistics do not take into account that the program encourages companies to reduce the amount of packaging that they are using in the first place and to use recyclable materials in package construction. DSD has reached agreements with approximately 450 local authorities, such as cities and municipalities, which are responsible for local waste management and recovery. These agreements, along with process innovation and technological development, have allowed DSD to become a truly efficient enterprise. A recent fee schedule for packaging by material is shown in Table 12.2.

German Attitudes and Beliefs About the Program

Household sorting of packaging waste and recyclables is well accepted throughout German society. "Ninety percent of citizens are in favor of the separate collection of waste and want to keep collecting their waste in yellow bags or recyclable waste bins in the future," claims Dr. Heike Schiffler of the DSD (PRO Europe, 2007, p. 15). In 2005, each consumer collected on average 63 kg. of packaging waste for collection by DSD. Many consumers see this as an important environmental contribution that they can easily make. DSD wants this attitude to continue into the future and therefore focuses on continual innovation in their collection processes to make it easier on the consumer.

Table 12.2

GD Fees by Material Type

Packaging material type	Fees in euro cents/kg valid january 1, 2006
Plastics	135
Composites	104.5
Composite Cartons	77.5
Aluminum	75.6
Tinplate	28
Paper/Cardboard	18
Natural Materials	10.2
Glass	7.6

Source: PRO Europe, 2007, p. 15.

In interviews conducted with German citizens, we noted that the German subjects viewed recycling their packaging much as Americans view recycling aluminum beverage cans (Zimmermann, 2008). It is important to do, but not because of any significant personal benefit and not because of any strong will to do well for the environment. In fact, other than their recycling, the German citizens interviewed did not personally have strong views on protecting the environment (Janda, 2008). It seems that, at least in this case, German citizens recycle because they view it as something that everybody else does. It ends up being self-fulfilling; if citizens think that nearly everybody does it, then nearly everybody will do it.

Successes Outside Germany

PRO Europe has brought the GD program to twenty-four countries besides Germany. Collectively, the programs using the GD symbol have provided untold environmental benefits throughout Europe; however, stories from specific countries often provide the best illustration of the program's successes. Some of the different approaches used by various European countries, and their successes, are described below.

"Valpak," in the United Kingdom, uses an interesting system for determining fees, one of which is market driven. Each participating company pays for the recycling of its allocated "obligation" through the purchase of Packaging Waste Recovery Notes (PRNs), the price of which is determined by the type of material that each note represents and the market for recycled content from that material (PRO Europe, 2007, p. 60). This policy ensures that the recycling industry for that material has enough money to invest in collection and infrastructure. It also inadvertently encourages the use of other materials for which there may be more demand. The Valpak system only requires companies creating more than 50 metric tons of packaging waste, with a turnover of more than £2 million, to register and pay fees for waste. It is not uncommon for countries acting under the EU Directive on Packaging Waste to place limits on the types of companies that are obligated to participate.

The French "Eco Emballages" program is similar to the DSD in that it collects fees from industry for its services (PRO Europe, 2007). It negotiates six-year contracts with collection companies to provide pickup and sorting of recycling. Recently, Eco Emballages began to develop the infrastructure to collect and recycle waste from electronics, a move that should encourage product design that allows for easy disassembly and recycling. The system is well accepted by the French public, with an estimated 80 percent of citizens participating daily (PRO Europe, 2007, p. 19).

Bulgaria, one of the more recent EU entrants, has a similar system for recycling packaging waste. The Waste Management Act of 2003 (WMA) requires the national manufacturers and producers of imported goods to meet specific targets for packaging recovery and recycling (PRO Europe, 2007). Although companies are not required to be part of an organization, "EcoPack Bulgaria" provides convenient collection services, and most companies choose this option. Producers and importers must pay a product tax if the goals are not met either individually or collectively in this system. Although the program is still in its early stages, EcoPack Bulgaria exceeded the goal set by the WMA and recycled 27 percent of packaging in 2005 (PRO Europe, 2007).

With many other successes such as those described above, the GD program in all its forms has contributed greatly to some of the larger objectives of sustainable development. Although these requirements are all government initiated, it is industry itself that implements these different collection programs. Together, business and government can have positive effects on the natural environment, and the GD program is a great example of what can be achieved through this cooperation.

Implementation in the United States

One of the main objectives of researching this material was to provide examples of programs in other countries that may guide implementation of a similar program in the United States. There are so many factors to consider in this matter, especially regarding the influence of politics and industry, that it is not possible to address them all within the scope of this paper; however, a noncomprehensive list of important factors that would affect a successful launch might include:

1. resistance from municipal and state governments,
2. industry cooperation in the venture,
3. consumer attitudes toward recycling, and
4. recycling capacities and technologies currently available.

Conclusion

The collection and recycling of packaging waste is an important issue for all modern societies and is something that must be addressed before the situation becomes irreversible. While some other types of waste are unavoidable, or unrecoverable, packaging can eventually be all but eliminated from the "single-use" waste stream. Recovering and recycling packaging not only saves raw materials that are in ever-shorter supply but also contributes to climate protection and other primary objectives of sustainable development.

Programs such as the GD are not an unbearable cost burden for business; rather, they offer the opportunity, and incentive, to rethink designs and processes that can be dramatically improved. Companies that embrace such a program early on, and make the necessary changes, will gain a competitive advantage over firms that do not. They not only will incur less in recycling fees but may also trim costs by reducing the amount that they waste. Government influence over business is frequently debated and doubtless many business interests would say "less is better"; however, because of the environmental issues that we now face, it is important for initiatives similar to the *Verpackungsverordnung* to be considered and, if feasible, implemented in the United States. These ideas are not new but, rather, tried and tested systems that have had great success in Europe and beyond. Packaging waste reduction plans, such as the GD, demonstrate proven tactics for accomplishing this goal.

References

Dueles System Deutschland (DSD). (2007). *Fakten: Informationen für Journalisten.* www.gruenerpunkt.de/fileadmin/user_upload/Seiteninhalt/Dateien/pdfs/0705_Fakten_final.pdf.

Dueles System Deutschland (DSD). (2008). *Der Grüne Punkt: Dueles System Deutschland.* www.gruener-punkt.de.

Environmental Data Services. (1993). U.K. to oppose EC targets for packaging waste. *The ENDS Report,* 217, 40–41.

Europe Information Service. (1993). Waste: New German law for economic recycling. *Europe Environment, 408,* II-2.

Fishbein, B. K. (1994). *Germany, garbage, and the Green Dot: Challenging the throwaway society.* New York: Inform.

Fuller, D. A. (1999). *Sustainable marketing: Managerial-ecological issues.* Thousand Oaks, CA: Sage.

Janda, R. (2008). Personal interview.

Gettelman, E. (2009). Aboxalypse now. *Mother Jones* (November/December). www.motherjones.com/environment/2009/11/aboxalypse-now.

Kahle, L. R., & Beatty, S. E. (1987). Cognitive consequences of legislating postpurchase behavior: Growing up with the bottle bill. *Journal of Applied Social Psychology,* 17(9), 828–843.

Kaufman, L. (2009, October 19). Nudging recycling from less waste to none. *New York Times*, p. A1.

McGlade, J. (2004, March 1). European packaging waste trends and the role of economic instruments. Speech, European Voice Conference. www.eea.europa.eu/pressroom/speeches/01–03–2004/.

Mintu-Wimsatt, A., & Lozada, H. (Eds.) (1996). *Green marketing in a unified Europe*. New York: International Business Press.

PRO Europe. (2007). *Europe goes green dot.* www.pro-e.org/Brochure__Europe_goes_Green_dot_.html.

PRO Europe. (2008). About PRO Europe. www.pro-e.org/Introduction.html.

Zimmermann, Z. (2008). Personal interview.

Part IV

Applications of Environmental Sustainability

As the concept of environmental sustainability encompasses various areas, it is important to see how this concept is implemented in those areas. Accordingly, Part IV introduces examples of environmental sustainability applications.

Cornwell and McAlister focus on the development of food preferences and food choices in early childhood and provide insights regarding interventions for more sustainable food consumption habits. Based on a thorough literature review, the authors show that preschool children are affected by marketing and advertising practices when they are shaping their food consumption habits. They conclude the chapter by providing suggestions for parents, caregivers, and marketers: Parents and caregivers should remove all packaging to reduce food and brand associations, package healthy food choices in fun ways, reduce the commercial content available to children, and be aware of the commitment that they are making with meal deals with collectible toys. Marketers can also support the sustainable food consumption initiatives through various methods such as offering only water as the default drink in kids' meals.

Russell, Flora, Strohmaier, Pöschko, Perez, Yu, Smith, and Rubens examined the online conversation about energy efficiency behavior by using the data collected on Twitter through the analysis of the messages, users, and content hashtags in tweets over a period of four months. Results indicate opportunities for text analysis on Twitter content to understand how to improve the relevance of energy efficiency communications and demonstrate user-friendly tools to visualize the semantics of vast quantities of user-generated content about energy and sustainability. The authors conclude that studying Twitter communications can be an important tool in assessing engagement and identifying influencers as well as word-of-mouth communities that can accelerate change in energy efficiency behaviors.

Moscowitz and Kahle examine the potential consequences of and problems in the revised Oregon Bottle Bill (OBB) from a comprehensive, marketing-based business perspective. The authors conducted telephone interviews and secondary research through media accounts to learn about the responses to the OBB revisions and to compare the revised OBB with bottle bills and container return programs in other states, such as California, Connecticut, Michigan, and Hawaii. Based on these phone interviews and state comparisons, Moscowitz and Kahle provide specific recommendations—for example, rebranding Oregon's container-deposit return program and increasing the deposit fee—and discuss how the implementation of these recommendations can make the program more effective.

Wiggin discusses how consumers select livable communities as well as the implications for consumers living in those communities. Using an Internet-based survey, the author found that community members define values and attributes of a livable community differently, which creates various market segments, and that a livable community and the identification with that community improves satisfaction and reduces mobility desires among those who reside there. Overall, Wiggin concludes that a livable community that provides a sense of social cohesion among community members drives sustainability in that locale.

13

Preschool Children's Preference for Energy-Dense, Branded Foods

An Unsustainable Trajectory

T. Bettina Cornwell and Anna R. McAlister

When one thinks of sustainability, many things may come to mind: miles per gallon or per liter, greenhouse gases, recycling, and eco-friendly behaviors of all sorts. Food behavior is likely not to be the first to mind when one thinks of our stewardship of the natural environment, although perhaps it should be a higher priority.

It has been recognized for some time that certain food behaviors, for example, choosing to eat beef (Sager, 1995), have a direct link to environmental degradation. In addition, the diet of most developed countries and large segments of many developing countries (Edwards, 2004) has put obesity center stage in issues facing world health. Health-care costs in many countries have an unsustainable trajectory in which continued increases threaten the ability to provide basic services. Of importance to the current chapter, "Health officials worldwide are concerned about the numbers of people who are overweight, particularly in childhood, putting them at risk for a multitude of chronic diseases as they age" (Edwards, 2004). In the interests of individual health, as well as the health of society and the capacity of health-care systems to cope with demand, change is needed. This chapter highlights the need for a better understanding of media and marketing exposure in early childhood and the development of food preferences and food choice. It delivers insights for interventions that can return society to a sustainable path.

The Case for Early Intervention

Changes in dietary patterns associated with environmental degradation and chronic disease must logically start with children. Eating patterns established in childhood are correlated with adult eating patterns and influence adult health (Kemm, 1987). Current weight-related disease in adolescents and children is found, for example, in type 2 diabetes and fatty-liver disease, and projections into adulthood suggest increased limb amputations due to diabetes and increased coronary heart disease, resulting in preventable deaths (Ludwig, 2007).

Behavioral change is known to be difficult, thus a move to more sustainable food behaviors early should have the greatest long-term benefit to individuals, society, and the environment. Unfortunately, basic knowledge of healthy food behaviors is not enough. People, even children, know that they should eat plenty of fruits and vegetables, but that goal fails to be reached by the majority of the population. In 2009, for example, only 32.5 percent of American adults met the goal of consuming two servings of fruit per day, while only 26 percent met the vegetable target of three servings per day (Centers for Disease Control and Prevention, 2010). Given that educational programs have largely failed in changing behavior, alternative thinking about the starting points of obesity is urgently needed.

The Potential for Early Intervention

On the positive side, restoring a healthy trajectory may be aided by the fact that preferences are malleable. Humans have the capability to adapt to the available food supply, and therefore flavor preferences retain plasticity throughout their lifespan (Myers & Sclafani, 2006). The golden opportunity, however, seems to lie in the formative years, when food preferences are initially established. Wardle et al. (2008) report an intervention in which children ages five to seven were exposed to raw red pepper and, after eight days, exhibited an increased liking for red pepper and an increased consumption of it. Skinner, Carruth, Bounds, and Ziegler (2002) argue that repeated opportunities to taste a food increase the chances that a child will accept or like the food. This logic of repeated exposure and trial extends to any food. Therefore, if children are regularly exposed to and sample French fries, then they are likely to develop a preference for them.

A central argument of this chapter is that the current way of thinking about food preference development and food choice intervention needs to be revised. Research investments and program interventions to date have largely centered on school-age children. One could reason that this is where many children are first affected by public policy. Unfortunately, even if food choices in school lunch programs are improved, as long as they have choice, children will largely choose according to established preferences. Therefore, early intervention in this discussion considers the preschool-age child.

One must ask why more attention has not been directed to researching this group. One reason is that it is difficult. Recruiting families, preparing materials for parents and for young children, and coordinating data collection sessions that are often individual are all factors that make the process time consuming and expensive. Another, perhaps more important reason for the limited emphasis on young children is that, from a marketing communications perspective, preschool children have been thought to be unresponsive and relatively unaware of marketing (for a review, see John, 1999). This view arose in the 1980s and 1990s, due in part to past research that did not consider the individual development of young children.

In the following sections, we briefly review the historical underpinnings of the popular notion that young children are relatively unresponsive to marketing and advertising and then provide a summary of recent studies that show how preschoolers are impressionable and how their thoughts and behaviors are shaped by their experiences with marketplace offerings. This chapter concludes with commentary regarding the potential for young children to engage in sustainable consumption behaviors, as well as suggestions as to how these behaviors can be encouraged at an early age.

Why Young Children's Consumption Has Been Largely Overlooked

Some of the earliest studies on persuasion knowledge concluded that children under the age of eight do not understand advertising persuasion (for a review, see Macklin, 1987). Ward and Wackman (1973), for example, concluded that children with "low cognitive ability" show little knowledge of advertising persuasion because they "cannot abandon their own perspective and take the perspective of the advertiser when viewing commercials" (p. 127). This conclusion was drawn after the researchers administered cognitive tasks to categorize their sample of five- to twelve-year-olds into one of three cognitive ability levels. Similarly, John (1999), after reviewing past literature, has asserted that children age two to seven view advertising as informative and entertaining because they have difficulty engaging in mental perspective-taking and hence fail to understand an advertiser's perspective until age eight. Reviewing evidence from multiple studies of persuasion knowledge, John (1999, p. 189) concluded that "there is little reason to believe that the vast majority of children younger than seven or eight years of age have a command of advertising's persuasive intent."

This dominant view in the marketing literature was largely unquestioned for many years. Donohue, Henke, and Donohue (1980), however, provided one exception. These researchers considered the fact that earlier studies relied heavily on interview questions to assess persuasion knowledge (e.g., "Why are commercials shown on TV?"). Donohue and colleagues argued that children's responses may have underrepresented their ability to detect persuasion, if their responses were unduly restricted by a lack of verbal skill. When Donohue et al. used a nonverbal task to assess persuasion knowledge in children ages two to six, 80 percent of children succeeded at the task. The findings from Donohue et al. suggest that tasks with low verbal demands allow preschoolers to demonstrate their knowledge of persuasion. However, attempts to replicate these findings have been mixed (see Ballard-Campbell, 1983; Kunkel, 1988; Macklin, 1987).

Other researchers examined the influence of premiums on children's preference for advertised products and concluded that children were not strongly influenced by the inclusion of a giveaway. For example, Shimp, Dyer, and Divita (1976) tested first- through sixth-grade children in an experiment assessing the effectiveness of an NFL team patch offered with an advertised cereal. These researchers reported no significant relationship between children's ratings of the team patches and their ratings of the cereal; however, they did acknowledge that the results may have been misleading because there was a ceiling effect in children's ratings of the premium. Heslop and Ryans (1980) conducted a similar study to assess premiums and reported that they might influence children's preferences but would ultimately have little impact on product choice. Although these studies contribute to an opinion that marketing to children might be harmless, the fact that distributors of cereal, fast food, candy, potato chips, and various other products continue to promote their wares with the inclusion of free premiums suggests that the marketing tactic is more successful than these academic findings would indicate.

Recent Studies with Young Children

Although much of the twentieth-century literature settled on the conclusion that children younger than eight are relatively unaffected by marketing, recent studies are painting a different picture. Studies in marketing did not keep pace with studies in developmental psychology that were challenging Piagetian views and broad groupings found in developmental stages. Developmental psychology was turning more and more to measures of individual differences in various developmental capacities. Using age-appropriate and individual testing methods, researchers in marketing and public policy have recently shown that preschool children are knowledgeable about brands and that food brands are particularly important in their lives. The evidence from these studies suggests that children's behavior—in terms of food choice—is significantly influenced by marketing tactics, and, unfortunately, the most persuasive tactics frequently lure children to consume energy-dense foods that are low in nutrient value.

A 2010 study by Mink and colleagues provides compelling evidence regarding the risk to children's health if they are persuaded to consume the foods that are targeted directly to them. Mink et al. (2010) report that a diet consisting of the types of foods advertised on commercial television would provide "5,560 percent of the recommended daily servings for sugars, 2,080 percent of the recommended daily servings for fat, 40 percent of the recommended daily servings for vegetables, 32 percent of the recommended daily servings for dairy, and 27 percent of the recommended daily servings for fruits" (p. 904). Young children are likely to request the foods that they see advertised on TV and marketed in their environment (Harris, Schwartz, & Brownell, 2010). Following is a brief review of some of the recent studies that detail early emergence of brand awareness and responsiveness to advertising in young children.

Brand Awareness

Some of the early literature on children's consumer socialization concluded that it is not until sometime around sixth grade that children develop an understanding of the ways in which brands serve as social symbols (for a review, see John,

1999). Our firsthand observations of young children suggested to us that surely something has been overlooked. The "cool" kids in preschools were the ones with the "right" foods at lunchtime. Whether it was Nemo on the yogurt container or SpongeBob on the sandwich bag, we observed how packaged foods containing brand logos and character endorsements served as symbols for identifying status in the preschool environment. Naturally, the possibility exists that this observation could be confounded. Perhaps the branded foods do not "make" these kids popular. Perhaps the popular kids happen to have the packaged foods, and some other underlying variable (e.g., family income) is at play. But there were also other hints that brands held strong meaning for these youngsters. For example, in casual conversation, a child asked to describe a favorite food would say "McDonald's" rather than naming a single item. So our anecdotal observations led us to design a study to test children's ability to recognize various brands and to see what meaning these brands hold for very young children.

Existing studies on the topic of brand symbolism had focused largely on the meaning of clothing brands (e.g., Achenreiner, 1997; Jamison, 2006). We suspected that very young children might be interested less in clothing brands and more in brands of toys and food, since these types of products feature more prominently in children's conversations and interactions with one another. To be sure, we tested three- to five-year-olds to determine their ability to recognize 25 child-oriented brands (e.g., Lego, McDonald's) and 25 adult-oriented brands (e.g., Nestlé, Nike). Recognition rates ranged from 0 percent to 93 percent across all 50 brands (McAlister & Cornwell, 2010a). Not surprising was the finding that McDonald's was the brand most easily recognized by preschool children. Recognition rates were significantly higher for children's brands as opposed to adult-oriented brands, and clothing brands showed one of the lowest rates of recognition for any product category that was tested. These findings suggest that young children are relatively proficient at recognizing brands and that their abilities have perhaps been underestimated in past studies that focused on product categories that are more relevant to teens and pre-adolescents.

Not only are preschool children capable of recognizing particular brand logos, but many of the youngsters in our study also had developed memory networks regarding the meaning of those brands. In a collage task, which required children to sort picture cards from two competing brands as well as distracter images, we found that many preschool children could tell a McDonald's drive-thru image from a Burger King restaurant image, they knew which characters were associated with which brand, and they also knew that a KFC bucket of chicken and a piece of broccoli did not "belong" with either McDonald's or Burger King. Likewise, preschoolers were relatively adept at distinguishing between Coca-Cola and Pepsi branded items and separating these out from images of beverage items offered by other brands. From a marketing and advertising perspective, the ability to recognize a brand and distinguish it from other competing offerings is brand differentiation.

The surprising (and somewhat disconcerting) finding came in a follow-up study in which children were asked their opinions about another child whom they had not yet met (McAlister & Cornwell, 2010a). Children rated their perceptions of the unfamiliar child's popularity and whether the unfamiliar child would be a fun play partner. The only information given about the unfamiliar child was information about his/her use of branded items (e.g., "This boy drinks Coke. Do you think he has a lot of friends or no friends or somewhere in between?"). Approximately one-third of participants in this study made meaningful judgments of the other child that were grounded in what they knew about the other child's brand usage. We were not so interested in whether the attributions were positive or negative but, rather, were more focused on the fact that children as young as three would inform their friendship decisions on the basis of whether another child ate McDonald's or Burger King or drank Pepsi or Coca-Cola.

Robinson, Borzekowski, Matheson, and Kraemer (2007) have also demonstrated preschool children's responsiveness to branding. Not only were the three- to five-year-olds in their study capable of recognizing the McDonald's brand logo, but these researchers also found that the preschoolers' perceptions of food taste were heavily influenced by packaging. Allowing the children in their study to taste various foods, Robinson et al. found that store-bought foods (e.g., carrots, milk) were perceived as tasting better when wrapped in McDonald's packaging, and the same effect also held for McDonald's food. That is, chicken nuggets and fries purchased from McDonald's were rated as tasting better when presented in branded packaging than when they were not known to have originated from McDonald's. Similarly, the presence of licensed characters on food packaging can shape children's perceptions of taste and their behavior when making snack food selections (Roberto, Baik, Harris, & Brownell, 2010).

Persuasion Knowledge

Another question of interest is whether children realize that advertising is typically a call to action for potential consumers. Do children know that the purpose of advertising is to prompt you to buy something? To address this question, we assessed three- to five-year-old children's ability to recognize persuasive intent in advertisements (McAlister & Cornwell, 2009). Like Donohue et al. (1980), we used a task with minimal language requirements. We showed children five different print advertisements and after each ad asked the question: "What does the [brand] man want you to do now?" Children responded by pointing to one of three picture response options for each ad. On each trial, one response option always depicted a purchase or consumption behavior. The other response options featured the advertised product in a manner unrelated to consumption or purchase (e.g., recycling the plastic Coke bottle). We found that approximately 35 percent of our sample selected the correct answer on three or more of the five trials. From our sample of 46 children, six children showed perfect ability to select the consumption option.

Are these findings more convincing than the opposite findings reported in earlier studies (e.g., Ward & Wackman, 1973)? We believe the answer is yes. Included in our testing of these children were developmental assessments. We recorded children's chronological age and took measures of their language ability and their social skills development. Using hierarchical multiple regression, we controlled for age and language and examined the relationship between social skills level and persuasion knowledge. Children with more developed social skills were better able to understand the intent of the advertiser than children with less developed social skills. Of particular interest was the fact that language ability was a significant covariate in the prediction of persuasion knowledge. These findings support the argument that the overly complex verbal requirements of earlier studies may have underestimated children's understanding. Our findings align with those of Donohue et al. (1980) who also detected persuasion knowledge in young children when using tasks with lowered verbal demands.

Given that one-third of our sample of preschool children showed above-chance ability to recognize persuasion attempts, we argue that preschoolers are relatively tuned in to advertising. They are aware that advertising is a part of their daily environment, and they know that a behavioral response is expected when one sees an advertisement. Does this mean that preschoolers are savvy consumers? Not necessarily so. What we have learned is that the preschool years are a time when young children become aware that an advertiser wants them to purchase the advertised product (or to request a purchase), but we have no evidence to suggest that children are skeptical of these persuasion attempts. With regard to food consumption, it may be problematic if children see foods advertised on TV or elsewhere and believe that the appropriate response is then to consume those foods without question.

Formation of Taste Palate and Links to Brand Awareness

Advertising has a dual function of both informing and persuading. As young people, children have limited information about the world, thus, they may find the information available in advertisements useful in terms of helping to guide their expectations. What drink might children expect to accompany the popcorn they get at the movies? If the picture on the sign at the concession stand shows a cup of soda, it makes sense that children would learn to associate popcorn at the movies with soda rather than juice, milk, or water. Likewise, because the majority of fast food burger restaurants typically offer burgers with fries on the side, children might come to expect fries with their burger, a soft drink as the beverage, and condiments such as ketchup. But what happens when a burger is served at home? Do fries necessarily come with that burger? Will the burger taste just like the one at Burger King, or can it be made to taste similar by the addition of condiments, such as ketchup? Chances are that children may have developed particular expectations via advertising and marketing exposures. Findings from our 2011 study suggest that children may actively seek to replicate behavior patterns learned with branded foods when they dine at home.

In our 2011 research paper, we report findings that children's brand knowledge is developed through TV viewing and through actual physical consumption (Cornwell & McAlister, 2011). Here we used the same collage task from our earlier research to measure children's memories for soda brands (Coke and Pepsi) and fast food brands (Burger King and McDonald's). As in our prior study, we again observed that preschool children showed evidence of established memory networks for these brands. Children who watch more hours of commercial TV each week scored higher in terms of their brand knowledge, as did children who ate at fast food restaurants more frequently. Interestingly, though, TV viewing and fast food consumption were not significant predictors of a child's taste preferences.

To measure taste preference, we developed and validated a survey measure for parents to report on the tastes that their children enjoy (Cornwell & McAlister, 2011). This scale measure shows good internal consistency and yields two scores, namely, a score reflecting a child's preference for food high in salt, fat, and sugar (SFS), as well as a score indicating a child's tendency to consume flavorful foods. Using structural equation modeling, we found that a child's preference for SFS foods was significantly related to their knowledge of fast food and soda brands. This preference, in turn, was related to "flavor hit behaviors" (e.g., consumption of flavorful foods like Doritos and candy such as sour worms, and addition of flavor to foods, such as by adding salt, ketchup, butter, or toppings).

It was somewhat surprising to find that a preference for SFS foods is related to brand knowledge but not to fast food consumption or exposure to commercial television. We argue that a palate that favors SFS foods may develop because children have very positive associations with the brands that offer foods matching this description. After children have information in memory regarding McDonald's and Burger King, Coke and Pepsi, they might seek exciting consumption experiences even in the absence of these brands. Indeed, we found that the children who knew the most about the brands we tested were the same children who were more likely to add ketchup, sauces, and spices to their meals, butter to their popcorn, and toppings on their ice cream. From this data, it appears that preschoolers who have stored information about these brands might seek to replicate their brand experiences with other food and drinks. Adding flavor to foods in this manner is arguably problematic, because it increases the consumption of overall calories as well as sodium.

Children's Responses to Strategic Marketing: The Case of Toy Premiums

Since the late 1970s, McDonald's has offered the familiar Happy Meal consisting of a sandwich, fries, soda, and a toy. In recent years, the company has faced pressure to improve the nutritional content of their kids' meals, so the offering has been altered slightly to include different meal options. A popular take on the meal today includes chicken nuggets, apple dippers (apple slices with, e.g., caramel dipping sauce), milk and, of course, the toy. Although McDonald's may have been the first to offer the three-item kids' meal with a free toy, numerous other restaurants have followed suit. In 2010, this practice came under fire amid claims that toys should be banned from kids' meals because the success of the toys in marketing fast food was thought to contribute to obesity in the United States (Bernstein, 2010). Even the alternative food offerings have come into question; for example, the apple dippers have been criticized for their caramel sauce accompaniment. Toys included in kids' meals are seen by some as "a powerful lure for children, encouraging them to eat unhealthy food, which then helps cause obesity" (Bernstein, 2010).

A handful of counties in California are testing a system in which restaurants are permitted to offer a toy with a combo meal only when the meal contains less than 500 calories, less than 600 milligrams of salt, less than 35 percent of total calories from fat, and less than 10 percent of total calories from added sugars or sweeteners and in which the meal contains half a cup of fruit or vegetables and one serving of whole grains (Frumkin, 2011). It has been acknowledged that "these types of toy bans take a lot of time and energy to address" (Frumkin, 2011), and the debate has been fueled by each side's passion for the questions at hand, rather than by empirical data regarding children's food choices. A question of central importance is whether banning the toys or restricting their use would result in an overall improvement in children's diets. This question has two aspects: Does the inclusion of a toy significantly increase a child's likelihood of wanting the fast food meal? Does restricting toy use mean that healthier foods could be marketed successfully such that they would be chosen over less-healthy foods?

To address questions regarding the potential efficacy of proposed interventions, we set about conducting research with preschool children to examine their choice behavior regarding meal deal offerings (McAlister & Cornwell, 2012). We examined a "less-healthy" meal and a "healthier" meal under conditions incorporating no toy, a collectible toy, or a noncollectible toy. Across two studies with separate samples of preschool children, we found that the healthier meal was rated just as favorably as the less-healthy meal when both meals included a collectible toy. In our second study, we found that children were significantly more likely to choose the healthier meal over the less-healthy meal when the healthier meal included a collectible toy and the less-healthy meal was offered without any toy. When each meal was offered without any toy, the less-healthy meal was more likely to be chosen.

These findings provide evidence that children's impressions of food are powerfully influenced by the toy offered alongside the meal. They also suggest that an outright ban on toys in kids' meals may not necessarily lead to the desired change in children's diets, at least not in the short run. If toys are banned from kids' meals, children who already prefer energy-dense foods may still not choose healthier alternatives. It must be noted, that most children age three to five have had experience with meal deals at restaurants, so it is difficult to say how taste preference might develop if children were not already introduced to high fat, sugar, and salt meal offerings. What our findings can clearly support on the grounds of developing food preference is that including collectible toys with meals that meet strict "healthy" nutritional guidelines could support preference for those foods.

Also of interest in our research were various findings showing that the allure of a collectible toy was much stronger than that of a noncollectible toy. This is especially important when we consider that the marketing strategy of including a collectible toy with a kids' meal supports not only brand knowledge and product trial but also repeat purchase. The sets of collectible toys offered by popular restaurants typically comprise five or six toys. Findings from our recent studies suggest that a child who has acquired items from a collectible set will likely be highly motivated to acquire the remaining items (McAlister & Cornwell, 2012; McAlister, Cornwell, & Cornain, 2011). Hence, when a restaurant offers kids' meals with collectible toys, they are likely to make five or six sales to each individual customer. If the meals are not nutritionally sound, this repeat exposure is cause for concern. Skinner et al. (2002) report that repeated opportunities to taste a food increase the chances that a child will like that food. Likewise, Birch and Marlin (1982) find that children prefer—and are more likely to choose—foods that are more familiar to them from prior exposure. Although restaurants might be using the marketing strategy of pairing collectible toys with their meals with the primary goal of the selling each meal, the use of collectible toys may inadvertently be having a much larger impact on children. Through repeat purchase of the meals, children's overall food preferences may be affected.

Summary and Suggestions Toward a Sustainable Future

The studies summarized in this chapter paint a picture of preschool children engaged with brands and influenced by marketing tactics. The important element that differentiates child consumers from adults is that they may not think to question how their behavior is being directed. Although preschoolers in our studies and Donohue et al.'s (1980) study showed an ability to detect persuasive intent in advertising, they did not demonstrate any skepticism about said persuasion. Given the nutritional value of the foods currently advertised to children, Mink et al. (2010) illustrate how an unquestioning response is problematic. Children who request and consume the types of foods advertised to them will consume sugar and fats in excessive amounts, and their daily intake of dairy, fruits, and vegetables will fall well below target levels.

New Trajectory Thinking for Parents and Guardians

Small-scale changes could commence in the home and in preschool settings to orient children toward a sustainable food trajectory early in their development. Findings reviewed here uncover some of the roots of children's preferences, thereby providing an evidence base to inform interventions. We now know that children recognize brand logos and use them as a foundation upon which to build memory networks of information. Although they may not possess the language skills to hold a sophisticated conversation about different brands and products on the market, children judge their peers on the basis of brand usage, and they form attitudes toward products and anticipate the taste of new foods according to the brand. All consumers rely on decision-making heuristics to reduce effort and energy committed to information processing (Scheibehenne, Miesler, & Todd, 2007), however, it appears that children rely heavily on brand logos to help them locate the products (including foods) that they desire. This sheds some light on the underpinnings of children's product preferences and may be helpful in terms of empowering parents and caregivers in interventions designed to counteract marketing efforts and orient children toward healthier food choices.

Parents could apply Robinson et al.'s (2007) findings regarding McDonald's wrappers to encourage their children to eat healthier foods. The approach could be twofold. First, if purchasing fast food for their children, parents could remove all packaging so that associations between the food and brand are reduced. Second, fruits, vegetables, and home-cooked meals could be "promoted" by packaging them in fun ways. One recent study showed how children's perceptions of taste are altered by the presence of a cartoon character on the container, whether for carrots, graham crackers, or gummy fruit snacks (Roberto et al., 2010). While these researchers reported a weaker effect in terms of the ability of cartoon characters to sway children's perceptions of carrots than of candy, we argue that the effect might be strengthened if parents remove fun associations from the energy-dense foods. In other words, innovative approaches like these might be most effective if children believe that fruits, vegetables, and other healthy options are the only foods available in cartoon-adorned packaging.

Parents and caregivers could also consider reducing the commercial content available to children. We have previously suggested that one of the simplest ways to achieve this is to replace TV time with DVD viewing, because DVDs do not contain as much advertising content as commercial TV (McAlister & Cornwell, 2010b). We also suggest that parents, other guardians, and preschool staff encourage a healthy level of skepticism by making time to talk with children about the advertisements to which they are exposed.

Many parents are familiar with the dilemma of wanting to set boundaries regarding the foods that they allow for their children but at the same time wanting to feel that they are not constantly saying "no." One way to deal with this problem is to shortlist the foods you will agree to and then permit your child to make the final selection. This allows your child a "safe" space in which to practice making independent decisions. If there are particular brands that you trust (i.e., you believe that the brand consistently offers high-quality, nutritious food) then those brand logos may come to serve as green lights to your child. Children will learn that "I'll get a 'yes' when I ask for [brand]."

Parents who struggle to say "no" to their children may find it difficult to deny a child's request for a meal paired with a collectible toy. Parents could say "no" if the meal on offer is of low nutritional value. Our findings indicate that having the "starter" items of a collectible set is likely to motivate children to want to complete the collection. Thus, what might start as one meal purchase may turn into a further four or five meals in order to complete the set. Parents should be aware of the commitment that they are making with that first purchase. Unless your state has regulations in place to restrict the pairing of collectible toys with meals that meet strict nutritional guidelines, we recommend that parents be wary of these toys. If your child's pleading for the toys is difficult to handle, think about visiting the restaurant without your child present to ask whether you may purchase the collectible set without purchasing the meals. Although it is not legally required, many restaurants offer this option.

New Trajectory Thinking for Advertising and Marketing

As micro-level initiatives nudge children in the direction of healthy food choices, it is important for policymakers to consider the ways in which macro-level systems can support these initiatives. From a transformative consumer research perspective, one that seeks to help consumers make better decisions, eating environments should foster positive dietary habits. In addition to the restriction of toy premiums in fast food promotion, other possible policies that might be considered as voluntary industry decisions or enforced limitations include offering only water as the default drink in kids' meals to reduce caloric intake from sugar-sweetened beverages. Likewise, buffet restaurants—where children frequently serve themselves—could limit visual and physical access to soda by replacing all-you-can-drink soda fountains with water fountains. While some of these changes may sound radical for a commercial enterprise, many are already being introduced in California preschools. The Healthy Beverages in Child Care Act was signed into law in California in 2010. The act specifies provisions, which went into effect in January 2012, that require licensed day-care facilities in California serve no beverages with added sweeteners (either natural or artificial) and make clean and safe drinking water readily available and accessible for consumption throughout the day (Robert Wood Johnson Foundation, 2010).

Of course, this is an overall system challenge that has many levels. Food companies, both restaurant chains and processed food manufacturers, in the pursuit of market share have emphasized taste and, under competitive pressure, salt and other flavor makers such as sugar and fat have seen an upward spiral. In this competitive landscape, any single company that makes a less flavored offering might not be chosen. Recent collaborative agreements among large food companies to reduce salt content (Associated Press, 2010) might drive an adjustment of people's palates to more healthful levels. Yet another part of the problem is that many of the niche health food producers that have products in line with advocated nutritional guidelines have limited distribution and even more limited promotional budgets. It seems, then, that micro-level changes may be needed while large-scale macro-level changes are contemplated.

If advertising is as powerful as suggested in its influence on children, one would expect that healthier foods could be successfully directed to them. While sustainable consumption must start with the right product offering (e.g., nutritious food items), marketing efforts could be made to invoke real change. Behavioral change might occur on a conscious or subconscious level, but what matters most is that consumers—including child consumers—are reoriented toward a pattern of repeat choices that is sustainable in the long term.

References

Achenreiner, G. B. (1997). Materialistic values and susceptibility influence in children. *Advances in Consumer Research, 24,* 82–88.

Associated Press (2010, April 26). 16 food companies agree to reduce salt. CBS News. www.cbsnews.com/stories/2010/04/26/health/main6434928.shtml.

Ballard-Campbell, M. (1983). Children's understanding of television advertising: Behavioral assessment of three developmental skills. *Dissertation Abstracts International, 44* (2–1), 314.

Bernstein, S. (2010, April 28). It's a sad day for Happy Meals in Santa Clara county. *Los Angeles Times.* http://articles.latimes.com/2010/apr/28/business/la-fi-happy-meals-20100428/.

Birch, L. L., & Marlin, D. W. (1982). I don't like it; I never tried it: Effects of exposure on two-year-old children's food preferences. *Appetite, 3*(4), 353–360.

Centers for Disease Control and Prevention (2010). State-specific trends in fruit and vegetable consumption among adults—United States, 2000–2009. *Morbidity and Mortality Weekly Report, 59*(35), 1125–1162.

Cornwell, T. B., & McAlister, A. R. (2011). Alternative thinking about starting points of obesity: Development of child taste preferences. *Appetite, 56*(2), 428–439.

Donohue, T. R., Henke, L. L., & Donohue, W. A. (1980). Do kids know what TV commercials intend? *Journal of Advertising Research, 20*(October), 51–57.

Edwards, B. (2004, April 26). Analysis: World Health Organization's proposal to fight global obesity epidemic. National Public Radio, Morning Edition. www.highbeam.com/doc/1P1–93852838.html.

Frumkin, P. (2011, April 8). NYSRA: Proposed toy ban is micromanaging. *Nation's Restaurant News.* http://nrn.com/archive/nysra-proposed-toy-ban-micromanaging/.

Harris, J. L., Schwartz, M. B., & Brownell, K. D., et al. (2010, November). *Evaluating fast food nutrition and marketing to youth.* Fast Food FACTS Report, Yale Rudd Center for Food Policy & Obesity. www.rwjf.org/content/dam/farm/reports/reports/2010/rwjf68794/.

Heslop, L. A., & Ryans, A. B. (1980). A second look at children and the advertising of premiums. *Journal of Consumer Research, 6*(4), 414–420.

Jamison, D. J. (2006). Idols of the tribe: Brand veneration, group identity, and the impact of school uniform policies. *Academy of Marketing Studies Journal, 10*(1), 19–42.

John, D. R. (1999). Consumer socialization of children: A retrospective look at twenty-five years of research. *Journal of Consumer Research, 26*(3), 183–213.

Kemm, J. R. (1987). Eating patterns in childhood and adult health. *Nutrition and Health, 4*(4), 205–215.

Kunkel, D. (1988). Children and host-selling television commercials. *Communication Research, 15,* 71–92.

Ludwig, D. S. (2007). Childhood obesity—the shape of things to come. *New England Journal of Medicine, 357*(23), 2325–2327.

McAlister, A. R., & Cornwell, T. B. (2009). Preschool children's persuasion knowledge: The contribution of theory of mind. *Journal of Public Policy and Marketing, 28*(2), 175–185.

McAlister, A. R., & Cornwell, T. B. (2010a). Children's brand symbolism understanding: Links to theory of mind and executive functioning. *Psychology and Marketing, 27*(3), 203–228.

McAlister, A. R., & Cornwell, T. B. (2010b). Children and advertising: Parents' role. *Pediatrics for Parents: The Children's Medical Journal for Parents, 26*(9–10), 18–19.

McAlister, A. R., & Cornwell, T. B. (2012). Collectible toys as marketing tools: Understanding preschool children's responses to foods paired with premiums. *Journal of Public Policy and Marketing, 31*(2), 195–205.

McAlister, A. R., Cornwell, T. B., & Cornain, E. K. (2011). Collectible toys and decisions to share: I'll gift you one to expand my set. *British Journal of Developmental Psychology, 29,* 1–17.

Macklin, C. (1987). Preschoolers' understanding of the informational function of television advertising. *Journal of Consumer Research, 14,* 229–239.

Mink, M., Evans, A., Moore, C. G., Calderon, K. S., & Deger, S. (2010). Nutritional imbalance endorsed by televised food advertisements. *Journal of the American Dietetic Association, 110*(6), 904–910.

Myers, K. P., & Sclafani, A. (2006). Development of learned flavor preferences. *Developmental Psychobiology, 48*(5), 380–388.

Robert Wood Johnson Foundation (2010). Healthy beverages in child care bill signed into law in California. www.healthyeatingresearch.net/news/271-healthy-beverages-in-child-care-bill-signed-into-law-in-california/.

Roberto, C. A., Baik, J., Harris, J. L., & Brownell, K. D. (2010). Influence of licensed characters on children's taste and snack preferences. *Pediatrics, 126,* 88–93.

Robinson, T. N., Borzekowski, D. L. G., Matheson, D. M., & Kraemer, H. C. (2007). Effects of fast food branding on young children's taste preferences. *Archives of Pediatrics & Adolescent Medicine, 161*(8), 792–797.

Sager, G. (1995). "A burger and a coke" and other environmental problems: Reflections on diet and the environmental crisis. *Sustainable Development, 3,* 149–157.

Scheibehenne, B., Miesler, L., & Todd, P. M. (2007). Fast and frugal food choices: Uncovering individual decision heuristics. *Appetite, 49,* 578–589.

Shimp, T. A., Dyer, R. F., & Divita, S. F. (1976). An experimental test of the harmful effects of premium-oriented commercials on children. *Journal of Consumer Research, 3*(1), 1–11.

Skinner, J. D., Carruth, B. R., Bounds, W., & Ziegler, P. J. (2002). Children's food preferences: A longitudinal analysis. *Journal of the American Dietetic Association, 102*(11), 1638–1647.

Ward, S., & Wackman, D. (1973). Consumer socialization: Initial study results. *Advances in Consumer Research, 1,* 120–125.

Wardle, J., & Cooke, L. (2008). Genetic and environmental determinants of children's food preferences. *British Journal of Nutrition, 99*(S1), S15–S21.

14

Semantic Analysis of Energy-Related Conversations in Social Media

A Twitter Case Study

Martha G. Russell, June Flora, Markus Strohmaier, Jan Pöschko, Rafael Perez, Jiafeng Yu, Marc A. Smith, and Neil Rubens

This chapter describes a large-scale social media data collection and research program focused on energy efficiency and climate change. The ultimate goal of this two-year program of work is to refine an energy and climate change taxonomy of terms, develop analytics that are robust in the face of an extensive database, and conduct iterative tests of simple and complex analyses (frequency of mentions over time; connections to social events, social networks and building, and maintenance of online energy related issue communities). The final goal of the program is to make the analytic tools and database available to energy-related scholars as well as others for the advancement of a social movement for environmental sustainability.

People influence others and are, in turn, influenced with respect to the actions, brands, products, and issues that they love and hate. This influence promotes awareness, motivates trial behaviors, reinforces purchase decisions, and sustains product or action loyalty. Large-scale social movements such as those for energy efficiency and sustainability require an initial articulate community with a shared belief to create virality. Word of mouth, online or in person, is essential to break down barriers, to spread ideas and actions, and to develop innovations. In fact, the ripple effect of word of mouth is estimated to have three times the reach and impact of traditional advertising (Hogan, Lemon, & Libai, 2004). Diffusion of information underpins the success of campaigns to drive change in behavior and the adoption of a sustainable lifestyle to reduce greenhouse gas emissions.

The term "social media" describes the online tools and platforms that people use to share opinions, insights, experiences, and perspectives with one another. Social media can take many different forms, including text, images, audio, and video. Understanding conversations in online social media has the potential to provide program planners and communication campaign managers with unique insights into individuals' thoughts and verbal productions about energy efficiency and climate change. Because of the increasing adoption of social media (73 percent of teens and 72 percent of young adults [Lenhart, Purcell, Smith, & Zickuhr, 2010]), new opportunities are available for studying the role of online conversation intended to persuade.

In 140 or fewer characters, the concerns, interests, and public narratives about energy efficiency and climate change are easily identified. Twitter conversations also reflect the social aspects of information diffusion through conventions such as retweets and other conversational responses, through the membership and social distance of these conversations, and in changes over time in the frequency and form of the networks. Twitter, a particularly popular type of social media that has proven relevant in a number of social challenges and conversations recently (such as the 2010–2011 revolutions in the Middle East), allows the social response to social or national events, as well as the media coverage of these events, and persuasive communication campaigns to be observed. Twitter is both a medium and the message (Savage, 2011).

This chapter outlines the broad aims of an ongoing research program to track and analyze social media conversations of more than 100 terms related to energy efficiency and climate change for insights about consumer attitudes and behavior. It describes in detail the first assessment of the project, which we have begun with an exploratory analysis, to investigate the extent to which Twitter conversations about energy consumption can be tracked and analyzed using a social media analysis framework for studying energy consumption descriptors, concerns, actions, and sources of information. Preliminary results from the initial phase of research confirmed the existence of energy-related conversations on Twitter and the usefulness of Twitter streams for assessing awareness of communication campaigns, brands, products, and policies related to creating communities of awareness, interest, and action regarding energy behavior. We examined the periodicity, content, and context of that conversation.

This arena of scholarship is essentially interdisciplinary. Our research team leverages expertise from multiple fields of scholarship: climate science, communications, systems analysis regarding marketing and advertising, and computer science (more specifically, machine learning, natural language processing, and network analysis). In our view, such collaborative work adds value to individual disciplines as well as providing actionable insights into the international concern of advancing energy efficiency and slowing climate change. While we find this interdisciplinary approach to studying energy-related conversations on Twitter fruitful and necessary, we are well aware of the challenges related to gauging and evaluating the research output of such an endeavor.

This chapter does not aim to provide definitive answers to the questions of whether, how, and to what extent public conversations on energy-related topics take place on Twitter. It does, however, identify concepts that can be used to initiate a research agenda on analyzing the semantics of conversations in social media regarding energy and climate change, in the hope of spurring further research in this domain.

Who Tweets, About What, and with What Impact?

Like other social media, Twitter was assumed to start with teens and then to move to other audiences. But Twitter took a different turn:

> Another reason that teenagers do not use Twitter may be that their lives tend to revolve around their friends. Though Twitter's founders originally conceived of the site as a way to stay in touch with acquaintances, it turns out that it is better for broadcasting ideas or questions and answers to the outside world or for marketing a product. It is also useful for marketing the person doing the tweeting, a need few teenagers are attuned to. (Miller, 2009)

Content analyses and user interviews reveal that Twitter is not focused on personal social issues but, rather, has a stronger emphasis on ideas. Recent data from Pew's ongoing media tracking studies (Smith & Rainie, 2010) reinforce the demographic diversity of Twitter users. Of the 72 percent of adult online media users, 8 percent are Twitter users. More specifically:

- Young adults: Internet users ages 18–29 are significantly more likely to use Twitter than are older adults. Also, these voting-age adults can significantly influence community and social policy as well as opinion regarding climate change.
- African-Americans and Latinos: Minority Internet users are more than twice as likely to use Twitter than are Caucasian Internet users. The uniquely deep reach of Twitter into this diverse audience may lead to more rapid diffusion of educational and vocational opportunities thought to bring about economic recovery in the United States.
- Urbanites: Urban residents are roughly twice as likely to use Twitter as rural dwellers.

Further, Twitter users vary in the frequency with which they check the site. Thirty-six percent of Twitter users check for material posted by others on a daily basis or multiple times per day—this is roughly comparable to users' engagement frequency. Forty-one percent say they check the site less than every few weeks or never do so. The remaining one-quarter of users say they check the site for updates a few days a week or every few weeks (Smith & Rainie, 2010).

Social media have been widely used for consumer goods and services. Market leaders such as Coca-Cola and Proctor & Gamble, specialty product companies such as Snap-on Tools, and cable channels such as CNN and MSNBC have incorporated Twitter into the media channels that they use proactively, creating communication campaigns that include social media for their consumer communities. In fact, the 2011 Superbowl featured the first-ever Twitter hashtag included in a television commercial as a call-to-action (Wasserman, 2011). A distinguishing feature of social media is that, while it may be initiated or catalyzed by communications in other channels, it is inherently consumer-generated content, and its virality depends on engagement. Even companies that do not actively sponsor social media have used it to monitor the nature and strength of consumer sentiment about their brands, products, and services (Wasserman, 2011).

Business metrics for social media measurement include subscriptions, traffic, and content and user profiles. The speed, breadth, depth, and rhythm of social media communications create a frame, or window, through which the volume, sentiment, and dispersion of consumer sentiment can be tracked. These metrics are considered early indicators and provide quick feedback on consumer response. Media effectiveness analysis typically focuses on a single metric: the number of click-throughs to views on YouTube, the number of friends on Facebook, the number of connections on LinkedIn, the number of followers on Twitter, the number of click-throughs on blogs, and the number of registrations on podcast downloads. Newer metrics that more accurately reflect the multidimensional nature of engagement are needed.

For example, early metrics based on buzz have proven useful for monitoring consumer opinions and behavior through social media noninvasively. Marketers have used metrics to guide their direct and indirect deployment of communications for awareness, trial, conversion, and loyalty campaigns (Russell, 2009, 2011a; Russell et al., 2011b). However, the known persuasive influences of communities and key opinion leaders have led to the development of revolutionary assessment techniques for diagnosing the health of a social media community and for identifying social roles in social media (Wu, 2009). The competitive value of metrics lies in being able to make early diagnosis for swift interventions in either sponsored or ad hoc social media—in order to achieve the most favorable results in influencing consumers' attention and behaviors—and in being able to marry traditional marketing, advertising, and promotional strategies and tactics with the viral potential of word-of-mouth influence through social media.

Twitter use is growing in prevalence among market leaders and innovators, and it reaches audiences essential to a social movement for sustainable lifestyles. Its use encompasses strong and weak personal and social ties, and it reaches previously untapped but affected audiences. Perhaps most important, Twitter content is issue-laden. Thus systematic access to data and conversations on Twitter allows us to study public conversations on a new scale.

Research Approach and Setup

Based on these observations, we selected public conversations and dialog on Twitter as a relevant phenomenon for our research on energy behavior change. To validate the decision, we asked whether, how, and to what extent public conversations on energy-related topics take place on Twitter.

In the first phase of our research program, our broad research question asks, "How do online conversations about energy efficiency behavior change over time?" We developed an eco-linguistic taxonomy of terms to describe energy use opinions, energy efficiency behavior, frames, metaphors, and technologies and to determine standard sources of energy information, such as the Department of Energy (DOE) and the Environmental Protection Agency (EPA). We captured tweets containing those terms, parsed identified elements of the communications, curated the data, and archived the data for access. We conducted a preliminary analysis of the messages, users, and content of the 18,338 hashtags that occurred at least three times in the 2.47 million tweets collected between September 3, 2010 and January 4, 2011. The analysis of this eco-linguistic-filtered social media was aimed at explaining the frequency, context, and potential persuasive influence of social media conversations about changing energy behaviors (Russell et al., 2011). We operationalized conversations to be mentions over time of our predetermined eco-linguistic terms and co-occurrence of related hashtags in Twitter. Three techniques were used to cull discernible patterns from the large quantities of data and portray the data visually: content analysis of the full tweets, network analysis of co-occurring hashtags, and semantic analysis of the co-occurring hashtags and their authors.

The Role of Social Media Conversations in Social Movements

There is a growing academic literature on the definition and measurement of persuasion, including social media conversations. Studies of argumentation pathways acknowledge the influence of source, attitudes, information processing, behavior, mental shortcuts, and sustaining reinforcers (Kaptein, Markopoulos, de Ruyter, & Arts, 2010). New insights advance our understanding of the complex interactions between the cognitive (resonance—"get it"—speaks to me); emotional (totally immersed, absorbed, the opposite of indifference); social (interactive, participative and involved); and temporal (longevity, a commitment to the future, seeing a long-term relationship) factors in interactive persuasion. Continuous partial attention characterizes the shift of attention from one medium to another in consumers' day-to-day multitasking and multimedia environments (Block & Schultz, 2009; Ophir, Nass, & Wagner, 2010). Programs focused on persuasive interactions address the management of attention to obtain total engagement (Reeves & Read, 2009).

The predominant one-to-many model of mass communication campaigns has undergone significant change with the proliferation of new channels and the advent of unstructured communication (Daft, Lengel, & Trevino, 1987), the declining audience of traditional channels (Livingstone, 2005), and the broad participation of users in generating content for single and mass audiences (Fogg, 2008). Effective messages must be increasingly targeted to smaller audiences, including an audience of one. The personalization of communications to an expanding number of individuals has depended on advances in several fields, including artificial intelligence, machine learning, psychology, sociology, and communication (Nass & Yen, 2010).

Further, the expansion of undirected and user-controlled communication forums, such as Twitter, offer the possibility of a new understanding of "grassroots" social

Table 14.1

Latest Messages Containing Energy-Related Keywords and Taxonomy

Term category	Number	Percent
1. Energy technologies/hardware and software (e.g., plug load sensors, smart meters, power strips, brands such as TED)	19	13
2. Communication behaviors, e.g., monitor energy bills	4	3
3. Energy and climate change frames, metaphors, and visualizations	41	28
4. Energy efficiency and climate change innovation programs (e.g., Carrotmob, 350, Earth Hour, Earth Day)	6	4
5. Issues such as renewable energy, global warming, energy insecurity	11	8
6. Utilities, venture firms and companies (all California)	9	6
7. Behavior: Low cost, high impact	20	14
8. Behavior: Low cost, lower impact	21	15
9. Behavior: High cost, high impact	9	6
10. Behavior: Higher cost, lower impact	4	3
Subtotal behaviors	54	38
Current total	144	

change. Thus both directed programs (such as socially motivated games) and less-well-defined and even spontaneous programs (such as a new YouTube video or a new climate calculator mounted on a credible Web site) have the potential to stimulate user-generated persuasion, in the context of technologically enhanced word of mouth. Along the continuum of intentions to influence how people think and act, persuasion depends on attention, engagement, and argumentation. Because it is user generated, social media includes all three of these elements. Either directly or indirectly, it evokes the presence of, or reference to, other people as social agents (Bailenson & Yee, 2005).

Tools for Data Acquisition, Curation, and Analysis

Data were acquired on a daily basis by using the NodeXL Twitter Importer module (Smith & Rainie, 2009), which captured the latest messages containing energy-related keywords, shown in Table 14.1. In addition to the message itself, acquired data include username of the message sender, along with the time and date of the message. The dataset was then parsed and analyzed by using Hadoop Map Reduce distributed processing on Amazon's EC2 computing cloud. By including 20 standard computing instances (~1 GHz, 1.7 GB memory), the complete dataset could be processed in less than an hour. The data processing selected tweets collected between September 3, 2010 and January 4, 2011, containing hashtags that occurred in at least three of the 2.47 million tweets. Data for these tweets were then passed to other applications—Excel, NodeXL, Gephi, and TwitterExplorer—for further analysis and visualization.

Using Energy-Related Terms to Filter Twitter Messages

A critical preliminary task in this research program was to create a taxonomy that describes the target behaviors, technologies, programs, information sources, issues, issue-frame metaphors, and visualizations related to a social movement for the development of sustainable lifestyles. Based on literature on the lexical framing of climate change, metaphors from analyses of climate-change journalism, risk communication, and public discourse, we constructed a taxonomy that included positively and negatively valenced frames, compound metaphors, frames that encompass moral imperative, values, and social movement frames, as well as energy reduction, conservation, and energy-wasting behavior (Lakoff, 2010). Tweets that contained these terms were selected into our dataset.

Although we used the conceptual underpinnings from the growing field of eco-linguistics and parent fields of rhetoric and linguistics, the actual wordings of behaviors and topics were standardized to match those used in several credible sources (e.g., Department of Energy, 2011; Environmental Defense Fund, 2011; Environmental Protection Fund, 2011). For our current investigation, standardization meant that the search terms for behaviors and topical issues were exactly as worded in source documents. If, for example, the behavior "take shorter showers" is worded differently in different source documents, all are included. Because there are myriad Web sites, nongovernmental organizations, government, and other sources for energy behaviors and terms, we are continuing to standardize those most closely aligned with the ones used in U.S. national policy. For example, all energy-related phases are derived from energy efficiency and renewable energy Web site and booklets from the DOE, the EPA, the National Academy of Science, and the Environmental Defense Fund. In the future, food issues and behaviors and transportation terms will be added and standardized to credible sources.

Table 14.1 shows the broad set of energy-efficiency terms selected for our research program, including metaphors for energy efficiency, behavior, and feedback as well as issues and four classifications of behavior.

In addition to Advanced Research Progress Agency (ARPA) energy-e salient terms, we also included indirectly related words on close contextualized issues, such as global warming and climate change, as well as broader but related social movements, such as "simpler lifestyle," "reducing consumerism." Finally, not included fully in this table but considered essential for the complete set of terms relevant to changes in energy-efficiency behavior, are behaviors related to broader issues: advocacy behaviors and food and transportation behaviors. Because many of the terms in the eco-linguistic taxonomy were already in common use, the creation of this taxonomy will allow an observation over time of changes in their use. The complete taxonomy of terms, their selection, collection, and specificity as well as standardization to known sources are described in more detail in a working white paper for Media X (Russell et al., 2011b).

Table 14.2

The Number of Tweets including Energy Terms, September 2010

Number	Energy term
11,629	power strips
21,600	smart homes
26,405	layer up
39,205	powermeter (Google)
40,145	thermostats (programmable)
52,287	remote + sensing
61,187	energy + Audi
81,023	cfls + lowlight
81,029	cfls + bad
81,232	cfls + ugly
83,097	cfls + mercury
83,128	alert devices
83,617	black balloons (visualization from energy campaign in Australia)
113,145	energy conservation
233,791	teds (the energy detective)
336,741	Energy Star (energy-efficient U.S. government-approved appliances)
340,533	smartmeters (utility-installed houly signal energy meters)
352,199	windpower
374,487	solarpower
395,495	cleantech
468,647	led
615,919	energy efficiency

Analyzing the Conversations

Several analytical lenses were tested in this exploratory study: frequency, periodicity, valence, co-occurrence, and context. Through several methods, we were able to describe snapshots and detect changes over time in the conversation as well as identify conversation-stimulating events, such as national policy, new technology launches, and media events.

Frequency of Mentions

The frequency of term mentions was counted as the number of tweets collected by filtering on the eco-linguistic terms. The frequency of September 2010 mentions of a sample of energy terms is shown in Table 14.2.

Periodicity

To understand the "drivers" of shifts in the conversation, changes in frequency over time were of particular interest. A sampling of tweets on all eco-linguistic terms over a two-month period revealed two rhythmic patterns: The social conversation

Figure 14.1 **Proportion of Tweets Containing Eco-linguistic Terms** (September–October 2010)

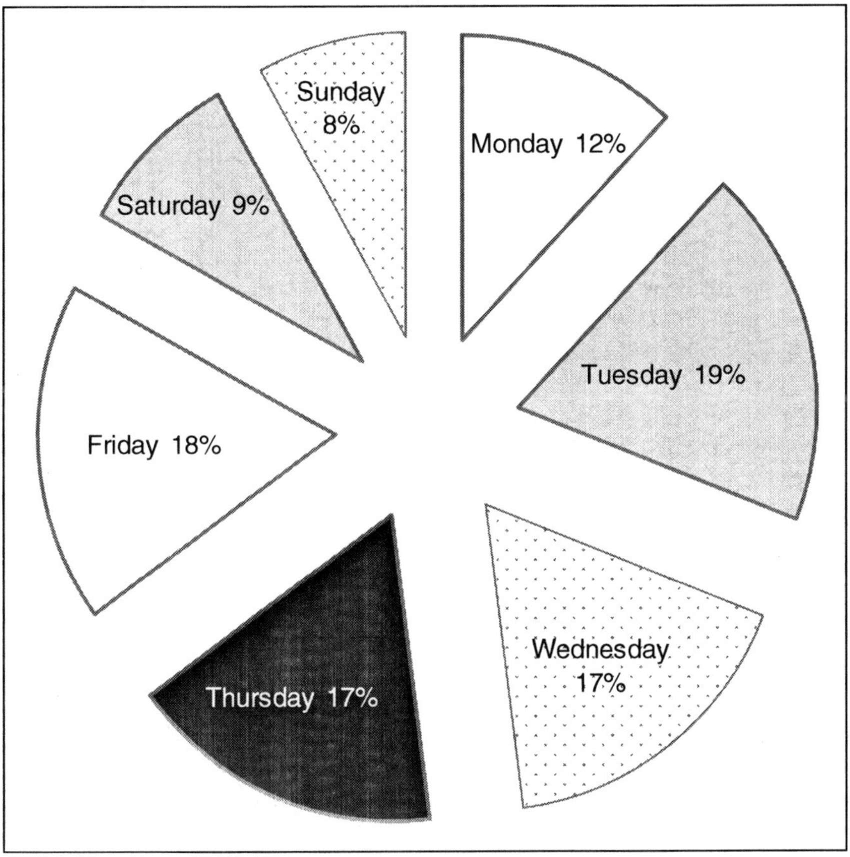

showed a day-of-the-week rhythm as well as consistently lower numbers of energy-related tweets on weekends.

The daily rhythm of all energy-related tweets collected in September and October 2010 are illustrated in a figure available at http://mediax.stanford.edu/ien/fig1.pdf. More analysis over longer periods is needed to determine whether this figure can be considered a baseline of "energy tweets," a growing trend, or a response to large media coverage of energy-related issues. The relatively lower frequency of tweets over the weekend was noted and prompted an inquiry about daily patterns.

Figure 14.1 shows the proportion of tweets containing the eco-linguistic terms that occurred by day-of-the-week during September and October 2010. In general, fewer tweets about energy occurred over the weekend and on Monday, while a higher proportion of tweets occurred between Tuesday and Friday. Further analysis would be necessary to see whether the content of workday tweets is qualitatively different from that of weekend tweets.

Closer analysis of one particular term over the two-month period revealed bursts of conversation during two periods (see the figure available at http://mediax.stanford.edu/ien/fig3.pdf). An analysis of the September–October 2010 tweets containing the term "smart meter" shows two periods during which a higher number of tweets about smart meters took place.

Word visualizations of the content of "smart AND meter" tweets during the two periods of heavy use revealed the influence of mass media on the Twitter conversations. Further analysis of the content of these tweets indicated reference to a political event and a media-promoted issue. In early September, the content in the "smart AND meter" tweets included many mentions of the announcement of a new rebate program for the installation of "smart AND meters," shown in a word cloud (see the figure available at http://mediax.stanford.edu/ien/fig4.pdf). In the 107 tweets, selected for their mention of "smart AND meters" during the period September 8–21, 2010, the relative frequency of "smart," "smart, AND energy" allow visibility of a wide diversity of other terms used in the tweets. "RT," the convention for retweeting a message, is also visible. An examination of the content of the tweets including URLs revealed interest in the announcement of a new federal rebate program for installation of smart meters and the release of a study about energy efficiency.

The content analysis of the full text of 210 tweets between October 25 and October 29, 2010, including "smart AND meters," is shown in a word cloud (via Wordle.com, in the figure available at http://mediax.stanford.edu/ien/fig5.pdf). Relative to the number of words in the tweets, the high proportion of the words "grid," "power," energy," and "security" revealed consumer concerns about the security of personal data and protection from hackers; URLs referred to several news stories on these issues. The strength of "RT" indicates the word-of-mouth value of some of the tweets. The selection criteria included the words "smart," "meters," and "meter"; and the prominence of those terms is perceptible.

Valence and Sentiment

Frequent positive or negative word associations with terms can reflect perceived and actual sentiment associated with the terms. Recalling Table 14.2 and the September 2010 test of a sample of the data, words with negative associations ("ugly" AND "bad") were observed in combination with the "cfls," forming compound terms (cfls AND . . .). These frequently occurring compound terms reflected time-specific negative attributes (perceived and actual) of compact fluorescent lights (CFLs), a highly touted energy-saving replacement for incandescent bulbs.

Sentiment analysis requires highly nuanced interpretations and represents a complex set of evaluations and other forms of social media indicators such as pronoun use (shared reality and social connection); verb use (particularly emotionally valenced or recommendation verbs); syntactical references; and style (immediacy—short words, first-person pronouns, low number of articles, positive emotion, more verbs than nouns). Sentiment analysis can provide important indicators of engagement, intimacy, and social connection to brands, products, or services. Linguistic markers and sentiment analysis can be used to diagnose engagement in online conversations and evaluate the customer context (Pennebaker, Mehl, & Niederhoffer, 2003). Because of the contracted lexicon and linguistic conventions of Twitter, new classification schema are needed for sentiment analysis of tweets. At the time of this writing, several unpublished proprietary tools for this are known to exist and are in use by businesses, but none are known to be available in an open-source format for scholarly use.

Context

Context is important in understanding how energy-efficient behaviors and actions, such as purchases, align with climate-change issues or with comprehensive lifestyle movements such as "low-impact lifestyles." This includes the network patterns created by co-occurrence of ARPA-e-related energy terms as well as the nature and extent of terms describing related issues such as energy insecurity, climate change, and environmental sustainability. In this preliminary study, context was visualized in the network patterns created by directed communication between tweeters, using the @Twittername conventions. Context was also operationalized as networks of hashtags occurring in tweets selected because they included one or more of the selected eco-linguistic terms. In addition, context was visualized as a tweetnomy (Wagner & Strohmaier, 2010), using Twitter Explorer (Wagner& Strohmaier, 2010).

Directed Communication Between Tweeters

In this chapter, Twitter messages are viewed as an element of conversation in one of three ways. The person sending the message, the tweeter, is intentionally addressing the message to a known individual, using the convention of @twittername (@ replies). The tweeter is referring a message or partial message that has been received from a known individual (retweets, indicated with the "RT" convention). Or, the tweeter is broadcasting a message to the broader social media community, for example, to an imagined individual or group of individuals, sometimes using key words or tags, such as #hashtag. Most Twitter users associate an image with their Twittername.

A network of directed communication between tweeters mentioning "smartmeters" or "smart AND meters" is shown in the Figure 14.6 available at http://mediax.stanford.edu/ien/fig6.pdf.[1] Each @Twittername creates a directional edge from the author to the intended recipient. Each RTtwittername creates a directional edge from the retweeter to the author. Roughly half of the 107 mentions in this sample of September 2010 tweets containing #smartmeter hashtags are not directed or connected; the tweets simply include the hashtag. In the remainder of the tweets, one large network focused on the Twittername "SFGate" dominates, with several other smaller clusters also evident, all showing a "reply magnet" social role (Gleave, Welser, Lento, & Smith, 2009). The network patterns show a simple star pattern, in which one node forms the center of the network, without interconnectivity across the other nodes.

Hashtag Network Visualization

Hashtag is a Twitter linguistic convention constructed by placing a # in front of a key word, abbreviation, or acronym. Hashtags provide a means of tagging, labeling, or adding context or metadata to Tweets. The use of multiple hashtags in a single tweet can be interpreted as a connection between the thoughts, terms, or issues by the author. We examined the co-occurrence of hashtags in the network analysis of 18,323 hashtags to evaluate the visibility of issues such as climate change, energy efficiency, and environmentalism.

A network visualization of the co-occurrence of 18,323 hashtags is shown in http://mediax.stanford.edu/ien/fig7.pdf. Each hashtag is represented by a node; the size of the node is proportional to the connectedness of that node to other nodes. In addition to #energy, other salient nodes with their own clusters of networks are #green, #solar, #climate, #eco, and #news. A more distal node with a significant network is the term #jobs. The spatial distance on the network indicates that the conversations about energy efficiency are separate from the conversation about clean technology or energy jobs.

The use of graphic images to represent network configurations is important because it allows investigators to gain new insights into the patterning of connections (Freeman, 2009). Information visualization amplifies human comprehension through an expressive view that can stimulate insight on a given phenomenon represented by the data.

The network visualization shown in Figure 14.7 available at http://mediax.stanford.edu/ien/fig7.pdf, was generated using the Network Explorer module (Rubens, Russell, & Perez, 2011) for Gephi (Bastian, Heymann, & Jacomy, 2009). The size of the node corresponds to the node's degree (number of edges), and the gradation of the node's color corresponds to the node's betweenness centrality (how well it connects the nodes, i.e., a measure proportional to the number of paths in the network that pass through a given hashtag). Thus, the term #energy has a high degree of centrality to all terms in the visualization. The position of nodes (network layout) was determined in two stages: (1) cluster-based and (2) relation-based compacting.

In the cluster-based stage, we use OpenOrd layout algorithm (Martin et al., 2011), because it produces a layout that allows us to better distinguish clusters based on the interconnections between the nodes. We then applied ForceAtlas (Bastian et al., 2009), to lay out the subgraphs (nodes repel one another, while edges pull nodes closer together). The network figure is embedded in a PDF document, which results from this process, by using scalable vector graphics, so it is possible to zoom in to look at finer details of the network without the loss of resolution. The data for the network structure were obtained by applying the tweetonomy concept (Wagner & Strohmaier, 2010) to the dataset. To produce a smaller subnetwork of higher "quality" we have kept only the hashtags that were connected to one another through edges with weight (number of co-occurrences between hashtags) of 100 or larger. The resulting network consists of 416 nodes and 1,103 edges.

Constructing Tweetonomies: Acquiring Latent Semantic Structures

"Tweetonomy" is a concept (envisioned and studied by Wagner & Strohmaier [2010]) that denotes the latent semantic structures that can emerge in social streams such as Twitter as a byproduct of online conversations. Based on analysis of messages and their content, as well as URLs and other user-based syntax such as hashtags, slashtags, or @ replies, tweetonomies can be constructed in a variety of ways. Emerging communication conventions on Twitter yield a large number of ways in which such taxonomies can be constructed by considering, for example:

1. the author(s) of messages;
2. recipients of messages;
3. retweets or diffusion of information;
4. contents of a message such as links embedded in messages, key words, or hashtags; and
5. the time of messages.

The term "tweetonomy" was inspired by research on social tagging systems (see, e.g., Helic et al., 2011; Koerner et al., 2010) in which the collective act of tagging resources (such as assigning the tag "news" to the resource; www.cnn.com) yields so-called folksonomies (VanderWal, 2007)—from folk-generated taxonomy. The idea of folksonomies is that a common structure emerges from the individual classification acts of a large number of users. Similarly, tweetonomies denote the emerging structures observed when large numbers of users collectively organize and structure conversations in online social media such as Twitter.

TwitterExplorer (Russell et al., 2011), a partial implementation of the concept of tweetonomies, is used to analyze and visualize the latent semantic structures embedded in energy-related conversations on Twitter, as seen in the figure available at http://mediax.stanford.edu/ien/fig8.pdf. TwitterExplorer is a user-friendly social stream analytics tool that was implemented based on the Django Web development framework, using Whoosh for indexing, NetworkX for network layout, and KMETIS for graph partitioning. TwitterExplorer visualizes semantic relations between terms used in Twitter messages based on different aggregation and similarity measures. In the following examples, semantic similarity between terms is calculated based on co-occurrence of terms within messages (tweets).

This analysis was performed on a sample of the 2.47 million tweets that contained any of the eco-linguistic terms included in this study. Tweets were selected into this sample on the basis of hashtags that were present in at least three tweets. Illustrative results demonstrate the use of this new tool for data acquisition, curation, and analysis. Three findings can be observed in this analysis; the entry term #smartmeter most often co-occurs with the terms #energy, #utilities, #cleantech, #greenjobs, #greentech, and #smartgrid; two locations, #Illnois and #California; and one brand, #deloitte. This first layer of co-occurring terms is then connected to a larger layer of co-occurring terms at the edge of the network circle. Interestingly, few of these networked terms convey the increased ability of customers to understand their energy use. Additional insight on the context of the conversation and the issues that it includes can be explored through examination of the content of the tweets.

TwitterExplorer: An Interactive Tool to Explore Tweetonomies

A screenshot of the Energy-TwitterExplorer showing details for the hashtag #energy is shown in the figure available at http://mediax.stanford.edu/ien/fig9.pdf. In the upper left, TwitterExplorer shows a list of tags related to #energy ranked by co-occurrence in tweets. In the upper midsection, TwitterExplorer shows a 2-hop ego-network of terms related to #energy based on co-occurrence in tweets. On the upper right, current tweets that include the hashtag #energy are pulled in real time from the Twitter Application Programming Interface (API). The chart on the left ("statistics") visualizes different properties for the #energy hashtag stream over time, including social diversity of the stream, which characterizes the extent to which tweets in the stream were authored by different users. The chart on the right ("environment statistics") plots the same properties for the hashtags semantically related to the #energy hashtag. Although this screenshot depicts semantic statistics for a single hashtag (here, #energy), TwitterExplorer provides an easy-to-use user interface to support analysts in exploring all other topics (hashtags) in the dataset in a similar manner. On the bottom, a list of all tweets that include the hashtag #energy in the dataset is presented.

Summary

The data, tools, and initial analysis presented in this chapter represent the first steps toward more refined analytical approaches that help explain the large-scale conversations taking place on Twitter and elsewhere. This case study has demonstrated the feasibility of using data-mining techniques to gather and analyze vast amounts of data from ongoing social media conversations and of analyzing the data for meaningful metrics that describe conversations about energy consumption behavior. The methods for this preliminary investigation included development of a list of energy-related metaphors, terms, and general descriptors as well as a list of energy conservation and reduction behaviors, monitoring term usage (location, frequency, context, clustering) on the Internet at frequent intervals, analyzing data for frequency and location of communication, clustering of terms over time—such as changes in their proximity and occurrence and the introduction of new terms and the fading of others.

Our initial exploration confirmed that conversations about energy-related issues are, indeed, taking place in social media, specifically Twitter, and that these communications can be studied to better understand how to use technologically enhanced word of mouth to stimulate user-generated persuasion. Using content analysis of full tweets, network analysis of co-occurring hashtags, and semantic analysis of the co-occurring hashtags and their authors, this preliminary investigation identified descriptors, concerns, actions, and issues. We confirm that studying Twitter communications can provide a means for assessing engagement, identifying influencers, and identifying word-of-mouth communities that can accelerate change in energy-efficiency behaviors.

An eco-linguistic taxonomy of more than a hundred terms was created, and included terms for energy technologies/hardware and software; communication behaviors; energy and climate change frames, metaphors, and visualizations; energy efficiency and climate change innovative programs; issues such as renewable energy, global warning, and energy insecurity; utilities, venture capital firms, and companies; and behaviors (high- and low-cost and impact).

For example, an issue-based sample of the tweetstream was captured and curated as a dataset. During the period from September 3, 2010 to January 4, 2011, over 2.47 million tweets that included one or more of the terms in our eco-linguistic taxonomy were gathered. These tweets contained 18,338 hashtags that were mentioned three or more times. Data analysis methods were applied to explore the aggregate of energy consumption-related conversations in vast quantities of Twitter data.

This case study demonstrated preliminary steps in tracking the extent to which energy-related terms are used by tweeters and the periodicity and content of their communications. Periodicity was observed by day or week and by topic in the Twitter conversation, as a whole and for hashtags of specific interest. The presence of emerging social communities was observed in a network of directional tweets. Content analysis of the tweets revealed a relationship between the volume of tweets on a topic (using a particular hashtag) and the visibility of social interest and concern in issues of broad significance. Analysis also showed that social media conversations can be used as a source of information about changing energy behaviors.

Using network analysis of hashtags, we analyzed and visualized contextual relationships among the salient terms used in social conversations and identified several clusters of related issues, revealed by the co-occurrence of hashtags. Through Twitter/Explorer, we demonstrated preliminary and partial application of the tweetonomy construct, with a network analysis of energy terms in Twitter streams, time-series analysis to track the evolution of consumer attitudes about energy efficiency, and metrics to characterize the conversations. We used social and linguistic structures of communication (repeat communications and varied types of Twitter communication conventions, such as pictures, hashtags, retweets, and URLs) to analyze the establishment of self-organizing communities of consumers. These communities share many of the characteristics of issue publics, which are small groups of people who follow one or more issues closely, and further research on similarities to and differences from other issue publics is needed to understand how to create, expand, and sustain word-of-mouth persuasion for energy behavior change.

We initiated exploration into the social aspects of information diffusion through conventions such as retweets and other conversational responses, through the membership and social distance of these conversations, and in changes over time in frequency and form of the networks. We demonstrated tools that permit visualization of vast quantities of user-generated content about energy and sustainability.

Results of this and related research and others like it that follow can guide program planners such as ARPA-e, utilities, or government agencies. For example, both agenda setting and priming are evidenced in the ebb and flow of smart-meter discussion. Thus trigger events can be created and promoted to enhance the discussion of how to best use a smart meter as a feedback tool. The rhythm and volume of that conversation could be observed in Twitter. Slater (2007) provides a provocative perspective on the mutual influence of media selectivity and effects and their impact on behavior, described as reinforcing spirals. In the case of energy behavior, change agents intend to be proactive in stimulating such reinforcing spirals that can lead to increasing energy efficiency and dampen those that led to greater consumption. The analytical methods and tools described here are a first step in this process-of understanding the energy discussion.

Recommendations

It is not yet known how social media will be integrated into the portfolio of communications that will achieve the tipping point of consumer behavior change in energy use. History has repeatedly shown that new media join rather than replace traditional media (Reeves & Nass, 1996). To achieve optimal results in minimal time, continual feedback is needed for the rapid iteration of innovative approaches. Openly available, rapid-response metrics that reflect consumer engagement with changes are vital. Social media metrics offer this opportunity. The identification and refinement of tools for analyzing conversations in social media are vital for confronting future social problems and challenges. Understanding energy-related conversations on Twitter can provide a steppingstone for detecting and potentially triggering changes in energy consumption behavior through social media. The social diversity of the tweets, for example, can indicate opportunities for exploring specific hashtags for deeper understanding of social roles in the conversation.

The results of this project have potential application for identifying new ways of tracking public opinion and behavior change related to sustainability and energy consumption and for analyzing domain-specific, user-generated content on social media platforms. Our research will continue to monitor the extent to which eco-linguistic terms appear in social media used by the general population. We will track the presence, participation, and meaning of energy consumption–related conversations in social media and, with these insights, support the development of initiatives to detect and potentially trigger changes in energy consumption behavior through social media. In addition, we believe that there are significant opportunities to monitor social media to examine the influence of larger social issues and contextual factors (environment, climate, and local and global events) on the conversation about energy, environment, and climate change.

Based on our initial results, we recommend continued collection of data and development of analytical methods and tools that can track public opinion related to energy consumption; analyze domain-specific, user-generated content on social media platforms; identify and track indicators such as semantics and social roles; identify and explore patterns and disruptions; identify and benchmark grassroots resources such as author networks; characterize opportunities for resource transformation; and build semantic models to understand the aggregations of conversation streams.

We have identified four major questions for persuasive technologies that lie at the intersection between people and information technology and require continued interdisciplinary exploration:

- What (and how much and what kind of) information is needed by consumers to drive changes in their energy use?
- What balance of technology-driven personalization, disambiguation, and privacy are optimal for building communities of awareness, interest, and action?
- How can the impact of best practice framing, empowerment, and compliance speed the adoption of technologies that encourage reduced energy consumption?
- What combination of persuasive technologies—both old and new—will make changing energy behavior contagious and persistent?

Analytical tools are needed for observation and interpretation of the millions of personal conversations already occurring online. Reliable and valid metrics are needed to measure the effectiveness of persuasive communications and enable meaningful interpretation of the impact. The semantic analysis of tweets containing eco-linguistic content in this chapter is a preliminary example of the data, tools, and metrics that can inform the timeliness, relevance, and positioning of persuasive communications.

To accelerate exploration of these important issues, we are making the eco-linguistic taxonomy, the Twitter Energy data, and the TwitterExplorer available for other researchers. Because of the urgency of addressing climate change and the need to mobilize widespread changes in energy consumption, we encourage other researchers to join us in a research agenda that includes analyzing and characterizing energy-consumption behavior; tracking public opinion related to energy consumption; analyzing domain-specific, user-generated content on social media platforms; identifying and tracking leading indicators of attitude and behavior change; and identifying patterns and disruptions that can accelerate change and provide alerts for emergency response.

Note

1. Data for this figure were visualized using NodeXL and its functionality for linking and revealing Twitter images, using the NodeXL Twitter Importer module (Hansen, Shneiderman, & Smith, 2010).

References

Bailenson, J., & Yee, N. (2005). Digital chameleons: Automatic assimilation of nonverbal gestures in immersive virtual environments. *Psychological Science, 16,* 814–819.

Bastian, M., Heymann, S., & Jacomy, M. (2009). Gephi: An open source software for exploring and manipulating networks. Paper presented at the International AAAI Conference on Weblogs and Social Media. North America, March.

Block, M., & Schultz, D. (2009). *Media generations: Media allocation in consumer-controlled marketplace.* Columbus, OH: Prosper Business Development Corporation.

Daft, R. L., Lengel, R. H. and Trevino, L. K. (1987). Message equivocality, media selection, and manager performance: Implications for information systems. *MIS Quarterly, 11*(3), 355–366.

Flora, J. A., & Russell, M. G. (2012). *A taxonomy of energy efficiency terms: Issues, frames, metaphors, sources and behaviors.* Technical Report, MediaX (Stanford University), Palo Alto, CA.

Fogg, B. J. (2008). Mass interpersonal persuasion: an early view of a new phenomenon. In H. Oinas-Kukkonen et al. (Eds.), *PERSUASIVE 2008: Proceedings of the 3rd international conference on persuasive technology* (pp. 23–43). Berlin: Springer.

Freeman, L. C. (2009). Methods of social network visualization. In R. A. Meyers (Ed.), *Encyclopedia of complexity and systems science.* New York: Springer.

Gleave, E., Welser, H. T., Lento, T. M., & Smith, M. A. (2009). A conceptual and operational definition of "social role" in online community. In *Proceedings of the 42nd Hawaii International Conference on System Sciences.* Big Island, Hawaii, January 7–10.

Hansen, D., Shneiderman, B., & Smith, M.A. (2010). *Analyzing social media networks with NodeXL: Insights from a connected world.* San Francisco: Morgan Kaufmann.

Helic, D., Strohmaier, M., Trattner, C., Muhr, M., & Lerman, K. (2011). Pragmatic evaluation of folksonomies. In *Proceedings of the 20th international conference on the World Wide Web* (pp. 417–426). New York: ACM.

Hogan, J. E., Lemon, K.N., & Libai, B. (2004). Quantifying the ripple: Word-of-mouth and advertising effectiveness. *Journal of Advertising Research, 44*(3), 271–280.

Kaptein, M., Markopoulos, P., de Ruyter, B., & Arts, E. (2010). Persuasion in ambient intelligence. *Journal of Ambient Intelligence and Humanized Computing, 1*(1), 43–56.

Koerner, B. (2010). How Twitter and Facebook make us more productive. http://www.wired.com/magazine/2010/02/st_essay_distraction/ (accessed June 22, 2013).

Lakoff, G. (2010). Why it matters how we frame the environment. *Environmental Communication, 4*(1), 70–81.

Lenhart, A., Purcell, K., Smith, A., & Zickuhr, K. (2010, February 3). Overview. In *Social media and young adults*. Report, Pew Internet & American Life Project. www.pewinternet.org/Reports/2010/Social-Media-and-Young-Adults/Summary-of-Findings/.

Livingstone, S. (2005). On the relation between audiences and publics. In Livingstone, S. (Ed.), Audiences & Publics: When cultural engagement matters for the public sphere. Changing media—changing Europe series (pp. 17–21) (2). Intellect Books, Bristol UK.

Martin, S., Brown, W. M., Klavans, R., & Boyack, K. (2011). OpenOrd: An open-source toolbox for large graph layout. Paper presented at the SPIE Conference on Visualization and Data Analysis (VDA), San Francisco, January 24–25.

Miller, C. C. (2009, August 25). Who's driving Twitter's popularity? Not teens. *New York Times*. www.nytimes.com/2009/08/26/technology/internet/26twitter.html.

Ophir, E., Nass, C. & Wagner, A. D. (2009). Cognitive control in media multitaskers. *Proceedings of the National Academy of Sciences of the United States of America, 110*(8). www.pnas.org/content/early/2009/08/21/0903620106.full.pdf+html.

Pennebaker, J. W., Mehl, M. R., & Niederhoffer, K. (2003). Psychological aspects of natural language use: Our words, our selves. *Annual Review of Psychology, 54*, 547–577.

Reeves, B & Nass, C. (1996). How people treat computers, television and new media like real people and places. http://www.humanityonline.com/docs/the%20media%20equation.pdf (accessed June 22, 2013).

Reeves, B., & Read, L. (2009). *Total engagement: Using games and virtual worlds to change the way people work and businesses compete*. Boston: Harvard Business School Press.

Rubens, N., Russell, M. G., & Perez, R. (2011). *Ecosystems network explorer*. Technical Report, MediaX (Stanford University).

Russell, M. G. (2009). A call for creativity in new metrics for liquid media. *Journal of Interactive Advertising, 9*(2).

Russell, M. G. (2011a). Evolving media metrics from assumed attention to earned engagement. In M. Eastin, T. Dougherty, & N. Burns (Eds.), *Handbook of advertising research* (pp. 125–144). Hershey, PA: Information Science Reference.

Russell, M. G., Flora, J., Strohmaier, M., Pöschko, J., Perez, R., & Rubens, N. (2011b). Semantic analysis of energy-related conversations in social media: A Twitter case study. Paper presented at the International Conference of Persuasive Technology (Persuasive 2011), Columbus, Ohio, June 3–6.

Savage, N. (2011). Twitter as medium and message. *Communications of the ACM, 54*(3), 18–20.

Slater, M. D. (2007). Reinforcing spirals: The mutual influences of media selectivity and media effects and their impact on individual behavior and social identity. *Communication Theory*, 17, 281–303.

Smith, A., & Rainie, L. (2010, December 9). *8% of online Americans use Twitter.* Report, Pew Internet & American Life Project. www.pewinternet.org/Reports/2010/Twitter-Update-2010.aspx.

VanderWal, T. (2007, February 2). Folksonomy. Vanderwal.net. www.vanderwal.net/folksonomy.html.

Wagner, C. & Strohmaier, M. (2010). The wisdom in tweetonomies: Acquiring latent conceptual structures from social awareness streams. In *Proceedings of the 3rd International Semantic Search 2010 Workshop*. New York: ACM.

Wasserman, T. (2011, February 2). Audi Superbowl ad claims first use of Twitter hashtag. Mashable. http://mashable.com/2011/02/02/audi-super-bowl-twitter-hashtag/#/.

Wu, M. (2009. Community health index for online communities. Lithium Technologies, White Paper. http://pages.lithium.com/community-health-index.html (accessed July 23, 2013).

15

Oregon's Iconic Bottle Bill

Ethan Moskowitz and Lynn R. Kahle

> *The [Oregon Bottle Bill] law, originally passed in 1971, has been an iconic symbol of Oregon's love of natural beauty and conservation, and fight against litter and the throwaway mentality.*
>
> —Former governor of Oregon Tom McCall (Gitlitz, 2001)

Originally voted into law in 1971, Oregon House Bill (HB) 1036 was the first of its kind to embrace sustainability in both public and private business sectors. This law, better known as the Oregon Bottle Bill (OBB), was designed around a bottle return system that encouraged and ultimately fostered participation from consumers and beverage companies alike. It was designed to communicate a social value for sustainability to everyone and to increase sustainable behaviors. Since its inception, the program has generated as much as a 90 percent return rate for eligible containers, and it has reduced roadside litter on Oregon roads to the country's lowest levels of accumulation (Container Recycling Institute, 2011). Today, ten other states and a number of foreign countries have enacted bottle bills modeled after the OBB.

In June 2011, a proposal supported by Governor John Kitzhaber was passed, which added amendments to the original OBB. "Since its passage 40 years ago, Oregon's bottle bill has resulted in the return of over 3 billion containers, helped discourage litter, and prevented waste from ending up in landfills . . . we have served as a national model for bottle redemption systems," proclaimed the governor at the signing of the new legislation on June 9, 2011 (Kitzhaber, 2011). The most significant revisions featured the inclusion of all glass, metal, and plastic containers; the opening of privately operated redemption centers; and the raising of the current 5-cent deposit to 10 cents per container if participation rates fall below 80 percent (State of Oregon, Department of Environmental Quality, 2012b). These amendments complemented an innovative revision passed in 2007 that added water bottles to the list of returnable containers (Container Recycling Institute, 2011). Public response has varied, with beverage distributors and retailers celebrating the newest legislation while political opponents remain wary of ever-increasing involvement by state agencies (Wong, 2011). Other critics are also concerned with how the OBB's most recent additions will effect overall program participation from all the diverse interest groups—including grocery and bottling businesses, politicians, consumers, and advocacy groups.

This chapter analyzes the potential consequences and problems resulting from the new OBB from a comprehensive, marketing-based business perspective. The revision's potential benefits and costs are considered, as well as the current and potential impacts for all the involved interest groups, focused on answering the following two questions:

1. How will the recent amendments to the Bottle Bill effect Oregon businesses, consumers, and ultimately the future of the container redemption program?
2. What changes need to be made to stabilize and increase Oregon's container return rate?

The second question listed above was inspired by casual research that highlighted the slow but apparent decline of the state's eligible container return rates. Since 1980, Oregon's container return rate has fallen 14 percentage points from 91 percent to 74 percent, and it has failed to yield an annual increase in 33 years (Spendelow, 2012). Although this decreased level of consumer participation might seem trivial to some, consider the following statistics regarding plastic and aluminum recycling from 2008 (Cummings, 2007):

- Manufacturing new aluminum cans from recycled containers uses 95 percent less energy than producing cans with virgin aluminum ore.
- In 2011, 54 billion aluminum cans were recycled, saving the energy equivalent of 15 million barrels of crude oil or the entire U.S. daily gas consumption.
- Americans use 50 billion disposable water bottles every year.
- Domestically manufactured plastics are made primarily (70 percent) from petroleum and natural gas.

Taking these facts into account, it is apparent that declining return rates can negatively effect Oregon's economy, environment, and quality of life. Progressive initiatives such as resource conservation and sustainability may be diminished or completely lost if support for programs such as the container-deposit system continues to decline.

Container-Deposit System Structure (1971–2012)

Before House Bill 3145's amendments were passed, Oregon's container return system had been structured and implemented in the same way as it had been since the program's inception (Spendelow, 2012). After HB 1036 was enacted in 1971, beverage manufacturers, distributors, and some commercial retailers created the Oregon Beverage Recycling Cooperative (OBRC) to establish the country's first bottle return system (Earth911.com, 2012). Today, the OBRC oversees all bottle deposits and returns in addition to processing any reusable container materials. It works with hundreds of grocery retailers throughout Oregon to transfer deposits to and from customers and to record return figures.

The new OBB establishes nonretailer redemption centers (Berger, 2012); however, these new locations are being implemented on a trial basis and are only just beginning to alter the retailer-based redemption structure.

Figure 15.1 illustrates how the container-return system currently operates without the use of the new BottleDrop container redemption centers, which were approved in the OBB's most recent legislative revisions. It is important to note that the other 10 states with bottle bill legislation and redemption programs use similar, if not identical, operational structures (Container Recycling Institute, 2007).

Consumers have several options from which to choose to redeem their deposit payments and to dispose of their used beverage containers. They may recoup their deposits through the processing of empty containers using reverse vending machines at participating grocery retailers. Almost 75 percent of containers sold in Oregon are recycled using this method. The OBRC reimburses participating grocery retailers for refunding consumer deposits and pays them a processing fee worth 1–3 cents per container upon collection of the returned aluminum, glass, and plastic materials. The processing fee is considered an incentive for continued retailer involvement in the container return program (WinCo Manager, 2012). Other Oregonians opt to pay private collection companies to process their used containers and forgo any deposit redemption in addition to paying extra for the additional service. This option is responsible for recycling roughly 12 percent of all eligible containers in Oregon every year (Shifflett, 2012). In contrast to the industry-sponsored system, private recycling companies are not mandated by the Bottle Bill to sustainably process their collected materials. This legislative loophole has raised concerns regarding operational transparency for these types of businesses. Oregon's consumers discard the remaining 18 percent of eligible beverage containers in the garbage, which ends up in landfill every year. All revenue generated from container deposits that are not recouped by consumers are allocated to distributors and bottlers to assist in financing the bottle return system.

A growing number of Oregonians are embracing another alternative return method by donating their used containers to charities and to low-income and homeless residents who frequent the retailer redemption facilities (WinCo Manager, 2012). These less-fortunate residents process the empty containers to receive deposit redemption funds for products that they did not initially purchase. Bottles and cans returned in this fashion significantly contribute to the program's overall container return rate; more important, this method is indicative of growing sentiment against the program's current return structure that has developed among many OBB interest groups over the past 30 years (Berger, 2012; WinCo Manager, 2012). The fact that consumers are sacrificing financial resources in return for more convenient and efficient recycling methods from nonprogram sources implies that structural changes are worth considering.

Figure 15.1 **Oregon's Container Deposit Return Program**

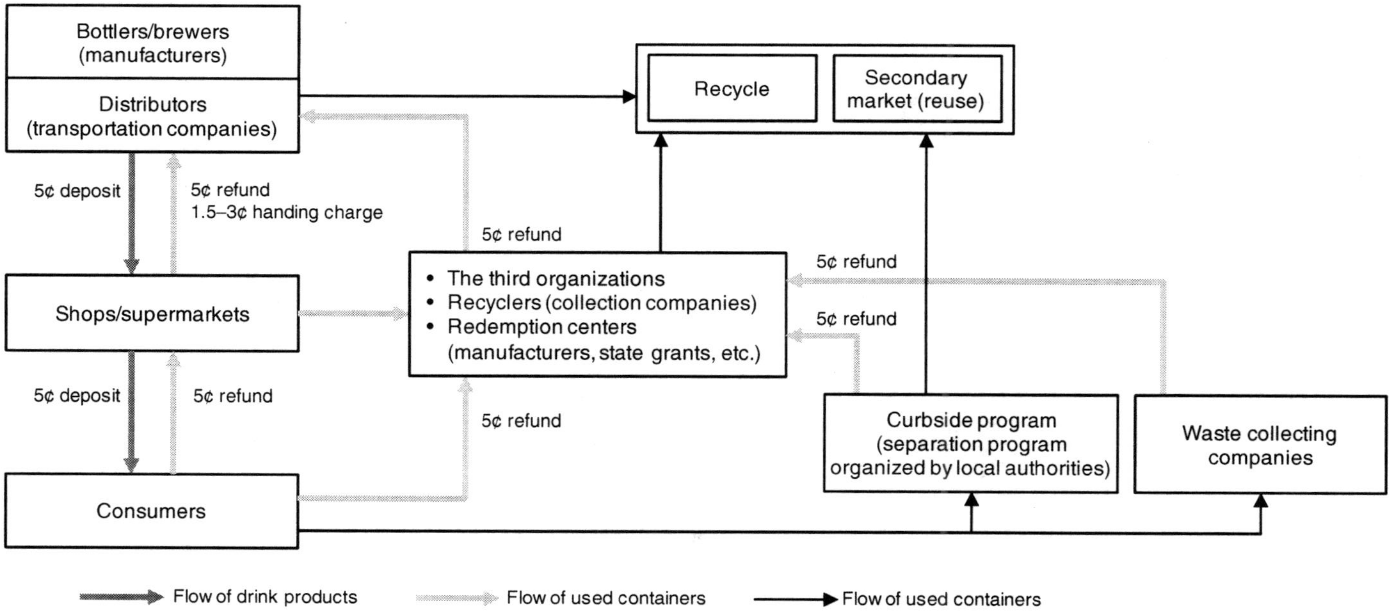

Declining Performance and Participation (1980–2012)

Beginning with the first year of the OBB's implementation in 1973, the annual rate for eligible containers returned increased every year before ultimately peaking at 91.2 percent in 1979 (Spendelow, 2012). Since then, program statistics have yet to reveal a yearly increase in the overall return rate, with the lowest level in the OBB's history, 74.4 percent, recorded in 2008 (Spendelow, 2012). Outdated accounting practices of eligible containers returned have created a three-year delay in producing accurate performance statistics. Barring any unforeseen changes, we can assume that performance either remained at its 2008 levels or likely continued to decrease. It is important to note that this problem is not confined to Oregon; declining beverage container recycling rates have been observed across all other bottle bill states beginning in the early 1990s, with the exception of Michigan (Gitlitz, 2001).

Although both local and national container return rates have continued to fall, Oregon retailers with redemption facilities reported a constant increase in the volume of processed container materials over the past 20 years (WinCo Manager 2012). The Bottle Bill Task Force, discussed below, also found that the volume of used beverage containers increased in direct proportion to projections of population increase in Oregon (State of Oregon, 2008). In turn, this fact implies that a higher proportion of return-eligible beverage products purchased are not being returned to redemption centers and are, instead, thrown away or recycled in another manner.

A variety of factors are responsible for the diminishing number of returns collected and processed by the redemption program. Across the country, recycling and processing rates of glass, plastic, and aluminum have not kept pace with increasing beverage sales, increasing to 173 billion containers a year, whereas waste disposal has grown to 34 billion containers annually (Gitlitz, 2001). Oregon's retailer-based processing facilities are a microcosm of this industry-wide problem with returning bottles. The current system presents consumers with an inefficient and somewhat unpleasant return process that is prone to technological malfunctions, sometimes requires waiting in line in unpleasant weather and is often dirty, ultimately resulting in fewer additional visits. The decline in the value of the nickel deposit fee has also negatively influenced overall return rates. As of 2012, a nickel was only worth 15 percent of what it was worth when House Bill 1036 was passed in 1971. To obtain an equivalent recycling rate today, the deposit would need to be 22 cents per container (Container Recycling Institute, 2011; Gitlitz, 2001). Although environmental stewardship is another incentive that continues to drive consumers to return their used containers, the financial component that past state legislators envisioned would help to maintain program participation in 1971 is virtually irrelevant as a factor today, if the deposit remains the same. Marketing strategies for the OBB's initiatives such as public service announcements or advertising campaigns to increase consumer awareness have also been underfunded and at times ignored. Studies examining the relationship between bottle bills and public support have found that public administrators can best facilitate acceptance of bottle bill laws by stressing the receptivity of significant community members to the new laws (Kahle & Beatty, 1987). Today, Oregonians born after the original OBB was enacted in 1971 make up a substantial proportion of the state's consumer base but may lack the education or experience necessary to understand how beneficial the container-deposit program is to the state. Ultimately, a combination of changing social norms, in-migration of people unfamiliar with the law's rationale, and other independent factors contributed to the decline in Oregon's overall container return rates from 1980 through 2012. More communication with the public could also improve compliance.

Amendments of 2007 and 2011

Recognizing the need for an improved OBB and return program, Oregon's state lawmakers crafted amended legislation in February 2007 (Mapes, 2011). The legislation's most important revisions and additions are the definition of beverages amended to include noncarbonated water products and the creation of a Bottle Bill Task Force (BBTF) to study and make recommendations for the future of the container collection and refunds.

At the time, Oregon joined Maine, California, and Hawaii as the only states whose bottle bills included plastic bottled water containers (Container Recycling Institute, 2011, 2012b, 2012d, 2013). Environmental groups were overjoyed with the amendment's passage, but members of the OBRC and participating grocery retailers were wary of how increased plastic container volumes would fit into an already struggling return system with limited processing capacity. State politicians alleviated their concerns by ordering the formation of the aforementioned BBTF (Nathanson, 2012). Using their recommendations as a framework, Oregon's House of Representatives voted in favor of new legislation in 2011 that meaningfully altered the future of the container-deposit program. This new law, titled House Bill 3145, featured three main amendments to the original OBB from 1971 (State of Oregon, Department of Environmental Quality, 2012a):

1. It expands the types of containers eligible for a refund to incorporate juices, teas, coffees, and sports drinks and any other beverage intended for human consumption with the exception of distilled liquor, wine, dairy, and infant formula.
2. It provides the possibility to increase the 5-cent deposit to 10 cents after the OLCC determines that, in each of two previous years, the number of containers returned was less than 80 percent of the total number of beer, soft drink, and water containers sold.
3. It promotes the development of additional "redemption centers" that will provide a convenient place for people to return their containers in addition to participating retail stores. Corporate distributor cooperatives (the OBRC) will be responsible for the operation of these redemption centers.

The biggest short-term problem that consumers will encounter is changing their deposit redemption habits to include the new BottleDrop return centers. Oregonians who currently rely on retailer-based facilities could be inconvenienced and alienated by the new redemption structure (Nathanson, 2012). In the long run, the focus of these new facilities is to improve the consumer's deposit redemption experience through more convenient return methods that are easier to use (BottleDrop, 2012). Consumers who adapt to the new structure the most quickly will be among BottleDrop's most loyal proponents (Berger, 2012). But how long will their loyalty last, and how many of them will encourage other Oregonians to start or continue to participate in the bottle return program after the change to redemption centers? What if the BottleDrop initiative is immensely successful but too costly to fully implement or maintain? These are the two most prominent concerns that politicians, businesses, and consumers will monitor closely as HB 3145's amendments are implemented.

Although operational design is the fundamental characteristic of the container-deposit program, the evolution of the program's social perception could change the system's overall performance radically. In 2007, Oregon Senate Bill 707's primary purpose was to include plastic bottled water containers on the list of products eligible for deposit and redemption (State of Oregon, 2007). A byproduct of that same legislation was the 2012 opening of ORPET. This $10-million plastic-recycling facility was developed in response to an increase in distributors' demand for plastic water bottle container recycling processes (Harger, 2012). Before ORPET's construction and opening in St. Helens, Oregon, the state's used bottled water containers were primarily shipped to China for processing and recycling (Harger, 2012). This issue garnered the attention of U.S. Senator Ron Wyden (OR-D), who championed a proposal that awarded the ORPET project $5 million in federal funding. "It is my hope that this facility will be the gold standard [for plastic recycling]," announced Wyden at the site's unveiling (Harger, 2012). Based upon ORPET's development and success, financial incentives offered by political and business leaders could encourage future innovations throughout Oregon's recycling industry.

Stakeholders

We pursued both interviews and media accounts to understand the views of stakeholders. Primary sources are exclusively telephone interviews with Oregon state politicians, beverage distributors, microbreweries, grocery retailers, and individuals with in-depth knowledge or personal experience with the state's container-deposit program. Interviewees included K. Becker, M. McClure, M. Ridge, J. Smith, and J. Sweet who provided information from the distribution, microbrewery and grocery retailer perspectives. Nancy Nathanson and Vicki Berger, two state politicians provided the legislative perspective. The majority of secondary research focused on other states with bottle bills and container return programs, such as California, Connecticut, Michigan, and Hawaii. These states were chosen because they exhibited similar demographic traits (population, culture) or possessed more recently created or structurally superior container return programs.

State Politicians

Oregon State Representatives Vicki Berger and Nancy Nathanson both voted for and currently support the OBB amendments for conflicting reasons. Berger was satisfied with the approved legislation yet wary of too much government involvement, whereas Nathanson argued that "community outreach at the local government level is needed to create additional incentives" to bolster container return rates (Nathanson, 2012).

Consumers

This political comparison underlines an ideological paradox that is both troubling and encouraging for the bottle bill's future. Even today, the two representatives cannot agree on how to revamp the container return system, yet they are two of many Oregon state politicians concerned with the program's continuing popularity decline among consumers. The overwhelming majority of Oregon voters are represented by elected officials who care more about the container return program than the citizens apparently do. Clearly, consumer attitudes toward the return program and recycling in general have to change before major improvements can be observed.

Psychologically, governments in democracies cannot get too far ahead of citizens. Laws encode or even guide public sentiment, but Americans learned from Prohibition that laws contradicting public opinion often have undesirable consequences. The OBB at first nudged public opinion toward sustainability (Kahle & Beatty, 1987), but the decline in communication in recent years has not retained popular support.

Local and State Businesses

On the more involved side of the deposit system sits one of Oregon's largest grocery retailers, WinCo Foods. Almost all WinCo locations in the state participate in the container return program, providing reverse-vending machine facilities for processing bottles and cans at the on-site facility. Recently, however, a WinCo store in Salem dropped its bottle return service following the opening of a new BottleDrop redemption center in the same neighborhood (Container Recycling Institute, 2011). The change pleased Dusty, the twenty-four-year store manager:

> Our business is predicated on moving larger volumes of inventory from the back of the store to the customer . . . and the container return program made operating our company's structure more difficult. It created a number of challenges for us, including a reduction in retail space to make room for bottle returns and time spent on machine maintenance. (WinCo Manager, 2012)

Dusty's comments shed light on some of the difficulties that retailers face when operating return facilities. Valuable store space is awarded to the consumer deposit redemption process, reducing the retailer's operational capacity. Lower capacity creates a significant competitive disadvantage; however, increasing retail and inventory space is a lucrative opportunity for grocers such as WinCo Foods, whose aim is to sell the largest possible volume of goods each day. Given the current 2- to 3-cent compensation retailers receive for processing container returns, they have little incentive to continue their involvement with the container-deposit program. "Any retailer would support [the OBRC] building new redemption centers . . . it's a no brainer," asserted Dusty (WinCo Manager, 2012).

Administrative Resources

The Oregon Liquor Control Commission (OLCC) is the government agency charged with the administration and oversight of the OBB's statutes. As the commission's liaison to Oregon distributors and wholesalers, Jesse Sweet works with OBRC and Department of Environmental Quality officials to ensure that all OBB initiatives are properly implemented. Sweet acknowledged the problems associated with serving rural communities using only specialized redemption centers:

> Rural redemption will definitely be a challenge going forward. The container-return system is not very profitable for the companies who make up the OBRC . . . these businesses will not invest additional resources in building new facilities if the consumer demand isn't there. (Sweet, 2012)

Sweet's analysis highlights a potentially detrimental situation for rural consumers. Without a significant metropolitan population such as those in Portland or Eugene, small coastal and eastern Oregon communities will have to rely either on the current return model or on the creation of redemption centers funded by private investments outside the OBRC. Grocery retailers, anxious to remove themselves from the deposit program, will be forced to remain involved for the foreseeable future and could drop their redemption service altogether. In the absence of return facilities, private collection companies and landfill would be the most likely destinations for rural consumers' used containers. Oregon ranchers, farmers, and agricultural workers would be forced to choose between paying more for container recycling services or throwing away their bottles and cans in the garbage at no additional cost. This situation has the potential to weaken or eliminate return programs in rural areas (McLane, 2011, 2012).

Alisa Shifflett, the OBRC's BottleDrop redemption center project manager, was the final administrative resource interviewed during the research process. Shifflet's role entails overseeing all operations of the current and planned BottleDrop locations, from the employee hiring process to coordinating container material transfers (BottleDrop, 2012). When asked about the possibility of future redemption center development, she outlined that "our Salem location will serve as the model we [the OBRC] will be using moving forward . . . in this model, the retailers' role consists of placing their names on the OLCC's application for establishing a convenience zone and paying a participation fee that pays for the new BottleDrop's operating costs . . . we're hoping for a 50/50 endeavor with the retailers" (Shifflett, 2012).

Reviewing Shifflett's model reveals that the OBRC's plan for expansion of its BottleDrop redemption structure could raise participation costs for distributors and consumers. The BottleDrop manager agreed with the OLCC's opinion that "the OBRC sees no profits from this venture . . . both distributors and retailers want to minimize their respective program costs" (Shifflett, 2012; Sweet, 2012). After the retailers are removed from the return process, the only way to reduce their program costs even further is by paying only a portion of the OBRC's participation fee or avoiding it all together. Without the retailers' funding, any additional distributor costs are passed on to consumers in the form of a decrease in eligible containers' redemption values. Therefore, the evolving relationship between retailers and distributors needs to be closely monitored by Oregon lawmakers to ensure the successful performance of the OBB's amendments.

BottleDrop's operational features were another topic discussed at length by Shifflett. Although the majority of consumers will use BottleDrop's reverse vending machines to redeem their deposits, the centers' premier "EZ-Drop" service is a "game-changer" for the deposit program and solves a numbers of problems that have driven down return rates (Berger, 2012). Oregonians value service qualities like convenience and ease of use, but EZ-Drop's deposit redemption bank account is the program's most significant component because it increases the container's overall return value for consumers. Under the current process, a person's time and labor is considered more valuable than redeeming any amount of container deposits. EZ-Drop condenses the current process into one step (container drop-off), increasing both the containers' relative value to consumers and the likelihood that they will use the EZ-Drop system again. The feature also presents consumers with a less-expensive alternative to private collection recycling services that allows them to reclaim their deposit fees (Association of Oregon Recyclers, 2012). Distributors' processing and transportation costs decrease as more containers flow through the OBRC's redemption centers, thereby streamlining the material recycling process through one facility instead of five separate retailer-based locations (Sweet, 2012). "While the model continues to be revised and improved, initial results indicate that we are bringing in more containers than the grocery stores ever did," noted Shifflett, highlighting the need for increased funding and consumer awareness to make BottleDrop redemption centers the new standard for Oregon's container return system (Shifflett, 2012).

State Comparisons

California

California is a suitable state for comparisons because of geographic proximity and the cultural similarities between California and Oregon residents. Both of the states' governments have supported environmentally conscious initiatives, and their citizenries embody a casual, laidback lifestyle that places great value upon natural resource preservation. In spite of its population (nine and a half times larger than that of Oregon), California boasted a higher overall container return percentage in 2010 (Marshall, 2011). The program increased recycling rates in the Golden State from 13 billion containers per year in 2006 to over 16.7 billion containers per year in 2011; those 3.7 billion containers are nearly 1.7 percent of the country's 224 billion containers that are consumed annually (Container Recycling Institute, 2012b).

Such strong support for the state's deposit return program can be attributed to two main differences between California's system and Oregon's current structure: curbside service registration and large container incentives. First, consumer containers that are processed by state certified recyclers are counted toward the state's overall return rate. This method of return accounting may initially seem like a strategy used to artificially inflate the program's overall success, but companies that practice curbside operations in California must incorporate the state's processing and payment structures into their operations (Container Recycling Institute, 2012b). State politicians included financial incentives funded by unredeemed deposits in the bottle bill legislation to mitigate potential backlash and encourage support from private collection companies (CalRecycle, 2012). The second endeavor that proved to be successful was the decision to double deposit fees to 10 cents on all returnable containers that hold more than 24 ounces of liquid (Container Recycling Institute, 2012b). This higher initial deposit fee, coupled with a more efficient weight-based return option at redemption centers, created a situation in which consumers were faced with fewer incentives not to return their used containers. Unmanned redemption sites have also proved to be an effective resource for consumers in less populated areas and are being rapidly introduced across the state's most underserved convenience zones (CalRecycle, 2012).

Michigan

California's recent success pales in comparison to the storied history of Michigan's container return program. Implemented in December 1978, the state's redemption system was the first to offer a deposit fee of 10 cents per container and has become the country's most successful bottle bill return system, boasting an annual return rate of around 98 percent (Container Recycling Institute, 2012e). Historically, Michigan's yearly return percentage has never dropped below 95 percent (State of Michigan, Department of Natural Resources and Environment, 2010). This 3-percentage-point decrease is even more remarkable when compared to Oregon's 16-percentage-point loss over the same time period, especially considering that both states offer only retailer-based redemption facilities (Gitlitz, 2001). Michigan residents' continued support of the redemption program resides in social norms established during the bottle bill's formative years that place value upon recycling used containers and recouping deposit funds (Container Recycling Institute, 2012e).

Although the financial incentive of having the dime deposit returned has been significantly diminished by inflation since 1978, the true power of the program's higher deposit fee lies in its ability to influence the attitudes and behaviors of Michigan's consumers (Kahle & Beatty, 1987). Another reason for the state's high return rates is the well-publicized use of its system revenues to fund other public programs. Known as the Michigan Bottle Deposit Law escheat, a percentage of unredeemed deposits are allocated to pay for environmental cleanup operations or educational seminars for businesses that use or handle hazardous materials on pollution prevention methods, technologies, and processes (State of Michigan, Department of Natural Resources and Environment, 2010). Using unclaimed deposits to fund programs that benefit all Michigan residents has worked to justify and to reinforce the value of the 10-cent deposit fee in the minds of legislators, businesses, and consumers alike.

Recommendations

We have two recommendations toward the overall goals to ensure the continued existence and future success of the Oregon Bottle Bill redemption program.

Recommendation 1

Design, organize, and execute a comprehensive rebranding of Oregon's container-deposit return program that emphasizes past, current, and future return incentives within the next three years. This cohesive campaign will feature marketing and advertising activities emphasizing the benefits of new BottleDrop redemption centers as well as the establishment and promotion of an education program supporting the Oregon school system and funded by unredeemed program deposits. The overall goal of the rebranding initiative is to reinforce or revise recycling attitudes for a younger generation of Oregon's consumers.

The two primary innovations of the bottle bill's rebranding campaign that should be featured throughout the marketing activities outlined above are the new BottleDrop redemption centers and Oregon schools education fund. Improvements like the "EZ Drop" consumer redemption service and 24-hour facility access at all BottleDrop locations are innovative features that all consumers need to understand. Hawaii's recent implementation of its bottle bill legislation demonstrates the positive correlation between consumer outreach and overall program success (Fassier, 2007). To realize the greatest return on their BottleDrop investment, the OBRC needs to direct resources toward educating Oregonians about their redemption centers' primary features. Another new incentive to be introduced is the Oregon Education Fund (OEF). The OEF is designed to help finance the state's public school system by donating a portion of all unredeemed container deposit payments to this underfunded public education program. Unlike their Michigan counterparts, Oregon's residents are currently offered a limited range of nonfinancial incentives to participate in their state's container return system. The OEF will solve this problem by increasing container return participation from both community leaders and average citizens who support public programs with wide-reaching social benefits (Kahle & Beatty, 1987). One additional feature of the bottle bill's rebranding will be the promotion of BottleDrop-sponsored redemption locations in rural Oregon communities. Based on models already being used in California, these unmanned stations are to be located in grocery retailer parking lots and will feed into the OBRC's overall processing network (CalRecycle, 2012; Shifflett, 2012). These "mini BottleDrops" are designed to alleviate retailers' participation concerns in sparsely populated areas without sacrificing rural consumers' container returns and overall program involvement.

Overall, the primary goal of this recommendation is to increase Oregon's annual container return rate by improving consumers' attitudes toward the bottle bill deposit program and sustainable business practices in general.

Recommendation 2

Work with Oregon state politicians to restructure the legislative amendment calling for an increase in the deposit fee to 10 cents per container beginning in January 2015. Any increase in the state's deposit value will be triggered if the implementation of new BottleDrop redemption centers fails to create a permanent incremental increase in return rates after three years of data analysis and feedback generated by new accounting technologies. An additional feature of the revised amendment will be a law banning the disposal of all used beverage containers in Oregon's waste receptacles and landfill.

Currently, House Bill 3145's second amendment mandates that January 1, 2017, is the earliest date that a 10-cent container deposit can be introduced (State of Oregon, 2008). Moving this deadline forward two years accomplishes two important objectives:

1. It prevents overall program participation from deteriorating to unrecoverable levels through a shortened three-year time frame for observation and analysis of all redemption centers' performance.
2. It necessitates investment in new accounting systems and technologies to improve the quality of the data being assessed prior to January 1, 2015.

Providing more modern, accurate accounting systems such as those that are currently being used in Michigan has two main benefits. First, more accurate and reliable container return data will decrease the turnover time required to analyze the influence of all amendments passed in 2011. Three years is more than enough time for these changes to be implemented and their effects assessed to reveal whether further action—such as an increase in the deposit level—is needed to reverse the pattern of declining return rates. Second, if the data produced by these feedback systems reveal that redemption centers are not the answer to the return program's problems, their technology will be an essential component when executing an increase to 10-cent deposit fees. Recall that Michigan was forced to invest in new processing technologies to reduce illegal container returns purchased outside its borders (State of Michigan, Department of Natural Resources and Environment, 2010). Although insufficient justification has been an important psychological mechanism in OBB success, the current level of deposit may be trending toward nonexistent justification.

The ban proposed above would make the disposal of any used beverage container illegal and a punishable offense under Oregon state law. It is important to note that the desired outcome of this new law is not to intimidate consumers and businesses to increase their level of involvement. Rather, its passage will function as a public service announcement to increase both program awareness and innovation within the state's recycling industry. Consumers are provided with another incentive to recycle used containers and redeem deposits that would have gone unclaimed. Furthermore, organizations operating within Oregon's material processing system will be faced with higher volumes of returned materials as well as the opportunity to provide convenient solutions to consumers effected by the new law. With funding from both the state government and the OBRC, new methods for material processing like ORPET's facilities could revolutionize recycling structures on a statewide or possibly nationwide level. A balanced combination of program redesign and private innovation is needed to ensure improvement in the container deposit system (Berger, Nathanson, 2012). Enforcement of this proposed law remains a concern; the technology to sort and remove recyclables from trash collection processes is not yet available. However, any existing or future business to offer consumers a sort-free recycling service will earn tremendous popularity from consumers looking for a convenient way to abide by the container disposal ban.

Conclusion

The OBB has contributed significantly to sustainable behavior with one type of solid waste. After 40 years, it has now received some updating and renovation that will we hope render it more effective in the future. The successful interplay of communication, psychology, and jurisprudence can provide a model for other efforts at increasing sustainable behaviors in society.

References

Association of Oregon Recyclers. (2012). AOR policies. www.aorr.org (accessed April 1, 2012).
Becker, K. (2012). Telephone interview. April 30.
Berger, V. (2012). Personal interview. March 10.
BottleDrop. (2012). What is BottleDrop? www.bottledropcenters.com/what/ (accessed April 14, 2012).

CalRecycle. (2012). California Beverage Container Recycling & Litter Reduction Act. Publication # DRRR-2012–0002, December. Sacramento: Department of Resources Recycling and Recovery. www.calrecycle.ca.gov/publications/Documents/1409%5C2012%5C2012002.pdf (accessed March 22, 2012).

Container Recycling Institute. (2007). What is a bottle bill? www.bottlebill.org/about/whatis.htm (accessed February 23, 2012).

Container Recycling Institute. (2011). Bottle bills in the USA: Oregon. www.bottlebill.org/legislation/usa/oregon.htm (accessed October 1, 2011).

Container Recycling Institute. (2012b). Bottle bills in the USA: California. www.bottlebill.org/legislation/usa/california.htm (accessed January 22, 2012).

Container Recycling Institute. (2012c). Bottle bills in the USA: Connecticut. www.bottlebill.org/legislation/usa/connecticut.htm (accessed January 25, 2012).

Container Recycling Institute. (2012d). Bottle bills in the USA: Maine. www.bottlebill.org/legislation/usa/maine.htm.

Container Recycling Institute. (2012e). Bottle bills in the USA: Michigan. www.bottlebill.org/legislation/usa/michigan.htm (accessed January 25, 2012).

Container Recycling Institute. (2013). Bottle bills in the USA: Hawaii. www.bottlebill.org/legislation/usa/hawaii.htm.

Cummings, L. (2007). Facts about aluminum recycling. Earth911.com, April 2. http://earth911.com/news/2007/04/02/facts-about-aluminum-recycling/.

Earth911.com. (2012). Plastic recycling facts. http://earth911.com/recycling/plastic/plastic-bottle-recycling-facts/ (accessed February 22, 2012).

Fassier, K. (2007, August 6). Hawaii recycling working out kinks. *Honolulu Advertiser*. http://the.honoluluadvertiser.com/article/2007/Aug/06/ln/hawaii708060361.html.

Gitlitz, J. (2001). Oregon's Bottle Bill at 30: How is it doing? Presentation, Association of Oregon Recyclers Conference, September 8. www.container-recycling.org/assets/pdfs/reports/2001-OregonBB30.pdf (accessed April 22, 2012).

Harger, S. E., III. (2012, May 9). ORPET recycling plant opens. *South County Spotlight* (St. Helens, OR). http://thetribonline.net/sustainable/story.php?story_id=133599366395491900/ (accessed May 11, 2012).

Kahle, L. R., & Beatty, S. E. (1987). Cognitive consequences of legislating postpurchase behavior: Growing up with the Bottle Bill. *Journal of Applied Social Psychology, 17,* 826–840.

Kitzhaber, J. (2011). Governor Kitzhaber signs bill updating Oregon's iconic bottle bill. Speech, June 9. www.oregon.gov/gov/media_room/pages/speechess2011/bottle-bill_060911.aspx (accessed October 8, 2011).

Mapes, J. (2011). How Oregon's bottle bill was greatly expanded in a legislative session made for killing bills. Oregon Live blog (*The Oregonian*), May 26. http://blog.oregonlive.com/mapesonpolitics/2011/05/how_oregons_bottle_was_greatly.html (accessed October 8, 2011).

Marshall, J. (2011). Biannual report of beverage container sales, returns, redemption, and recycling rates. Notice, November 7. www.bottlebill.org/assets/pdfs/legis/usa/CA-2011Nov-rates.pdf (accessed April 12, 2012).

McLane, M. (2011). Bottle Bill extension is flawed. Southern Oregon.com blogs, Legislative Outtakes, May 6. http://blogs.esouthernoregon.com/southern-oregon-legislators/2011/05/06/bottle-bill-extension-is-flawed/ (accessed October 1, 2011).

McLane, M. (2012). Telephone interview. March 15.

Nathanson, N. (2012). Telephone interview. March 10.

Shifflett, A. (2012). Telephone interview. May 10.

Spendelow, P. H. (2012). Personal correspondence, March 22 and March 29.

State of Michigan, Department of Natural Resources and Environment. (2010). *Michigan Bottle Deposit Law: Frequently Asked Questions.* April 8. www.michigan.gov/documents/deq/dnre-whmd-sw-mibottledepositlawFAQ_318782_7.pdf.

State of Oregon. (2007). Senate Bill 707. 74th Oregon Legislative Assembly, 2007 Regular Session. www.leg.state.or.us/07reg/measpdf/sb0700.dir/sb0707.a.pdf (accessed March 22, 2012).

State of Oregon. (2008). *Oregon Bottle Bill-Task Force Final Report.* October. Salem, OR: Publication of Legislative Administration. www.deq.state.or.us/lq/pubs/docs/sw/BBTaskForceFinalReport.pdf (accessed March 21, 2012).

State of Oregon. (2011). House Bill 3145. 76th Oregon Legislative Assembly, 2011 Regular Session. www.leg.state.or.us/11reg/measpdf/hb3100.dir/hb3145.intro.pdf (accessed October 1, 2011).

State of Oregon, Department of Environmental Quality. (2012a). Oregon bottle bill: Then and now. www.deq.state.or.us/lq/sw/bottlebill/thenandnow.htm.

State of Oregon, Department of Environmental Quality. (2012b). Oregon's evolving bottle bill. www.deq.state.or.us/lq/sw/bottlebill/index.htm (accessed February 20, 2012).

Sweet, J. (2012). Telephone interview. May 10.

WinCo Manager, Dusty. (2012). Telephone interview. April 22.

Wong, P. (2011, May 25). Rep. Berger's comments on House Bill 3145. *Oregon Statesman Journal.*

16

Defining Livability

How Livable Communities Contribute to and Benefit from Social Cohesion

Kyra L. Wiggin

> *Livable Communities provide and promote civic engagement and a sense of place through safe, sustainable choices for a variety of elements that include housing, transportation, education, cultural diversity and enrichment and recreation.*
>
> —Walkable and Livable Communities Institute, 2011

Broadly speaking, a community is a social system consisting of multiple, interdependent, and interacting social units (Hillery, 1955; Sanders, 1966). Although urban planners have touted the benefits of "livable" communities from an economic standpoint, they have neglected the psychological benefits that communities afford to those who reside in a livable community. Generally speaking, "livability" refers to an urban system that contributes to personal development and the physical, social, and mental well-being of its inhabitants. For example, livable communities enhance residents' sense of community awareness and social bonding. The resulting social cohesion among community members contributes to fostering a community identity, which in turn further bolsters the social cohesion that sustains communities and keeps them livable. This self-perpetuating circle is herein defined as the "social cohesion of livable communities."

Although owning a home in an ideal community tops many consumers' wish lists (Fournier & Guiry, 1993), consumer behavior research has neglected the study of livable communities. Researchers have, instead, adapted the community framework to explore psychologically formed brand communities in which consumers may never interact or encounter one another and yet still feel a sense of social cohesion based upon their shared purchases (Carlson, Suter, & Brown, 2008; Muniz & O'Guinn, 2001). Purchasing a product with a brand community may psychologically initiate a consumer into that community; however, purchasing a home psychologically and physically injects the buyer into a community of neighbors and involves a greater purchasing commitment than does the typical consumer product. However, little is known about the dynamics that drive consumers to move into livable communities and the post-choice psychological consequences. Furthermore, the very concept of what constitutes a livable community from the perspective of different consumers has not been articulated or assessed. Hence, enhancing understanding of consumer perceptions and behavior regarding livable communities will contribute to both consumer researchers and community planers.

The purpose of this chapter is to address the aforementioned gaps regarding livable communities and to lay the foundation for understanding the processes through which various customer segments select and secure a home in a community based on its ability to meet their livability standards. Further, it explains how a livable community bolsters its members' post-selection satisfaction. Finally, this chapter demonstrates how consumers who are satisfied with their community form a loyalty toward their community and incorporate the community into their sense of self.

An Integrated Theory of the Community

A community fulfills the vital need of individuals to belong and affiliate with others (Baumeister & Leary, 1995). Livable communities satisfy this need by bringing neighbors together to become interdependent, thereby forming a psychologically harmonious group. The interaction among individuals allows for sharing of values and meanings that are deemed relevant for defining their community, despite any perceived insignificance or triviality to individuals outside the community (Tajfel, 1981).

In this context, the term "community" conveys a sense of homogeneity among neighbors through shared values and lifestyles that distinguishes members of the community from non-members, or those who are outside the community. This commonality is what gives a community meaning to the individuals who reside within it. However, shared meanings are localized and anchored to a specific community, and over time that meaning can change due to shifts in the community (Kates & Goh, 2003). This leads to the creation of "subcommunities," which can be compared to market segments. Subcommunities co-create meanings that define their own core values to maintain a sense of homogeneity within their segment and heterogeneity from other subcommunity or market segments (Kozinets, 2001; Schouten & McAlexander, 1995). Because subcommunities set their own standards for what makes a community livable, the ranking of attributes that determine livability will vary across segments. Consequently, one should not expect a stable, universal definition for a livable community but, rather, a constantly evolving, multidimensional definition based on the shared experiences and changing values of subcommunity members.

Selecting a Community and Weighing the Alternatives

Consumer decisions involve a series of trade-offs that often require justification for selecting or rejecting certain options and affirming one's decision to avoid post-decision regret. Purchasing decisions are often based on more than just their expected utility. Consumers may also consider the ability of a potential purchase to make them feel socially connected to parallel purchasers (Algesheimer, Dholakia, & Herrmann, 2005). For example, purchasing an Apple product may be motivated just as much by the desire to be a part of the Apple community as it is by specific features of the product.

Brand research has examined "community" in a context in which post-decision regret about joining a community is inconsequential because the consumer has the option to dissociate from the brand community or to replace the product with another product that is associated with a more desirable community or to no community. However, when selecting to become part of a residential community, the consumer faces a substantial risk that making the wrong decision will contractually create an obligation to become a member of the residential community for a defined period or else face extensive exiting costs. This decision can be a source of emotional discomfort, ranging from mild dissonance from uncertainty over whether it was the right choice (e.g., when the outcome is still unknown) to acute regret from the conviction that it was the wrong choice (e.g., when the outcome is known). However, selecting a residential community whose attributes align with the consumer's core values will increase post-decision satisfaction and contribute to what is perceived as a livable community.

During the selection phase, the attributes that are weighted as most important may vary across consumer segments based on individual values and goals. For example, some consumers may emphasize safety and security needs by finding a safe community with available health-care services while others prefer communities that will enable advancement and nurturance (Higgins, 2002). This may include such attributes as employment opportunities and housing options with different price points that enable the consumer to move up the social ladder without leaving the community. While some consumers may desire to have all their needs met by their community without the need to venture outside it, for others not having the ability to move around freely may threaten their sense of personal freedom (Brehm, 1966; Brehm & Brehm, 1981). Thus, a community must make it easy for members to arrive where they desire to go by providing a variety of mobility options, such as public transportation, sidewalks, and dedicated bike paths.

Hypothesis 1: The values ascribed to attributes that define a livable community vary across community members in a way that creates distinct market segments.

Ultimately consumers must select a community that satisfies their need to belong and assimilate as well as their need to feel distinct and unique (Brewer, 1991; Brewer, Manzi, & Shaw, 1993). Not unlike the resource-based perspectives of the firm in which organizations prevail when their resources are valuable, uncommon, and difficult to imitate or substitute (Barney, 1991), successful communities adopt similar principles to attract and retain permanent residents. Applying this perspective, a livable community should be vibrant and diverse. It must provide the type of services and retail establishments that are needed and wanted by community members. Houses that vary in type and price will not only bring diverse community members together through some shared similarities but will also allow for a sense of uniqueness that is usually absent from suburban communities in which the houses are mirror images of one another. However, a livable community must not be so unique that it prevents neighbors from engaging in creative and challenging activities as a community and reflecting on those events. Such actions are necessary for improving overall satisfaction with the communal relationships and creating and reaffirming a sense of belonging (Broemer, 2001; Reis et al., 2011). These activities can be fostered by parks, recreation, and entertainment opportunities.

Post-Decision Evaluation of a Livable Community

During the final stage in the decision-making process, consumers make an evaluative assessment of their decision. At this phase, consumers ask themselves whether their selection of a residential community is congruent with their goals. The degree of satisfaction may depend on individual differences in decision-making styles. For example, maximizing consumers aspire to accept only the absolute "best" on every criterion and standard that they hope to attain, whereas satisficers are willing settle for something that is "good enough" so long as their choice meets their predefined criteria (Parker, de Bruin, & Fischhoff, 2007; Schwartz et al., 2002). To avoid post-decision regret, maximizers must remain committed to values that they believe define a livable community, consider the benefits of their selected community, and neglect any contradictory information that may arise (Puca, 2001; Taylor & Gollwitzer, 1995). Because the attributes of a livable community are goal congruent, consumers should be more satisfied with their choice and less likely to experience post-decisional dissonance and regret when they are able to locate in a livable community.

Hypothesis 2: Residents in a community that aligns with their livability standards will be more satisfied with their community and less likely to desire mobility.

Social Cohesion of Livable Communities

An individual's sense of self-concept is partially based upon membership in social groups. Members will assign value and emotional significance based on their degree of attachment to group membership (Tajfel, 1981). Attachment to a group is stronger when the group has been self-selected (Ellemers, Kortekaas, & Ouwerkerk, 1999) and therefore aligns with an individual's core values. Social cohesion arises out of this collective identity and becomes the "social glue" that brings neighbors together to sustain a livable community.

Individuals form evaluative judgments about their social group or community across four dimensions that define and make up collective self-esteem (Luhtanen & Crocker, 1992). Collective self-esteem represents the feelings of self-worth that one derives from one's group memberships. The first dimension, membership, refers to how valuable the individuals perceive themselves to be to the larger community. The second dimension, private esteem, measures the attitude of the member toward the group and the value placed on that membership. In contrast, public esteem—the third dimension—is how the member thinks others feel about their group. The last and most important dimension, identity, indicates how central that community is to the individual's self-concept (e.g., how strongly they identify with the group).

As a self-selected community in which members have shared values, desires, and lifestyles, livable communities should strengthen each of these dimensions. Because of this commonality, members of a more livable community should be more likely to want to interact and establish relationships with their neighbors. Peters and Kashima (2007) suggest that even the simplest social interactions facilitate the sharing of emotions and establish a coalition between those involved in an event that elicits the same emotional response. This social cohesion among community members strengthens their collective self-esteem, which in turn determines the extent to which individuals value their livable community and the importance that they place on maintaining it. Research on identification has shown that high identifiers are motivated to suppress their self-interests and maintain a strong sense of loyalty to the group. Conversely, low identifiers are more concerned with personal gain than with the interests of the group and are therefore unmoved about becoming more distant from or leaving the group (Ellemers, Spears, & Doosje, 1997; Jetten, Branscombe, Spears, & McKimmie, 2003). As a result of having residents that are highly identified with their community, a livable community is more sustainable over time because this identification serves as a buffer against post-decisional dissonance and regret that would otherwise lead to desires to relocate to another community.

Hypothesis 3: Increasing identification with a community (e.g., collective self-esteem) increases satisfaction with that community and decreases desires for mobility.

Study Overview

The proposed predictions were tested in a survey of actual community members that was designed and administered by Northwest Research Group. The results help to determine what defines a livable community and how those definitions vary across segments (H1). Next, it analyzes whether being in a livable community increases satisfaction with the community by reducing mobility desires (H2). Finally, it tests whether social identity with a community is predictive of community satisfaction (H3).

Methodology

Sample

A random sample of adults was drawn from a large Internet-based panel of U.S. residents who were compensated for their participation with e-Rewards® dollars. A total of 1,122 participants completed the online survey.

To ensure equal representation across the United States and of communities of different types and sizes, the sample was stratified by census region (Northeast, South, Midwest, and West) and community type (urban, suburban, and rural). The data was weighted by type of community within census regions based on data from the 2005 American Housing Survey (U.S. Census Bureau, 2006), making this sample an accurate representation of the general population.

Procedures

Northwest Research Group administered an online questionnaire to community members who were selected to participate. The questionnaire asked them to think about what a livable community means to them and to determine the importance of various attributes in defining a livable community. The survey followed a procedure that uses Maximum Difference (MaxDiff) scaling to determine the relative importance of community attributes. MaxDiff scaling is a choice-based trade-off technique in which participants select the "most important" and the "least important" attribute from a list of four (Finn & Louviere, 1992; Marley & Louviere, 2005). This process was repeated nine times in order to capture all twelve of the selected attributes that comprised the Livability Scale.

After completing the MaxDiff scaling task, participants were asked a series of social comparison questions in which they indicated how their community measured up to other communities in terms of overall livability and for each item of the Livability Scale, using a seven-point scale anchored by (1) much less livable and (7) much more livable. Furthermore, they were presented with the 16-item Collective Self-Esteem Scale (Luhtanen & Crocker, 1992) so that the target social category was their respective community. The scale consists of four interrelated, but distinct, subscales:

1. Membership: I feel I am a worthy member of my community;
2. Personal Esteem: I am glad to be a part of my community;
3. Public Esteem: My community is considered good by others;
4. Identity: My community is a reflection of who I am.

Participants answered several demographic questions, including what type of community they currently live in (rural, suburban, urban) and what type of community they would like to live in given their lifestyle.

Livability Scale

Items used to develop the Livability Scale were selected from an extensive review of articles and research studies on livability, such as a conference proceeding on livability (Hahlweg, 1997), Walklive.org, and the U.S. Department of Transportation. After the findings were synthesized, twelve common attributes were selected that seemed to best describe livability across sources and to form a reliable scale (Cronbach's α = .85). Table 16.1 provides the intercorrelations and descriptive statistics for the items, based on the responses to the social comparison questions comparing their community to other communities.

Results

Livability as Defined by Market Segments

To test H1, results from the MaxDiff scaling were analyzed by Northwest Research Group using Hierarchical Bayes (HB) techniques. This technique permits the estimation of individual-level utilities and yields a relative value for each item. This method specifies how much more important one item is compared to another.

Results showed that safety was the most important characteristic of a livable community, but there was also substantial discrimination between the other attributes (see Table 16.2), thereby supporting H1. Using a *K*-cluster analysis, the results indicated that the three-factor model was a better fit than the two-factor model but no different from the four-factor model. Furthermore, there was discriminant validity between each of the three segments on all twelve items, $F(2, 551) = 12.37–207.82$, $p < .001$. Based upon the attributes that each segment perceived provided the most utility to their concept of a livable community, the three segments were named Hipsters, Economist, and Recreationalists.

Community Satisfaction

To determine whether a livable community enhances satisfaction and reduces mobility desires, a difference measure was created between the type of community in which they live and the type of community in which they would like to live. The community satisfaction measure was contrast coded (–1 unsatisfied; 1 satisfied).

Overall, participants reported high satisfaction with their choice of community, with only 20 percent reporting the desire to move. The desire to move to a less densely populated community dominated this shift. In particular, the desire to move from an urban community to a suburban community accounted for 30 percent of unsatisfied community members, and 25 percent wanted to abandon their suburban community for a rural community.

Table 16.1

Summary Statistics and Correlations for Relative Livability of Their Community

			Correlation										
Variable	Mean	SD	A	B	C	D	E	F	G	H	I	J	K
Availability of public transportation	4.21	1.70											
Availability of sidewalks and bike paths	4.66	1.56	.44										
Easy to get to places I need to go by car	5.02	1.41	.14	.32									
Availability of different types of housing	4.49	1.36	.33	.33	.30								
Availability of housing with different price points	4.31	1.33	.20	.26	.24	.56							
Access to parks, recreation, and entertainment opportunities	4.96	1.43	.34	.56	.37	.34	.24						
Access to different types of retail and services opportunities	4.70	1.48	.46	.49	.37	.34	.23	.49					
Availability of jobs nearby	4.24	1.43	.29	.35	.16	.33	.27	.35	.40				
Access to health-care services	4.74	1.47	.31	.31	.38	.30	.21	.38	.49	.39			
Community is diverse	4.52	1.39	.41	.35	.20	.47	.43	.34	.36	.29	.27		
Vibrancy of the community	4.50	1.39	.30	.49	.21	.28	.18	.51	.40	.30	.26	.35	
Community is safe	5.08	1.49	.02	.29	.36	.18	.13	.39	.25	.28	.22	.09	.40

Note: All correlations were significant, $p < .001$. Safe community was less correlated with diversity, $p < .05$ and there was no correlation between safe community and the availability of public transportation, $p = n.s.$

Table 16.2

Community Market Segments

Hipsters	Economists	Recreationalists
Safe community	Safe community	Safe community
Diverse community	Availability of jobs nearby	Easy to travel by car
Vibrant community	Health-care services offered	Access to retail and services
Recreation/Entertainment	Housing at different prices	Recreation/Entertainment
Public transportation	Easy to travel by car	Health-care services offered
Sidewalks and bike paths	Different types of housing	Vibrancy of the community
Different types of housing	Access to retail and services	Sidewalks and bike paths
Housing at different prices	Recreation/Entertainment	Availability of jobs nearby
Health-care services offered	Community is diverse	Public transportation
Access to retail and services	Vibrancy of the community	Community is diverse
Availability of jobs nearby	Public transportation	Housing at different prices
Easy to travel by car	Sidewalks and bike paths	Different types of housing

Perceived Relative Livability

A binary logistical regression with community satisfaction as the dependent variable and the social comparison of overall livability as the predictor ran against the null model with no predictors was significant, $\chi^2 = 7.67$, $p < .001$. The perception that one's community was more livable than other communities distinguished between community members who are satisfied with the community in which they live and those who desire a different community. The results of this regression directly support H2. The extent to which community members perceive their community to be more livable than other communities significantly predicted whether they were satisfied with their community ($b = 0.23$; $SE = 0.08$), $Wald(1) = 7.65$, $p < .01$). According to the Nagelkerke formula, the approximate variance in community satisfaction accounted for by the perceived livability was 0.22. The overall hit rate for the model was 81 percent.

Social Identification

Next, the role of social identification on community satisfaction was analyzed. A binary logistical regression with community satisfaction as the dependent variable and the four components of the collective self-esteem scale (membership, private esteem, public esteem, and identity) as the predictors was run against the null model with no predictors was significant, $\chi^2(4) = 47.53$, $p < .001$. In support of H3, collective self-esteem attached to a community reliably distinguished community members who were satisfied with their community from those who were not. The Nagelkerke formula indicated that the approximate variance in community satisfaction accounted for by collective self-esteem was 0.13 with an overall hit rate for the full model of 81 percent. Closer examination of the predictability of collective self-esteem on community satisfaction indicated that only public esteem ($b = 0.06$; SE = 0.03), $Wald(1) = 4.07$, $p < .05$) and identification ($b = 0.74$; SE = 0.02), $Wald(1) = 10.60$, $p < .001$) were predictive of community satisfaction.

Discussion

This chapter suggests and offers support for the proposition that a definition for "livable" communities is best provided by those who matter most, that is, the residents of the community. This definition further shows that livability extends beyond simple economics. It is multidimensional in that it encompasses the physical, social, and psychological well-being of all its inhabitants as well as providing opportunity for growth and personal development.

As hypothesized, with the exception of the need for safety, the attributes that define a livable community are not universal. Different segments emerged within each community that value a community based on its ability to provide different needs. The Hipsters place a high value on culture and having a community that is vibrant and diverse, and they care less about service needs and accessibility. The Economists take the exact opposite approach. For them, survival is critical, and the community must offer jobs nearby, access to health-care services, and housing options. Conversely, they do not value some of the community attributes that create social cohesion. For example, they value drivability over other, more social transportation options such as public transportation or sidewalks. To them, vibrancy and diversity are of average value. The Recreationalists emphasize accessibility and want a community that offers opportunities for retail, services, parks, recreation, and entertainment. However, this segment is most likely to prefer a homogenous community that lacks overall diversity and different housing options.

There is no doubt that livable communities enhance the residents' sense of community awareness and social bonding. The more they perceive their community to be livable, the more likely they are to be satisfied with their community and to want to stay within their community. The bond between community members further bolsters this satisfaction. In particular, community members who strongly identified themselves as members of a community and felt that others valued their community were the least likely to desire mobility. Taken together, these findings suggest that a community that is perceived as livable and provides a sense of social cohesion among community members drives sustainability of that community.

Acknowledgments

The author is grateful to Northwest Research Principal and its Managing Director, Rebecca Elmore-Yalch, for collecting and providing the data used in this chapter and for its collaborative support in questionnaire design and MaxDiff analysis. The author also thanks Richard Yalch for his helpful comments on various drafts of this chapter and Lynn Kahle with providing this opportunity.

References

Algesheimer, R., Dholakia, U.M., & Herrmann, A. (2005). The social influence of brand community: Evidence from European car clubs. *Journal of Marketing, 69*(3), 19–34.

Barney, J. (1991). Firm resources and sustained competitive advantage. *Journal of Management, 17*(1), 99–120.

Baumeister, R. F., & Leary, M. R. (1995). The need to belong-desire for interpersonal attachments as a fundamental human-motivation. *Psychological Bulletin, 117*(3), 497–529.

Brehm, J. W. (1966). *A theory of psychological reactance.* New York: Academic Press.

Brehm, S. S., & Brehm, J. W. (1981). *Psychological reactance: A theory of freedom and control.* New York: Academic Press.

Brewer, M. B. (1991). The social self: On being the same and different at the same time. *Personality and Social Psychology Bulletin, 17*(5), 475–482.

Brewer, M. B., Manzi, J. M., & Shaw, J. S. (1993). In-group identification as a function of depersonalization, distinctiveness, and status. *Psychological Science, 4*(2), 88–92.

Broemer, P. (2001). Ease of recall moderates the impact of relationship-related goals on judgments of interpersonal closeness. *Journal of Experimental Social Psychology, 37*(3), 261–266.

Carlson, B. D., Suter, T. A., & Brown, T. J. (2008). Social versus psychological brand community: The role of psychological sense of brand community. *Journal of Business Research, 61*(4), 284–291.

Ellemers, N., Kortekaas, P., & Ouwerkerk, J. W. (1999). Self-categorisation, commitment to the group and group self-esteem as related but distinct aspects of social identity. *European Journal of Social Psychology, 29*(2/3), 371–389.

Ellemers, N., Spears, R., & Doosje, B. (1997). Sticking together on falling apart: In-group identification as a psychological determinant of group commitment versus individual mobility. *Journal of Personality and Social Psychology, 72*(3), 617–626.

Finn, A., & Louviere, J. J. (1992). Determining the appropriate response to evidence of public concern: The case of food safety. *Journal of Public Policy & Marketing, 11*(2), 12–25.

Fournier, S., & Guiry, M. (1993). An emerald green Jaguar, a house on Nantucket, and an African safari: Wish lists and consumption dreams in materialist society. *Advances in Consumer Research, 20,* 352–358.

Hahlweg, D. (1997). Making cities livable. In S. H. Crowhurst Lennard, S. von Ungern-Sternberg, & H. L. Lennard, *International making cities livable conferences,* ed. Carmel, CA: Gondolier Press.

Higgins, E. T. (2002). How self-regulation creates distinct values: The case of promotion and prevention decision making. *Journal of Consumer Psychology, 12*(3), 177–191.

Hillery, G. A. (1955). Definitions of community: Areas of agreement. *Rural Sociology, 20*(2), 111–123.

Jetten, J., Branscombe, N. R., Spears, R., & McKimmie, B. M. (2003). Predicting the paths of peripherals: The interaction of identification and future possibilities. *Personality and Social Psychology Bulletin, 29*(1), 130–140.

Kates, S. M., & Goh, C. (2003). Brand morphing: Implications for advertising theory and practice. *Journal of Advertising, 32*(1), 59–68.

Kozinets, R. V. (2001). Utopian enterprise: Articulating the meanings of Star Trek's culture of consumption. *Journal of Consumer Research, 28*(1), 67–88.

Luhtanen, R., & Crocker, J. (1992). A collective self-esteem scale: Self-evaluation of one's social identity. *Personality and Social Psychology Bulletin, 18*(3), 302–319.

Marley, A. A. J., & Louviere, J. J. (2005). Some probabilistic models of best, worst, and best–worst choices. *Journal of Mathematical Psychology, 49*(6), 464–480.

Muniz, A. M., & O'Guinn, T. C. (2001). Brand community. *Journal of Consumer Research, 27*(4), 412–432.

Parker, A. M., de Bruin, W. B., & Fischhoff, B. (2007). Maximizers versus satisficers: Decision-making styles, competence, and outcomes. *Judgment and Decision Making Journal, 2*(6), 342–350.

Peters, K., & Kashima, Y. (2007). From social talk to social action: Shaping the social triad with emotion sharing. *Journal of Personality and Social Psychology, 93*(5), 780–797.

Puca, R. M. (2001). Preferred difficulty and subjective probability in different action phases. *Motivation and Emotion, 25*(4), 307–326.

Reis, H. T., Maniaci, M. R., Caprariello, P. A., Eastwick, P. W., & Finkel, E. J. (2011). Familiarity does indeed promote attraction in live interaction. *Journal of Personality and Social Psychology, 101*(3), 557–570.

Sanders, I. T. (1966). *The community: An introduction to a social system.* New York: Ronald Press.

Schouten, J. W., & McAlexander, J. H. (1995). Subcultures of consumption: An ethnography of the new bikers. *Journal of Consumer Research, 22*(1), 43–61.

Schwartz, B., Ward, A., Monterosso, J., Lyubomirsky, S., White, K., & Lehman, D. R. (2002). Maximizing versus satisficing: Happiness is a matter of choice. *Journal of Personality and Social Psychology, 83*(5), 1178–1197.

Tajfel, H. (1981). *Human groups and social categories: Studies in social psychology.* Cambridge: Cambridge University Press.

Taylor, S. E., & Gollwitzer, P. M. (1995). Effects of mindset on positive illusions. *Journal of Personality and Social Psychology, 69*(2), 213–226.

U.S. Census Bureau. (2006). *American housing survey for the United States: 2005.* Current Housing Reports Series H150/05, August. Washington, DC: Government Printing Office. www.census.gov/housing/ahs/data/national.html.

Walkable and Livable Communities Institute. (2011). Definition: Livable communities. www.walklive.org.

About the Editors and Contributors

Nicola Berth received her Master of Business (Hons) in 2010 from Auckland University of Technology, where she conducted some of the research for this book. She has a passion for sustainable business with a particular interest in green marketing. Though she currently lives in New Zealand, she is originally from Germany. She is currently the Marketing Coordinator at Gerard Lighting Group.

Rajesh Bhargave is an assistant professor of marketing at The University of Texas at San Antonio. In addition to the issues examined in his chapter, he studies consumers' memory for experiences, time perception, and judgment and decision-making topics. He holds a Ph.D. in marketing from the Wharton School of the University of Pennsylvania as well as a bachelor's degree in business administration from The University of Texas-Austin.

Melissa G. Bublitz is an assistant professor of marketing at the University of Wisconsin–Oshkosh. Her research work examines the intersection of marketing and public policy in the areas of environmental sustainability, food and exercise decision making, positive marketing, and multicultural marketing. Her research interests also include multisensory marketing, packaging cues, emotional intelligence, nutrition, as well as food, financial, and media literacy. Her research has appeared in the *Journal of Consumer Psychology, Journal of Business Research,* and *Journal of Research for Consumers.*

Alex Cavallero is a fifth-year senior at the University of Massachusetts–Boston pursuing a B.S. in management with a double concentration in marketing and finance. He currently works in the investor relations department of a private equity firm, where his responsibilities include international marketing, outbound marketing, capital acquisition, and investor relations.

Meng Cheng is a second-year MBA student at the University of Massachusetts–Boston with a concentration in international management. She is interested in marketing research and sustainable operations in management.

T. Bettina Cornwell (Ph.D., The University of Texas) is the Edwin E. and June Woldt Cone Professor of Marketing at the Lundquist College of Business, University of Oregon. She is also director of research for the Warsaw Sport Marketing Center at the University of Oregon. Prior to joining the University of Oregon, she was a professor of marketing and sport management at the University of Michigan. Her research focuses on marketing communications and consumer behavior and typically includes international and public policy emphases. Dr. Cornwell's research has recently appeared in the *Journal of Advertising, Journal of Advertising Research, Journal of Consumer Research, Journal of Experimental Psychology: Applied, Journal of the Academy of Marketing Science,* and *Journal of Public Policy & Marketing.*

June A. Flora (Ph.D.) is a senior research scientist at Stanford University's Human Sciences Advanced Technologies Research Institute. Her current research focuses primarily on the study of energy reduction and conservation via social media, Facebook interfaces, and interpersonal communication programs. Dr. Flora runs an energy behavior project, studying the behavior change attributes of energy reduction behaviors. In collaboration with Professor Banny Banerjee, Dr. Flora is testing three motivation-framed, Facebook energy-reduction applications. Along with her colleagues, she is also examining the relationship of extreme weather experience and attention to weather news and climate change communication and information-seeking. With more than twenty years at Stanford University's Department of Communication and Stanford Prevention Research Center, Dr. Flora brings an extensive background and publication record in community studies, health communication, and social marketing to the field of energy reduction.

Eda Gurel-Atay (Ph.D., University of Oregon) serves the marketing community by researching and teaching in the consumer behavior area. Her research interests center on the impact of social values on various consumer behaviors, lifestyles and psychographics, celebrity endorsements and advertising effectiveness, and materialism. The shopping process and its impact on retailer evaluation and shopping well-being of consumers are other topics that attract her attention. Current studies explore the relationship between celebrity values, brand values, and consumer values; the impact of lifestyles on health-related behaviors; the impact of values (such as materialism and happiness) on consumer well-being; and the relationship between self-expressiveness in shopping, shopping well-being, and overall subjective well-being. Her work has appeared in peer-reviewed journals such as *Journal of Advertising Research, Social Indicators Research,* and the *International Review of Retail, Distribution*, and *Consumer Research.*

As an educator, Dr. Gurel-Atay has taught consumer behavior, marketing research, and principles of marketing courses. She engages her students by blending marketing theories with real-world applications and through hands-on activities such as preparing promotional campaigns to increase sustainable consumption, to encourage time/money donations to nonprofit organizations, and to improve the effectiveness of social media usage for nonprofit organizations. In addition to research and teaching, Dr. Gurel-Atay serves the marketing community by taking active roles (e.g., being a webmaster or a session chair) in conferences and by being an ad hoc reviewer for journals (such as *Journal of Consumer Research, Journal of Macromarketing*, and *Journal of Retailing and Consumer Services*) and conferences (such as American Marketing Association conferences, North American conference of the Association for Consumer Research, and Society for Consumer Psychology winter conferences).

Sidney Su Han is a Ph.D. candidate in marketing and consumer psychology at the University of Guelph (Canada). His research focuses on consumer social cognition and sustainable behavior. His primary interest is in investigating the role of information processing and consumer psychographics in persuading behavioral change, with a focus on coping with inconsistency in attitudes and behavior when promoting sustainable lifestyle and behaviors, as well as examining the effectiveness of public policy or strategy and its boundary conditions in changing individual behaviors to improve ecological, social, and personal well-being.

Lukas Jones graduated from the University of Oregon in 2008 with a bachelor's degree in business administration. His areas of study were marketing, international business, and the German language. He now resides in Seattle, Washington, and works as a project manager in the tech industry.

Lynn R. Kahle is the Ehrman Giustina Professor and head of the Department of Marketing at the University of Oregon, where he was founding director of the Warsaw Sports Marketing Center. He has served as president of the Society for Consumer Psychology and as chair of the Sports and Special Events, Special Interest Group of the American Marketing Association. He was previously editor of *Sport Marketing Quarterly*. He is a fellow of the Society for Consumer Psychology as well as the American Psychological Association and Association of Psychological Science. He is an executive member of the American Marketing Association.

Dr. Kahle has been an active researcher. His research topics include sustainability, social media, international marketing, lifestyles and psychographics, sports marketing, attitudes and values, and communication. His research has been published in such journals as the *Journal of Personality and Social Psychology, Journal of Consumer Research, Journal of Consumer Psychology, Child Development, Public Opinion Quarterly, Journal of Advertising*, and the *Journal of Marketing*. His twelve books include *Creating Images and the Psychology of Marketing Communication* (edited with Chung-Hyun Kim), *Sports Marketing and the Psychology of Marketing Communication* (edited with Chris Riley), and *Values, Lifestyles, and Psychographics* (edited with Larry Chiagouris). His two most recent books are: *Consumer Behavior Knowledge for Effective Sports and Event Marketing* (edited with Angeline Close) and *Marketplace Lifestyles in an Age of Social Media* (with Pierre Valette-Florence).

Sommer Kapitan is a Ph.D. candidate in marketing at the University of Texas at San Antonio. As a Canadian-American (she became a U.S. citizen in 2010), Ms. Kapitan parlays her attraction to sacred natural landscapes into her research on consumer behaviors that support sustainable living. She earned her B.S. in 2004 and an M.A. in communication from Texas A&M University, where she spent two years lecturing in business before joining the program at San Antonio in the fall of 2009.

Yun Lee is a Ph.D. candidate in marketing at the University of Iowa. Her research examines affective, cognitive, and motivational determinants of consumer behavior and advertising/marketing communication effectiveness. She has presented her research at various conferences, including those for the Association for Consumer Research, the Society for Consumer Psychology, and the American Marketing Association. She has received the Graduate College Doctoral Dissertation Fellowship at the University of Iowa as well as the M. Bhanu Murthy Memorial Prize for Excellence in Teaching. Prior to joining the doctoral program in marketing at the University of Iowa, she earned a master's degree in public administration at the University of Illinois at Springfield, a master's degree in business administration at Dankook University, South Korea, and a bachelor's degree in theater and film at Dankook University, South Korea.

Diane M. Martin (Ph.D., University of Utah) is an associate professor of marketing at Aalto University, Helsinki. She is the winner of the International Communication Association W. Charles Redding Outstanding Dissertation Award and Senior Fellow of American Leadership Forum. Her scholarship is published in numerous journals in marketing and communication, including *Consumption, Markets and Culture, the Journal of Business Ethics,* and the *Journal of Applied Communication Research.* In her recent textbook *Sustainable Marketing*, written with John Schouten, Dr. Martin brings her keen sense of the power of marketing to the problem of how to remain competitive while restoring the earth's natural capital and creating greater well-being for a global population.

Anna R. McAlister is an assistant professor in the Department of Advertising, Public Relations, and Retailing at Michigan State University. Prior to joining Michigan State, she worked as a lecturer in the Department of Consumer Science at University of Wisconsin–Madison. Having earned a Ph.D. in developmental psychology, she had a special interest in the application of theories of developmental psychology to the study of children's consumer socialization. Her work is largely policy-oriented, with a focus on children's knowledge of food brands and their responses to food advertising. Recent papers were published in *Journal of Public Policy & Marketing, Journal of Advertising*, and *Cognitive Development.*

Elizabeth Minton is a Ph.D. candidate in marketing at the University of Oregon. She received her MBA from Idaho State University and her BBA in marketing from the University of Alaska Southeast. Before starting the doctoral program, she conducted tourism development reviews for a rural tourism development agency and worked in marketing and accounting for an aviation tourism company in Alaska. Her research interests are consumer behavior, social marketing, sustainability, and religion as a determinant of consumer behavior. She has published research in *Tourism Analysis* and presented research at the World Marketing Congress and the Religion as Brands conference.

Jill Mosteller (Ph.D., Georgia State University) is an assistant professor of marketing at Portland State University. Her areas of research include emerging trends in consumer behavior, online consumer behavior, and environmental influences across various consumer contexts. She has published research in the *Journal of Consumer Affairs* and *Journal of Business Research*, in addition to presenting work at a variety of conferences, including those of the American Marketing Association, Academy of Marketing Sciences, Advertising and Consumer Psychology, and the American Psychological Association annual conference. Prior to entering academia, Dr. Mosteller worked in the wireless and telecommunications industry, in various field and strategic management corporate roles.

Ethan Moskowitz, an Oregon native, attended the Robert D. Clark Honors College at the University of Oregon. After graduating with a bachelor's degree in 2013, he relocated to Southern California to work as a scientific recruiter for Aerotek. He hopes to turn his passions for music, sports, microbreweries, and the environment into a successful business venture someday.

Dhananjay (DJ) Nayakankuppam received his Ph.D. in marketing from the Ross School of Business at the University of Michigan at Ann Arbor. He is currently an associate professor of marketing at the Tippie College of Business at the University of Iowa in Iowa City. His research examines evaluative processes and draws substantively upon theories in social cognition. He has published articles in the *Journal of Consumer Research, Journal of Consumer Psychology, Marketing Science, Journal of Marketing*, and *Psychological Science.*

Scott Owen works for the U.S. Fish and Wildlife Service's National Conservation Training Center in Shepherdstown, West Virginia, training service employees in environmental education. Previously, Mr. Owen worked for two years at the headquarters office in Arlington, Virginia, creating policy and workshops for youth programs. Scott received his M.S. in marketing from the University of Oregon. Previously, he was employed as an Experiential Education Coordinator at the University of Missouri-Columbia, where he led team-building courses and rock-climbing trips for students and members of the community.

Andrew Parsons is the head of the Department of Marketing, Advertising, Retailing, and Sales at Auckland University of Technology (New Zealand). He earned his Ph.D. in management from the University of Auckland. His research interests lie in the broad area of shopper responses to (retail) marketing stimuli, and he has published on a variety of topics in this area, ranging from store atmospherics and online shopping to advertising regulations and social marketing impacts. His interest in sustainability and green issues stems from the shopper demands and responses around current marketing practices.

Laura A. Peracchio (Ph.D., Northwestern University) is a professor of marketing at the University of Wisconsin–Milwaukee. Dr. Peracchio's areas of research interest focus on consumer information processing including food and nutrition issues, visual persuasion, and language and culture. Her work has appeared in the *Journal of Consumer Research, Journal of Marketing Research, Journal of Consumer Psychology, Journal of Public Policy and Marketing*, and *Journal of Advertising*. Dr. Peracchio is editor of the *Journal of Consumer Research* and has served as president of the Society for Consumer Psychology.

Rafael Perez is a senior data scientist at the App Annie, China. He earned an M.Sc. degree in computer science at the University of Electro-Communications (Japan). His research focuses on correlation and causation between signals. He has applied developed methods in e-learning, stock markets, recommender systems, and social networks. His current interests include clean energy and optimization of energy conversion in food technologies.

Jan Pöschko is a software developer interested in analyzing and visualizing data, discrete mathematics, and interface design. He received a master's degree in mathematical computer science from Graz University of Technology (Austria). Mr. Pöschko loves creating Web applications and believes that information, combined with proper tools to make sense of it, can help make our world a better place. He enjoys photography and bicycling and is often seen wearing green shoes.

Neil Rubens is an assistant professor at the Knowledge Systems Lab at the University of Electro-Communications in Japan. He is also a member of the Innovation Ecosystems Network at Media X, Stanford University. Dr. Rubens received an M.Sc. degree from the University of Massachusetts and a Ph.D. from the Tokyo Institute of Technology, both in computer science. He studies concepts of learning and intelligence from computational and cognitive aspects. He pioneered a concept of Active Intelligence—a system that learns actively in an unsupervised or semisupervised manner. Systems based on Active Intelligence have been used in a variety of projects in the domains of e-learning, business intelligence, and knowledge management. Dr. Rubens wrote chapters on machine learning, active learning, and recommender systems for books published by MIT Press and Springer. His research has received funding from corporations and the governments of Japan, the United States, and Sweden.

Dr. Martha G. Russell is senior research scholar at the Human Sciences and Technology Advanced Research (H*STAR) Institute and Executive Director at Media X, Stanford University, and senior fellow at the Institute for Innovation, Creativity, and Capital (IC2) at The University of Texas at Austin. Dr. Russell has established collaborative research initiatives in technology leadership and information sciences for national science agencies and technology companies, pioneering early public-private partnerships in microelectronic and information sciences and in manufacturing technologies. She has led interdisciplinary research and leadership programs for national agencies and consortia. Dr. Russell has developed planning/evaluation systems and consulted regionally and internationally on technology innovation for regional development. She studies innovation ecosystems using data-driven visualization methods for systems analysis and is promoting the development of new media metrics for the persuasive impact of interactive, place-based, and social media. She serves on the advisory board of the *Journal of Technology Forecasting and Social Change*.

Sigal Segev (Ph.D., University of Leicester) is an assistant professor in the Department of Advertising and Public Relations, School of Journalism and Mass Communication at Florida International University (FIU). Her research interests focus on several areas of marketing communication with a special focus on consumer behavior, ethnic identity and acculturation, green behavior, responses to advertising, and consumer decision-making processes. She teaches at both graduate and undergraduate levels in the Department of Advertising and Public Relations. Prior to joining FIU, Dr. Segev held various marketing communication positions in both corporate and government organizations.

Kim Sheehan (Ph.D., University of Tennessee–Knoxville) is professor of advertising at the School of Journalism and Communication at the University of Oregon. She serves as director of the Master's Program in Strategic Communication and on the leadership team for the Green Product Design Network, an interdisciplinary program recognized as one of the University's "Big Ideas." One of the founders of the Greenwashing Index, Dr. Sheehan is also the author of several books and articles in *Journal of Advertising* and *Journal of Public Policy and Marketing* as well as numerous other academic journals.

David Silvera earned a B.S. in mathematics and a MBA at the University of California at Irvine. He earned his Ph.D. in social psychology at the University of Texas at Austin. After graduating, he joined the Psychology Department at the University of Tromsø (Norway). He moved to the Marketing Department at The

University of Texas at San Antonio. His primary research interests are attributions, consumer decision making, and self-regulation.

Marc Smith is a sociologist specializing in the social organization of online communities and computer-mediated interaction. Mr. Smith leads the Connected Action consulting group and lives and works in Silicon Valley, California. Smith cofounded the Social Media Research Foundation (www.smrfoundation.org), a nonprofit devoted to open tools, data, and scholarship related to social media research.

Samuel Soo is a senior campaign manager at the VivaKi Nerve Center. The VivaKi Search Hub provides back-office search operations to the Australia/New Zealand region. VivaKi is the global umbrella for the media assets of Publicis Groupe. Key Brands internationally include Starcom Worldwide, ZenithOptimedia, Digitas, and Performics. Samuel has a Master of Business (Hons) from Auckland University of Technology, which is where he conducted some of the research described in this book.

Markus Strohmaier (Ph.D., Graz University of Technology) is an assistant professor on the faculty of computer science at Graz University of Technology (Austria). He was a visiting assistant professor at Stanford University during the 2011–12 academic year. His research interests include social software engineering, web-science, social and semantic computing, network-theoretic algorithms and analysis, agent modeling, and data mining.

Jill Sundie is an assistant professor of marketing at The University of Texas at San Antonio. She holds a B.A. in economics from the University of Arizona, an M.A. in economics from the University of Southern California, and a Ph.D. in psychology from Arizona State University. Her research focuses on evolutionary biological approaches to consumer behavior, including motivations for status consumption. She also studies emotions experienced in status consumption contexts, such as envy and *schadenfreude*, the effects of materialistic values on intimate relationships and well-being.

Dr. Lefa Teng is an associate professor of marketing at the University of Guelph (Canada). Dr. Teng's research interests include two broad streams: marketing and consumer behavior. In the marketing area, his research focuses on branding and promotional strategies; in consumer behavior studies, he investigates consumer information processing and the purchase decision-making process. Most of his research contexts are related to cross-cultural consumers and international markets. His research has been published in *Journal of Business Research, Journal of Consumer Marketing, Journal of International Marketing,* and *Journal of Service Marketing.*

Kristin Trask was a Ph.D. student at the University of Texas at San Antonio. She currently resides in North Carolina and works with entrepreneurs and small businesses.

Kai-Yu Wang (Ph.D., University of Wisconsin–Milwaukee) is an assistant professor of marketing at Brock University, Ontario. His research interests include consumer information processing and marketing communications. His work has appeared in *Journal of Business Research, Service Industries Journal, Industrial Marketing Management,* and *Advances in Consumer Research.*

Kyra L. Wiggin is a fourth-year Ph.D. candidate in marketing at the Michael G. Foster School of Business, University of Washington. Prior to pursuing her Ph.D., Ms. Wiggin graduated *summa cum laude* from Boise State University with a business degree in economics and psychology. Her current research centers on social identity, attributions, and how consumer curiosity influences processing, judgments, and decisions. Ms. Wiggin cowrote a book chapter in *Cracking the Code: How Managers Can Drive Profits by Leveraging Consumer Psychology,* and her research has been presented in several conference proceedings for the Association for Consumer Research and Society for Consumer Psychology.

Guang-Xin Xie (Ph.D., University of Oregon) is an assistant professor of marketing at the College of Management, University of Massachusetts–Boston. Dr. Xie's research interests focus on persuasion knowledge and marketplace deception. He has published research articles in a number of academic journals, including the *Journal of Advertising Research, Journal of Social Psychology,* and *Marketing Review.*

Nara Youn (Ph.D., Northwestern University) is an associate professor of marketing at Hongik University, Seoul (South Korea). Her research activities to date have focused on social relationships and their impact on consumer behavior. She takes an experimental and empirical modeling approach to examine dynamic market phenomena through specific social mechanisms of communication and consumer learning. Her research has been published in various academic journals such as *Marketing Science* and *Information Systems Research.* She previously taught at the University of Washington, Seattle, and the University of Iowa, Iowa City.

Xiaojing Yang (Ph.D., Indiana University) is an assistant professor of marketing at the University of Wisconsin–Milwaukee. Dr. Yang's research examines how advertising in general, and creativity in particular, influence information processing and consumer behavior. He has published articles in journals such as *Journal of Consumer Research, Marketing Science, Journal of Consumer Psychology,* and *Journal of Advertising.*

Jiafeng (Camilla) Yu is a product manager at White Night Technology, which delivers fun products to help women and their BFFs stay in touch with, support, and gift one another. Prior to this, Ms. Yu worked for Media X at Stanford University and the Silicon Valley Innovation Institute. Her research interest and work experience covers social media, online marketing, mobile applications, and project management in Silicon Valley, Austin, and Shanghai. A recent study analyzed Twitter to understand the branding and reputation of innovation hubs. She earned a master's degree from The University of Texas at Austin. She currently collaborates with Innovation Ecosystems Network. Her passion is building connections between people, companies, and regions in the Innovation Ecosystems Network.

Dr. Ying Yu is an associate professor of strategic management at the School of Management at Shanghai Jiaotong University (China). Dr. Yu's research interest focuses on strategic management and marketing management. He provides management consulting services for many public, private, or crown companies in China, and he is an external strategy consultant for several large firms in China. He has published over thirty articles in a variety of academic journals in China and overseas. He is an influential scholar in strategic management, and his research has gained wide exposure in several popular media in China.

Author Index

Subject Index

Italic page references indicate figures and tables.